REFRAMING BRITI

At the Villa Rose (1920)

Reframing British Cinema

1918–1928

Between Restraint and Passion

Christine Gledhill

 Publishing

For Matt and Luke. In love and solidarity.

First published in 2003 by the
BRITISH FILM INSTITUTE
21 Stephen Street, London W1T 1LN

The British Film Institute promotes greater understanding of,
and access to, film and moving image culture in the UK.

Cover design by Ketchup
Cover image: *Squibs Wins the Calcutta Sweep* (1922)

Set by Fakenham Photosetting Limited, Fakenham, Norfolk
Printed in the UK by St Edmundsbury Press, Suffolk

British Library Cataloguing-in-Publication Data
A catalogue record for this book is available from the British Library

ISBN 0–85170–889–7 (pbk)
ISBN 0–85170–891–9 (hbk)

Contents

Acknowledgments

Thanks must follow to the many who have encouraged, supported, constructively critiqued or goaded me to persist over a number of years in this mapping of the practices and films of 1920s British cinema. Of course, while acknowledging my debts, none of those named below bear any responsibility for the shortcomings and errors of this book. Thanks begin with former heads of BFI Publishing and the NFTVA, Ed Buscombe and Clyde Jeavons, who responded to my initial proposal for an investigation of a cinema then almost unviewed since the initial release dates of its films. And then to Elaine Burrows, Bryony Dixon and Kathleen Dixon of the NFTVA and to Janet Moat and Saphron Parker of BFI Special Collections, who put up with my occupation of viewing cubicles and valuable office space over years of trawling through films, scrapbooks, collections of notes and unpublished materials. They offered not only their invaluable expertise but belief in the project during times when it hung in the balance. Help from BFI Library staff has been unfailing, and in particular from Janice Headland, who shared her researches into the biographical data of key film-makers of the period. Latterly, Andrew Lockett and Sophia Contento, new forces in BFI Publishing, have patiently endured delayed deadlines and steered the shaping of an unwieldy manuscript into something like manageable proportions.

Time spent in libraries and archives has depended on the generous support of the Leverhulme Trust, who awarded me a six-month Research Fellowship in 1997–8 to lay the foundations of this project, and of the Arts and Humanities Research Board, who awarded funding in 2001–2 for teaching relief to complete writing and preparing presentations and outlines for film seasons. Public funding was underpinned by support from Staffordshire University Research Initiative in the form of an initial sabbatical and latterly periods of unpaid leave, for which I must thank the Dean of the School of Humanities and Social Sciences and my colleagues in the Department of Media, Journalism and Cultural Studies, who tolerated my repeated absences. Versions of sections of this book have already appeared in *Moving Performance: British Stage and Screen, 1890s–1920s* (Linda Fitzsimmons and Sarah Street [eds], 2000), a collection of essays first presented at a cinema centenary event organised by Bristol University Drama Department in 1996, and in publications following the Nottingham Silent British Cinema weekends – all edited by Alan Burton and Laraine Porter and published by Matthew Stevens of Flicks Books, who is to be thanked for his support of new work on often recondite areas of British cinema.

My intellectual debts are many and I must acknowledge first the generous, thoughtful and constructively critical support of David Mayer and Martin Meisel. Their work has been a major inspiration and they have encouraged me to trespass into intellectual territories beyond my own. In the field of film studies, I owe an inestimable debt to Charles Barr for changing the questions we can ask of British cinema. Throughout this process the growing interest and confidence in British film-making in a number of arenas changed my situation as an isolated researcher into one among a fast expanding community. Lorenzo Codelli, co-organiser of the annual Pordonone Silent Cinema Festivals, offered encouragement and a format for logging the results of viewings. The screening of British 'taster' strands at these festivals, followed by the more intensive annual British Silent Cinema weekends initiated between Laraine Porter, Sue Porter and Paul Marygold at The Broadway, Nottingham, and Bryony Dixon and Elaine Burrows at the NFTVA, were of inestimable value. The change from the editing table, with its small, silent and stop-start images, to expertly projected films, wonderfully accompanied by such sympathetic musical interpreters as Neil Brand, Jon Sweeney, Phil Carli and Stephen Horne, offered an entirely new experience of and perspective on this cinema. The Nottingham weekends have been marked by the unfailing interest, excitement and generosity of participants, as also by the emergence of a new generation of researchers, now the authors of some remarkable PhD theses, soon to be published, from whose work and thinking I have learned a lot. For stimulating discussions, access to their work and general encouragement, I thank in particular: Michael Allen, Jon Burrows, Michael Hammond, Andrew Higson, Laurence Napper, Amy Sargeant, Michael Williams. I owe much also to three cohorts of Film, Television and Radio students at Staffordshire University, who have raised productive questions and insights while testing my ideas about 1920s British cinema against its later decades.

Among film collectors and the wider archival community, I thank Kevin Brownlow and Patrick Stanbury for advice and access to material; Tony Hillman and Valerie Bradley for sharing their knowledge about Maurice Elvey; and Tony Fletcher for his fund of knowledge about early British cinema and indefatigable enthusiasm. For very material help with research, I must thank Maggie Womersley, who gave me two years of research assistance, funded by Staffordshire University, rooting through trade, fan and review press in search of clues to the reigning values and assumptions of British film-makers and audiences. Also heartfelt thanks to Amy Sargeant, who helped complete these searches and has been unstintingly generous in sharing her own research and offering hours of telephone support. To all my colleagues at Staffordshire University, my friends and family who have listened to and discussed my obsession and perplexities, thanks are owed. Many thanks, in particular, to David Mayer, Martin Meisel and Lynda Neade, who have read and commented on sections of the manuscript. And finally my gratitude to Jim Cook for last-minute, but assiduous and clarifying, editorial help in finalising the book.

Introduction

To those of us involved in the late 1980s in BFI-sponsored projects on melodrama and British cinema,[1] the encounter with British films of the 1920s suggested a body of work more interesting, quirky and rich than was generally allowed. A few years later, with the support of BFI Publishing and the National Film and Television Archive (NFTVA), my investigation began. Starting with a few well-known figures – Brunel, Cutts, Pearson, Novello and Balfour – I also wanted as far as possible to avoid cherry-picking the few titles already feted in the British historical canon: the silent Hitchcocks, Duponts and Asquiths. Thus, using the invaluable groundwork laid by Rachael Low's pioneering volumes, my search fanned out from these central points to explore the lesser byways and backwaters of British film-making in this period.

What was I looking for? And why the 1920s? The answer to the latter is that my question is not concerned with film history as such – in the sense of focusing on who did what, when, or in terms of chronicling origins and influences, whether of auteurs or key works. However, starting from an interest in the fate of melodrama in British cinema, the 1920s offered a period when the feature film is becoming an established format and the nature of the consolidations that will ground future directions is discernible. At the same time the terrain is still shifting, with British film-making poised between a nineteenth-century past of popular visual narrational traditions and a future divided between the hegemony of Hollywood over mainstream entertainment and European movements laying claim to film as art. Feature film-making in Britain during the 1920s is thus a productive site of multiple, intermingling currents, crossing between past traditions and future practices. My investigation, then, in asking how these films work, sought to establish the parameters of an aesthetic and cultural context within which to evaluate and make sense of their peculiarities and intriguing features.

For Rachael Low (1971), British film-making in the 1920s is interesting because symptomatic of the problems confronting a modernising entertainment industry seeking to develop a visual narrative language. Her work in charting and profiling the rise and fall of numerous production companies, together with the shifting fortunes of key players, offers a crucial starting point. Her approach to the films themselves, however, is based on cinematic values vested in the montage editing and expressionist camerawork established in European cinemas as support for the claim of film as art. In the only other, and more recent, book-length study of the period by Kenton Bamford (1999), the films are assessed within a post-1968 ideological frame. This focuses on their failure to deal either with the social problems of their times or to provide entertainments for the working classes comparable to those offered by Hollywood. Bamford does valuable work unearthing a range of contemporary critical comment. But his book neither examines the films themselves nor moves beyond a demand for representation that is largely oblivious to the work of aesthetic practice and wholly unsympathetic to what can now seem at best quaint and at worst pernicious liberal bourgeois values. The word 'silly' haunts such retrospective evaluations of the period's popular fiction, which, whether print, pictorial or filmic, to modern generations hardly seems grown-up.

At first glance such perspectives are understandable. For many at the time, the First World War and the absence of forward-looking political leadership in the postwar period demanded the end of everything tainted as Victorian. Cinema heralded a new social as well as artistic medium. The 1920s saw the emergence of a lively British film culture that itself ignored native product. Rather it looked to French,

German, Scandinavian and Soviet cinemas for signs of a new art in the making, and, with some ambivalence, to America for signs of a democratic modernity for the new century. In the second half of the decade the London Film Society, the journal *Close Up*, early film historians and critics such as Iris Barry, Ernest Betts and Paul Rotha provided the terms for defining the specificity of film as an art form distinct from literature, theatre and painting. In the process they laid down the values of film history and criticism for decades to come, wielding, as Laurence Napper (2001) suggests, a disproportionate influence in later definitions of this period in terms of modernist or avant-garde practices, the principles of which were only just coming into view. However, the 150-odd films that rolled past me on the NFTVA's viewing tables suggested sources in a different and, at first sight, almost alien culture of middlebrow tastes and fantasies, still infiltrated with Victorian and Edwardian tropes and resonances. Any encounter with modernity appeared here in oblique and ambivalent ways, registering largely indirectly the shocks of a war that had undermined belief in progress promised by the machine and scientific rationality while accelerating social and economic change. On the one hand, an inevitable democratisation was transforming a social structure stratified by deeply ingrained rifts of class, gender, region and ethnicity. At the same time, high-toned revivals of disappearing folk and artistic traditions – harlequinade and verse drama, for example – intermixed with expanding popular consumption of late-Victorian pictorial iconography and sentimental fiction and a rising heritage and rural tourist industry. These trends fed a culture of fey, escapist, if often whimsically ironical, fantasy and make-believe. British film-making of this period, not least through its penchant for theatrical and literary adaptation and close affiliation with West End theatre, is rooted in these peculiar forms. It is, then, small wonder that an intelligentsia seeking to champion cinema as a new and modernist art form should look beyond a native cinema that remained enmeshed in a culture seemingly retrogressive and middlebrow.

Eighty-odd years later, film is securely established as a distinctive art form within a network of histories, theories and aesthetic practices. A new form of cultural history among theatre, visual arts and film scholars is increasingly concerned with interdisciplinary investigation. It is now possible to revisit these films that are crossed by multiple, often contradictory, cultural and aesthetic currents in a more open-minded way, less threatened by British cinema's association with theatre, print fiction and popular visual iconography. Moreover the coexistence of past and present practices within the new medium of cinema contributes to more subtle and richer articulations of aesthetic perception and cultural change than a model of linear progression from one form to another allows. The concern of this study, then, is to propose a framework within which the work of these films can appear in terms of their own culture, rather than to prematurely assess them against standards of Hollywood 'classic' narrative or European art cinema. I want to evaluate the films for what they *do* rather than what they fail to do. Such an approach questions the relegation of this cinema as 'old-fashioned', rethinking its relation to the practices and values of its surrounding and preceding cultures, which to a critical intelligentsia appear all too easily as regression from the modernism promised by film. In his study of English painting between the wars, David Peters Corbett (1997) makes the argument that the turn away from Vorticism and Futurism by postwar English painters must be investigated as itself a response to modernity, rather than a failure of modernist imagination defined by Continental examples. This response, as he and others such as Paul Fussell (1975) and Jay Winter (1995) show, is marked by the trauma of the First World War as humanity's first experience of mechanised mass destruction. Escape, Richard Dyer (1992) convincingly argues, is shaped between the two poles of what we seek to avoid and what we imagine as a healing substitute. Escape is, then, as worthy of study and as revealing as polemical encounters with social problems, and in many ways, perhaps, more so, in that the constraints of facticity are dissolved to allow more liminal, unconscious imaginings to appear.

All this granted, it was not easy, Friday after Friday in the NFTVA's basement cubicles, to fathom these films that offered often opaque and bemusing images such as the bizarre skiffle-playing, animal skin-clad troupe in *She* (1925), scattered like comic-book cut-outs across hillsides, strumming their makeshift instruments. Or to adjust to the mix of understated acting, literalising mime and melodramatic gesture in films as different as *The House of*

Peril (1922) or *The Little People* (1926). Or to find a stable viewing position within the magic-lantern-like alternation of views and pictures taken from a range of different angles, flashing by, in films such as *Call of the Road* (1920) or *Mademoiselle d'Armentières* (1926). Or, in a film such as *At the Villa Rose* (1920), to accommodate a narrative carried by static figures explaining and counter-explaining the moves of a detective plot through a plethora of titles and flash-backs to its long title-less central sequence of dream-like events folding one into the other. Such strategies create sudden, intriguing effects, while failing, it seemed, to cohere into the focused fictional worlds offered by American cinema of the period or to yield the aesthetic distance of the surreal, expressionist or constructivist visions found in French, German and Soviet films. Instead, I was collecting iconographic moments that had all the force of magic-lantern slide or picture-postcard images; gestural acts that cele-brated the dexterity and skill of a performance; shots constructed with the architectural complexity of a theatrical staging; plot devices that turned on public occasions in which the most private feelings had to find their expression; or generic motifs that used Continental settings as occasions for dressing up and disguise.

The point of explanatory coherence, then, was not going to be found in a body of national themes that 'reflected' the social realities of the 1920s. Nor in a style that could be said to characterise a philosophic or aesthetic sensibility in specifically cinematic terms. And certainly not in terms of a radical break with the past of the kind valorised by the avant-garde and that is the goal of many intellectuals and literary practi-tioners of the period and since. Rather, starting with an interest in the impact of British cinema's own aes-thetic and cultural inheritance on its practices, what gradually emerged through my viewings was a set of strategies derived from preceding and neighbouring narrational, theatrical and pictorial forms. For exam-ple: a persistent framing of characters that did more than create a picture, but served to articulate the pro-tagonist in his or her social location; the organisation of social spaces into theatricalised stages for public enactment; editing that organised pictorialised images in a form of collage – images framed, articu-lated, acculturated, symbolic, serving both as social documents and dramatic portents – building cumu-latively in a kind of flicker book or kaleidoscopic

configuration and reconfiguration of patterns made from pre-given pieces. Inevitably, then, a structure for this study emerged in terms of those very features that have been used to dismiss it: theatricality, picto-rialism and a dependence on pre-told stories.

However, in turning to theatrical, pictorial and performance histories, I am not seeking to construct a 'baton passing' version of history focusing on influ-ences and transmissions, still less to count numbers of adaptations and theatrical personnel involved in British film-making – the facts and figures that offer a mechanical, economistic explanation of this cinema. Rather, this study seeks to locate the force of such an inheritance in aesthetic practices that repre-sent a way of perceiving and shaping events and characters. In so doing, it confronts and attempts to articulate the aesthetic dimension of what Christo-pher Williams (1996) has named the 'insistently social' nature of British cinema. Too often, as Williams points out, this has resulted in a sociologi-cal account as substitute for consideration of deviant aesthetic characteristics dismissed as uncinematic. Equally problematic, as Pam Cook (1996) argues, is the recourse to a coherent, singular national identity that involves excluding alien, unwanted elements: for example, the valorisation of the social-realist tradi-tion running from Grierson's documentary move-ment through the home-front movies of the 1940s, Ealing comedies and Woodfall's New Wave and so into British television drama, at the expense of dis-reputable, lowbrow genres such as Gainsborough costume melodramas, crime films, Hammer Horror and Carry On films. However, while this opposition has served the polemical purpose of bringing the 'underside' of British generic film-making into view, merely to reverse values does little to develop under-standing of how film-making works as *both* aesthetic and social practice. As Charles Barr (1986) suggests, both sides – documentarist observation and subjec-tive fantasising – belong not only to British cinema as separate strands of film-making, but to each other as recto and verso of a composite cultural aesthetic practice.

While it is possible to analyse what British cinema's theatrical, pictorial and storytelling practices do *formally* with images, protagonists and dramatic and narrative devices, historicising such practices enables us to locate them *culturally*. We see not only what drives their development, but what is culturally

enacted through the aesthetic formations they produce, and what possibilities are thus made available
for aesthetic experience and fictional imagining. The
twin histories of melodrama and music hall, for
example, both fundamentally important to the practices of British film-making, are intertwined with
issues to do with class performances, representations
and audiences. British society has experienced class
division in historically specific ways, in particular
through the displacement of revolution by reform,
the crucial point of which for my argument is a
resulting deeply embedded perception of social difference and division governing social structure and
cultural identity. Whether you are born British
(whatever that means) or not, to live in Britain is to
be caught up in social forms, twists of language,
habits of thought that emerge out of this social structure to form what is variously and with different
emphases termed a 'cultural mode of perception',
'horizon of expectation' or 'cultural imaginary'. This
does not, however, make aesthetic practice and its
fictions reflections – direct or distorted – of social
realities. The practice of underplaying and the value
of restraint, for example, do not merely 'reflect' the
grip of middle-class ideology over theatrical performance. Cultural practices are more dynamic than
that, for out of them may be spun particular aesthetic
effects, engagements, frissons and patterns of dramatic enactment.

Equally, in using the adjectives middle- or working-class, I am not invoking the idea of authentic
cultures belonging exclusively to objectively identifiable classes. On one level, it is precisely because class
and gender identities are always in flux that the effort
to demarcate and maintain cultural boundaries is
intensified. On another, the process of democratisation not only strives to amalgamate cultures in one
mass popular sphere, but provides increasing opportunity for cross-cultural experience through education, entertainment and the marketplace. The terms
middle- and working-class culture refer here to representations of forms through which we know and
think about different social groups, representations
that themselves come to serve cognitive, symbolic
and imaginative functions, not least in the circulation
of pictures, performances and stories from one
medium and cultural site to another. Thus I read the
significance of the practices and patterns of British
film-making through the dynamics of the encounter

between cultures and aesthetic perception. In seeking
to situate the working practices of British film-
making within these broader perceptual frames, this
study attempts to delineate a cultural poetics capable
of explaining and valuing the peculiarities of the
films of the 1920s while offering signposts to contemporary cinema.

I arrive at such delineation through three intersecting and equally important routes: 1) a reading of
histories of theatrical, visual and narrative arts and
entertainments in the period roughly spanning the
1850s into the 1920s; 2) listening to the varied voices
interweaving through trade, journalistic and fan
press, or speaking through autobiographies, notebooks and other memorabilia, expressing comment,
advice, criticism and longing around the project of
producing British films for British audiences in the
1920s; and 3) close analysis of the practices and
strategies of the films themselves. Often quoted is
Michael Balcon's comment that 'hardly a film' of the
interwar years 'reflects the agony of their times'.[2]
However, this partly depends on what you think
films can reflect. Vested social and economic interests
at different points both resist and require democratisation and modernisation. But changing mental
frameworks within which people think and act is an
inevitably slow and uneven process, controlled neither by promotional nor regressive fictionalising. The
imaginary work of fiction production, particularly of
a popular generic kind, provides space for transfor-
mative work that includes reaction, contest and
imaginary futures. Such processes take place not only
in fictions but *around* them in the struggles for control that they set in motion. Thus I have sought to
pay attention to what producers and audiences say
and think as a means of entering into the mindset of
the period, while at the same time constructing an
interpretive frame through which to understand the
wider cultural significance of such debates, arguments and convergences.

Inevitably, perhaps, this study falls short of both
the ambition I started out with and the experience
garnered along the way. There are many voices and
perceptions not included or excised; many films and
film-makers whose excellences or interesting insights
have been squeezed out. While the idea of a 'cultural
imaginary' is implicitly at work in my analyses of
these films and would, given fuller attention, reveal
much about the social and ideological strains and

negotiations of the period, this remains a future project. My focus has concentrated on the practices and strategies deployed in these films, on their cultural sources and aesthetic outcomes. Thus this study emphasises continuities and the middlebrow mainstream rather than the breaks and avant-garde transgressions that on the whole have inspired the critical imagination. There is, of course, a marked caesura in the decade, when the shutdown of film production in November 1924 signalled the demise of many filmmaking companies and careers, and galvanised attempts by survivors and newcomers to modernise and above all seek collaboration with Europe and/or America. Again a close analysis of the differences involved in these changing production methods and their stylistic outcomes is an inviting project yet to be undertaken. But without investigation of the cultural conditions and aesthetic context of particular practices, any attempt to chart stylistic developments chronologically remains at the mercy of prevailing historical assumptions and values, and it is the former project that this study addresses.

It is true, as Pam Cook, Andrew Higson and others have argued, that no study of a national cinema can assume a hermetically sealed cultural space. Britain, Europe and America have interchanged cultural artefacts, personnel and ideas through the centuries. Nevertheless, when calling for a 'geography of art' in *The Englishness of English Art* (1993), Nikolaus Pevsner argues for the locatedness of art practices, while acknowledging their shifting intersections with currents from other cultures and climes. Ideas, practices and influences circulating internationally do not get subsumed into a blank space. If notions such as 'cultural poetics', 'horizon of expectation' or 'cultural imaginary' hold any force, then ideas and practices crossing national and cultural boundaries are subject to locally conditioned uses and interpretations even as they contribute to shifting, expanding or contracting the frames within which local cultural practices operate. It is within this local perceptual environment that this study seeks to locate British cinema. In this context, geography takes on more than contingent significance, infiltrating the perceptual frameworks and aesthetic strategies that shape British filmic imagining. If geography and biography are the twin poles of fiction-making, then the organisation of cinematic space, performance, protagonists and narrative emphasises the

power of social location and the boundaries that demarcate as they define, in contrast to the heroic biographic trajectory emphasising progress through time that characterises American cinema.

In seeking to establish the impact of cultural location, my discussion moves backwards and forwards between late nineteenth-century and 1920s practices as well as between the early and later years of the decade. While this may frustrate the desire for chronological, linear order, the experience of crossing the symbolic boundary represented by the millennium was something of a revelation to me. As I worried about presuming a connection between what G. H. Lewes wrote in the 1850s and 1920s filmmakers, I recalled my intellectual initiation through the work of F. R. Leavis, and that I had read *Hamlet* at school through my father's take on A. C. Bradley and Harley Granville-Barker. Once I included my parents' experience in my personal conceptual map, then what I had been told involved figures born not only in the early 1900s but in the heart of the 19th century. A cultural imaginary is not ordered in neat chronological stages but rather as a web or, to use a metaphor popular in the 1920s, a kaleidoscope of intersecting, fluctuating memories and motifs, different elements of which wax and wane, shift into the foreground and recede, as particular questions predominate. This is the metaphor I would choose to represent the mix of theories, analysis, anecdote and commentary involved in this exploration.

Some structure, however, there has to be if a framework for a cultural poetics of British filmmaking is to emerge. The three themes of theatricality, pictorialism and storytelling intertwine throughout the book, but contribute also chapters that focus particular practices and values under these separate heads. But these themes are also gathered in two different ways, the model for which is borrowed shamelessly (but with permission) from Martin Meisel's ground-breaking interdisciplinary study of nineteenth-century narrative, pictorial and theatrical forms, *Realizations* (1983). In Part One, chapters on theatricality, pictorialism and performance construct three 'Co-ordinates' that weave together to form what I propose as the cultural poetics of British filmmaking. In Part Two, 'Conjunctions', these practices are brought together under three categories of film production: *authorial* – focusing on the solutions found by particular directors to the problems of turning pictures into films; *generic* – emphasising the thematic and aesthetic constellations that facilitated and exploited British performance practices with their emphasis on role-playing, dressing up and disguise; and finally, the weaving of all these practices, motifs and themes into *stories* told and exchanged within the cultural and aesthetic space represented by British cinema.

Within this framework, I attempt to delineate a 'cultural poetics', which shares many of the features attributed to the 'cultural geography' of English art by Nikolaus Pevsner, which in turn chimes with the antimonies structuring British film-making set out by Charles Barr. In particular, Pevsner's study identifies: the separation and juxtaposition of elements, creating an architectural montage of differentiated rather than unified spaces; an emphasis on concrete observation combined with the non-corporeal, the ambiguous and the uncanny; an anachronistic appropriation of elements from past or foreign styles as a kind of 'fancy dress', disregarding formal purity or consistency; a preference for the understated combined with a self-reflexive delight in paradox and the illogical; an emphasis on story over aesthetic form. Such features add up to a hybrid amalgam of image and narrative materials captured by Andrew Higson in the title and introduction to his recent anthology on British cinema, *Dissolving Views* (1996). Equally they point to the interplay of social and imaginary boundaries and the fantasies of boundary crossing and masquerade that Pam Cook finds in her study of costume and identity in British cinema, *Fashioning the Nation* (1996). If, as I argue, the concept of the boundary resonates with the ingrained social division so frequently blamed for the class-bound regressiveness of British cinema in comparison with the apparent democratic egalitarianism of Hollywood, the strategies of the 'geographic imaginary' outlined in this study work not like American cinema to produce the homogeneous identity of the cultural 'melting pot' but to keep shifting boundaries in play and difference in circulation.

PART ONE

CO-ORDINATES

1 Theatricalising British Cinema

Standard theatre and film histories resolve critical debates between stage and screen in favour of their separation. The idea that each 'art' or 'medium' is distinct has been so successful that 'staginess' and 'theatricality' have become self-evident faults in a film.[1] British cinema's use of stage plays and actors, its 'theatrical' performance mode and *mise en scène* are therefore dismissed as uncinematic. Such polarisation simplifies stage–screen relations, obscuring their significance for each other and the role of theatre in the 'cultural imaginary' of English life in particular. Hugh Hunt opens an account of the social and literary context of the modern period with a quotation from Henry James, commenting in 1879 on the popularity of the London theatre:

> It sometimes seems to an observer of English customs that this interest in histrionic matters almost reaches the proportions of a mania. It pervades society – it breaks down barriers . . . Plays and actors are perpetually talked about, private theatricals are incessant, and members of the dramatic profession are 'received' without restriction. They appear in society, and the people of society appear on the stage; it is as if the great gate which formerly divided the theatre from the world had been lifted off its hinges.[2]

Fifty years later these observations still hold true. All that has changed by the 1920s is the extension of this 'mania' to cinema with an even wider social range of aspirants.

If debates about acting and performers on stage and screen wage furiously throughout the period from 1880s to end of the 1920s, this is partly because intensifying pressure to modernise class and gendered codes of behaviour is played out in the crossover between theatre and social life. In *Modern Memory and the Great War* (1975) – a study of soldiers' perceptual experience of war – Paul Fussell devotes a chapter to theatricality:

> A major reason for the British tendency to fuse memories of the war with the imagery of theater . . . is the vividness of the sense of role enjoined by the British class system . . . In contrast to the American scene, British life is pervaded by the sense of theater allied to this instinct for class distinctions. It is the British who praise one another by saying, 'Good show!' During the war, it was the British, rather than the French, the Americans, the Italians, the Portuguese, the Russians, or the Germans, who referred to trench raids as 'shows' or 'stunts', perhaps because it is in British families that charades and amateur theatricals are a convention'.[3]

Fussell's observations not only recall Henry James's comments but suggest a productive approach to British cinema. The infiltration of theatrical metaphor into common phraseology, into modes of thinking and imagining, shapes in turn approaches to film-making – for example, the theatricalisation of spaces for public enactment or the delivery of performance as role-playing. The interchange between theatre and British films, then, is not simply a matter of the proximity of West End to film studios or the economics of adaptation, but concerns a set of shared perceptual frames. This is not to deny distinctions between the two forms, nor to deny the influence of standard-setting developments in America and Europe, but to recognise that such influences are absorbed within this locally conditioned cultural and aesthetic framework.

In this chapter I begin by suggesting the sheer variety of theatrical production and film exhibition during the 1920s that results from major upheavals in dramatic and performance practices. This leads to an investigation of debates provoked by such developments that, running between the 1880s and late 1920s, form a crucial context for the postwar development of British cinema. My focus here is on key notions that circulate from one generation to the next through theatrical and film trade, fan and review press. Building on these ideas, I outline a conception of theatricality that illuminates certain characteristics of British film-making practice, with examples from a range of representative films and film-makers of the period roughly bounded by the period from 1918 to 1928.

PROGRAMMING AND EXHIBITION PRACTICES

If cinema was to establish its place within a national cultural scene it was bound to engage with the theatre. And if histories based on great plays and playwrights, films and directors conceive theatre and cinema as distinct, singular entities, on the ground we find a far greater variety of forms, practices and personnel, interchanging and contesting with each other. Something of the theatrical variety of the period is captured by James Agate's annual volumes, *The Contemporary Theatre*, published between 1924 and 1927. These list plays under categories such as, Greek Play, Elizabethan Drama, Foreign Plays, Modern Plays, Melodrama, Revivals, Morality Plays. Coward's Ruritanian romance, *The Queen Was in the Parlour* (1926/play; 1927/film), is here a 'Modern Play', while his *Easy Virtue* (1926/play; 1927/film) counts as a 'Morality Play' along with Novello and Collier's *Downhill* (1926/play; 1927/film). However, their earlier *The Rat* (1924/play; 1925/film) is listed under 'Melodrama', as is E. Temple Thurston's *The Blue Peter* (1924/play; 1929/film). There were also plenty of nineteenth-century revivals, such as Charles Reade's *The Lyons Mail* (1877/first performance; 1923/revival, with several film versions, including Ideal's film of 1917). In the volumes for 1924 and 1926 Agate also includes a few film reviews, including British war films such as *Réveille* (1924), *Ypres* (1925) and *Mademoiselle d'Armentières* (1926).

Standard drama histories of this period focus on the growth of the independent theatre movement from the 1890s onward, including the influx of naturalist, symbolist and expressionist drama from the Continent and a native 'new drama', which contributed to the emergence of a middle-class intelligentsia in its support. However, the 'great' actor-managers (many knighted for their services to the nation and each lauded as the 'last' of their kind) – among them Charles Wyndham, John Martin-Harvey, Gerald du Maurier – still mounted their

most successful productions into the 1910s and some into the 1920s. Their presence, if resisted by modernisers, exerted a continuing force on the theatrical and cinematic scene. In the teens, Matheson Lang forsook the Shakespearian and Shavian repertoire in which he came to prominence for romantic melodrama, later taking up film-making to finance his management of the New Theatre, where he mounted a range of romantic and exotic popular productions during the 1920s. Mrs Forbes-Robertson, Basil Dean and W. A. Darlington all thank cinema for syphoning off melodrama and spectacle from the theatre.[4] However, James Agate, if a little confessionally, declares not only his pleasure at the appearance in the West End of new melodramas, but, even, of enjoying a visit to a Wardour Street trade show: 'Will it be believed that I was held by this arrant rubbish? . . . I went out to lunch and then *came back and saw some more films!*' (original emphasis).[5]

According to *The Bioscope*, the big theatrical event of 1919 remained the Drury Lane autumn melodrama. That year Louis N. Parker and George Sims' *The Great Day* was offered 'on a scale only possible at this famous old house, with its huge stage and extraordinary facilities for realistic effects . . . [which] have . . . become household words'. Drury Lane's success, the writer adds, with a clear nod in the direction of 'new' and experimental drama, lies in 'never attempting to become psychological, never going over the heads of the majority of people . . . the normal man in the street'. That the film rights had been secured by Famous Players–Lasky British, along with permission to use the original scenery, properties and costumes, and a guarantee of advisory support from Arthur Collins, the play's producer, was a matter for general congratulation.[6] A few years later, Herbert Wilcox acknowledges the continuing draw of Drury Lane by opening *Decameron Nights* (1924) there with full orchestral accompaniment. When Walter West decided to make another adaptation of *Maria Marten* in 1928, he was guilty less of being out of date, as Rachael Low suggests, than of recognising the pleasures of the audiences who had made its recent stage revival at the Elephant and Castle a success (see Chapter 5).[7]

In closing his first volume of *The Contemporary Theatre 1923*, then, James Agate concludes not that theatre is dying from the competition of cinema, but that it looks remarkably healthy. Five independent theatre companies, serving the intelligentsia, intersected with a broadly popular middlebrow West End theatre of classical revivals, romantic drama and melodramas and the more lowbrow entertainments offered by the music hall, variety, vaudeville. At the same time, a host of amateur theatrical and play discussion groups were active up and down the country, while 'barnstorming' melodramas still toured provincial towns.

CROSSING THE BOUNDARY BETWEEN THEATRE AND CINEMA

Actors and productions circulated between these different entertainment sectors. Michael Sanderson records how, for a number of reasons including the growing respectability of the music hall, legitimate actors were, from 1910 to the end of the 1920s, drawn to the halls. During the 1920s, for example, Godfrey Tearle appeared in an A. A. Milne sketch about demobilisation, while the young John Gielgud re-enacted his successful role as Romeo in the Balcony scene.[8] Conversely, John Stokes notes that J. T. Grein's Independent Theatre soon dropped its outright hostility to the commercial theatre, seeing its role as a seedbed for new dramatic practices that if more widely successful might transfer to the West End.[9] Lillah McCarthy, an actress firmly associated with new and experimental drama, appeared with Matheson Lang in both stage (1913) and film (1919) versions of the romantic *Mr Wu* (see Chapter 5). In their early days, both she and Lang had been advised by their mentors – respectively Shaw and Louis Calvert – to play melodrama and romantic drama in the provinces to gain experience and broaden their audience.[10] Conversely, in the 1910s we find Maurice Elvey – who was to become the most prolific of any British film director – playing small roles in the romantic dramas mounted and toured by Fred Terry and Julia Nielson's company. In 1911, however, seeking intellectual challenges, he formed the Sunday evening Adelphi Play Society at the Little Theatre, staging and acting in plays by Ibsen, Strindberg, Schnitzler and Chekhov, including the first English production of *The Seagull* (1912). As a result, Granville-Barker invited him to take Shaw's *Fanny's First Play* to New York in 1912, where, Elvey claims, he saw his first film and shortly thereafter converted to film-making.[11]

This permeability between legitimate and popular forms suggests the wider role of theatre and per-

formance in the reorganisation of British society in the fifty-year span stretching roughly from 1880 to 1930. The rise of amateur dramatic societies during the late 19th and into the 20th century not only contributed to the reform of the theatre but offered an escape route to the sons and perhaps especially the daughters from constricting social-class backgrounds.[12] As site of 'role-play', amateur dramatics offered vicarious experience of a social fluidity increasing in society at large. Thus Brian Aherne records how his mother's theatrical ambitions were confined by her family to association with Barry Jackson's, originally amateur, Pilgrim Players, with whom he also gained his first experience on stage.[13] By the turn of the century, however, the efforts of reformist actor-managers such as Henry Irving (the first to receive a knighthood, in 1895) had raised the social status of theatre. With the growth of media-produced 'fame' and 'celebrity', the nation's political and industrial leaders and members of the aristocracy increasingly sought the company of actors alongside writers and painters at their social gatherings. If the consolidating respectability of the theatre offered new opportunities to the children of well-to-do families, the cinema – caught between its low-class status as fairground and mass entertainment and its growing reputation as art form (in Europe) and leading industry (in America) – offered more challenging social movement. Thus, while coming from upper- or middle-class professional backgrounds, Ivor Montague, Anthony Asquith, George Pearson and Adrian Brunel founded a cinematic intellectual elite; as filmmakers they espoused cinema as a site of cross-class industrial production and popular cultural imagination. Conversely, the autobiographies of Noel Coward, Herbert Wilcox and Harry Rowson, cofounder of Ideal, repeatedly express surprised pleasure in a success that enabled them to rub shoulders with the politically powerful and titled alongside the intelligentsia.[14]

The crossover between theatre and cinema, extensively documented by Jon Burrows, began in the early teens, led by star actor-managers such as Herbert Tree, John Forbes-Robertson, Charles Wyndham and Ellen Terry, who allowed their productions to be recorded for the fees they generated, for the access it gave them to wider audiences and with an eye on posterity.[15] By the 1920s many younger actors were moving flexibly between film and stage:

for example, Henry Edwards, Guy Newall, Ivy Duke, Ivor Novello, Fay Compton, Gladys Cooper and Leslie Banks, among others.[16] Some of the most adventurous film directors of the early 1920s were actors such as Henry Edwards, Kenelm Foss and Guy Newall, who seemingly transferred the practice of actor-management to the as yet more open arena of cinema, combining scriptwriting, acting and directing (see Chapter 3).

MIXING LIVE AND FILMED PERFORMERS

An equally significant aspect of the cultural interpenetration of theatre and film in Britain is the return in the 1920s of a mixed-media exhibition context. Rachael Low records that by the early teens the practice of including films as turns in music-hall or fairground sideshows had all but ceased due to the increase in specialised cinemas. But the use of theatres and large concert halls for showcasing new prestige films – and creaming off first-run profits – had led to some tension between theatre managements and film exhibitors.[17] However, in 1919, an exhibition practice inaugurated by D. W. Griffith for *Broken Blossoms*, opened up the stage–screen relation to more than an economic stratagem. This special presentation involved not only dressing the theatre and usherettes in Chinese fashion (including hanging up cages of canaries that sang throughout the film) but beginning the performance with an elaborate prologue in which Mabel Poulton made her first appearance, miming Gish dying in a Buddhist temple.[18]

On one level, association with the established arts lent cultural prestige and respectability that would attract a better, higher-paying class of clientele. *Kinematograph Weekly*, reporting on 'The *Broken Blossoms* furore', notes how 'the higher-class audiences which have been flocking during the past few days to the Alhambra, consisting of people who have never been inside a film theatre . . . come away impressed . . . that here is an art . . . well worthy of cultivation'.[19] But this strategy opened up an interface between live and screen performance that British entertainment culture was quick to exploit. Trade press and newspaper reviews for the period record numerous elaborate prologues devised for prestige productions at trade shows, London openings and at more ambitious provincial venues. Sometimes they would meld into the screening itself, so that *Flames of Passion*

(1922), which opens with a close-up of a femme fatale in flames, must have emerged seemlessly out of the prologue representing Dante's Inferno.[20] The 'sky lights' that illumined the prologue for *Decameron Nights* remained shining throughout the screening, 'giving a very artistic effect'.[21] More ambitious provincial exhibitors would utilise such grand openings or devise similar ones.[22]

Kinematograph Weekly records an experiment by the Provincial Cinema Theatres circuit in mounting a 'revuette', titled *Speed*, which had been 'specially written, composed and produced' as a preamble to a Betty Balfour vehicle, *Monte Carlo* (1925), showing at the Globe, Acton. *Speed* lasted thirty minutes, included 'six scenes, a full cast of players as well as dancers and a beauty chorus' and was, apparently, enthusiastically received by the audience. The intention was to tour the 'revuette' with the film to all PCT venues.[23] Clearly, these developments represent a fluid combination of live and film entertainment. Reversing an earlier order whereby films were inserted into live entertainments, a practice of interspersing the film programme with variety turns became more systematic and organised in the second half of the 1920s. As a result, the Variety Artistes' Federation, having secured local authority licensing for such acts in cinemas throughout the country, went on to inaugurate a successful membership drive among the performers.[24] The *Daily Herald,* under the heading 'All Moving to the Movies', quotes the Secretary of the VAF to the effect that 'the tendency nowadays . . . is to combine vaudeville turns with a cinema programme, and many houses interpolate singing and dancing turns between pictures'.[25] Film trade and theatre press suggest that the economic insecurity that affected in different ways both cinema and music hall during the 1920s contributed to the growth of mixed-media shows. *Theatre World* complains that music-hall and variety acts are invading the cinema and depriving unemployed film artistes of business.[26] However, *The Stage* emphasises the social and aesthetic implications of such programming: 'Kinema proprietors are more and more seeking in the variety turn that fillip to their picture programmes which is so essential to the maintenance of old and the creation of new patronage.'[27] By the late 1920s, *The Kine Year Book* declares a new form, 'Kine-Variety', now 'definitely established . . . as a regular feature in a large number of the houses'. This was supported by 'orchestral work . . . of a far higher quality . . . than ever before', along with 'the most wonderful organs in the world . . . installed in all kinemas of any pretensions'.[28] Rachael Low records, with some amusement, the lengths to which this particular form could be taken when the London Palladium opened as a 'cine-variety' house in 1928:

> The stage curtains parted, Reg. Foort, the well-known cinema organist, lulled the house to silence with the opening bars of 'The Lost Chord', and then a spotlight traced De Groot standing before a transparent background, on which was seen 'the golden gates'.
>
> His music! Then the gates opened as the one hundred performers took up the harmony, which swelled into a terrific crescendo, as dazzling light fell upon a crystal fountain playing in the background. Then the fountain disappeared as 'The Lost Chord' gave place to 'The Blue Heaven', and suddenly the symphony died, it was gradually merged into syncopation, and an elevator rose at the back of the De Groot party, bearing Teddy Brown and his band, furiously working out the same melody according to the more popular and more modern conceptions of musical entertainment.[29]

This spectacular example also underlines the essential part played by music in the mixed-media context of pre-sound cinema, as it did in much theatrical performance.

Rachael Low sees the showmen as 'complacently abrogating the functions of the film maker', but in some cases theatrical and film showmen were prepared to work hand-in-hand in even more audacious experiments.[30] *Kinematograph Weekly* reports the integration of film with live performance in Boston by George Beban, an American character actor.[31] This impulse found fertile ground in Britain as part of theatrical as well as cinematic entertainment. The *Daily News* describes how in 1926 a film sequence – for which the actors provided spoken dialogue – was incorporated into the play, *Dr Knock*, at the Little Theatre in Leeds.[32] Conversely, in 1927 at the Plaza, Regent Street, Ivor Novello performed a section of the film, *Downhill* (1927), live, which according to *The Bioscope* melded into the film without visible breaks in continuity.[33] David Mayer offers further examples of filmic projections employed in live drama.[34]

Such practices met with varying approval from different audience groups, distinguishing the broad popular audience from an intelligentsia concerned with the potential of film as a distinctive art form. According to the *Daily Sketch*, students in an unnamed university town stamped every time a musical interlude interrupted the screening of films.[35] Similarly, *The Motion Picture Studio*, warning against mixing forms, declared: 'we always regard film "prologues" with resigned boredom and, if our observation goes for anything, the average audience does, too'.[36] On the other hand, *Kinematograph Weekly* reports that the 'artistically conceived prologue' devised by C. B. Worrall of the New Bohemian Cinema, Finchley, for *Decameron Nights* 'elicited so much appreciation that at many of the screenings the public wouldn't let the picture go on until the principal vocal number had been rendered three times'.[37] Reiterated complaints about musical interludes and interminable prologues recur with increasing impatience in the second half of the 1920s, particularly among campaigners for cinema as an autonomous art who, like Iris Barry, excoriated these 'abominations called prologues'.[38] But it is clear from reports in the provincial press that at the very least the prologue or variety interlude contributed a community function to the cinema, showcasing the 'splendid talents of our children' and of local dancing, dramatic or elocution schools.[39] From such contradictory reports, it is logical to assume that there were good and bad prologues and variety turns, just as there are good and bad films and plays. Equally, good and bad meant different things for different audiences. Arguments that polarise high-cultural and popular uses of theatre or cinema capture only a part of what was happening on the ground.

In a 1930 BBC talk, Desmond MacCarthy suggests a pragmatic solution to the tension between critical values and actual practices when he recommends the critic develop a multiple personality. 'The mind of the ideal spectator must, like a good motor-car, run on several gears; and from different plays you must ask not only different experiences, but be content with different qualities of enjoyment, sometimes with trivial ones.'[40] As David Mayer suggests, there is no clear-cut dividing line between the performance arts of stage and screen, and, despite the 'baton' conception of many theatre or cinematic histories, no single, nor even uni-directional, route of transmission or influence between them.[41] In Britain, especially, for reasons I shall suggest later, the two forms impact on each other. This is recorded in *The Picturegoer* in a 1926 article commenting that theatrical hostility to cinema seemed supplanted by raids on its techniques, citing in the staging of *Chu-Chin-Chow* the effects of close-up, fade-in and fade-out, achieved through masking techniques.[42] Furthermore, it claims the use of prologue and epilogue in recent stage plays to be derived from film-making practice. In his biography, Cecil Hepworth records his cinematic farewell in 1923 as a purely theatrical event. With his business in receivership and his precious films soon to be melted down for their silver content, Hepworth stage-managed a swansong screening of his remake of *Comin' thro' the Rye* (1923). For this he devised a prologue involving the play of light on his actors, and so successful was the live act that he toured it round the country without the film:

> [The show] . . . gave the effect of a huge picture in a gilt frame which at first showed nothing but the ordinary title familiar on every silent film. This gradually dissolved into a stage scene with the *living* actors going silently through their parts. That dissolved into another title filling the frame to be replaced again by the appropriate scene and so on . . . the effect was quite magical and as the actors were 'personal appearances', the whole thing went with a swing.[43]

However, after one performance, he recounts, he was accosted by a disappointed lady who had 'come up all the way from the country to see Alma Taylor in the flesh and had been put off with a coloured film'.[44] The only way Hepworth could pacify her was to take her behind the scenes to meet the star herself. Here we have a staged event that, for this spectator at least, creates the perfect illusion of film. On the other hand, we have films that work hard to incorporate the theatrical as live event. Such practices are supported by a discourse running through the commentaries of the 1920s that attributes 'flesh and blood' as a key value of the live performance and, like Hepworth above, assigns the more ambivalent terms 'mechanical' and 'shadows' to cinema. Terms such as 'shadowland', 'shadow puppets', 'grey shadows' proliferate through the trade and review press. The argument is in part about which medium is the more lifelike and therefore 'truthful' or 'realistic', and which the more artificial and therefore false.

At the heart of this opposition lies the complicated relationship of life and art, which does not align with but cuts across the theatre/cinema boundary and is worked through British culture in distinctive ways. In this respect, the adoption by one medium of techniques and effects created by another is not merely an outcome of commercial competition. It follows a culturally endemic practice of nineteenth-century arts and entertainment forms, strengthened by adaptation, reproduction and intertextual exchange between painting, fiction, theatre and reportage. I will be arguing that there are deeply embedded social reasons why British culture in particular should rely so heavily on representing itself through the artefacts and practices of different social constituencies. These social underpinnings belong in part to pressure on the arts for connection with the lived experience of a wider social range as part of a slow movement towards greater social participation and democratisation. Arguments encouraging stage actors' appearances in music hall or, later, in cinema stressed the educative effect of these new mass-mediated forms, reaching audiences for whom the theatre was inaccessible either socially or geographically, and encouraging them to try the 'real thing'.[45] But a more nuanced class-based pleasure may have been involved. Michael Sanderson, recording the different social backgrounds of legitimate actors and music-hall or variety artistes, speaks of 'the almost magnetic relations of attraction and repulsion between the halls and the actor'. He argues that 'the *frisson* of incongruity and contrast' of crossover appearances of actors or music-hall performers in each other's medium 'tells us much of what the Edwardians found attractive in this fusion of the two theatrical traditions'.[46] This class-based frisson arising from the exposure of difference lies, I shall argue, at the core of the peculiar, culturally derived aesthetic that informs British cinema practice.

THEATRICALISING FILM

In the context I have outlined, then, economic pressures are reinforced by cultural predispositions to combine the exhibition and performance practices of theatre, music hall, variety and cinema. From this perspective, it is the cultural and aesthetic significance of theatre and acting that concerns this study. It is this that I now want to trace by examining the considerable 'bleeding' between the theatrical and filmic in terms not only of source material and personnel but of acting styles, staging and narrational practices.

Scores of films of the period involve theatrical performers as characters and theatrical performances as narrative events. For example: a West End actress in *The Lure of Crooning Water* (1920); a faded music-hall performer in *Nothing Else Matters* (1920); the minstrel wandering incognito as Paragot in *The Beloved Vagabond* (1923); the fallen maestro, Lewinski, and violinist pupil in *The Blackguard* (1925); Italian puppeteers in *The Little People*; a Chinese nightclub dancer in *Piccadilly* (1929) and so on. The cultural importance of theatre and performance is documented in *Guns at Loos* (1928) by a hilarious cross-dressed First World War 'camp' theatrical, recalling Paul Fussell's observations quoted above. The entertainment takes place in a shed open to an audience of weary servicemen. But the camera set-up from behind them looks beyond the performers through an opening at the back of the improvised stage, to where armoured vehicles are preparing for the front – the 'real' Theatre of War. Here both 'scenes' function as social documents, a notion to be discussed in more detail in Chapter 2.

The theatrical, however, is not confined to literal representations of the stage. In 1926 The *Westminster Gazette* comments, 'no modern film is complete without a magnificent ball-room or cabaret scene'.[47] The internationalism of the period and the pressure to compete with Hollywood spectacle may well underpin the numerous films featuring European settings involving carnival, casinos, masked balls and cabarets: for example, *Carnival* (1921); *At the Villa Rose* (1920); *The House of Peril* (1922); *The Triumph of the Rat* (1926); *The Sea Urchin* (1926). However, their emphatic recurrence suggests an attempt to incorporate theatrical and performance presence into the film's story world and *mise en scène*. Such events or settings draw into the body of these films something of the razzmatazz that often accompanied their exhibition, drawing similarly unfavourable comment from certain quarters as to their taste, morality or truthfulness.[48]

Fig. 1.1. Lucia dances the 'Dying Puppet' as prologue to the puppet show that opens George Pearson's *The Little People* (1926)

On the other hand, the live-action prologue led some film-makers to tap into more self-consciously artistic practices, by integrating the prologue into a film's opening. George Pearson, for example, opens *Nothing Else Matters* with a danced harlequinade, before shifting into the story of a music-hall artist's attempted comeback, entangled in marital misunderstandings. This interpolation foreshadows and at the same time points up the story's themes and outcome. Fred Leroy Granville does something similar with *The Beloved Vagabond*, opening the film with an extra-diegetic mime in which Carlyle Blackwell as a Pied Piper-like figure cavorts with sundry children. *General Post* (1920) uses the children's game of the same name as prologue to a tale of shifting class relations following the war. The Italian heroine of Pearson's *The Little People* dances the 'Dying Puppet' both as diegetic prologue to the puppet show (Fig. 1.1) and fateful anticipation of her later disastrous appearance in a Mayfair nightclub as the story plays out its conflict between folk tradition and the sexual exploitation of stardom (see Chapter 6). Numerous films incorporate ballets or performed spectacles into their storylines at points where the characters are arriving at some crisis or high emotion. Ballets are staged at country-house balls at critical moments for respectively hero and heroine in *Flames of Passion* and *The Beloved Vagabond* (the latter giving Jessie Matthews her first film dancing role). In *The Pipes of Pan* (1923), Hepworth superimposes a fairy ballet over a woodland pond, called up by the heroine to preserve the faith of the little boy she has befriended, which later is to serve as a lesson to the more disillusioned adults (see Chapter 4).

At one level, cabaret, carnival and the masked ball serve as a means of releasing characters from an everyday world into the theatricalised costumes, gestures and actions that such events permit (see Chapter 5). On another, they point to the metaphorical significance of the public performance as a space for playing out tensions in British culture between life and artifice, private emotion and public presentation. In particular, the social changes of the postwar world renewed earlier debates in theatrical and now film criticism about what could or should be represented and how – issues involving questions of class and gender verisimilitude. The flesh and blood/shadows, live/filmed performance pairings suggest an overlap between such issues. Flesh and blood implies the

dynamic of living bodies but also an offending grossness, while the distance created by the absences of the cinematic image – bodily presence, colour, the voice – promises, for an intelligentsia concerned with cinema as 'art', access to more refined and spiritual reaches of artistic experience.[49]

HISTORICISING THEATRICALITY

The 1920s are marked by a class-informed struggle for cultural 'ownership' of cinema between showmen, intelligentsia, financiers and audiences, whose different interests circulate competing critical values and aesthetic preferences. Continuing late-nineteenth-century debates about the reform of the theatre, much of this discussion concerns acting, explored further in Chapter 3. Victorian acting, George Rowell argues, responded to the needs of melodrama and the huge theatres that had been built to accommodate large-scale entertainment for a growing mass and urban public in the first half of the 19th century.[50] But melodrama, like the theatre itself, comprises many things. And just as there is no singular, uni-directional line from stage to screen, so neither is there a singular line of progression from melodrama to the modern forms so often characterised in opposition to melodrama as 'realist'. As Thomas Postlewait shows, rather than neat alignment, complicated cross-relationships run between the critical values of melodrama, realism and particular playwriting or performance practices.[51] Thus the play, *The Green Goddess* (1921 New York; 1923 London), by William Archer, champion of dramatic realism, is, according to *The Oxford Companion to the Theatre*, 'an improbable melodrama'.[52] However, a British reviewer of the American film adaptation (1923) declares it a 'powerful melodrama', the effect of which nevertheless depends upon 'the meticulous realism both of plot and of character'.[53] Melodrama, then, constitutes a critical and aesthetic space in which a range of social and cultural tensions are played out, contested, negotiated. Crucial to my arguments are the class and gender-driven shifts in the history of melodrama's evolution.

REFORMING MELODRAMA

Historically, melodrama was forged from the convergence of two broad class-based cultural traditions: one, excluded from official culture, which contained a mix of folk and new urban entertainment forms, and another, more formally coherent, deriving from an increasingly influential middle-class fiction and theatre of sentimental drama and comedy. This forging comes about in the West from the commercial potential of new entertainment markets and the requirement of an industrialising, democratising society for a redefined and enlarged public sphere. Melodrama – a particular mode of imagining and dramatising – emerges as a new kind of entertainment machine capable of generating a range of genres for different audiences fashioned out of a variety of materials, continually adapted and transformed as they circulate in an expanding culture. News events, popular paintings or songs, romantic poetry, successful high dramas or circus acts offer sources for theatrical enactments.[54] Melodramatic sub-genres, specialising in particular materials, effects and spectator address, compete for the loyalty of differentiated audiences, while each production site seeks to maximise them by inclusive programming achieved by mixing its offerings. In the absence of copyright laws, competition for audiences was furthered by plagiarism, piracy and adaptation.

From its inception, melodrama was held in considerable ambivalence. In one manifestation, drawing on proscribed and marginalised popular entertainments, melodrama provokes, much as today, establishment anxiety as to the cultural degeneration and insubordination of the lower orders. Equally, however, providing an excitement and moral fervour lacking in sentimental drama and comedy, melodramatic materials are poached from London's East End and Surreyside to invigorate the repertoire of the legitimate theatres and stem the flow of more adventurous middle-class audiences in the opposite direction. As a result, the tactics of class-differentiated forms of entertainment for a while combine. Thus action and sentiment, pathos and spectacle are drawn into a composite but highly flexible aesthetic modality, capable of different and often contrary emphases, orientations and generic manifestations. Wedding two cultural traditions, and drawing together different audiences into a new public mass, melodrama becomes a source of both fascination and threat.

A central feature of melodramatic modality is its polarisation of antagonists in terms of emotionally defined moral identities that are eventually aligned with the guilt of the villain and the innocence of the heroine. Class opposition – intersected by gender and race – provides a key source for such dramaturgy. Much nineteenth-century melodrama cues into the visual and social oppositions made visible by the startling juxtapositions of fast expanding, heteroglot cities – rich/poor, upper class/working class, luxury/squalor – as well as by social experiences of sudden rise and fall accompanying the boom and bust cycles of industrialisation.[55] Class opposition is repeatedly enacted in the antagonism of decadent aristocrat or ruthless agent of capitalism against the virtuous poor.[56] In France at the turn of the eighteenth century and in Russia in the early 20th century, this aesthetic of justice could briefly serve revolutionary ends.[57] But in emerging social democracies, outright class opposition required containment at both symbolic and social levels. Arguably, American melodrama, driven by an egalitarian ideology, displaced class into other oppositions, a major one being the opposition America/Europe, which permitted the association of class with the old country. But in England, seeking to stem revolution by reform, there remains a tension between the shift to a social democratic society in which 'all sorts and conditions of men' are supposed to be of equal value and the historically ingrained fact of class demarcation.[58] If initially melodrama invaded the cultural space of an aristocratic elite through the expansion of middle-class and new urban working-class audiences, by mid-century the middle classes dominated the centre, providing an all-inclusive norm against which other cultural formations would be marginalised. Theatrical reform begins in the latter half of the 19th century, with the mutually reinforcing bids by certain theatrical managements to raise the status of the theatre and acting profession. They sought to woo a middle-class audience frightened off by the more popular manifestations of melodrama, and by a fraternity of dramatic critics, playwrights and actor-managers avid to regain the theatre for 'serious drama' and a new kind of intelligentsia. Key to these ambitions was reform of the repertoire and performance mode in terms of greater 'truth', 'verisimilitude' or 'realism' in which middle-class audiences could recognise themselves and their concerns.[59]

From the 1860s new theatres were built on a smaller scale, thereby allowing for more detailed staging and performance effects, and an increasing role for verbal language over spectacle. The programmes became shorter, starting later in the evening to suit middle-class working and dining hours, and, together with the practice of dimming the house lights, focusing attention on the play. The pit was reconstructed as stalls seating, and, with the elimination of the half-time, half-price entrance and an overall rise in prices, forced its traditionally lower-class occupants up into the gallery out of sight.[60] Changing the physical conditions of theatre-going and play-production in this way facilitated the refinement of melodramatic codes of action, staging and performance in line with changing codes of verisimilitude aimed at the recognition and support of the middle-class and emerging intelligentsia. As Michael Sanderson notes, 'characters wore modern dress, inhabited recognisable interiors and spoke the educated parlance of the day', a change that both encouraged and drew from the entry of the upper middle classes into the acting profession and consequent 'gentrification of the stage'.[61]

Paradigmatic in their contribution to shifts in theatrical practice, critical values and cultural publics is the work of three dramatic critics – G. H. Lewes, William Archer and J. T. Grein. In support of reformist actor-managers such as the Bancrofts, and new dramatists such as Ibsen and Shaw, they campaigned to raise the status of the theatre as a national institution. Between them they spanned a period from the mid-19th century into the 1920s. G. H. Lewes – philosopher, actor and drama critic – published a collection of reviews in *On Actors and the Art of Acting* (1875), which was a source of inspiration to George Pearson. W. A. Archer, translator of Ibsen and drama critic, delivered *The Old Drama and the New* (1923) as a series of public lectures commissioned by the London County Council in 1920–1. J. T. Grein, founder of the Independent Theatre Club in 1891 and member of the Stage Society (1899–1939), campaigned, along with Archer, for the New Dramatists and Ibsen. His drama criticism for the *Illustrated London News* was collected in 1921 and 1924 as respectively *The World of the Theatre* and *The New World of the Theatre*. Alongside Clement Scott, these three contributed key ideas and values to the cultural and aesthetic environment in which British film-making practices and critical debates would eventually evolve. Their support was crucial for the refinement of melodrama as a mode of perception and aesthetic practice.

Their campaigns effectively shifted the terms of verisimilitude in conformity to a middle-class outlook. Since melodrama depends on recognition to authenticate its moral claims, it must adapt its strategies to new circumstances. Thus G. H. Lewes praises the performance of Charles Mathews and Madame Vestris in *A Day of Reckoning* (1850) in terms that seek to 'naturalise' the class-based protagonists of melodrama:

> Vestris and Charles Mathews were *natural* – nothing more, nothing less. They were a lady and gentleman such as we meet in drawing-rooms, graceful, quiet, well-bred, perfectly dressed, perfectly oblivious of the footlights. He is a polished villain – a D'Orsay without conscience, and without any of the scowlings, stampings, or intonations of the approved stage villain. There are scoundrels in high life – but they are perfectly well-bred [original emphasis].[62]

This account represents not the proscription of melodrama but its refinement in conformity with middle-class codes of decorum. Indeed, Lewes implicitly recognises a retraction of audience reach for this new mode of performance when he speculates how far such nuances would be understood in the pit.[63] William Archer similarly reveals the class underpinnings of the new dramatic values in his complaint about a lapse of verisimilitude in Tom Robertson's melodramatic comedy, *Society* (1865). Sidney Daryl, a lovelorn barrister, 'seeks consolation in champagne, and insults Maud before a ball-room full of people'. 'Are we', asks Archer, 'to conclude that manners have greatly improved since 1865 or merely that the author did not know what was possible in a mid-Victorian drawing-room?'[64] As a result, comments Michael Sanderson, by the start of the inter-war years, mainstream acting style had changed from 'full-blooded and rhetorical to a quiet, muted conversational naturalism, fitted for the drawing-room play'.[65]

Significantly, it is the *public* expression of feelings that Lewes and Archer want to see restrained, separating private emotion from public life, both in terms of the scope of dramatic plots and of the theatre as a public arena. Action retreats to the drawing room as a place of social interactions governed by polite behaviour, while the new villain no longer engages an audience in his social malignity or furious plotting for revenge, but is self-contained, 'perfectly oblivious of the footlights', inscribing a distance between audience and enactment. In the British context, this aesthetic of social decorum and distance between persons is a condition of middle-class hegemony in which a gradual shift towards democratic representation depends on clearly class-demarcated spaces and rituals for social and dramatic interaction. In fact, to return to Archer's complaint about Sidney Daryl in *Society*, the exchange in question *did* start in private, in that Sidney begins his protest to Maud while they are both alone in an ante-room where a buffet is laid out. Coincidentally – but dramatically opportune – as his emotional temperature rises the folding doors to the ballroom are thrown open, transforming his accusation into the disgraceful and melodramatic public display of which Archer complains. Sidney hysterically – and cinematically – runs through the assembled company to the sounds of crashing chords and images of swirling dancers. Crucial to this dramatic switch from private to public is the arrangement of the stage into different spaces and the possibility of their intersection.

GEOGRAPHY VERSUS BIOGRAPHY

Reform comes also from another direction. If G. H. Lewes's comments on *A Day of Reckoning* suggest a universal human nature, Archer's concern with what *really* happens in middle-class drawing rooms demands the close observation of social behaviour that has become the goal of a new documentarist impulse. This is increasingly apparent across a range of art, entertainment and journalistic forms as the century progresses. For instance, W. P. Frith's paintings, *Ramsgate Sands* (1854), *Derby Day* (1856–8) and *The Railway Station* (1862), popularised the social panorama embracing new public sites for inclusive social gatherings, bringing 'types' from different social classes into proximity. Pierce Egan's much recycled *Tom and Jerry* (1821), in which two young bloods found excitement exploring the dens of Seven Dials, was to be followed by sensational melodramatists, investigative journalists and social documentarists, such as Henry Mayhew's *London Labour and the London Poor* (1849–61) and Gustave Doré and Blanchard Jerrolds's collaboration, *London, A Pilgimage* (1872). George R. Sims (1847–1922) worked across melodrama (e.g. *The Lights of London*, 1881), journalism (*How the Poor Live*, 1883) and ballads (e.g. the

ever popular, *The Workhouse, Christmas Day*, filmically illustrated by George Pearson in 1914).

An emphasis on increasingly documented rather than metaphoric location becomes central to the identification of protagonists and dramatic events according to their social position and interactions, impacting on staging and scene-setting. The programme for *Real Life* (1882), for example, notes the division of the play into the following geographically located 'scenes':

ACT I.
A LODGING HOUSE IN DRURY LANE.
The Two Roads in Life.

ACT II.
THE LONDON DOCKS.
The Decoy. Departure of the 'Magnet' for Ostend.

ACT III.
A BELGRAVIAN MANSION.
A Woman Wronged.
VICTORIA RAILWAY STATION.
Departure of the Dover Mail. A Deed of Vengeance.

ACT IV.
BRANDON HALL, SUSSEX.
The Ebony Casket.

Such spatial juxtapositions record the impact on perceptual experience of city and rural spaces divided by class, as well as the significance of new urban sites that bring people separated by social position into contact.

This slippage between melodrama and social document attenuates the polar oppositions that fuel melodramatic conflict. In their different ways melodrama reformists and documentarists seek to stem the disruptive potential of class conflict by appealing to the sympathies and social responsibility of middle-class conscience. Thus, if documentary mapping extends social reach it also contains by demarcating class-defined protagonists.

Similarly, reform of melodrama's exteriorised passions through separation of private from public expression institutes psychological boundaries, inhibiting cross-class infiltration of personal or subjective space. Illuminating in this context is Martin Meisel's analysis of the tension in narrative painting between the temporal movement of narrative and the located moment of the picture, the theme of Chapter 2.[66] Significant here, however, is the implied translation of a biographic narrative trajectory into geographic *mise en scène*. While the panoramas of Frith and others freeze the social juxtapositions of new democratising activities such as train travel or seaside outings, the socially documented scene-setting of melodramas like *Real Life* suggests a geographic staging of juxtaposed social spaces. Such locales are peopled by contrasting types identified by the social signifiers of dress, gesture, habitat and trade, reinforced through the processes of 'character drawing' and 'character acting' discussed in the following chapters. *General Post*, for example, introduces us to Gentleman's Tailor, Edward Smith, as he surveys his appointments calendar, the week mapping time across the activities of socially located players:

Date	Day	Time	Particulars
15th	Mon	4p.m.	Committee Meeting
21st	Tue	5p.m.	Children's Tea
19th	Wed	7p.m.	Girls' Social Evening
5th	Thurs	6.30	Ragged School Gym Drill
10th	Fri	9a.m.	Soup Kitchen Accounts
14th	Sat	2.30p.m.	Territorial Inspection by CO

The role of the 'boundary' in such socio-geographic staging suggests the different ways in which approaches to narrative and *mise en scène* developed in British and American cinemas. If American melodramatic genres largely displace class conflict into oppositions more amenable to egalitarian ideology, narrative can then be organised into a temporal, biographical trajectory following the projection of a hero or heroine's life story through time and across a *mise en scène* of natural and social divisions. Arriving at new and democratic positions, biography conquers geography. Verisimilitude in British culture, on the other hand, requires a geographic mapping of social-class-defined spaces that inhibits the individual's progressive trajectory through time, working to reinstate the boundaries that divide protagonists. Geography rules. Representation itself becomes a means of rational control through class identification and social mapping. The social boundaries explored by social investigators, melodramatists and painters are internalised through a lexicon of character types,

their habitats and appropriate behaviours, while 'control' as a middle-class ethos not only ensures that the personal does not spill into public life, but maintains a proper distance between persons *tout court*. Thus concern with behaviour appropriate to drawing rooms is not simply a condition of verisimilitude for one class only, but essential to the boundaries on which perception of differentiated social identities depend. Class formations shift, but the mode of cultural perception they give rise to bequeaths a set of aesthetic practices that suggest the wider significance of theatricality and performance for British filmmaking.[67]

In this sense three interrelated aspects of cinematic theatricality emerge. First, the *stage* as a site for a public enactment, an architecturally designed and theatrically lit space that organises the physical and narrative movements of the drama's protagonists. Second, *acting and role-play* (discussed in later chapters) as the means by which public performers occupy this space. Finally, the placing of the *audience* in the generation of expressive performances and public acts. A key question for understanding British film aesthetics is the orchestration of these relationships and how theatricality may be rendered cinematic – or cinema theatricalised – in a way that identifies a British style of film-making.

THE THEATRICALISATION OF CINEMATIC SPACE

Theatricality in British cinema begins with the shot composed as a stage, bounded by the proscenium arch – tripled as picture and film frame, the concern of the next chapter. If the theatrical proscenium arch and footlights separate the public space of the stage from the private space of the individualised audience member, the stage is itself a means for the public but contained expression of private dilemmas. Through dramatic construction, set design, performance mode and role-playing, protagonists are not only separated from the audience but from each other by divisions between private and public spaces. Similarly, characters are internally divided between private and public selves. Thus theatre is paradigmatically important for British culture as a site in which private selves may be realised, and often *only* realised, through public stagings. In this sense theatricality informs British cinema aesthetics through its production of sites of action as metaphorical stages for social performances.

CINEMATIC STAGES

In an exhibition site still calling itself a theatre, cinema offers its own set of frames, beginning with its proscenium arch framing the screen. As noted above, a fictionalised stage is a site of action in many 1920s films. In *Duke's Son* (1920), Billy, showgirl mistress and recently made wife of the tuberculosis-stricken card-sharper, Sir Robert Sheen, is going through her song routine, 'Wait for Me My Husband', when she collapses on stage under the weight of premonition. The crisis of *Nothing Else Matters* occurs as Jimmy Daw attempts to make his music-hall comeback to a stony audience. *The Rat* finds Zelie de Chaumet bored at a spectacular musical show. And in *Downhill*, Ivor Novello – apparently making ends meet as a waiter and purloining a forgotten cigarette case – unexpectedly starts jigging as the camera pulls back to reveal his role in a swaying chorus line of similar waiters. But aside from literal 'stagings' of this kind, the performance event can be extended to other arenas of public or semi-public 'acts': for example, the law court, the concert, the already mentioned carnival, nightclub and cabaret, the country-house ball, wedding breakfast, harvest festival, civic ceremony, birthday party and so on.

Such events, involving social performances for a gathered assembly, are perhaps prone to theatricalisation, but many films deploy all means – scene construction, location, *mise en scène*, camera position, action and performance – to produce the event as a staging. Action, for example, is often segmented as a series of discrete 'scenes'. *General Post*, scripted by Eliot Stannard from a stage play and directed by Thomas Bentley, produces through its much admired and experimental use of horizontal and vertical wipes the effect of the closing in or opening of theatrical wings or curtain drops to end and open 'scenes'. Such scenes may be internally segmented by the use of straight cuts when shots are part of a composite unit, reinforcing the theatrical effect of the wipe as a definitive scene end. *Nobody's Child* (1919) uses gestural rhetoric to close a scene. On reaching a door the actor will look back, give and perhaps receive a disengaging gesture such as a lifting or turning of the head, a raising of the hand, a sigh or a lingering look, followed by a swift turn and exit. The Cutts/Hitchcock collaboration, *The Blackguard*, signals each temporal shift in the hero's biography by opening onto an imposing, theatrically conceived stage set, viewed as if from the stalls. This recalls not simply the structure of stage and auditorium, but the charged atmosphere when the audience hushes as the curtain rises to reveal the first images and sounds of an as yet unvisited theatrical world in which people are going about their business. Thus the film opens onto the medieval twisting streets and deeply sloping roofs of a twilit, misty Bavarian town as the lamplighter performs his task. The next scene opens with a view across a street at a pavement café, where under the awning a down-and-out violinist and well-heeled artist sit with their drinks on opposite sides of a table-strewn stage. In from the wings wanders the hero as child, soon to be torn between their conflicting influences. The third scene reveals the steps of a filmically contrived cathedral (a replica of Milan Cathedral), at the top of which stands a crippled beggar. A few stage extras pass from left to right in the foreground, a flight of doves wing down from right to left, creating an atmosphere of religiosity, pathos and hope.[68]

Domestic set construction may also reproduce metaphoric stages for dramatised enactments. Country- and town-house architecture is graced with sweeping staircases arriving in large halls serving as communal meeting places. Half-landings or upper galleries, onto which various bedroom doors open, provide a network of often complexly conceived, interlinked stages for formal encounters or private exchanges: for example, *The Hound of the Baskervilles* (1921), *The Passionate Adventure* (1924), *Guns at*

Fig. 1.2. Country-house gardens provide stages for narrative encounters with their terraces, flagged ponds, stone balustrades and steps (*Comin' thro' the Rye*, 1923)

Loos, *Kitty* (1928) and, most spectacularly, Cutts's *The Queen Was in the Parlour* (see Chapter 4). Country-house gardens such as we find in *The Bargain* (1921), *Passionate Friends* (1921) and *Comin' thro' the Rye* provide similar locations for staged encounters, with their terraces, flagged ponds, stone balustrades and steps (Fig. 1.2). Public buildings such as the 'great cosmopolitan hotel' of *Human Law* (1926), or the ballrooms and dinner-dance venues in *The Man Without Desire* (1923), *The Triumph of the Rat* or *Champagne* (1928), provide arenas for heterosexual entanglements within complex networks of multi-level, large- and small-scale, fully public and semi-private spaces. Thus the drama of the newly wed but paranoid Henry Radcliffe in *Human Law* depends on the theatrically designed hotel set of multiple levels, perspectives, exits and entrances. Action starts with a medium shot of a small mezzanine refreshment area where the boredom of an adolescent seated with his mother instigates an unpleasant little social comedy of mischievous glances aimed at the legs of a neighbouring woman. Spotted and rebuffed, his wandering eyes focus in a narrowing iris shot on the newly wed bride below, left waiting at an intersection of stairways and passages, while her husband inspects the bridal suite. The boy moves down to circle around her and then, casting insinuating looks through a wrought-iron screen, sidles, despite her rebuff, onto the sofa beside her, eventually to be assaulted and killed by the jealous husband. But in the meantime the action has cross-cut to the husband inspecting the bridal suite – a stage-managed scene that through framing and montage editing suggests a similar prurience. Under the gaze of manager and bellboy, the husband slyly takes in the public signs of a sexual consummation he will not experience: the lacy pillow slips, the semi-pornographic Venus and Cupid over the bed – all to the smirks of onlooking staff.

By utilising the multiple and shifting possibilities of internal staging and framing through set design, personal and private moments become available within public modes of address. So, for example, in *The Prude's Fall* (1924) Andre, expecting to reunite with the bride who, through misrecognition, he has spurned, finds himself witnessing her suicide. He is posed on a small landing, looking across the well of her room, to a dais where she sits gazing into a dressing-table mirror. Swivelling round, she returns his gaze as the poison she has drunk takes hold, the personal drama both contained and intensified by the space between them. Similarly, internal curtains are repeatedly used for the theatrical presentation of personal and private moments. In *The Little People*, the middle-aged writer Lyn, realising his love for the Italian dancer and puppeteer, Lucia, whom his entrepreneurial friend has tried unsuccessfully to turn into a Mayfair sensation, is pacing his study, separated from the hallway by a diaphanous curtain. His serving man now draws it aside to allow Lucia's entrance, revealing Lyn, lit at the back of the room, his hand held in a gesture of hopeless proposal to her. In a similarly overdetermined moment in *The Blackguard*, the premises of the art dealer Vollmark set up behind what looks like a proscenium arch flanked by two velvet curtains. In long shot we look through into the showroom behind, where the now grown-up princess admires the painting of Michael done when he was a poverty-stricken protégé of the famous artist mentioned above in the café scene. The picture recalls her childhood visit to the studio when she fell secretly in love with the boy model and his music. Planning to stage Michael's imminent arrival as a surprise for both of them, Vollmark has his servant close the curtains to the hallway. Standing silhouetted before them like a stage compère, he greets the now rising violinist, and, promising to delight him, pulls the cord, making the curtains swing open with a grand flourish to reveal the princess at the back of the room. Startled, Michael catches his breath, as the dealer takes him by the arm, gently leading him into the theatrical scene. In *Human Law* the three-year-old daughter of Henry Radcliffe is seized from his estranged wife. Still clutching a huge toy cat, she is brought to meet her awkward and embittered father on what functions effectively as a fore stage before a proscenium-like curtain topped by a pelmet. This is hastily drawn to shroud the degenerate party in progress in the inner room behind and will soon be torn down to produce a discordant clash of moral identities and feelings.

GEOGRAPHIC STAGES AND SOCIAL MAPPING
In this way the multi-level sets and internal frames of private and public spaces produce bounded stages for actions controlled and contained within public codes of performed behaviour (Fig. 1.3). If frames and stages contain, the documentarist impulse to identify

Fig. 1.3. Geographic staging in *The First Born* (1928)

protagonists through socially defined locales contributes to geographic dramatic construction, mapping boundaries that demarcate characters and their actions according to class and social position. The internal organisation of country mansion and town house may be used for the upstairs/downstairs dynamic. For example, in the opening scenes of *Guns at Loos* ambivalence about the First World War is dramatised not only in the enacted opposition between management and factory hands but in the opposition between the farewell ball 'upstairs' and the carnivalesque party held 'downstairs'. Here heroics are submitted to the realistic pragmatism of servants who have been called up and unlikely to return. In *General Post* and *Blighty* (1927) corridors and hallways offer sites for unexpected encounters between employers and servants, and in *Passionate Friends* and *Human Law* for the constraining presence, observation and sometimes spying of servants or staff. For example, in the sequence titled 'Her Wedding Night' in *Human Law*, the new bride spends her marriage night not in honeymoon bliss but alone after leaving her new husband in a prison cell. Her return to the now redundant bridal suite is nevertheless staged as a public event, under the observing eyes of hotel staff, so that the intense privacy of the moment we are interested in must be signified in public images and gestures. Her entrance to the wedding suite is framed in an oval mask, her gaze vacant so that she almost walks into a table, which is caught by an attentive waiter, the camera left to point out the nuptial wreath suspended from the ceiling.

The countryside produces similarly spatialised social divisions between the manor house and gentry, the small town or village high street with its shopkeepers, local professionals and community gossips, and on the social margins a lone cottager, gypsy caravan, outsider or vagrant. In *Tansy* (1921) the heroine and her grandfather are made vagrants when turned out of their tithe cottage because of Tansy's entanglement with a travelling harvester. In *Comradeship* (1919), the coming of war turns social relations in Melcombe on their heads, as the daughter of the manor converts the Great House into a hospital and woos for the cause the shy, pacifist and potentially socialist owner of the local tailoring business (see Chapter 4). *General Post*, offering a similar geography, uses a wartime drama to challenge even more explicitly the territorial demarcations of rural communities (see below and Chapter 2). City geography, if appearing more rarely in 1920s films, orchestrates mass conurbations as stages for social action (Fig. 1.4), producing starker (because physically closer) juxtapositions between East and West End, between the dark alleys of terraced slums and the porticoed and pillared steps of town houses and public buildings, between workers' pub or dockside and glittering department store or dinner-dance club. *The Passionate Adventure* juxtaposes the alienated life of a Mayfair mansion with the hero's adventures in the tenements of East London's docklands. Juxtaposed scene-construction in *Kitty* makes Lady King's country seat, shot through an imposing gatehouse facing left, the recto of her town house, which opening onto the right frame abuts the lower-middle-class street where Kitty and her mother run a tobacconist's shop. As suggested above, this propensity for dramatic contrast was utilised by melodramatists and social documentarists alike to combine shock, pathos and social message.

Such use of social locales as bounded public stages rarely visualises the coherent spatial totality that is the goal of a continuity cinema. This lack of integration, however, serves to intensify the sense of social juxtaposition that in some cases is deliberately emphasised through strategic cross-cutting and

titling. For example, *Flames of Passion* pointedly contrasts the newly wed bliss of Dorothy Hawke (Mae Marsh) – singing in her little mob cap at the piano for her elderly barrister husband – with a violent domestic row between lower-class Kate (Hilda Bayley) and her chauffeur husband, Arthur Watson (Herbert Langley). An intertitle underlines the dramatic geography: 'in another part of town another drama plays itself out'. Arthur, now sacked by the Hawke family after getting Dorothy pregnant, is sinking into drink, while Kate struggles to bring up, unbeknown as yet to Dorothy or Arthur, their illegitimate baby. The town has only featured once, in what is effectively a comic prologue in which the tomboy schoolgirl, Dorothy, is caught mimicking a prim, middle-aged lady. But the film's sense of divided social arenas and the different destinies played out in each could not be more explicit.

An equally schematic if differently valued contrast juxtaposes the city's nervous exhaustion with country living. Thus *The Lure of Crooning Water*, in which a flighty actress on the verge of a breakdown is sent for a rest cure on the farm, identifies the city with theatrical allure and the country with the stability of family. In Hepworth's later films such disjunct social locations take on an almost allegorical function. For example, in *The Pipes of Pan*, an itinerant tinker and his daughter are transported for the sake of their traditional metal burnishing recipe to a country mansion, which is both home and head office of nouveau-riche manufacturers out to exploit their simplicity (see Chapter 4). *Kitty* augments the country seat/urban back street opposition by annexing the values of country life to the Thameside cottage its heroine turns into a successful café and home for her war-damaged husband. To achieve this, however, she must literally kidnap him from the town house where he has been languishing in the clutches of his aristocratic mother.

Many films, seeking more exotic opportunities, intermix locations in Europe or the outer reaches of the Empire with familiar scenes of the home country, creating more startling juxtapositions while at the same time displaying different social-value systems. Thus *The Bargain* contrasts the harshness and semi-criminal desperation of an outcast son's gold-prospecting life in the Australian outback with his father's nouveau-riche success in England. This in turn is measured against the pastoral idyll of 'Wood-

Fig. 1.4. Geographic staging in *The Sign of the Four* (1923)

lands', foregone through upward mobility to landed gentrification at 'Bewley Court', and remembered only in flashback. The cost is a family divided. *The Little People* shifts action between the community of southern Italian puppeteers to London Mayfair nightclub life and back again in a poetic meditation on the cultural relations of traditional and commercial forms of entertainment.

One Colombo Night (1926) juxtaposes London stock-exchange corruption and its ideological support, a home counties country vicarage, against on the one hand the economic and sexual exploitation practised in a Ceylonese rubber plantation, and on the other the spiritual retreat of a convent mission. As a programmatic film, made up of melodramatic set pieces – the villain's attempted seduction of the heroine, displacement of the hero to Australia, the intercepted and then destroyed letter, engineered misrecognition, stolen documents, last-minute rescue – the film offers a clear illustration of the spatial theatricalisation of British cinema. Nearly all these actions are set in public locations, framed through arches, or curtains, or from a high angle, turning both documented locations and studio sets into stages or arenas for action. Here are played out social and moral interactions of imperial colonisation and finance capitalism, enacted as conflicts between familial obligations and personal choices. So, for example, the film opens with a high-angle view through a civic archway onto the main thoroughfare of Colombo, setting up a stage for multiracial but unequal encounters between colonials, tourists, Eastern businessmen and beggars, mingling together on the street. The colonial interior of villain, Richard Baker's mansion, with its pillars and stairways, and the exterior shots of his rubber plantation provide a *mise en scène* for further stagings of colonial power and servitude. Colonisation of the economy becomes sexual colonisation at the entertainment put on for Baker's business associates, in which his reception room is effectively set up as a private nightclub for the display of the Ceylonese girl, Lalla, who dances for the card-playing, whisky-swilling male guests, over whose heads her performance is shot. Less successfully, Baker is attempting to apply the same force to the Englishwoman, Rosemary, whom she encounters in the opening colonial city spaces as she arrives to visit her sister, the Mother Superior at the nearby convent.

The shift of action back to England and the Stock Exchange introduces further public stages for the enactment of finance capital's power relations, not only in the dealings of the stock market itself but in the way they are entwined in the fabric of English bourgeois life. For example, at a tea dance Jim, the soon to be misrecognised hero, courts Rosemary under Baker's brooding gaze. Baker attempts to insinuate himself into the daily routines of her guardian uncle's country vicarage, where, framed oppositionally in an archway of light, Rosemary resists male authority, defending her integrity, freedom of choice and steadfast loyalty to Jim. Later, back in the Colombo convent, the church, with its pillars, arches and steps to the surrounding garden, provides another stage for a final emotional enactment. As Jim arrives at the moment of her ordination and Rosemary tears away from the altar to reach him, the nuns stand holding out her veil. The echo from Lalla's earlier dance of the veil suggests two very different but equally culturally ambivalent images of female sexuality. Such images are taken up again in Powell and Pressburger's postwar *Black Narcisus* (1947).

NARRATIVE AS BOUNDARY-CROSSING: *THE RAT* AND *UNDERGROUND*

Geographic locale, then, produces both cultural definitions and stages for action. The emphasis on boundaries set in place both by the limits of a social stage and the manipulation of scenic space produces its own distinctive narrational dynamic. If boundaries divide protagonists from each other, juxtaposition is also a form of contact that provokes border crossings. In *Flames of Passion*, for example, the action crosscuts between Dorothy's pampered existence on a landed estate and Kate's experience of domestic violence in a worker's cottage. Three times in the film Kate appears in great agitation at the Forbes's mansion, twice to be met by Dorothy's protective aunt. The last time, however, knowing that her baby is dead, Dorothy takes charge, the frisson of the impending encounter announced by the title: 'Here the two women are together for the first time.' The difference between them is marked in their dress and stature – Dorothy, petite in flowered chiffon, Kate, statuesque in her black dress. For a moment, social class power is reversed. Kate's veiled threat to use her knowledge of the baby's parentage to further her own needs is also a declaration of social justice: 'You are the murderer of this child.'

Graham Cutts's 1925 film, *The Rat* – made for Gainsborough and staring Ivor Novello in a vehicle he and Constance Collier developed for the stage[69] – demonstrates in a romantically energised manner how stage, frame and boundary contribute in both their literal and metaphoric senses to the theatricalisation of cinematic space. The action of the film is divided between three social locations. The Parisian underworld centres on the White Coffin, haunt of the Apache Rat (Novello). A tiny apartment in a tenement block is the stage for domestic scenes featuring Odile (Mae Marsh), a poverty-stricken waif and the film's sign of virtue, who secretly adores the Rat but figures for him only as a playmate sister. And, finally, the Parisian demi-monde delivers Zelie de Chaumet (Isabel Jeans), high-class courtesan to the vampire-like Baron Stetz, who will be the undoing of the young couple.

Zelie, adorned in fur and jewels, is taken to the legitimate theatre for a spectacular variety show. However, Stetz, knowing that she is bored, arranges for her party to bring her to a low dive known as the White Coffin. The architecture of the White Coffin underlines the role of class difference as stimulus to her jaded senses. The set – by C. W. Arnold, among the first of British cinema's 'film architects'[70] – is constructed as a series of distinct areas, with a lower dance floor overhung by an upper mezzanine reached by an open stairway. This structure demarcates distinct class spaces. The mezzanine functions as a kind of dress circle, coffin-shaped arches allowing the fashionable crowd seated above to look down on the lower floor, while framing alternately the action below or the upper-class spectators eagerly waiting for something to happen. They are not disappointed. At the centre of the lower 'stage' is the charismatic Rat, soon provoked into a knife fight by a rival's provocative remarks about Odile. The fight functions as a working-class ritual performed for the upper-class viewers, who are caught by the camera leaning eagerly forward to watch through the openings. If, however, such framing and staging contain characters within separate social spaces, the coffin-shaped arches enclose a three-dimensional arena pulsating with movement, while spatial juxtaposition facilitates boundary transgression. The ritualistic 'performance', then, refuses to stay within the bounds of its own framed stage. The

two combatants, followed by their supporters, push up the steps onto the mezzanine floor, galvanising Cutts's highly mobile camera and bringing a triumphant Rat under Zelie's desiring gaze.

Novello's Paris provides an imaginary social architecture for such romantic class oppositions and encounters, centred on the figure of the apache as a boundary figure much in vogue in the 1920s (see Chapter 5). In contrast, Anthony Asquith's *Underground* (1928) draws on the documentarist's awareness of the contemporary, democratic city as evolving a set of public sites and practices – in particular, travel and shopping – that enforce mixing and contact (Fig. 1.5). This in turn reinforces efforts to demarcate social identities in which class and gender boundaries are constantly slipping in the process of modernisation. The modern urban daughter is thrust into a world of dangerous social mixing, where girls earn their living not in service but in offices and department stores and in order to work must venture unchaperoned into the crowded tunnels and carriages of the underground system. Asquith introduces his characters through a comedy of class/gender interactions, as a variety of social types defend personal space against the pressure of proximity in a crowded tube train. However, melodrama will ensue from the harassment by raffish, working-class Bert (Cyril McLaglen) of 'nice' girl Nan

Fig. 1.5. The democratic city enforces mixing and contact in *Underground* (1928)

(Elissa Landi), which is intercepted by upwardly mobile station porter, Bill (Brian Aherne), whose task is to guard the underground's passageways, both directing passengers and keeping social order.

Bert chances across Nan again, when, standing at a department-store counter considering the slogan, 'Look at Your Hat: Everyone Else Does', he glimpses her in the distance serving in haberdashery. By 1928 a cut between a look and its object is enough to theatricalise space. A close-up captures Bert's glance cutting across the distance between store departments. In the next shot his body has followed. We find him leaning flirtatiously on Nan's counter, to be repelled not only by Nan's pointed consignment of the scarf he has fingered to the 'greatly reduced' pile, but by the freezing stare of the supercilious floor-walker, bent on maintaining class and sexual propriety. Bert leaves, but that evening is hanging around the tube station, where he observes Bill returning a dropped glove to Nan. The vulnerability of public space to transgression and violation is emphasised as

the film shifts from comedy to melodrama. An innocent exchange between Bill and Nan is intercut with the shadows of a passionately kissing couple hidden on the spiral stairway just above them. And the sequence concludes following Nan's departure with the intrusion of Bert's malevolent stare into the left frame of a shot focused on Bill's ethereal smile and distanced gaze, dreaming of their coming Saturday date (Fig. 1.6). These moments from *The Rat* and *Underground* suggest the significance for a geographic drama of the look as a means of transgressing social space (to be explored in Chapter 4).

Such boundary crossings may be provoked through the action of desire or reversed through social failure and disgrace, while characters move up or are forced down the social scale. In *Downhill*, for example, Rod's downward progress activates not only the material force of the boundary as, ejected from his home in disgrace, he takes the escalator into the underground system, but the double meaning of 'stage'. The biography of a human life story becomes

Fig. 1.6. Bert's malevolent stare intrudes into the space of Bill's daydream in *Underground* (1927)

a series of positionings, of arrivals and departures to and from socially definable and significant locales. *Downhill* literalises this perceptual structure as Rod shifts from one social/life 'stage' to another: from the playing fields of public-school England, to the London musical stage, to backstage husband of a celebrated London star, to gigolo in a Parisian nightclub, and finally to drugged delerium in a Marseilles brothel. Thus whether narrative movement entails social rise, as in the Great War dramas, or fall, the boundary can rarely be eliminated, for it is the dynamo of dramatic action and narrative possibility.

Transgression of boundaries, however, produces the problem of reconstituting home. If, to take films at either end of the decade, *Flames of Passion* and *Underground* use the boundary to point up social contrasts and incite transgression, the end result in both is the ejection of troubling class elements: Arthur Watson is arrested and found guilty of murder; Bert is killed by an underground train. However, as well as division the boundary may represent a meeting point, as in fictions tentatively exploring the social aftermath of the Great War. In *Comradeship*, *General Post* and *Blighty*, military service enacts a reorganisation of social boundaries. Elevation through the ranks enables a hero from the mercantile or serving classes to marry a defiantly modernising daughter of the aristocracy as a symbolic pivot for the construction of community, not in place of, but across, social difference. In all three films, a combination of document and fiction is used to bring socially defined and demarcated figures into juxtaposition, representing, as the vernacular has it, 'all sorts and conditions of men' from 'all walks of life'. Thus different social identities are held in tension, with implicit irony or pathos. In *General Post*, recognised by *The Bioscope* as 'a social history of our times . . . in miniature',[71] this process clearly touched a nerve. *Kinematograph Weekly* commented on 'its levelling ideology' and somewhat nervously on the dramatic licence that allowed

a member of the aristocracy to be 'put through it' in the interests of home defence, by his own stableman, an ex-sergeant of the Guards. This very funny episode concluded with an incident which 'brought down the house' at an exceptionally enthusiastic premiere, showing the stableman-sergeant imploring Heaven for patience to endure the stupidity on the drill-ground of his highborn employer.[72]

The Territorials (founded in 1908) are anathema to Sir Dennys Broughton, who early in the film fumes with indignation to his tailor, Edward Smith, about a servant's attendance at Saturday inspection: 'I march beside my butcher, my baker, my tinker, my tailor!' A large close-up follows of his Blimp-like face, eyes bulging over his moustache, rendered comic by his immediate submission to Smith's tape measure. The regression to nursery rhyme reappears in an odd little vignette of Saturday drill, which plays on the dissolution and reconstruction of class boundaries both necessary to and reinforced by the war. A title, correcting the nursery-rhyme line Sir Dennys jumbles up – 'The tinkers, tailors and candlestick-makers' – introduces newsreel footage of troops marching through the high street. At the park, Teddy Arundell as the stableman CO energetically drills his men, bizarrely shadowed by a group of children lined up behind him with tin drums and paper hats. As he orders his men to fall into line, the child soldiers fall in on either side of him, while a crowd composed of all classes of people watch in a semi-comic representation of an emerging democratic public sphere not yet accepted nor fully understood.

Such films, then, utilise social mapping to bring their protagonists, initially geographically demarcated, into contact rather than confrontation, working towards negotiated cohesion across the boundaries of difference rather than engineering the ejection of class-challenging figures. The alternation between demarcated social locations serves as convergence as well as contrast.

PERFORMER AND AUDIENCE

A corollary of this theatricalised cinema's conception of its narratives as a series of stagings or performances is the 'audience', both in the film and of the film. For a performance is always for someone whether given publicly or in private. As suggested above, the terms of a reformed melodrama allow socially differentiated protagonists to meet on the same stage only by observing the public codes of behaviour that constrain personal feeling. If the psychological boundary between players and audience is not to be threatened, personal feelings must appear in appropriate public forms – they must be 'performed'. Thus paradoxically, the private/public tension in English culture develops a theatricalised mode of imagining that at high moments of personal crisis requires a mediating audience or spectator.

In the case of the theatrical or ritual performances noted above – such as Jimmy Daw's attempted music-hall comeback in *Nothing Else Matters*, or the Rat's knife fight and Apache tango in the White Coffin – a watching audience is staged on screen. But where a literal theatrical performance is not in question, a variety of public situations generate fictional audiences as witness to the public exposure and containment of a private event, whether for their constraining presence, constructive support or implied social comment. Thus in *Comradeship* a number of melodramatic devices (for example, misrecognition) and performative strategies (for example, masculine restraint) are used to thwart the recognition of heroine and the (now blinded) hero that they love each other. It is only at a public meeting to inaugurate a local branch of the Comrades Club in Melcombe that through the language of hands (see Chapter 4) the woman finds the public means to break through both masculine reserve and the constraints on private expression. Public witness is crucial here to a movement of private desire that cautiously uses heterosexual romance to refigure class relations – the man in question is a local businessman, the woman, the lady of the manor. Similar public witness is used at the conclusion of at least three other Great War dramas, *General Post* (see Chapter 2), *Blighty* and *Guns at Loos*. *Blighty* brings together the Villiers's ex-chauffeur, Marshall (Jameson Thomas), now awarded a permanent commission in the army, and their daughter, Ann, in an Armistice-Day montage that unites her aristocratic family with workers on a nearby building site in the two-minute silence. *Guns at Loos* resolves the competition between the munitions factory owner, John Grimlaw, and Lady Cheswick's adopted son for the hand of her daughter, when, lit and posed as a Christ-like figure, and, like John Armstrong, blinded, Grimshaw calms his striking workers and wins Diana.

Stories about performers, or figures who bear a weight of public representation, as in the First World War dramas, might be expected to utilise public occasions to perform their symbolic work of uniting the personal and social. But their use of the on-screen audience suggests the role of the more general frontal shooting position in effectively constructing the British cinema spectator as witness. Even when obvious framing and staging is absent, the camera position makes the viewer an often distanced observer of action presented for public reception. For example, in *Flames of Passion*, an encounter between Dorothy, newly arrived home from finishing school, and her father's chauffeur, Arthur, translates theatrical *mise en scène* and spectatorship into cinematic frames and points of view. At the same time, it maintains the distance that ensures a performance witnessed rather than immersion in the action – the goal of continuity cinema. So we watch Dorothy in medium-long shot, framed by a trellis, coming down the garden path towards us, her hands clasped. Transformed from schoolgirl into young womanhood by a change of clothing, she pauses in mid-shot as her gaze is caught off screen. A medium long shot gives us her view: a man in shirtsleeves, stood, legs apart, striking a match by an open car. A close-up reveals a heavy jowled face, indicating a powerful and threatening masculinity. Three medium long shots focus first on Watson polishing the car, then on Dorothy circling in and out of shot, the final one bringing her into his space. The distance of camera from performer in these shots separates the viewer from the action. We watch a look that engenders anticipation of the inevitable. Similarly, long shots, framed by trees, observe at a distance the driving lesson that Watson offers Dorothy, until the car pulls up in a wood. Dorothy jumps out, while Arthur follows more deliberately, leaning languorously against the car, sexual innuendo marking his smile as, tipping back his cap, he watches her movements. A close-up iris shot foregrounds his intense look as a warning sign for the audience, while in the next shot she wanders carelessly into the woods. Watson's movement out of frame left is followed by a cut to a long shot of the pastoral scene, viewed across a pond, distancing us from the action, and revealing at the back of the frame Watson's pursuit of Dorothy out of sight. In these sequences the framing of tree-lined roads, or a garden trellis, produces the distance of narrating/ viewing perspective, from which it is possible to cut into close shots or iris shots in order to witness more closely – rather than participate in – the action.

At the end of the decade Maurice Elvey's *High Treason* (1929) futuristically anticipates the use of telecommunications both to reconfigure the boundaries of national and political difference and to blur the boundaries between world and personal stages. These new communication media invade personal space but also engage the personal in political public ends, creating new forms of private/public encounter and new forms of witness. Michael (Jameson Thomas), son of the belligerent President of the European Confederation, uses the Tele-Radio to woo an independent-minded Evelyn (Benita Hume), daughter of the leader of the World Peace League (Humberstone Wright). Unknown to Evelyn, however, this official communication channel, besides previously scanning bathing belles on the beach to the amusement of male office clerks, now picks up a reflection in a mirror that catches facial expressions she thinks hidden from Michael. Later, the simultaneous derailment of a cross-Channel train and explosion at the World Peace League headquarters lead to immediate mobilisation. Attempting to get her father away in a last-minute bid for peace, Evelyn and a band of newly mobilised women, uniformed in white boiler suits, confront the black-leather-clad Michael at the head of troops sent to guard the airport (see Chapter 4). Cross-cutting between close-ups on eye exchanges between Evelyn and Michael enacts a private drama between potential lovers who are political opponents within a theatrically choreographed, gendered stand-off between peacemakers and warmongers as their respective audiences. Here the cut itself is theatricalised, the juxtapositions between gendered groupings producing the frisson of contact across the cut that nevertheless maintains separation. In such dramas neither public nor private can be expressed without the other.

In this chapter, I have argued that the theatricalisation of British cinema represents neither a mechanical reliance on stage plays and personnel nor mechanical placement of the camera in the stalls. Rather, in so far as the theatrical crosses the boundaries between stage and life, it acculturates cinematic perception, framing ways of seeing and organising narrative. In so doing, it provides a theatrical-cinematic dramaturgy capable of releasing the private into public arenas that are always socially defined and therefore distinguished and bounded according to the categories of difference that structure British society. This is not to suggest that a theatrical *mise en scène* and dramaturgy is a mere reflection of a regressive class structure that compares pejoratively with the biographical egalitarianism of Hollywood or the modernist negations of European art cinemas. Hollywood's biographical mode of narration has been equally critiqued for illusions of homogeneity and social progress that deny difference. Rather, in developing a conception of the cultural poetics underpinning British film-making practices, I want to suggest that social experience and its determinations provide materials and modes of perception that act as a stimulus in the process of cultural imagining – of generating dramatic enactments, stories and aesthetic sensations. A cultural poetics, in that it is rooted in place and time, constrains but also provides opportunities. This is not to imply that aesthetic practice overrides ideology. Rather that it makes something out of ideologies, something experienced in a different dimension. The encounter at the social boundary – the dialectic of private and public – represents a dynamic that homes in on the neuralgic centre of an ideology, squeezing from it an aesthetic frisson.

Of the many films mentioned in this chapter, *The Rat* is pivotal for this discussion, a theatrical 'love-child' of Novello's burning desire for the stage. It is a film that fully realises the potential of the moving camera to reorganise spatial divisions, and a sign that, after the dire November of 1924, when no films were in production in Britain, rising talents were renewing popular success out of the stage/screen collaboration. It was a film also that, in its use of staged performances and rituals, and of Novello's charismatic theatricality, put a new twist on the relationship of restraint and passion that continues to be so central to the British conception of 'good' acting. It is to this issue that I turn in Chapter 3. Before doing so, however, it is necessary to make a diversion through the proscenium arch, and, taking account of its exchangeability with a picture frame – often hinted at in this chapter – to enter the stage picture beyond. Here I want to explore the significance of pictorialism in British popular culture and its entwinement with theatricality as a lasting influence on the modes of perception and aesthetic practices of its cinema.

2 Going to the – British – Pictures

Although for some time the term 'picture' dominated common-sense perception of film both in the US and UK – as in picturisation, picture palace, picture-goer – it is only in self-consciously American mode that in Britain we go to the movies. This designation would be unfurled as a polemical banner in the title adopted by *Movie*, which in 1960 opened with a now familiar attack on the failings of British cinema. By the 1920s 'movie' had infiltrated the language of film journalism. Nevertheless, trade-press titles consistently retained the term 'picture' whenever 'movement' was referenced – as in *The Motion Picture Studio* and *The Film Renter and Moving Picture News* – while fans were resolutely served by *Pictures*, *The Picturegoer*, *Picture Show* and so on. Even the modernist Iris Barry appealed to her readers in 1926, *Let's Go to the Pictures*.[1]

The dominance of the picture in British conceptions of film-making emerges from the array of pictorial practices of late-nineteenth- and early twentieth-century popular culture. Accompanying the foundation of major metropolitan art galleries and museums came the development of reprographic technologies and photography, the print shop, the illustrated press, the art of book illustration and advertising. A plethora of visual devices made drawn and photographic pictures move, offering entertainments and education for home and public use. According to George Sadoul, 'during the second half of the nineteenth century, the magic lantern enjoyed a popularity in Britain unknown elsewhere',[2] while amateur photographic clubs mushroomed in larger numbers than in either Europe or America.[3] Meanwhile the emergence of the department store, utilising the new technologies of plate glass and electric lighting, offered proscenium-like window displays for the equally new pastime of 'window shopping'. The regularity and intensifying speed of new means of transport from suburbs into metropolitan centres

made the panorama an everyday experience, with the passing of 'scenery' framed in the windows of trains, trams and automobiles or viewed from the aerial perspective of the balloon.[4] The Victorians, says Michael Booth, 'learnt to look at their world through the medium of pictures'.[5]

A world experienced pictorially encouraged visual modes of understanding, representing and narrativising. Just as I have argued that the connection between British film-making and theatre arises from the cultural significance of theatricalised space and performance, so a prevailing value for picture-making suggests a resonance beyond simple repetition of Victorian traditions. Rather, insistent pictorialism indicates a further dimension of the culturally specific mode of perception this study seeks to delineate, one in which pictures serve different functions and relate to narrative differently than in received notions of the 'cinematic'. In particular, the converging etymological histories of 'picture' and 'document' point to a relationship, based in the technologies of reproduction, whereby pictures, circulating across media and social spaces, function as cultural documents in a process of narrative and potentially dialogic encounter.

This chapter, then, beginning from the perspective of nineteenth-century pictorial traditions that functioned as reference points in the 1920s and beyond, investigates the wider cultural resonance of the 'picture' and 'pictorialism' for British film-making.

PICTURES AS POPULAR CULTURE

Crucial to the role of the picture is its extension into a variety of media. Martin Meisel's seminal study, *Realizations*, charts the diverse forms taken by the nineteenth-century drive towards visible fiction across painting, serial novels, book illustration and theatre, showing how techniques and materials were borrowed from, and exchanged between, media under a dominant pressure to pictorialise narrative and to narrativise pictures.[6] Thus painters thought of their canvas as a stage and their figures actors thereon, theatre producers sought to create stage pictures, while both sought to tell stories: 'the boards of the theatre and the canvas . . . [became] . . . the same thing'.[7] This convergence embraced film in the early 1910s in the private theatre at Bushey built by the painter, Hubert von Herkomer (1849–1914), whose last endeavours sought to realise the symbiosis of all the arts in film-making.[8]

In this proliferation of pictorial-narrative forms Martin Meisel discerns 'the matrix of a style and . . . a way of structuring reality'.[9] A pictorial habit of mind establishes a set of formal practices and of socio-cultural exchanges within the marketplace for a mass-mediated popular culture. These, then, contribute to the production contexts, perceptual frameworks and aesthetic strategies of British film-making.

PICTURING THE WORLD: FROM PAINTING TO PICTURES

Part of a drive towards visual apprehension of the world, pictorialism is underpinned by the development of the optical sciences and photography, which in turn support commercial exploitation of new art forms and leisure opportunities. In this context, the narrative picture-maker is caught, Meisel argues, between the 'appetite for reality' and 'a requirement for signification'.[10] However, what counts as real or significant is relative, involving a contest between ideas of truth, beauty and realism to which pictorialism is central. Since the argument between 'reality' and 'significance' produces different emphases and strategies, a range of pictorial-narrative practices was generated and there are as many uses for, and ideas about, pictorialism as there are for theatricality.[11] Its legacy, then, contributes a mix of practices and ideologies to British cinema.

The pictorial habit of mind consolidates with the growth of painting as both artistic production and cultural institution. Two recent studies of Victorian painting by Christopher Wood and Lionel Lambourne follow Martin Meisel in stressing the popularity of paintings in nineteenth-century culture.[12] This was facilitated through the early invention in Britain of the processes of mechanical reproduction that ensured their circulation through cheap prints, the illustrated press, magic-lantern slides and picture postcards. This indicates the changing role of painting from fine art to a broadly popular source of entertainment, information and education, proliferating into the public sphere a host of pictorial images as the foundation of a mass-mediated visual culture. Thus *The Oxford English Dictionary* records how the term 'pictorial' shifts in the early 1800s from reference to the practice of painting – the work of the painter – to the product, the 'picture' itself. By 1826 the term has infiltrated the culture more widely to denote something 'illustrated' or having the quality of a picture, gradually incorporating 'picturesque', which loses its specialist meaning. By the 1880s it attains independent status as a noun, naming a new kind of journal: 'the pictorial'. By now, 'picture' includes not only painting but the new art of photography.

Henry Peach Robinson (1830–1901), a prominent and widely influential Victorian photographer, believed that to be counted as art the photograph must become a picture, popularising practices that contributed to the crossover between pictorial painting and cinema. Robinson struggled to unify truth to nature promised by the photograph and the aesthetic effect of artistic composition against the rise of naturalists such as P. H. Emerson (1856–1936) and Paul Martin (1864–1942). Trained in journalistic wood engraving, Martin advocated 'the real snapshot – that is, people and things as the man in the street sees them', as opposed to the pictorialists' ambition 'to make their photographs as much like a painted picture as they could'.[13] To this end Martin adapted his camera so he could take candid shots of 'Street Characters', such as 'A London Flower Girl', 'Hop-pickers at Rye' or night scenes.[14] Thus, like the meeting of melodrama and investigative journalism noted in Chapter 1, pictorial vision engages with reportage, leading to the rise of photo-journalism and twentieth-century media such as *Pathé Pictorial* and *Picture Post*.[15] In this respect pictorial apprehension of the world brings the search for idealised beauty and truth – as sources of significance – into tension with the 'appetite for reality' or, in Peter Brooks's illuminating term, the 'document'.[16]

This appears in two related forms: on the one hand, a fascination with the reproduced appearances of a fast expanding world of perceptual realities both homely and exotic; and on the other, a focus on 'ordinary' lives. A shift from the epic and historical subjects of academic painting and classical drama to narratives of everyday life opened up two sets of questions. First, who should occupy what cultural space? Second, how can ideal truths be related to the contingent and random detail needed by contemporary realism? Walter Scott aligned himself with Coleridge in warning against the 'demoralizing falsehood of the pictures' spread by the democratising aesthetic of melodrama, which attributes 'noble and virtuous sentiments to the persons least qualified by habit or education to entertain them'.[17] W. P. Frith's experiment in pictorialising modern life in *Ramsgate Sands* was judged 'a piece of vulgar Cockney business unworthy of being represented even in an illustrated paper'.[18] Similarly, British social-realist paintings by, for example, Richard Redgrave, Hubert von Herkomer and Luke Fildes provoked cries of outrage against their imaging destitution and poverty.[19] However, fast growing urban centres, creating challenging proximities between reorganising social classes, provided both urgent social need and economic opportunity for the expansion of representation in a market for visual culture developing as a source of social imagining.[20] Frith's social panoramas, in particular, attracted such large crowds to the Royal Academy's summer exhibitions that they required a barrier and a policeman to protect them.[21]

In one respect, then, the foregrounded aesthetics of pictorialism eased the approach to new subject matter. Thus Frith, who mid-century abandoned literary and historical subjects, found a means of reconciling pictorial qualities with the unpicturesque attributes of modern life in the variegated compositions afforded by the new public sites of mass society: the seaside outing; Derby Day; the railway station. Similarly, while conceding that the new demand for realism checks overindulgence in 'sweetness and affectation', H. P. Robinson nevertheless identifies the moral significance of art with aesthetic perception: 'The stage heroine studies her part in the hospital and dies before the audience without emitting a cough, a gasp, or a groan, but she cannot do without the idealism imparted by slow music and the limelight.'[22]

If, then, the 'picture' is the focus of formal exchange between novel, picture, theatre and eventually film, its aesthetic attractions also make it a medium of cultural exchange between social groups. The mechanics of reproduction work both to draw

forms together in collaboration, while also leading to proliferation and diversification in the intensifying circulation of pictorial images from one medium or social arena to another. In this respect the circulation of pictures participates in 'the expansion of discourse' observed by Martin Meisel, contributing to the emergence of a mass-mediated popular culture in the late 19th and early 20th century.[23] In pictorialism – as medium of exchange – emerges a new kind of public sphere, constructed as 'middlebrow', broadly popular and capable of a certain democratic inclusiveness. Such a process makes problematic the interpretation of cultural forms and practices solely in terms of their class origins, an issue taken up in Chapter 4 in relation to the critique of pictorial and pastoral imaging in British cinema.

THINKING IN PICTURES

By the 1920s, pictorial values and attitudes circulate in a diversity of practices and discourses, the review press providing copious evidence. So, for example, *The Bioscope* notes of *Lady Clare* (1919), Mary Odette 'always makes a charming picture'.[24] It praises Elvey for his 'keen eye for well-composed pictorial effect',[25] and Hepworth for his 'keen feeling for atmosphere and pictorial effect'.[26] Reviews in *Stoll's Editorial News* declare of *Duke's Son* (1920), 'the pictures are always first rate', and that in *The Rocks of Valpre* (1919), 'the sea pictures are wonderful'.[27] The *Kinematograph Weekly* notes of the trade show for *The Call of the Blood* (1920), 'the startling scenic effects make an extraordinary appeal to the eye and almost compelled applause'.[28]

Kenelm Foss, himself he says trained as a painter, has no hesitation in endorsing the centrality of the picture as a central preoccupation of the film-maker:

> Also, it being PICTURES we're dealing with, don't you think that perhaps some aesthetics, a decorative sense, some knowledge of composition, would help a little? No matter what brain stuff is in one's picture, what plot, what acting, the simple-minded public will, first and last, expect to see pleasing PICTURES, with the edge of the silver screen as their frame. And I, for once, am happy to count myself in this respect one of the simple-minded public.[29]

Foss's contention is borne out in the delight in Hepworth's films expressed by Gertrude Allen in *Pictures and the Picturegoer*:

No artist has ever given us with a paintbrush more beauteous pictures to gaze on than some which have flashed (alas! their impression is all too fleeting through the medium of the screen) before our charmed vision during the screening of any one of his famous productions.[30]

REALISATIONS

Although pictorial perception is diffused widely through a range of visual practices by the 1920s, both film-makers and critics drew copiously on the popular culture of painting inherited from the 19th century, in particular the use of paintings as source material. Literally, the realisation entails the reproduction on stage of a well-known painting, in which setting, character grouping and gesture come together before our eyes to replicate the moment of the picture. However, as Martin Meisel shows, there are several types of, and uses for, the realisation. A painting might provide narrative material, or apposite reference, or serve as comic counterpoint. But *as realisation* its key function is the pleasure of reproduction itself. The realisation offers not only recognition of a familiar image but the 'increment of reality' provided by living bodies; not only is curiosity satisfied through narrative extension of the picture's premises but admiration is invited for the technical skills involved.[31] In broader terms the realisation contributes to the formation of a more inclusive public sphere through wider intertextual circulation via mass-cultural marketing that extends into cinema.

This practice gave Maurice Elvey his entry into film-making. On leaving the romantic-pictorial theatre of the Nielsons, he took as subject for his first film the talking point of the 1913 Royal Academy summer exhibition, the Reverend John Collier's *A Fallen Idol* (see Fig. 2.6), to which I will return below. Elvey continued this practice in many of his films of the teens and 1920s. *The Loss of the Birkenhead* (1914) uses a print found in numerous public houses of the time and, like *A Fallen Idol*, reproduced as a folded insert in Christmas editions of The *Illustrated London News*.[32] *Nelson* (1918) draws on Romney portraits. *The Wandering Jew* (1923) realises Leonardo da Vinci's *The Last Supper* (Fig. 2.1), *The Royal Oak* (1923) reproduces celebrated portraits by van Dyck of Charles I and II and for its concluding scene draws on Yeames's popular *And When Did You Last See Your Father?*[33]

If Elvey found in *A Fallen Idol* both narrative pretext and a topical talking-point, his use of Leonardo da Vinci's *The Last Supper* in *The Wandering Jew* compresses a number of functions into a brief moment. Calling on its familiarity, the film uses the painting not only for its solemnity and prestige as the work of an 'old master' and its capacity to obviate censorship rules against the representation of Christ but also for its communicative power as an image of ultimate betrayal. Preceding the realisation, Matathias, 'proud aristocrat of Judea' (Matheson Lang), unable to buy healing from the Nazarene for his captive mistress, Judith, has declared Jesus an imposter, whereupon she collapses. A title shifts from the domestic to the universal story: 'So for some short span of days, mankind's great tragedy nears its consummation.' The scene fades up on a long shot of a sunset over a rocky landscape tinted red and fades out to a red screen, establishing a pictorial sense of portentous finality. An ochre title announces, 'The Last Supper', and in the next shot, a cross superimposed over a heart floods the screen with light, followed by the fading in of Leonardo's painting, the cross substituting for the image of Christ at its centre (Fig. 2.1). The completed painting, set in a heavy gilt frame, is held as a tableau for several seconds, before coming to life, the disciples turning to chat to each other or reach for bread. A title then pinpoints the key figure for the film – 'Judas' – followed by a medium close-up of a balding man talking to a disciple on his right. Judas then leans frontally towards the camera and across to the left, his raised fingers playing speculatively across his lips, and his bulbous gleaming eyes swivelling repeatedly from right to left as the image fades out. The painting is thus used as a solemn but economic means of filling in the film's biblical back-story. The camera's capacity to change scale and isolate a relevant detail enables this reference to Judas's betrayal to anticipate the awesome curse that in the next scene will turn Matathias into 'The Wandering Jew'. At the same time the status of the tableau as realisation – as reproduction – is emphasised by its enclosure in the gilt frame within the borders of the screen.

If the realisation seeks a literal reproduction of a familiar painting, the reach for metaphor in reviewing discourse reveals the currency of pictorial genres and styles, which act as reference points, informing aesthetic perception. *Narrow Valley* (1921) offers 'an

Fig. 2.1. Leonardo da Vinci's *The Last Supper* 'realised' in Maurice Elvey's *The Wandering Jew* (1923)

amusing portrait gallery of rustic worthies . . . sketches a trifle exaggerated . . . realistically executed . . . effective studies in the grotesque'.[34] *The Bioscope* reviewer of *Comin' thro' the Rye* (1923) perceives Hepworth's pictorialism as reminiscent of art nouveau: 'a lyric touch in some of these screen pictures, showing dainty white columbine figures gliding like rose petals blown by the wind though flower laden arbours'.[35] In many cases films are linked to named painters. George Pearson is credited with 'a Hogarthian touch' in *Love, Life and Laughter* (1923) and Hepworth's *Tansy* (1921) offers 'a beautiful Stott study'.[36] The *Westminster Gazette* responds positively to the 'clever Rembrantesque preliminary section showing various London scenes' that opens Henry Edwards's *A Girl of London* (1925).[37] At the end of the decade, *Cinema World* comments on a picturesque Betty Balfour in Denison Clift's *Paradise* (1928), 'gliding in and out of the magnificent Monte Carlo ballroom set, looking as if she had 'stepped right out of a Joshua Reynolds painting'.[38]

OLD AND NEW MASTERS: POPULIST AESTHETICS

The cultural valency of pictorial reference, then, takes several forms, underpinning a widespread mode of aesthetic response and reading. This orientation is summed up in a four-page spread in *The Picturegoer* for January 1924. While the writer, Marjorie Mayner, credits the New World for the gift of the new kind of 'picture' represented by cinema, nevertheless she claims it is the old masters of Europe who provide techniques whereby 'camera craft takes the place of the artist's brush and palette', painting with 'living materials'. And among European directors who lead in pictorialising film-making, 'so far as originality goes, British directors are well to the fore. Their canvases have been of necessity smaller . . . but their out-of-door effects are unequalled, except perhaps by those of D. W. Griffith'. For Mayner, Maurice Elvey and George Pearson stand alongside Seastrom, Stroheim, Ingram, Lubitsch and Gance as masters of both pictorial effect and the painterly reference. She concludes with an implicit recognition of the cultural conditioning of perception. If the 'old masters' can be frequently recognised in the work of Hepworth and Henry Edwards, this is 'largely unconscious . . . [arising] out of the real similarity between the form of paintings on canvas, and screen pictures *as they see them*' (my emphasis).[39] Indeed, recourse to painting is recommended by cameraman, L. G. Ergot, who, in *The Motion Picture Studio*, recommends 'observations from the old masters, from prints, engravings and photographs' as guides to the composition of figures, backgrounds and use of light and shade.[40]

On one level the association of films with 'old masters' is a claim on the cultural prestige that the British theatre had earlier won through the production of 'stage paintings', emulating the aesthetic status bestowed by the Royal Academy on artists. Thus *The Bioscope* finds in *Daniel Deronda* (1921) 'not the Venice known to tourists but an unknown Venice of Whistler's etchings, byways and corners'.[41] There were, indeed, international precedents for linking film with fine art practices, both in Hollywood's establishment of art direction as a recognised element in film-making and in the emergence of distinctive European film movements drawing on Expressionism or Surrealism. The latter were championed by the London Film Society (1925–39) and the journal, *Close-Up* (1927–33). However, aside from this developing minority strand in international cinematic culture, British trade and press commentaries by film-makers and critics alike suggest a nationally specific approach to 'art' and the 'artistic', detached from any nameable movement. Rather it is the 'picture', with its traditional appeals and pictorially disposed aesthetics, that is felt to represent a nationally particular visual sensibility. 'Charm' and 'atmosphere' are key terms used to identify the felt value of the style. Thus Hepworth's 'keen feeling for atmosphere and pictorial effect' represents a 'typically British school of picture-making'.[42] The *Daily News* reviewer, disliking the story of Guy Newall's *The Garden of Resurrection* (1919), nevertheless admits that 'the pictures, as usual in British films, are finely seen'.[43] Charles Dalmon – performing unusually early the role of art director for George Clark Productions and admired for his work on *The Lure of Crooning Water* – argues the importance of design in creating 'atmosphere'. However, he demands that British film-makers band 'together in the laudable

effort to work out our own salvation' rather than depend on imitation of American practices.[44] 'Atmosphere' comes together with 'charm' in S. R. Littlewood's response to Fay Compton. Her value, he suggests, 'is expressly that she is utterly different from the ordinary Hollywood film type and that she conveys something of the repose, wistful poetry, beauty and silences . . . [of] our island-home even in these notorious days'.[45] If Littlewood links pictorialism with English pastoralism, another critical strand links it with historical period. Thus *The Bioscope* is aware of *Lady Clare*'s slowness in relation to 'American high-speed drama'. Nevertheless it perceives in its realisations of Tennyson's poem scenes that 'transport . . . [us] . . . back to the very heart of Georgian England', something 'no foreign producer or players could catch'.[46] The relationship of pictorialism to the pastoral and the past is both central to the cultural and aesthetic territory occupied by 1920s British film-making and a source of critical misgiving – issues to which I return in Chapter 4.

The populist aesthetics implied here were supported by a frequently expressed belief that the visual senses respond unconsciously to beauties that might remain opaque if expressed verbally. *The Bioscope* declares that 'to see the spoken word visualised on screen has on most people a greater effect than the actual speaking'.[47] It suggests that in *Don Quixote* (1923), Elvey 'has produced pictures of the Knight of the Doleful Countenance . . . which will appeal not only to the very small minority familiar with the book but to all lovers of pictorial effect'.[48] Frederick Talbot, in the revised version of his book, *Moving Pictures: How They Are Made and Worked*, claims:

> The photographer must be an artist. Pictorial charm makes appeal to one and all in varying degrees it is true, and perhaps to the great majority, unconsciously. But . . . no section of the huge picture-playgoing public is so fiercely denunciatory of a photographically weak picture as the majority, the artistic sense of which is generally supposed to be in sore need of development.[49]

N. G. Arnold, named by Edward Carrick as the 'ablest Art Director in the country',[50] makes a similar argument in 1927 in an article decrying mechanistic approaches to set building that disregard 'beauty of line, form, composition or expression of personality'. He claims that the 'public have an inherent appreciation of beauty and an unconscious appreciation of a dramatic setting', while actors and cameramen work better in a 'true atmosphere' provided by artistically designed sets.[51]

Taken together such pictorial referencing in both film-making practices and reviewing perception suggests three things about the aesthetic parameters within which British film-makers worked. First, pictorialism represents a source of aesthetic pleasure that must be visible in order to be enjoyed. It therefore, as Andrew Higson notes, contributes to the presentation, the foregrounding of the image, as a picture.[52] Second, the picture is a source of cultural reference, of discursivity. As *The Picturegoer*'s feature writer cited above suggests, the film-makers of the period and their cameramen draw on popular traditions of aesthetically pleasing or familiar images. And third, and perhaps most problematically for contemporary tastes, the picture accesses, and circulates, a cultural legacy; the pictures induce recognition by reference to the past. I shall return to the last two points on p. 57. But in the next section I want to examine further the aesthetics of pictorialism as it intersects with theatricality to produce a distinctive presentational, gestural style that, in producing images as acculturated signs or references, contributes to the cultural poetics of British cinema.

GESTURE AND PICTURE

Central to the symbiosis of picture and story is their shared dependency on the organisation of figures to produce the 'telling scene'.[53] The new focus on the individual in the industrialising West emphasised human personality as the source of meaning and truth, and emotion as both the material and goal of aesthetic production.[54] This was still a major concern of film-makers who in the 1920s pondered the aesthetics of cinema. Colden Lore, scenario writer and author of *The Modern Photoplay and its Construction*, declares, 'nearly the entire resources of the widespread empire of art are devoted to the portrayal of emotions'. He goes on to argue: 'More than in the Drama, the persons in the Photoplay are to us, first of all, subjects of emotional experience, and it is the expression of their emotions, their portrayal, that gives meaning to, that becomes the central object of, the photoplay.'[55] This emphasis makes the actor crucial, as George Pearson records in his notebooks and public lectures: 'An artist author feels certain emo-

tions that he desires others to feel keenly. He selects as his medium or material the physical body of the Actor. He has to fashion that material with the tools of the silent screen.'[56]

In *Realizations*, Martin Meisel charts the shift from eighteenth-century identification of gestures with abstract, universal, idealised passions underpinning the rhetoric of neo-classical painting and drama towards their function as signs of individual emotion and character. Brought into visual relationship, these gestural indexes of emotion body forth a story.[57] Narrative, then, arises not from the linear sequence of causally linked actions of classical drama, but from composition – frequently a tableau – which focuses emotional conjunctures and situations, often based in a protagonist's perception of, or response to, another.[58] Gesture serves narration 'by expressing the simultaneous relationship of several figures . . . in a static configuration . . . symbolis[ing] a dramatic situation'.[59] The consequent assumption that emotionally pregnant situations depend on the actor's contribution to a picture runs across debates about screen as well as stage acting. Thus Henry Neville (1837–1910), a distinguished Victorian actor and actor-manager, contends in a lecture to the Society for the Encouragement of Fine Arts that the stage 'gives to the observer living pictures'.[60] Forty-odd years on, the brochure for the Victoria School of Cinema Acting tells applicants that it is the business of the film artist 'to secure effective pictures' and 'to make a succession of telling pictures'.[61] This pictorial conception of acting has proved problematic for film criticism, assuming first that the tableau is defined by stasis and frontal framing, and second that it demands exaggerated gestures and artificial poses from the actor. Such practices, it is commonly argued, inhibit the defining features of film: movement and the registration of 'natural' inflections of muscle and glance. Closer examination, however, suggests that the pictorial traditions inherited by British cinema are more complex.

STAGING PICTURES

In their respective accounts of nineteenth-century pictorial-theatrical practices, Louis James and Martin Meisel show that the theatrical tableau was neither entirely static nor wholly dependent on an enclosing frame to produce its effects. Rather, it is formed by the *movement* of figures into a significant

arrangement. This depends on the dynamic interaction between lines of force created by the direction of
gestures and looks, momentarily held for the aesthetic and interpretative pleasure of the audience,
only to be dissolved as the figures break away.[62] Nevertheless, the transformation of the proscenium arch
into an all-enclosing gilt picture frame by Squire and
Marie Bancroft at the Haymarket in 1880 served to
consolidate pictorial staging and to intensify the
pleasure of the tableau as picture. Its heavy, ornately
carved and gilt embrace of the playing arena defini-
tively separated audience from the enactment. This
was further enhanced by the dimming of house lights
in the 1880s.[63] The result concentrated the spectator's attention on the distant scene, pictorialising its
three-dimensional existence with visual effects
organised by set design, lighting schemes and crowd
arrangements, anticipating the movement into position of a key protagonist. According to Michael
Booth and Martin Meisel, this mode of stage painting was perfected during Henry Irving's reign at the
Lyceum.[64] Thus Irving, about to stage *Faust*, in
which he was to play Mephistopheles, allays Bram
Stoker's fear that his elaboration of spectacular pictorial effect for Walpurgis Night will overpower the
actors:

> I have studiously kept as yet all the colour scheme to
> that grey-green. When my dress of flaming scarlet
> appears among it – and remember that the colour will
> be intensified by that very light – it will bring the whole
> picture together in a way you cannot dream of . . . You
> shall see too how Ellen Terry's white dress, and even
> that red scar across her throat, will stand out in the midst
> of that turmoil of lighting.[65]

Crucially, then, the picture is the climactic result –
the apotheosis even – of movement, so that part of
the aesthetic pleasure is seeing a picture put into
place.

Such an effect marks the culmination of the
encounter between the Rat and Zelie in the pictorially demarcated spaces of the White Coffin. As
described in Chapter 1, narrative springs to life, with
the underclass intruding onto the mezzanine occupied by the *haute bourgeoisie*. At the close of this
sequence, the excitement over and the upper-class
visitors gone, the Rat leaps into one of the coffin-
shaped arches and, posing picturesquely for the

crowd, relocates himself, as it were, in the picture.
Thus a dynamic tension runs between movement in
theatricalised space and the containment of pictorial
framing that is so important to the aesthetic of
restraint discussed in the next chapter.

If Irving and Tree had perfected the art of the
stage picture, cinema's capacity to bring to life a
screen canvas was, as Albert Chevalier, ruefully comments, enhanced by the employment of nature as
'scene painter'.[66] Thus the *Aberdeen Evening Press*, on
location for *Christie Johnston* (1921), describes how
'about 60 fisher people of Auchmithie and district
make groups and figures for the scenes'.[67] The
Dundee Argos comments appreciatively of the same
picture: 'the Viscount is seen climbing the steep
narrow path leading from beach to the east end of
the village and stopping to look meditatively over the
sea, and into this scene Mr Rome succeeded in
introducing some fine artistic touches'.[68] A frequently noted feature of Elvey's films is their presentation of 'many beautiful screen scenes, notable for
their artistic grouping, lighting and photography'[69] –
effects exemplified by the trysting and training-camp
scenes of *Comradeship* discussed in Chapter 4.

If, however, pleasure lies in seeing the picture
form as the culmination of a movement, the dynamic
forces out of which the tableau is created also serve
to dissolve the picture back into movement. As Netterville Barron insists against the presumed artifice of
the pose in expressive acting, 'dramatic movements
include pauses and poses, since the essence of both is
there before and there after. A pause is only dramatic
because of its context, which, of course, is always a
movement.'[70] The movement into and out of the
picture relates, Louis James argues, 'to the emotive
inner structure of each scene . . . the actors . . . react
to each other with the direct intensity of a magnetic
field'.[71] The tableau, then, represents a pause within
a pattern of choreographed, almost balletic, gestures,
with bodies constantly bending towards, twisting or
turning away from each other.

FIGURES IN A LANDSCAPE: *TANSY*
The dynamic potential of this dramaturgical structure for a culture in the throes of change orchestrates
Cecil Hepworth's *Tansy*, to which I return in Chapter 4. Here, my concern is the film's exploitation of
the tension between movement and pictorial tableau
to dramatise the conflict between the stasis of a ret-

rogressive patriarchal order and the movement of revitalised pastoral. Patriarchal stasis, based on retrogressive memory, possession and social convention, is represented in different ways by the bereaved Joad Wilverley and his widower father, and maintains its grip on the present through a rootless agricultural mechanic, Clem. In contrast, the figure of Tansy (Alma Taylor), who takes on the job of shepherd to the Wilverley flock, combines contact with past roots through her grandfather with the regenerative, free-flowing energy of the modern land girl. While Tansy courts the younger son, Will, as they perform together the tasks of the farming calendar, she becomes the object of matrimonial and sexual schemes nurtured respectively by Joad and Clem. The growing crisis between the film's pictorial, narrative and ideological tensions comes to a head in the Wilverley farmhouse. In the BFI print, this scene opens on a tableau of patriarchal familial dysfunction, enclosed within an unfeminised domestic space, the father emblematically rooted to his fireside chair, caught between his antagonistic sons. Will stands over Joad in a hiatus of incipient confrontation, to be broken as the brothers lunge at each other. The fight is suspended as Joad, breaking free and twisting towards the camera, freezes, hand to head, horrified both at their fratricidal impulses and the dawning truth: 'My God, you and Will. Is it true?' He demands Tansy be fetched, but, rushing in from the back of the set, she is already there, moving towards Will, who swings miserably away from her, as he hovers behind his immobilised father.

Joad turns back to the camera, as he takes money from his pocket, a title declaring: 'My brother and I give ye a month's money instead of notice. Do ye understand? Now go!' Slapping the money on the table, he crosses the room to lean on the mantle over the hearth, centre of patriarchal authority, while Tansy moves frontally towards the camera to pause in suspended emotion, her fists clenched. Then Tansy breaks the tableau, moving to the left of frame, while Joad answers the shifting figural balance, extending arm and index finger to cast her out.[72] The circling of figures within the tableau continues as Tansy, at first repulsed, steps back into profile, frame left, Will starts forward with head turned away from her, while Joad blocks the right-hand frame, his open palm gesturing to his brother as he accuses her of causing their conflict. She crosses to

Will, dragging on his arm, demanding that he confirm their mutual understanding. Will, still refusing to look at her, shakes her off and she retreats to left frame, bewildered, looking to the family retainer, Robert, who sadly shakes his head. At this moment of apparent stalemate, the image fades out and up, indicating a portentous moment in the balance and a switch in emotional and narrative direction. Tansy slowly turns half towards the camera, and then, picking up the money, hurls it at Joad, who stands immobile, hands in his pockets. Pivoting sharply, she marches out back left, Will staring after her. Joad continues to stare off front, just past the camera, as Robert comes to him, reconfiguring the now all-male tableau and declaring that Tansy had 'loved the lad all along'. Will remains gazing after Tansy, his father still transfixed in his chair between the worried Robert and discomfited Joad, with Tansy the only object moving in a now imaginary, off-screen landscape. *Tansy* thus demonstrates the choreographic work of the tableau, which brings movement to a pause in dramatic encounter, producing both pictorial effect and narrative significance within a pattern of gestures that originate in one action and move towards another. Crucially, Hepworth, rather than making a break with the pictorial-dramaturgical practices of British popular culture, exploits the cultural resonances of their aesthetic dynamics in a negotiation of the tensions between continuity and change, past and future.

Martin Meisel, noting the analogy between pictorial theatre and the 'dissolving views' of the magic lantern, distinguishes its dramaturgy from that of the linear, causal progress of classical drama: 'Each [stage] picture, dissolving, leads not into consequent activity, but to a new infusion and distribution of elements from which a new picture will be assembled or resolved.'[73] Desmond MacCarthy, reviewing Noel Coward's *Conversation Piece* in 1934, describes how the impending loss of the picture as the play moves on only intensifies its pleasure:

> the pictures which the play forms continually before our eyes . . . inspire indeed an astonished pleasure . . . Had I seen a painting which was a facsimile of, say, the tableau of the Regency party in Act II, I would not have given it a second glance, but on the stage it riveted me; perhaps because I know that in a moment it would vanish and change.[74]

The narrative painting, Meisel suggests, inhibiting forward movement and directing our attention to forces from the past that meet in the tableau, is resonant with this sense of loss.[75] While hidden truths are made visible, the future hangs in the balance, since in losing the picture the chance of restitution is threatened. Tansy flees the Wiverley farmhouse straight into Clem's trap. Thus, as Peter Brooks explains, the last-minute rescue of melodrama enacts a bridge between the recognition offered by the tableau and the power to act on which restitution depends.[76] Will finally breaks his immobilisation, rushing into the landscape to rescue Tansy from Clem's clutches. The film concludes in a final embrace of regeneration, silhouetted on the skyline and framed by trees. The dramatic tableau, then, instigates a double movement. Bringing various lines of action into a pictorial-theatrical conjuncture, it realises the culmination of events leading up to it. In this sense, our perspective is turned to the past, rather than to the forward movement of the heroic trajectory of 'classical' narration. But, pausing on the dramatic, aesthetic and moral 'effects' of the moment, the significance of the tableau lies in anticipation of its consequences, when the future must be rescued from, or reconciled with, the past.

GESTURAL AESTHETICS

The drama of the tableau depends on the legibility of gesture, for which pictorial organisation is crucial. In this sense, gesture links actor to painted figure. The actor-manager, Dion Boucicault, describes the gesture as itself 'a sort of picture'.[77] While painters drew on acting manuals for bodily poses and gestures of their figures, so actors are advised, by for example Henry Neville, 'to attend picture galleries as source of appropriate attitudes'.[78] Equally, the body and face of the film actor is required to visualise for the spectator the emotions that drive a protagonist and characterise his or her personality.[79]

This focus on gesture had been established through a web of discourses spun over two centuries around the significance of bodily movements, posture, face and eyes, interweaving philosophical and aesthetic theories of language and bodily expression with the rising sciences of natural history, anthropology and physiology.[80] These ideas not only informed actors' handbooks but filtered into popular practices such as phrenology or the collection of cartes-de-visite, postcards and cigarette cards featuring actors exhibiting particular gestures or poses. This fascination enters early cinema in the popular 'facials' genre – films consisting of dissolving poses and 'face-pulling', discussed respectively by Amy Sargeant and Joe Kember.[81] It can be found in the photographic strips or collages, offering updated poses and facial expressions by popular film actors, scattered through actors' handbooks and the trade and fan press up to the end of the 1920s (Fig. 2.2).[82]

Recent historiography has produced considerable scholarly discussion of actors' manuals and of the acting style variously described as rhetorical, histrionic or pictorial, which was often derived from rudimentary line drawings in actors' handbooks, and characterised as a set of crude, exaggerated and artificial poses inappropriate for film. However, theatre historians, and not least the manual writers themselves, warn against confusing the abstract systems represented by the handbooks with performance *practices*.[83] In *The Road to the Stage* (1827), Leman Thomas Rede argues against the notion that 'some

Fig. 2.2. 'The Expressions of Clive Brook' from *Picture Show*, 28 January 1922, p. 7

general rule of performance' will automatically guarantee dramatic effectiveness. 'If the actor cannot feel what he utters, it will be useless to attempt to make him run the gauntlet through a set of emotions by rule.' Thus it is for its provision of *training exercises* that Rede reprints 'a celebrated analytic review of the effect of various emotions on the human frame'.[84] Similarly, a century later, Netterville Barron dismisses fears that codification of gestures will lead to mechanised acting by analogy with the pianist practising scales.[85] As David Mayer points out, taking actors' handbooks as guides to finished performance deracinates technique from the aesthetic totality that configures a moving stage or cinematic picture.[86] Moreover, there is an inevitable gap between training exercises and the practices of particular performers. Rather than determining performances, these handbooks provide access to shifting ideas about techniques for linking emotion, character type and the body. In the next chapter I shall follow some of these debates through changes in dramatic writing, staging and performance, the afterwash of which impacts on British film production as a *performed* cinema. In this section, however, I want to focus on the contribution of the performer to the creation of a picture.

In Martin Meisel's study it is in melodrama that the tension between 'the appetite for reality' and 'demand for significance', between 'the temporal movement of narrative and the frozen moment of the picture', achieves aesthetic resolution as dramatic action climaxes in tableau, delivering significance made legible through gesture.[87] Although in North European cultures, the rhetorical performance associated with melodrama, especially if badly performed, has always been open to ridicule – and indeed, its high-flown claims to emotional significance were frequently subject internally to counterbalancing parody from supporting comic roles – it was not necessarily perceived as 'unnatural'. Indeed, according to Peter Brooks, the philosophical theories that first codified the language of the body conceived gesture as, precisely, 'natural' because involuntary, instinctive and therefore uncontaminated by the evasions or duplicity of social convention and verbal language.[88] Thus, Henry Siddons argues:

The Soul speaks the most frequently, and most easily, in those parts where the muscles are *pliable* and *ductile* . . . most frequently in the *eyes*. These operate so spon-

taneously, and so easily, that they hardly leave an interval between the sentiment and its effect [original emphasis].[89]

At the end of the century Henry Neville writes, 'The eyes are the "index of the mind" . . . their complicated fibres serve no purpose but to convey impressions to the soul, and to give external expression to them'.[90]

While, however, physiology guarantees authenticity, gestures require system and repeatability if they are to signify. Thus declaring that 'the gestures are the exterior and visible signs of our bodies', Siddons argues, 'every incomplete picture . . . of internal or intellectual ideas, ought to embody itself by *images*' (original emphasis).[91] In 1923 Colden Lore explains that the artistic imagination is concerned with 'reproducing copies of original sensations once felt . . . and of all sense impressions, those most easily reproduced are visual sensations'.[92] While gestures may be drawn from everyday life, as expressive signs they are honed by pictorial organisation in order to communicate with an audience. Thus Dion Boucicault admonishes actors:

gesture must be subordinate to the spectator himself . . . It is a sort of picture . . . do not let your gesture be too short . . . You do not know how long you can rest upon a good one. It tires you, but it will not tire the spectator.[93]

If this style did not strike its advocates as exaggerated or artificial, this is partly because the gesture appears within a total pictorial-theatrical ensemble, underscored by music.[94] Its appeal, then, was doubly expressive: narrative meaning bound up with aesthetic affect. However, the tension between the 'appetite for reality' and what counts as 'significant' means perceptual and aesthetic codes diverge. By mid-century, the arrival of naturalist practices from the Continent and gradually extending boundaries of representation challenged the aesthetic values that produce significance. Pondering on the distinction between illusion and representation (in Meisel's terms between the 'appetite for reality' and 'signification'), G. H. Lewes wrestles with the continuing need for symbolic expression – 'the internal workings must be legible in the external symbols'.[95] At the same time, he rejects traditional codifications of bodily gestures, which increasingly seemed too emphatic and too public to capture the new, smaller dimensions of private existence that naturalist practices and photography were bringing into representational view. In real life, Lewes argues, 'men and women express so little in their faces and gestures or in their tones of what is tearing their hearts'. Yet it is by 'looks, gestures, *position in the picture*' that the actor must generate the signifiers of inner life (my emphasis).[96]

In this context, an increasing domestication of painting and drama in terms both of expanding middle-class markets and subject matter produced a gradual shift from the public arena of *coups de théâtre* and polarised confrontation favoured by large-scale painting and melodrama. Instead, more personal scenarios turn on problems of perception, choice and indecision. This attempt to bind together the natural and typical, the ideal and the psychologically authentic is heralded in the work of the Pre-Raphaelites, who contributed to refiguring the gestural rhetoric captured in acting handbooks. Thus Martin Meisel suggests how the Pre-Raphaelites reversed the drive to externalise conflict in melodrama's tableau of crisis in favour of a contrary pressure to internalisation. The focus shifts to narrative moments that anticipate rather than arrive at the climax, the incidental, apparently spontaneous gesture, look in the eyes or domestic detail pointing towards an internal dilemma that decorum may not allow to be expressed. For example, in Millais's *The Black Brunswicker* (1860), the girl's hand, in the moment just before parting, reaches to press the door shut as her soldier fiancé moves to open it. In Holman Hunt's *Valentine Rescuing Sylvia from Proteus* (1851), Julia unconsciously twists her ring, as, disguised, she watches the discovery of her former lover with Sylvia.[97] Such moments substitute, Meisel suggests, the plausible 'situation' or inward perception for the emblematic tableau – a pause in the flow of time, rather than the climactic freeze-frame.[98]

This shift in the rhetoric of narrative painting was shared by the pictorial stage in the refined performance and staging modes that arose with the new theatrical managements ushered in by the Bancrofts, Charles Kean and Tom Robertson (see Chapter 3). A mid-century essay in *Blackwood's Edinburgh Magazine* questioning 'the meaning of all this realism' points to Kean's 'style of acting . . . [as] remarkable for the specification of little traits and details that

serve to realise the character as much as possible in that style which has been called Pre-Raphaelite'.[99] William Archer makes a similar connection between the Pre-Raphaelites and Robertson, citing the pictorial detail of Robertson's stage directions in *Ours*: 'throughout the act the autumn leaves fall from the trees . . . [which] shows a wholly new desire to produce an illusion of reality by minute but characteristic touches. Robertson was a pre-Raphaelite of the theatre.'[100]

THE INTERVENTION OF THE CAMERA

Such shifts were reinforced by the advent of photography, which promised to break through the increasingly apparent conventions of gestural language to capture ever smaller facial and bodily inflections, intimations less of a 'soul' than of the hidden self of modernity. William Archer uses the newness of photographic vision as a metaphor for artistic representation: 'the most familiar things exist in our consciousness as in an undeveloped negative; artistic presentation is like the developing "bath". Do we not sometimes find a revelation in a photograph of a dearest friend?'[101] Advocates for cinematic art were not slow to claim the advantage of the close-up, which compensated for loss of words by the 'greater intensity of gestures and facial expressions on the screen':

> In the theatre the spectator uses his opera glass to follow the play of the actor's facial muscles, the narrowing of his eyelids, the quiver of his nostrils, the twitching of his lips . . . and it is precisely this type of emotional expression for which the screen is so suitable.[102]

Similarly, M. P. Prout, reporting for *The Motion Picture Studio* on a meeting at the Royal Photographic Society, declares the kinematographer's art as 'essentially kine-portraiture': 'It is watching the changing expressions of the artistes . . . [by] . . . which the story is being unfolded that constitutes the absorbing interest of the good photoplay.'[103]

In intensifying the scope of observation and, through cinematography, capturing the vagaries of the moving world, the camera collaborates with and extends the innovations of Pre-Raphaelite vision, bringing into view a new gestural lexicon for the expressive and narrative work of the painter, actor and film-maker. In the process, as the boundaries of social representation are extended, the painter and camera alike fish out of the flow of daily living often startling gestural signs of the modern: Holman Hunt's conscience-stricken courtesan in *The Awakening Conscience* (1853); Ford Madox Brown's navvies in *Work* (1852–63); Ivy Duke, in *Lure of Crooning Water*, lighting a cigarette as she sardonically surveys the narrow confines of her farmhouse retreat while contemplating seducing its owner (Fig. 2.3); Cherie Bouchier blowing bubble gum in defiance of male and class power in *Palais de Danse* (1928).[104]

This modernising process is evident in the changing terms deployed in actors' handbooks and advice columns. For example, in 1827 L. T. Rede offers a robust description of mirth, which 'opens the mouth . . . towards the ears, crisps the nose, lessens the aperture of the eyes, and sometimes fills them with tears; shakes and convulses the whole frame and, appearing to give some pain, occasions holding the sides'.[105] In 1919 Violet Hopson retains Disgust along with other designations found in early guides – Mirth, Surprise, Pleasure, Uncertainty, Indignation, Mollification, Rage and Terror.[106] However, allowing for gender differences, Hopson suggests more constrained and anodyne renderings of these emotions. Mirth is 'a wistful smile', while 'disgust' involves 'a petulant look, corners of the mouth drooping'.[107] Significantly, too, Hopson finds it difficult to describe precisely what an actor does to convey such states, suggesting the increasing dissolution of gestural codes under the pressure of naturalist detail and a less expressive, normative verisimilitude.

Fig. 2.3. Updating the 'Pre-Raphaelite touch'. Ivy Duke, in *Lure of Crooning Water* (1920), surveys the narrow confines of her farmhouse retreat while inwardly contemplating seducing its owner

THE REGISTERS OF GESTURE

The acculturation of gesture, however, ensures both its retention as a signifying element and a persistent mixing of rhetorical and naturalist styles. At the end of the 19th century, Dion Boucicault and Henry Neville each elaborate models that attempt to hold together the expanding range of performance modes, accommodating the apparently spontaneous transparency of naturalist practices to the typifying gesture or character trait capable of signification because of its repeatability. Boucicault develops a conception of multiple character discussed in Chapter 3. Neville similarly provides a tripartite conception of gesture that identifies three 'registers' of address. The *colloquial* captures 'the actions most in use in daily life', employing gestures that stay close to the body, not rising above the forearm; while 'voluntary and vivacious', they are also governed by 'taste'.[108] The *rhetorical* includes gestures employing the upper arm to shoulder height, which are used to support emphatic or persuasive communication; while the *epic* gestures, rising above shoulder height, 'depict all that is grand, lofty and sublime'. Neville notes regretfully that 'the commonplace drama of to-day does not particularly call upon this class of action, and numberless actors know no more how to use them than a footman knows how to handle a flail'.[109] In relation to British film acting these comments highlight both multiple and shifting codes of gesture. Second, different levels of stylisation bring the demands of naturalism into line with a socially coded signifying system, accommodating private to public forms of expression. Significantly, the colloquial should, in Neville's terms, avoid, as much as the epic requires, the 'picturesque'. Neville concludes by saying:

> The exigencies of public taste, which may desire the Epic to-day, the Rhetoric [sic] to-morrow, and the Colloquial the next day, require you to be ready and practised for every style . . . The knowledge of one style . . . gives a charm and distinction to the other; cultivation in any branch of plastic art brings us nearer to perfection.[110]

Such changes in performance mode, moral scale and social values can be traced from the centrepiece of Augustus Egg's triptych, *Past and Present* (1858 – Fig. 2.4), via a mid-nineteenth-century press illustration for the melodrama, *East Lynne*, figuring a

Fig. 2.4. The centrepiece of Augustus Egg's triptych, *Past and Present* (1858) (© Tate London 2003)

Fig. 2.5. Epic gestures in a mid-nineteenth-century press illustration for the melodrama, *East Lynne* (Courtesy of Theatre Museum © V&A Images)

similar familial crisis (Fig. 2.5), to the more ambivalent, private scenario envisaged in John Collier's *A Fallen Idol* (1913 – Fig. 2.6a), which formed the basis of Maurice Elvey's first film. Both the *East Lynne* illustration and *Past and Present* confirm established morality in the rigid and retributive figures of patriarchal righteousness, deploying the drawing room as public centre of the bourgeois household, with relatives and children as witness to the act. But while the *East Lynne* illustration advertising the theatrical melodrama deploys a fully epic gestural vocabulary, *Past and Present* utilises a more mixed and contradictory rhetorical repertoire. Here, the clenched fists of the husband and the foot that grinds his rival's letter into the ground contrast with his sunken posture and spread legs, whereas his wife displays epic abasement, her arms and clasped hands stretched above her head but at floor level. However, if introducing greater

naturalism, the rhetorical force of the scene is hardly diminished, but is, rather, displaced into the geography and iconography of setting. Public morality is clearly stated in the open door reflected in the mirror, sign of an expulsion both behind and before the actors, in the precarious house of cards built by the children and in the allegorical paintings on the walls. By 1913, Collier's *A Fallen Idol* retreats to the privacy of the library, where a similar scenario is played in low-key colloquial gesture, commended in *The Bio-*

Fig. 2.6a. (top) John Collier's *A Fallen Idol* (1913), the controversial exhibit at that year's Royal Academy summer show (Permission of Auckland Art Gallery Toi o Tamaki). This formed the basis of Maurice Elvey's first film, *The Fallen Idol* (1913). The film's realisation of Collier's painting, fig.2.6b. (bottom) was reproduced in *The Bioscope*, 6 November 1913, supp. xxxv

scope review of Elvey's film version for its restraint: 'The facial resemblance of the two protagonists to the figures in the original picture is quite remarkable and they faithfully preserve the spirit of the latter by their restrained and dignified acting.'[111] In this case, less determinate gestures and the absence of public symbols produce a similarly understated moral dilemma opening up the question at the film's end, 'Will he forgive her?' – a question that would have been inconceivable in its earlier picturisations.

However, the expansion of the performing lexicon, the proliferation of visual detail and the potential anarchy of moving pictures threaten the stability and discriminations necessary for configurations that articulate looks and gestures as legible signs of emotional meaning. George Pearson quotes from G. H. Lewes in his notebooks: 'gestures, to be effective, must be significant and to be significant they must be rare'.[112] This sentiment is echoed by Boucicault, who warns against meaningless fidgets that will lose the interest and attention of the audience: 'Let the gesture be exactly as pertains to what you say, so as to help the meaning, and no more.'[113] Similarly, Henry Neville reminds his reader 'that gesture is rendered insignificant by frequency'.[114] Towards the end of the 1920s Lilian Bamburg advises aspirant film actors to 'avoid all needless movements'.[115]

PICTORIAL ARTICULATION: FRAMES, VIGNETTES AND BOUNDARIES

'Rarity' is the condition for the differentiation on which articulation and signification depends. Pictorialising gestures and movements selected from the vastly expanded repertoire now drawn from everyday life offered a means of isolating and slowing down what would otherwise appear undifferentiated, meaningless and therefore unappealing. Henry Neville, declaring that 'Beauty is Power', recommends the performer practise sinuous and graceful movements reminiscent of the snake charmer: 'sway slowly and frequently, and acquire by practice and patience that unconscious excellence which fascinates beholders'.[116] In this style David Mayer sees the influence of art nouveau.[117] Its impact is demonstrated in the deliberately slow and graceful arm and hand movements of Lily Elsie, heroine of Elvey's *Comradeship* (discussed in Chapter 4). In this respect, art nouveau returns the potentially profuse detail of Pre-Raphaelitism to the clarity of decorative design

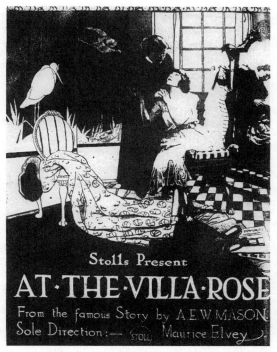

Fig. 2.7. A decorative edging part-frames this mix of photograph and drawing in an advertisement for *At the Villa Rose* (1920) in *The Kinematograph Weekly*, 15 April 1920, p. 90

that enables gestures and images alike to exercise their fascination: for example, the 'dainty white columbine fingers gliding like rose petals blown by the wind' perceived in Hepworth's films.[118] The prevalent use by trade advertisements throughout the 1920s of decorative edgings to frame photographs mixed with graphic design seeks similar effects (Fig. 2.7) while in 1924 Sidney Bernstein argues the artistic importance of proscenium design as 'the setting which has to frame so many hundred pictures'.[119]

In this context, the transformation of the proscenium arch into a picture frame served both to compensate for naturalism's diminution of gestural rhetoric and to stabilise the detail of Pre-Raphaelite staging into pictorial configurations earlier sustained by the emphatic figure relations of the dramatic tableau. Film-makers made similar use of the mask, vignette and iris to pictorialise the film frame and to stabilise shifting shot scale and focus when 'the proscenium opening of the theatre is changed into the adjustable limits of the screen edge'.[120] Quoting Edgar Allan Poe, Martin Meisel suggests that the enclosing frame, as well as concentrating action into a particular 'effect', provides 'an indisputable moral power in keeping concentrated the attention'.[121] In focusing on the 'telling point' of the picture, the film frame contributes to the articulating power of the gesture or glance. At the same time, it accrues a narrational function through its figurative shape. The vignette – heart-shaped for love, lozenge-shaped for battlefields, and so on – identifies theme, while the degree of sharpness or softness of iris or mask contributes to mood and affect. Such vignetting enables Maurice Elvey to pioneer the film biography as a discursive form, different-shaped frames presenting images as narrative pictures while also articulating a wider historical or cultural significance. So, for example, *Nelson* makes use of the spot-iris to encircle Nelson's little sister at their mother's deathbed;[122] a heart-shaped mask to represent his East Indies venture, enclosing a ship's figure-head in its left half and a malaria-stricken Nelson in the right; on the eve of battle an oval to capture his mental image of home, with wife at the piano and father seated next to her; a full circle, edged by an exotic tracery of palm fronds, into which sweeps the temperamental Queen of Naples; lozenge and diamond shapes to produce battle vistas, and so on. Thus a picture or view is offered not only for aesthetic response but for a reading, guided by the process of articulation instigated by the frame and developed by the pictorial composition within it.

Crucial for the poetics of British cinema, pictorial articulation produces not only legible signs but contributes to the work of differentiation. If theatrically framed spaces serve to socially locate and demarcate characters, pictorial framing collaborates with this process, isolating, identifying and presenting to the viewer not only social types, character traits and environmental 'views' but drawing attention to social or psychological encounters emphasised by the frame boundary. *Call of the Road* introduces irascible Uncle Silas (Ernest Douglas) in a circular mask that frames his screwed-up features as he peers out from under a top hat and takes pinches of snuff. The following two-shot introduces an ingratiating innkeeper, rubbing his hands together nervously. The replying circular mask frames Silas giving a wickedly calculating grin. In another episode, a spot-iris encircles his scapegrace nephew, Alfred (Victor McLaglen in his first screen role), gazing thoughtfully after the departing youth, Lord Ullswater, following his humiliation at the hell-

fire club that Alfred is running in his uncle's absence. The mask serves to single out this moment, asking us to appreciate how Alfred differs from his irresponsible aristocratic companions and pointing to his potential redemption. Graham Cutts in *The Wonderful Story* (1922) deploys oval and circular masks to differentiate his protagonists. Thus the rugged, masculine but egocentric Robert is presented in vignettes that highlight him pulling laconically on his pipe, often detached and watching others, sometimes intruding into their frames, and associated with a large black laborador. In contrast, his more retiring but sympathetic younger brother, Jimmy, is framed in domestic activity – digging, washing, repairing a roof (thus vulnerable because unaware of the other observing) – accompanied by a playful kitten.

By the mid-1920s the norms of continuity editing had displaced the mask and iris shot. However, the pictorial conception of theatrical scene and framed shot persists in British film-making and alternative means are found to produce the effect of framing within a cinematographic *mise en scène*. The scriptwriter, P. L. Mannock, attacking Hollywood's trend towards ever larger sets that dwarf the actor, quotes from Frank Vernon's *Modern Stage Production* (1923), which makes similar complaints about current stage practice. Vernon's answer explains how to produce a theatrical reduction in scale presumed to be the prerogative of the camera:

> If a spacious room is . . . indicated . . . let the whole stage space be employed: if a stuffy room is . . . indicated, contract your flats. There are triangular and circular settings, too little used; and there is a whole field of

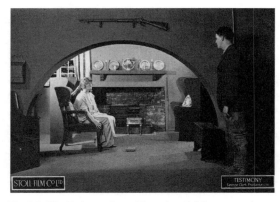

Fig. 2.8. The kitchen arch provides an internal frame to enclose a filmic picture in *Testimony* (1920)

'suggestion' to be explored by the use of permanent false proscenium curtains with the *little picture of salient import in the centre* . . . focusing attention where attention should be focused – on the acting [my emphasis].[123]

The arches, pillars, looped curtains, doorways or trellises, which duplicate the proscenium arch through naturalised internal framings discussed in Chapter 1, may equally open onto filmic pictures and views (Fig. 2.8). Towards the end of *Blighty*, for example, when the Armistice coincides with the anniversary of their son's death, a door is discretely opened and closed on his parents in a tableau of grieving memory, hands held and half-turned to the clock that marks the hour. Equally, external locations and landscapes offer 'natural' frames. H. P. Robinson notes of the popular rural drawings of Birket Foster that he 'takes every opportunity of enclosing his picture with graceful lines' provided by sloping roofs, curving foreground water or overarching branches.[124] As Andrew Higson has shown, Hepworth exploits such compositional frames,[125] but the practice is common throughout British films of this period. In the early 1920s this strategy may be combined with the mask or vignette. In the duel scene in *Call of the Road* a thick tree trunk cuts the frame vertically just off-centre, its curve to left and right extended by overhanging branches that meet on the right with an answering half-curved mask, enclosing the encounter of the duelists and their supporters. The curve to the left frames a second smaller space to the side of the action, where Lady Rowena conceals herself with her maid to watch the antics of her as yet unknown cousin. In Cutts's *The Wonderful Story* an oval mask framing a shot of just married Kate, pausing at the door before confronting her former fiancé, her husband's now paralysed brother, is softened by the art nouveau-like tracery made by an overlapping ring of garden greenery.

IVY DUKE: PRE-RAPHAELITE OF THE CINEMA
The films of Guy Newall and Ivy Duke, postwar newcomers from the theatre to film, were warmly greeted for their freshness of performance and camerawork. A new repertoire of unfamiliar pictorial gestures, suggesting a filmic Pre-Raphaelitism, interlaced often emotionally laden melodramas. In *Testimony* (1920), directed by Newall, and in *The Lure of Crooning Water*, directed by Arthur Rooke, Ivy Duke creates her respective characters in a series

of delicately drawn gestures, looks and movements. Precisely timed, they startle because they are 'rare', in the sense of being both non-redundant and new. In both films Duke is called on to represent the modern woman from town entering a rural backwater. Pictorial articulation – achieved through the use of circular masks in conjunction with played gestures – is doubly important as the unfamiliar is brought into view. In *Testimony* Duke plays Althea May, whose arrival as a new teacher is first observed by Lucinda, the woman whom she will replace in the affections of Rachel Lyons's only son, Gillian. In a soft-edged circular mask Lucinda pauses as she leaves Rachel's kitchen, framed by the whitewashed stone porch, her attention caught off screen left. In medium close-up Althea peeps curiously over the garden gate, her arms encumbered by packages and a basket, caught within a frame created by the wicket gate and foliage clustering round her on either side. A reverse shot returns to Lucinda, looking puzzled at the sight of the stranger, followed by a mid-shot of Althea, her gaze distracted, her nose wrinkling as she absorbs a new rural sensation, revealed by a circular mask as a butterfly. Again we return to Lucinda watching, and in the next shot, Althea, realising her curiosity is observed, clumsily drops her parcels in embarrassment. *The Bioscope* reviewer speaks of Ivy Duke's 'delicate beauty and extraordinary personal charm': she has 'just that touch of refinement and distinction which might be resented in a village'.[126]

The conflict between the displaced mother and potential daughter-in-law is intensified through the increasing pictorial clash of traditional and new gestural iconographies. Althea, now installed as a new bride in Gillian's family home, has been set to domestic tasks by his mother. An abandoned bucket and mop tell Rachel that Althea has absconded, and she instructs her son to find and reprimand his wife. A circular mask encloses Ivy lying on her stomach in the pasture, followed by a smaller circle framing the picture she is watching: a cow suckling a calf. Gillian eventually enters her shot, kneeling beside her. She does not move, but still staring ahead, her chin resting on one hand and a hint of smile, she reaches for his hand, pulling it under her chin. He looks down puzzled at her apparent indifference to his reprimanding calls, and bending closer follows her gaze to the picture of the cow and calf – an intimation of impending maternity. Sliding his right hand over her back and his left under her shoulder, he turns her over, her head twisting up to him as he folds over her, burying his head in her neck. The shot irises out. Here, newly recognised gestures of maternal sexuality combine with traditional pastoral icons to introduce a contemporary femininity. In a later sequence the power of the enraged mother crushes these signs. Under a heavy arch that frames the fireside (see Fig. 2.8), Althea sits reading (in itself a bone of contention), while Rachel, sat in shadow, sews. Pausing, she takes a pair of bootees from her sewing box, cupping them protectively to her breast, a close-up emphasising indecision. Kissing them, she takes the bootees to Althea. A close-up catches a quizzical look from Althea, who, failing to recognise the significance of the gesture, lightly shakes her head. Rachel's outrage is heightened by a big close-up and in the following shot she snatches the bootees back to hurl them on the fire in a violent outburst that acts like a maternal curse. With Gillian's entrance, the scene culminates in domestic estrangement.

SERIAL DISCONTINUITY

While the practice of theatrical realisation and stage painting of the kind perfected by Irving united picture and drama, a second set of relationships, emerging from an increasing diversification of cultural markets and forms, instigated a movement towards dispersal and discontinuity. If the tableau depends on convergence in the unifying situation, the strain of narrative movement breaks the confines of the singular picture, producing a variety of picture/story relations. For example, the picture series or progresses of Hogarth, Cruikshank and Frith; the triptych of the Pre-Raphaelite painters; and the 'before and after' or socially contrasting duos popular in Victorian narrative or anecdotal paintings, such as Abraham Solomon's *Waiting for the Verdict* (1857) and *Not Guilty* (1859).[127] Furthermore, the marriage of the picture with the printed text – for example, the use of literary quotations to accompany paintings and the illustrated press – extended the narrative moment of the picture through the word.

THE ILLUSTRATIVE MODE

Seeing the world in pictures benefited from the early development in Britain of reprographic technologies and a consequent flowering of illustrative techniques.

While common sense conceives the illustration (assumed to be visual) as serving an original (assumed to be verbal), Martin Meisel shows that pictures were not necessarily integrated into nor dependent on prose narrative, but often followed a parallel trajectory, offering 'not just decorative embellishment but narrative enrichment'.[128] The illustration might constitute independent 'realisation' or 'parallel imaginative creation', but in either case it delighted through the 'illuminating extension of one medium by another'.[129] Crucially, the illustration marked a relationship between different discursive fields. Nor was it confined to the relation between picture and print. The *Daily Telegraph*, reviewing Henry Neville's performance as the hero of *Henry Dunbar* (1865), notes not only the stir of appreciation on his first entrance, which realised perfectly 'the description given of the reputable handsome-looking gentleman' (familiar from the novel), but that 'the character received at the hands of Mr. Neville the most complete illustration'.[130] Henry Neville himself conceives of gesture as a process of illustration, hovering between productive and passive conceptions. Colloquial gestures 'must be analogous to . . . those sentiments you would *illustrate* or *force*' (my emphasis).[131]

Illustration was encouraged institutionally by serial publication in magazines or multi-volume editions of novels. Pictures bridged the gap between instalments, gaining not only a certain emblematic autonomy in generating a story image that takes life in the reader's mind but reconciling the pleasures of tableau and narrative movement. For the 'picture' prolongs a dramatic or piquant situation kept alive in 'ocular reality', while the narrative hurries on to its resolution.[132] Not only, then, does serialisation make reading discontinuous, but the pictures are consumed *in parallel* with the written fiction. The narrative relationship between picture and text was, Martin Meisel suggests, one of 'serial discontinuity' rather than symbiosis, encouraging the mental collaging of picture and text rather than a unified and singular experience.[133] This process continues into British film-making. Appreciation of filmic pictures operates in parallel or in tension with the coalescing of a fictional world and apprehension of a narrative thread.

MAGIC LANTERN AS INTERTEXTUAL RELAY

As semi-autonomous realisations or fictional emblems, popular illustrations could spin off from collaboration with the printed page to join a host of other images retailing fictional characters, tourist views, personalities, documented types and scenes circulating in the culture. Almost by definition a 'picture' is available for reproduction, offering sources for further production. In this sense, illustrations, realising popular fictional characters or story moments – for instance, George Cruikshank's 'Oliver Asking for More' – function as intertexts, forming the basis, as Martin Meisel shows, of various dramatic and later filmic adaptations.[134] Across the 19th and 20th centuries, emblematic images circulated through popular forms such as cartes-de-visite, stereoscopes, picture postcards, magazine 'novelisations', cigarette cards, magic-lantern entertainments, advertisements and, eventually, films. Gaining in this way a certain independence from the narrative text, the illustration served culturally and institutionally as an 'intertextual relay',[135] contributing to the circulation of affective and cognitive perception from one social arena to another. One of the most prolific 'machines' for activating this relay was the magic lantern. As noted above, the take-up in Britain of the magic lantern was particularly strong, arguably becoming as influential a mediator as photography between nineteenth-century pictorial forms and British cinematic poetics.

Stephen Humphries and Mervyn Heard describe in their respective accounts the shift from the late eighteenth- and early nineteenth-century lantern shows, using music and chiaroscuro lighting effects to create an all-enveloping sensual and sensationalised phantasmagoria of gothic mystery and apparition, to more heterogeneous practices later in the century, employing the lantern as an instrument of home and public education and entertainment.[136] More like a television schedule than a singular aesthetic experience, magic-lantern entertainments offered highly varied programmes, comprising stories, songs, fairy tales, tricks, travel documents, news images and, from the 1860s, mixing painted and photographic slides. Attempts to create synthesis and flow were developed by techniques such as dissolves – sometimes involving multiple lanterns – moving slides, and accompanying music, songs, recitations or a lecturer's commentary. However, heterogeneity was reinforced by the mix of painted, drawn and photographic styles, by different-shaped frames, an absence of logical sequence, and different types of vocal or musical presentation.

The Yorkshire firm established by James Bamforth – 'King of the Lantern Slides' – effected an influential shift towards the illustrative mode in the early 1870s with the life model genre. This offered photographic slide sets based on popular songs and story recitals illustrated by tableaux posed by the Bamforth family and workforce against realistic backgrounds.[137] Frequently, woodblock illustrations to these songs and stories served as 'the basis for the arrangement of the stage-settings and models'.[138] The form became a staple genre of magic-lantern entertainment, providing by the 1890s employment in more than a dozen studios.[139] As with the illustrated book or magazine, the images, assuming audience familiarity with song or story, developed a parallel set of visual relationships rather than attempting to deliver the substance of a plot. In the early 1900s, Bamforth moved into film production, while, following the craze for collecting picture postcards that was spreading from the Continent, they also inaugurated a 'new and soon extremely popular line of cards illustrating pantomime and other popular songs', which would found the world's largest postcard company. Significantly, the connection with theatre persists, for while 'local residents, staff, and family members . . . continued to "model" for the cards . . . professional actors and actresses, "borrowed" from the Huddersfield theatre or music-halls, played an increasing part'.[140]

PICTORIAL VIEWS AND TRAVELOGUES

Magic-lantern slide, picture postcard and film travelogue, frequently interchanging images, offered their audiences views of home and foreign landscapes, cities, architectural monuments and customs. Such forms emerged on the one hand from the European tour and the socially widening access to travel, and on the other, from the adventures of an expanding imperialism. As the 'jewel in the crown', India, Stephen Humphries finds, 'probably inspired more lantern sequences than any other country'.[141] Early cinema quickly locked into this process of shrinking the world. Such pictorial pleasures persisted throughout the 1920s, as is evident in reviewers' responses to the 'views' found in British cinema's use of local rural or foreign exotic locations. So *The Bioscope* finds 'no special moral or message' in *Carnival*, but rather, 'lovely pictures of Venetian canals'.[142] In *A Romance of Wastedale* (1921), it notes 'admirable pictures of the lake and mountain district of Wastedale which reflect great credit on the photographer, John J Cox'.[143] Elvey's *Don Quixote* offers 'scenes among the mountains of Andalusia, with their superb effects of light and shade, [which] give a romantic interest to the figures of the knight and his humble squire'.[144] Paris and Venice are subject to repeated visitation by British film-makers in this period.

Such travel pictures and tourist views interleave the fictions of British cinema in the 1920s and after, offering both discrete pleasures as pictures and icons of social and cultural recognition, thereby contributing to the geographic mapping of narration. Squibs, and Betty Balfour with her, becomes a national icon as the Piccadilly Circus flower seller, holding up London traffic to fling herself at her policeman boyfriend when she learns of her sweepstake win in *Squibs Wins the Calcutta Sweep* (1922). The swings of emotional temperature between music-hall skit and tragic melodrama that structure this film are heightened by the contrasting associations of London and Paris in which they are alternately played out. *The Man Without Desire* uses the tourist imaginary, fed by pictorial views of Venetian canals, crumbling palaces and gloomy alleyways, to lock into a tale combining English science fiction and Pre-Raphaelite fantasy. Elvey speaks of the value of London landmarks as 'selling-points' – a strategy he used for the boat chase along the Thames in *The Great Gold Robbery* (1913), and repeated in *The Sign of the Four* (1923).[145]

SERIAL DISCONTINUITY AND PARALLEL PLEASURES

The notion that films 'illustrate' familiar stories is widespread in 1920s reviewing. *Around the Town* declares, 'a novel can be wonderfully presented by a series of pictures'.[146] *Films* sums up *The Rocks of Valpre* with the judgment that it 'will mean crowded and appreciative houses, for it illustrates a really good story in the best possible way'.[147] *Films*, while emphasising that the book should be read beforehand, says of *The Garden of Resurrection*, 'the spirit of the novel is beautifully caught and as finely illustrated'.[148] The illustrative mode, then, continues to provide parallel rather than integrated relations between film and novel. Thus in its opening title Elvey's *Bleak House* (1920) announces that Dickens's novel contains 'material for many dramas', from which this film has selected 'the most dramatic of all

the tales . . . the story of the hunting down of Lady Dedlock and the discovery of her secret'. A quote from the *Daily Herald* used in its trade advertisement notes the mediation of the illustrative intertext: 'The costumes, make-up and scenic effects are all excellently modelled on Phiz's drawings.'[149] The discreteness of the illustrative picture, its parallel relation with the written story and the consequent habit of parallel consumption described by Martin Meisel, instigates a different reading mode from the one usually associated with continuity cinema. Thus G. A. Atkinson writes in the *Daily Express* of Dinah Shurey's *Second to None* (1926) that the 'ingenious narrative is *interleaved* with many fine pictures of Her Majesty's ships going about their stately business'. Since such images are beloved of audiences, 'there is much to be said for writing a story around official pictures of this type'.[150] Gertrude Allen, already quoted above, regrets the speed at which Hepworth's 'beauteous pictures to gaze on' flip by.[151] Seriality of pictorial pleasure is clearly enhanced by a *mise en scène* that treats each filmic set-up as a picture, emphasised by the varieties of pictorial framing described above. Thus many film reviewers' responses suggest a magic-lantern or picture-gallery experience. For example *Lady Clare* – in which Mary Odette makes such a 'charming picture' – offers 'as beautiful and truthful a succession of pictures as have ever been presented in photo-dramatic form'.[152] Moreover, the resulting parallel mode of reception afforded by pictures 'interleaved' with narrative enables reviewers to register conflicting responses. Thus *The Bioscope* finds Elvey's *Romance of Wastedale* a 'rather conventional melodrama' with unclear narrative that nevertheless yields 'some really excellent pictures of mountain climbing'.[153] *The Motion Picture Studio* suggests that *The Bigamist* (1921) has a weak story and needs cutting, but offers 'the most beautiful views of the South of France'.[154]

The impact of the mode of serial discontinuity on British cinema style, particularly in the first half of the decade, is marked. It is anticipated not only by the practices of the illustrated book, magazine and magic lantern but theatrically by the turns or acts of music hall, variety and the new form hitting the stage in the 1920s, the revue. These forms deliver entertainment in 'segments', the impact of which on filmic narration I shall explore in Chapter 6. Here, though, it is worth noting the frequency with which scenes are constructed not simply pictorially, but in imitation of the magic-lantern slide or dissolving view. *The Call of the Road*, for example, uses the picaresque tale of Lord Alfred/Victor McLaglen's vagabondage to string together a number of pictorially enacted vignettes reminiscent of magic-lantern images or music-hall turns. Alfred and his companion, a wandering gypsy fiddler, rest outside a country alehouse. This provides the vantage point for what is effectively a lantern joke enacted across the river. A lazy miller is beaten by his harridan wife, to the comic moralising commentary of Grandfather Mullins who sits drinking with them: 'e deserves it, says I, for lettun 'er wear the trousers'. At the conclusion of this little entertainment, the music staves and words appear over the picture as the characters – and probably the film audience – sing, 'There was a jolly miller once . . .' in a manner familiarised by the magic-lantern show. Maurice Elvey's *Nelson*, among a range of pictorial devices, uses a telescope frame to re-create young Nelson's fight with a polar bear as a magic-lantern story – the painted arctic landscape and pantomime animal rendering with self-conscious quaintness an event otherwise difficult to film. The prologue to *General Post* was much praised by *The Bioscope* for its 'introductory dissolving views of Sir Denys's ancestors'.[155] Recalling another visual toy, *Decameron Nights* is praised as 'pictorially . . . a work of almost kaleidoscopic variety'.[156]

PICTORIALISM AND MODERNITY

Such an explicitly pictorial and illustrative mode tends to disappear following the collapse and revival of the British film industry in the mid-1920s. After the watershed year of 1924, and in the wake of the growing importance of set design and art direction in Europe and America from the mid-teens onwards,[157] concern shifts from the framed picture to pictorial habitation of the three-dimensional set. But while painterly allusion and art design in film had an international currency – not least in the spread of the 'art-title'[158] – such influences were absorbed into a perceptual context already deeply imbued with a long tradition of circulating and consuming cultural forms as pictures.

PROBLEMS OF CONTINUITY

The struggle to compete with American product and increase European co-production provoked concern to keep up with practices emerging elsewhere. British pictorialism, with its different cultural roots, presented a problem for developing modern film fiction. According to Kristin Thompson, the form consolidating in American studios as a world standard emulated the internally integrated condition of the short story.[159] Into the illusion of a fully consistent world, the spectator was to be led through techniques of analytic editing, a process barely considered in Britain, where editing was still understood as 'cutting' and 'joining' in order to excise 'wasted footage'.[160] *Kinematograph Weekly*, the more hard-nosed of the two major trade journals, aggressively promoting the American standard and therefore critical of British practices, complains that *The Bohemian Girl* (1922) is 'too much a series of beautiful photographic studies'.[161] Significant, then, is its appreciation of *Carnival*'s 'series of gorgeous scenes', despite not being 'properly blended' with the story of the love triangle.[162]

In this context, trade admiration for the Balcon/Saville/Freedman production, *Woman to Woman* (1923) clearly lay in its successful integration of 'spectacular effect', which through its grasp of analytic editing 'never clogs the unfolding of the narrative'. But in explaining why the 'continuity is free from ambiguity', *The Motion Picture Studio* reviewer does not abandon, but rather accommodates, the needs of continuity to a pictorial sensibility:

> Early scenes in Paris are full of tiny glimpses of character and types (in the best sense) which convey the picturesque entourage of the setting . . . [and function] not as digressions but contribute to explain the action . . . British productions either neglect them as extraneous or insert them half-heartedly and inadequately. How useful is an 8-ft close-up of a tiny piece of acting in conveying the spirit of a scene which contains numbers of people.[163]

One can almost see the canvas depicting Clive Brook's 'stern faced protagonist of passionate events' being carried onto the set![164]

There is much discussion of 'continuity' throughout the trade press of the 1920s, especially by *Kinematograph Weekly*, which uses the term as a frequent measure of the failings of British films. Continuity is designated 'bad' in *Flames of Passion*, 'uneven' in *The Beloved Vagabond* and generally 'ragged' by W. J. Elliot, a prominent scriptwriter of the period.[165] In this respect, Edward Thompson's advice that producers pay an expert 'to write a continuity that is something more than a mere sequence of events' suggests the dominant problem.[166] The 'something more' is not specified but thinking in sequential segments rather than analytically is clearly commensurate with imagining a fiction in serial pictures or in the parallelism of narrative and illustration, often explained, as *Kinematograph Weekly* complains of *Carnival*, in titles.[167] Perhaps, then, it is not surprising that British film-makers had difficulties with the term – damned by George Pearson as a 'shibboleth' and 'that blessed word from America', in his 1923 'Address to the Faculty of Arts'.[168] Such comments focus on the production of drama or story, rather than the coherence of a fictional world.

Thus, despite awareness of the need for 'punch', 'pep' and 'vim' – terms that attempted to catch the very different attractions of fast-paced American editing and acting – there is a reluctance to let go of the picture as the centre of pleasurable perception. As late as 1926 the influence of the pictorial mode of thinking persists. Reporting from the Imperial Conference, the *Daily Sketch* laments the failure of British authors, 'conservative and contemptuous of modern developments', to write for the cinema. As an example of someone who would be an 'admirable writer of film stories', the report cites Heine, because his 'poems are a succession of dissolving photographs, a picture in each line'.[169]

PICTURE COLLAGE

If the pictorial frame cuts into the fluidity demanded by American continuity, animation of pictures had been long prefigured by the theatrical tableau discussed above, as well as by the visual toys and magic lantern that preceded cinema. In arguing against the claim of the Impressionists to record more precisely what the eye actually sees by focusing only on the centre of vision closest to the eye, thereby rendering surroundings indistinctly, H. P. Robinson seeks to expose the fallacy that the eye is a 'fixed instrument'. Rather, the eye, changing focus, adapts, kaleidoscope-like, 'to every plane so instantaneously that we practically see the whole of a scene in focus at the same time'.[170] Martin Meisel discusses the 'unfixing' of vision induced by the moving panorama and diorama that offer the spectator both comprehensive vision, taking in a wide sweep, and the possibility of

focusing on detail. This fostered a cinematic mobility of vision noted in many nineteenth-century novelists, especially Dickens and Thomas Hardy.[171] While new forms of travel and movement-based entertainments link the concept of the 'mobile eye' most obviously to the continuously moving camera, the realisation of such mobility in a pictorial cinema fosters other techniques, producing, as I shall explore in Chapter 4, a flicker-book mode of perception. For Robinson, it is as if the eye deployed its own internal shutter, the brain refocusing one picture after another as vision takes in a scene, forming a composite whole from distinct parts. For Robinson, this led to the practice of combination printing, building up photographic pictures from a range of different negatives, sometimes taken over a period of several years. Hepworth describes his own conception of compositing pictures as a 'mosaic'. Thus, rather than analytic editing or constructionist montage, 'collage' may suggest more precisely the way many British films of this period are put together.

A scene from *The Call of the Road* – in which Uncle Silas discovers his scapegrace nephew sleeping off the after-effects of the previous evening's chaos – exemplifies this approach in a startling combination of pictorial composition and collage, exploiting both the penetrability of scenic space and multiplication of points of view. Following a pictorialised title, 'The Dawn's Approach', and an iris-out onto a long shot across tree-fringed lawns, a carriage pulls up outside the Truscott mansion. Cut to a tableau of the scene that awaits the uncle's unexpected arrival. A high-angle shot catches Alfred slumped at a table front right, facing the camera, surrounded by overturned furniture, empty wineglasses and scattered playing cards. His figure is caught at the apex of three rays of light, streaming into the darkness through the half-curtained windows at the back of the frame. After the irascible entrance of Silas, we are treated to a second view of this painterly composition from behind him, as, thrusting aside the agitated servants, he stands appalled, gazing into the scene of devastation as it were from the wings, framed by the two door leaves and trembling flunkies. They discreetly close the doors behind him as he marches into the scene, temporarily shutting out our view too. Cut to the previous shot, with Silas now inside the picture, a threatening presence standing directly behind his nephew, arms behind his back. A series of close-ups flick between his grim face and high-angle shots of scattered cards and a fallen candelabra. Alfred rouses into wakefulness, twisting back to camera to see Silas glaring at him and then, glancing downwards, registering the scene in his uncle's perception. This is the dramaturgy of pictures, the cumulative effect anticipating a traumatic encounter. The sequence ends with Silas pointing Alfred out of the door, to take up a life of vagabondage.

Kenelm Foss similarly orchestrates contrasting points of view in the sadly incomplete *The House of Peril*, which at suspenseful high points combines subjective moving camera and objective pictures, anticipating Hitchcock's celebrated practice by some years. The murder of Anna Wolsky, lured by the villainous Wachners to her death in their gloomy house in the woods, is constructed as a collage of performed actions and reactions, isolated in discrete, symbolic pictures. As Anna concentrates on the seance set up by the Wachners, the following sequence takes place:

MS three-shot	Watched by his wife, Herr Wachner, raised mallet in his hands, sidles up behind Anna, who is seated at the table.
MCU	Madame Wachner's intense eyes seem both to direct and register the blow as the mallet descends.
CU	A terrier chained in its kennel outside, howls.
MLS	The living room: Frau Wachner stiffens as she rises, the table and a chair overturned, Anna's body lying in a heap on the floor. Frau Wachner bends, bringing her clasped hands up to her face, while the husband, stooping over the body, lifts the cover of a trap door under the carpet.

Various reaction shots follow, deploying rhetorical gestures of horror, and the sequence ends with the following images:

H/A CU	The howling dog.
MCU	Herr Wachner at the window, his hands over his ears.

This is a titleless sequence, depending on traditional gestures and signs of melodrama: raised mallet, fallen chair, howling dog. But elsewhere the marriage of picture and word through intertitles not only contributes to articulating images as signs but sets up dialogic perspectives on types and encounters replayed with a difference. A collage of points of view, things seen and observers' reactions produces interpretations and readings, slipping from ocular to mental perspectives. Thus newly widowed Sylvia negotiates the traditional role of 'True Woman', travelling against advice unescorted to the gambling resort of Deauville and, moreover, insisting on taking with her the symbol of her independence – a priceless string of pearls her late husband gave her. Her emancipation, however, falters when at the casino she encounters a good-looking foreign Count in need of moral guidance:

Title:	'Sylvia, the Saver of Souls.'
Shot 1:	Iris-up on a group of gamblers.
Shot 2:	BCU. Sylvia's hand, palm turning over and outwards.
Shot 3:	CU. The Compte de Virieu, registering agitation at the gambling table.

The title both locates Sylvia within a female typology and comments on it, ironising the pictorialised gestures that follow on cue.

Later in the story, Bill Chester, Sylvia's phlegmatic English lawyer, alarmed by a newspaper expose of the Deauville gambling scene, comes to rescue her, but too late to prevent the suspicious disappearance of her worldly-wise friend, Anna. Pictorial documents and knowing titles here manage the boundary between a documented contemporary reality and the onset of the supernatural. Reading newspaper headlines against the background of Tower Bridge, Bill decides to go to France. As he settles down to spend his first night in Deauville, a title marking the limits of normal expectation – 'Your ordinary, healthy European is not a believer in Ghosts' – heralds the eruption and imposition of an alternative fantasised world on the solid environment of a French hotel bedroom. Drawers appear to open of their own accord. Bill settles down again to sleep, then starts up with a look of disbelief. Cut to Anna's reflection in the dressing-table mirror, which moves across the room, passing through furniture towards him, then disappearing. Checking that the brooch the ghost lays on his bedside table is really not there, Bill is able to sleep again. But in the morning his belief in the prosaic world of everyday appearance is confounded when the hotel manager confirms from Bill's sketch that Anna really does possess the brooch.

MONTAGE OF EMOTIONS

Frames and titles used to demarcate shots inevitably prolong the habit of thinking about performance in terms of gestures, while an approach to filmic construction as a collage of discontinuous images generates tensions and confrontations anticipating the dynamic of montage. In her pamphlet on film acting, Violet Hopson describes a letter exercise used to train actors to express the nine principal emotions mentioned earlier.[172] This exercise aims not only to make gestures into legible signs of emotion. Emphasising shifts between contrary states, it conceptualises the narrative potential of gesture − like that of geographic staging and the production of the tableau − as a process of montage juxtaposition, requiring the actor to switch across gestural and emotional boundaries. Thus Louis James, in his account of the rhetoric of melodrama, describes the emotional as well as physical acrobatics required of the melodramatic actor in producing the bodily signs of swift-changing and often reversing emotions.[173]

Exemplifying this process in practice, *The Picturegoer* reports on the training of Lady Diana Manners for her first screen role in *The Glorious Adventure* (1922): 'For three hours and a-half one afternoon Blackton worked on the vivid personality of Lady Di, and taught her the art of registering the emotions of horror, surprise and sorrow.'[174] In similar fashion, George Pearson puts Betty Balfour through her emotional paces when, as Squibs, she must confront the corpse of her sister's husband: 'never raise your eyes from the body. And remember the four emotions, Surprise, Horror, Hope, Fear −− one, two, three, four − we'll take it by numbers.'[175] The letter exercise recorded by Violet Hopson is indeed numbered, emphasising the unfolding of narrative as a succession or juxtaposition of feeling states enacted in, and making considerable demands on, the actor's body. As Violet Hopson warns, 'Surprise and pleasure succeed one another naturally, but disgust at this stage is difficult . . . The sudden transition from rage to mirth is very trying.'[176] Hugh E. Wright is admired for precisely this skill: 'His remarkable power of expression . . . will be a feature of the new

film, for he plays the part of a man at one time torn with emotion, and at another the gayest devil-may-care.'[177] *Picture Show* speculates that the conditions of film-making increase this challenge, commenting on Clive Brook's performance in *This Freedom* (1923):

> the constant change of expression and general bearing from the enthusiastic young man to the broken-hearted father made considerable demands on his histrionic versatility, not easy to command under the peculiar conditions of film acting with its lack of psychological continuity.[178]

Such emotionally kaleidoscopic performance represents the actor's skill, a source of viewing fascination, and a means of pictorially building a story. It requires support from shot or scenic framing, segmented narration and pointed intertitles to mark the juxtaposition between, or change from, one emotional or moral state to another. George Pearson is perhaps the director who responded most acutely to the potential for emotional montage, exploiting the pictorial impact of images to evoke a drama of feelings unhooked from their logical place in an extra-cinematic world and from the demands of narrative progression. While retaining pictorial and theatrical impact − partly through creating protagonists who are performers − Pearson's images break free from the frame and stage. As a preface to his autobiographical account of making *The Little People*, he says, 'Novels, plays, pictures, poems, may suggest ideas, but with that their contribution should end . . . Cinema, if true to itself, should be a lawless medium, free as the vision of the human eye.'[179] Here he draws on the conception of mobile vision discussed above: 'Without conscious guidance our eyes rove over a score of images in a moment of time, they dart on some point of interest, leave it, return to it, fly elsewhere, return again, as free as a bird in flight.'[180] However, Pearson's free combination of images brought tradeshow complaints about narrative clarity, leading to the re-editing of *The Little People* by other hands. G. A. Atkinson wryly comments: 'Pearson is a genius, and if he can be prevented from writing his own stories and scenarios . . . then he will beat the world.'[181] For Pearson, however, it is the feeling of the image that creates the structure of the montage rather than plot logic. Quoting Griffith as his authority, Pearson writes in his notebooks of his aim to build films 'emotion by emotion'.[182]

Something of the impact of this approach is registered in his synopsis for *Réveille*, which reaches for a 'great light . . . from unseen sources . . . fantastic dream shapes without locations . . . the scenes the cinema will make on the day of its liberation from the pedant worshippers of the word and the material'.[183] Pearson's challenge in this film was to envisage the return of the dead from the First World War in an act of solidarity with the living. Before arriving at this vision, however, Mick, the film's Squibs-like heroine, learns on Armistice night of the death of the young soldier whose child she bears:

> It was 2 in the morning when they all returned from Trafalgar Square . . . they danced a final merry-go-round in the old passage . . . till Mother found she was dancing on a letter that lay on the mat under the slit in the street door. Her old eyes needed her glasses . . . she tried to see in the dim candle light . . . she thought she saw OMS on the letter . . . as Mick and the spinsters danced up the stairs to bed.
>
> . . . Mick stopped her clown's antics . . . to lean over and shy a last handful of confetti through the door at Mother . . . but the light in Mother's room went out . . . only a candlestick rolling slowly sideways on the floor . . . smoke trailing upwards . . . only a white-faced girl leaning over the stair rail . . . only two white-faced women clutching at each other . . . then . . . flesh and blood became stone . . . a great silence . . . and all the while mad men and women were dancing round Britannia in the Savoy Hotel.[184]

Pearson's films represent a distinctive cinematic development of the national emphasis on the pictorial, acculturated image, taking film in a direction quite different from that consolidated in Hollywood. 'I sometimes thought the arbitrary convention of "visual continuity" was too rigidly applied; a little license might do much to illuminate an emotional moment.'[185] Like Hepworth, Pearson's emphasis on pictorial-emotional values fights to retain the moral idealism of an earlier age, now vested in the innocence and bird-like freedom of the image in the postwar world of mass-mediated modernity, and in a refiguring of 'woman'.[186] It is Hitchcock, following the trail marked out by the predilections of Graham Cutts, who would marry the pictorial image, positioned within a montage of voyeuristic looks and exhibitionist displays, with the identifications ensured by continuity. Rather than Pearson's commitment to 'hope', Hitchcock's more brutal modernism would bring to the surface the full ambivalence of an image not only acculturated but sexualised. But this is to jump ahead to Chapter 4. The pictorialism of the early 1920s is still locked into an aesthetics of pictorial affect.

PICTORIALISM AND THE AESTHETICS OF AFFECT

The focus of *affect* is pleasure in beautiful form and the feelings it provokes. Thus H. P. Robinson comments: 'All these things are intended to be felt more than seen.'[187] Christopher Hussey, writing in the 1920s on the 200-year tradition of the picturesque, now the popular vernacular of commercial art, speaks of the deeply inculcated 'habit of *feeling* through the eyes'.[188] Cecil Hepworth declares: 'Much of my success, I am sure, is in the aesthetic pleasure conveyed, but not recognised, by the beauty of the scene and generally mistaken for some unknown other quality in the film.'[189] Aesthetic perception and response is in such arguments the guarantor of significance, which, despite the observational bent of English art, is rarely considered self-evident. However, as we see in discourses running from G. H. Lewes and H. P. Robinson to Cecil Hepworth and George Pearson, the proliferation of detail introduced by naturalist practices and intensified by the camera threatened the visual aesthetics of affect and meaning. Rejecting photography as a mechanical device for recording what he variously describes as the 'intolerable solidity', 'self-satisfaction', 'ugliness' and 'dirt' of fact,[190] Robinson argues:

> impressionism has induced the study of what we see and shown us that we all see differently; it has done good to photography by showing that we should represent what we see and not what the lens sees . . . the struggle is now to see pictorially and to represent pictorially . . . we see what we are trained to see, and if we are lucky, perhaps a little more.[191]

The 'little more' is down to the human observer, who uses photography, like the alchemist, to convert raw nature into a picture.[192] Nevertheless, however aesthetically pleasing, the picture must 'tell you something worth telling', a choice of term that emphasises selective articulation as opposed to the accumulation of incidental material that supports the impression of unprocessed reality.[193] For a slowly democratising but demarcated society, reality is of necessity already deeply acculturated and culturally deeply fissured. It is not surprising, therefore, that British painting, photography and film generally found it almost impossible to escape the urge to narrate reality as itself a process in construction through various forms of 'telling', the subject of Chapter 6.

AESTHETICS AS HERITAGE

The importance of pictorial 'telling' is registered reflexively in a series of popular nineteenth-century paintings depicting the circulation of the pictures themselves. This process entails a range of social encounters: at the print-shop window, in the public gallery and museum, in the artist or photographer's studio, in the art-dealer's shop and on the walls of nearly every domestic interior created as a backdrop to some family scene. Dramatising the entry of the picture into the expanding universe of discourse, this focus on the picture as both commodity and cultural document may provoke observational humour or sympathetic recognition. However, the conviction of the pictorialist is that aesthetic response acts as a stimulus to empathy and social perception. For example, William MacDuff's *Shaftesbury, or Lost and Found* (1862) enacts an exchange between two types of cultural 'document': two picturesque shoe blacks gaze at an etching of the philanthropist, Lord Shaftesbury, set among well-known contemporary paintings in the shop window of Messrs Graves, London print publishers. The pathos of the pictorialised little 'urchins', appealing to the sympathies of a middle-class viewer, combines with the documentary facticity of location. Conversely, this 'increment of reality' is embedded in an equal increment of artistic perception, dramatising the process through which a wider populace gains entry to aesthetic sensibility and symbolic imagination. Thomas P. Hall's *One Touch of Nature Makes the Whole World Kin* (1867) is an explicit pictorialisation of this idea. Positioning the viewer inside a print-shop window, behind and to the side of a new exhibit, we observe, pictured within the window-pane frames, a cross-section of urban street life gathered to gaze. Among them are pictured: a top-hatted, monocle-peering dandy, a street-sweeper, bourgeois housewives, a par-

lour maid and, paused in the background, a horse-drawn omnibus, its driver pointing out the picture to his curious passengers.

Reproduction and circulation through the print shop and illustrated press widens access to artistic works and aesthetic sensibility as part of a democratising nation's 'heritage'. The cult of the picturesque began within upper-class culture as a new way of appreciating hidden aesthetic values in the vagaries of Nature. This mode of perception evolved through the cultivation of landscape gardening, the European tour, pastoral poetry and painting.[194] Nevertheless, the growth of the illustrated press and cheap prints, the rise of the magic lantern, expansion of domestic and foreign tourism, and above all the spread of photography with its various spin-offs made aesthetes and travellers of a far larger and more inclusive public. In an essay that explores the mass mediation of landscape, John Taylor suggests the role of photography in popularising – and inadvertently making more widely available to urban populations and the rising tourist industry – the aesthetic perceptions of the landscape painters who had first defined the picturesque: 'Photographers had long practised the salvation of the picturesque ... these pictures ... became talismans or touchstones, evidence that the landscape really did exist.'[195] Summarising Richard Keene, writing in 1884 in the *British Photographic Almanac*, Taylor lists a by now familiar pictorial lexicon produced by the 'sign-ification' of the landscape:

> suburbia might be growing but within five or six miles of every photographer's door there were abbeys, ancient places, birches, brooks, canals, cattle, churches, cottages, crags, crosses, dingles, farms, ferns, foxgloves, gables, ivy, lanes, locks, oaks, ponds, rustic bridges, rustics at work, tombs, watermills, windmills, walls and woods.[196]

Such images circulated through lantern slides, picture postcards, illustrated magazines, amateur snapshots, advertising, packaging and the mania for scrapbooks and collectables, enabling families and community groups across the social classes to exercise aesthetic sensibilities and cultural identities through a pictorial capturing of the world.

Such sensibilities underpin reviewers' responses not only to pictorial allusions in British films but to the so-called 'heritage properties' and artefacts that provide locations and interiors, especially for costume films. *Lady Clare* is praised in *The Bioscope* for its 'rich tone of rare old mahogany, the soft deep polish of fine silver', while the 'country wedding of the merry bachelor' – itself recalling rural genre painting – 'transports us back to the very heart of Georgian England'.[197] 'Heritage' as a product of upper- and middle-class culture is a contaminated concept in contemporary analysis. However, the macro-analysis that ideologically identifies artefacts with the class, gender or race of their producers or owners takes little account of the gaps, twists and shifts involved in reproduction and circulation, nor of the slow, micro-movements in perception and feeling that bring about larger social and ideological changes. For example, what exactly is at stake in the complexly democratising negotiations with high art in Marjorie Mayner's *Picturegoer* article quoted in Section I? Here she claims cinema not only as a new source of beauty but equally a point of access for the millions to the 'old masters':

> In lonely state, paintings by the Old Masters hang in palace, cathedral and picture-gallery. The New Masters cover a wider field, for their work is multiplied and sent to every corner of the globe . . . the New Master works for the appreciation, not of the few, but of the many . . . bringing . . . beauty to beauty-loving eyes which otherwise might never behold them. The film reaches the poor as well as the rich, the ignorant as well as the cultured and sooner or later, all must benefit by the artistic lessons it teaches, apart from its entertaining qualities as a story-teller.
>
> Where the masterpieces in canvas lie enshrined in big cities to which pilgrimage must be made, the masterpieces in celluloid are just round the corner and within reach of everybody, whether rich or poor . . . Who has not consciously or unconsciously seen and learned something about Beauty from one or other of the New ones?[198]

The critique fielded by this writer focuses on elite institutions not the art works they house, laying claim on the value of and right to aesthetic sensibility for all. The advertisement for Elvey's *The Fallen Idol* declares as a selling point: 'Everyone Can Appreciate It', while, in demanding tasteful cinema design, Sidney Bernstein argues that 'for the power class of patron, as well as for those in more expensive seats, there is an inborn sense of beauty'.[199]

This pictorial sensibility, mixing aesthetic pleasure and sentiment, is central to the perceptual habits into which the practices of 1920s British filmmaking locked. However, whereas pictorialism identifies aesthetic *affect* in idealist terms with subjective pleasure in beautiful form, modernist thinking locates aesthetic *effect* in the objective productivity of the work's construction, enabling it to interpellate viewers' responses ideologically.[200] Pictorialist aesthetics are therefore condemned on two counts. First, aesthetic feeling is produced from the passive, voyeuristic position of consumer. Second, the pleasure itself deceives, avoiding the unpalatable truths confronted by a materialist practice of realism. Robinson, for example, is notorious for his advocacy of excision of the ugly and, through combination printing, replacing any 'unbeautiful' features of his usually pliable working-class models by the more refined body parts of middle-class ladies.[201] Consequently, materialist aesthetics demand objects that distanciate the spectator, in order to produce space for intellectual critique. However, in so far as pictorialism through frontal camera, intrusive framing and discontinuous cutting intervenes between spectator and film object, it is also condemned for inhibiting involvement in a fictional world according to the norms of Hollywood – norms otherwise critiqued for their seamless suture of the spectator into an ideologically contaminated narrative system.[202]

PICTURES AS DISCOURSE

Despite the competitive pressure of American continuity cinema and the challenge to pictorialism from Continental modernism, these broadly popular and intertextual conditions of pictorial existence persisted into the 1920s as a continuing set of culturally determined modes of perception and meaning-making. Indeed, as noted by Andrew Higson, *Kinematograph Weekly*, reporting a Royal Photographic Society lecture, declares cinema heir to the pictorial values promoted by 'that great photographer, artist, and scientist, H. P. Robinson'.[203] As the evidence discussed above shows, seeing the world in pictures – turning experience into pictorial form – was inculcated as a widespread habit through a variety of cultural practices and media across the social spectrum. The extension of 'pictorialism' from fine art to photo-journalism and the travelogue, generalising the 'picturesque' from landscape painting to gardening and tourism through the accelerated expansion in reproductive technologies, contributed to merging picture and document as a crucial factor in the development of British cultural poetics. Pictures, as aesthetically crafted signs, become potent cultural documents, equally economic as sources of communicated meaning and aesthetic pleasure and as units of mass reproduction.

PICTURE AS CULTURAL DOCUMENT

The social panorama pioneered by W. P. Frith contributed to this mode of pictorial observation, while, as noted in Chapter 1, the social documentary emerged out of a conjunction of melodrama, graphic art and sensational police reporting, giving rise to the social surveys of philanthropists and incipient sociologists like Charles and William Booth or B. S. Rowntree.[204] At the same time the magic lanternists disseminated photographic slides documenting the social and economic conditions of England's working people and rural poor.[205] The interchange between such practices was crucial in establishing the specific mix of document and fiction that came to characterise British cinema, bringing into expressive conjunction the theatrical, pictorial and observational eye. Thus *The Bioscope*, reviewing *General Post*'s focus on the social effects of the Great War, praises the opportunities afforded by Eliot Stannard's script 'for introducing on his bigger canvas many characteristic glimpses of social transformations', noting 'flashes of such significant commonplaces of wartime as the sugar queue and medical examination'.[206] From the documentary perspective, *Ypres* was one in a series of reconstructions of wartime battles mixing newsreel footage and re-enactment pioneered by Bruce Woolfe. *The Bioscope*'s review suggests a viewing protocol established by the magic lantern and anticipates some of the appeal later to be developed by *Picture Post*:

> In thrilling and majestic war pictures – partly real, partly reconstructed – is told the epic story of the Ypres Salient . . . more graphically, perhaps, than any war film yet produced does it depict the atmosphere of the battlefield as seen by the soldier in the trenches . . . Interspersing this main narrative are innumerable vivid incidental touches, including historic 'topical' glimpses of the King and the Prince of Wales, Haig and the Crown Prince of Germany, besides wonderfully staged pictures of individual feats of heroism.[207]

Pictures of battlefield and sugar queue, alike providing stages for public enactment, serve a similar function to the social panorama, offering juxtapositions of social classes and types that fascinated their publics then and since.

These new techniques of social documentation, stimulated in part by a democratising process that sought social reform as protection from revolutionary upheaval, participate in a process frequently analysed in terms of class surveillance.[208] The figure of the policeman haunted the graphic artists' and documentarists' excursions into the nether reaches of London as well as engravings that circulated images of destitution and despair. Stephen Humphries quotes one lanternist writing for *The Optical Magic Lantern Journal* of 1899: 'I was nagged . . . by a church society for pictures of the outcast . . . we were mistaken . . . for police officers obtaining portraits of suspected persons'.[209] However, the significance of such pictures can only be unravelled as they enter into textual relationships and circulate in public discourse. The policeman is one agent among many, a figure of ambiguity threading through British popular culture, to be exploited most notably by the fertile imagination of Hitchcock.

Like melodrama, the picture, negotiating conflicting demands for aesthetic significance and local recognition, combines, in Peter Brooks's terms, both vision and document.[210] The *Oxford English Dictionary*, in tracing the evolution of the term 'document' from teaching or warning (medieval), to evidence or proof (19th century), to cultural artefact, 'something written, or inscribed . . . as a manuscript, title-deed, coin' (20th century), suggests the symbolic, aesthetic and cultural reach of this composite. The production of the document as proof and currency of social exchange – recalling the role of missing and discovered documents in the denouements of melodrama – serves the narrative rhetoric that seeks to establish the moral and social identities of protagonists divided by social position and personality type. Central to the production of such documents is the cultural function of reproduction and repetition, brought to its high point in the 'realisation' and then dispersed through proliferating media forms. For in the consolidation of an evolving repertoire of character types, locations, performance gestures and narrative actions, the emphasis is on *re*-presentation, *re*-cognition and perhaps, *re*-invention. In discussing this process, Martin Meisel stresses 'the road to reality is not back to an original but from the word to the picture to the flood-lit stage' and thereon, he suggests, to the screen.[211] Indeed, the notion of an 'original' is something of a paradox for a stratified society, needing to capture social difference through type and iconography. However, the reproduction participates in the re-codifying and diversifying processes of re-presentation. Thus in a class-divided society, repetition and circulation across different class entertainment forms of acculturated images and sounds serve to consolidate cultural documents that, once established, can be called on in a process of contest and exchange. This becomes central to British cinematic practice as it negotiates the changing contours of modern life. Pictorialism, derived from painting but practised in different media, foregrounds the work of the picture, emphasising its role in turning nature into culture – a sign of human desire, intervention and control. Reproduction and realisation can be seen, then, as participating in a cultural reconstruction of reality, in which the process of re-presentation and efforts to augment realism collude. Thus the picture participates in Martin Meisel's concept of the 'expanding universe of discourse', introduced at the start of this chapter.[212] In this context, circularity is perhaps a more appropriate metaphor than the linear progress of Meisel's proposition. The picture is representation, document, sign, whose acculturation intensifies the more it is reproduced and circulated from one cultural arena to another. Arguably, in Britain this process contributed towards a gradual democratisation of culture capable of acknowledging and bringing into contact bounded signs of social difference.

THE DISCOURSE OF PICTURES

General Post and *Nell Gwynne* (1926) represent different uses of the pictorial document in this transformational process. As suggested in Chapter 1, *General Post*, in its focus on the impact of the First World War, emphasises the socially integrating dimension of the document. *Kinematograph Weekly* describes the film as 'a panorama . . . of the revolutions brought about by the war in social ideas and prejudices'.[213] Early in the film, Betty Broughton's aristocratic family are disturbed to read a newspaper report of her involvement in the philanthropic work of the Sheffingham Social Democratic Guild (see Chapter

1). The family row that ensues intercuts her protests that she 'can't sit here doing nothing when there's so much misery at our very door' with flashbacks documenting her work in the local soup kitchen and, again, assisting a sick working-class mother. The pressure of shifting gender identities on class boundaries is marked discursively by irising into and out of the flashbacks and by Bentley's attempt to realise graphically Betty's vocal opposition to her family. Following her explosive 'You're all content to grow up like vegetables', titles flash consecutively onto the screen: 'I'm NOT', 'and I must', 'and I will work', after which she throws down her napkin and storms out. As the story progresses, this pictorial discourse juxtaposes (via wipes) or draws into each other (via dissolves and iris) public images, popular representations, social documents and newsreel footage from across a range of class cultures. Vignettes, enacting moments of social comedy or pathos, recall familiar features of wartime life: for example, the medical board noted by *Kinematograph Weekly* with a frisson of recognition as featuring 'pictures of shivering recruits undergoing the perfunctory, "Say ninety-nine!" '[214]

The discursive work of pictorial narration is visibly active as in many such films in its concluding sequence, when the town band gathers with crowds at Sheffingham station to welcome returning soldiers. Here, as suggested in Chapter 1, alternation between different social locations and converging actions develops social mapping as an integrative as well as a demarcating device. Thus, while fiction stages Edward Smith's triumphant return to Sheffingham as a colonel, and Betty discovers her mistaken perception of his emotional distance as neglect, newsreel footage captures the victory crowds milling round Buckingham Palace. These are interrupted by a quotation: ' "It is difficult to smile with an aching heart": Chas. Dickens.' The following vignette focuses not on Betty but on an unnamed woman nursing her baby, who, attracted to her window by the celebrating crowds, turns to a photograph on her wall. This dissolves into an oval-framed filmic image of war graves and charred trees, then back to the photograph. Cut to the woman weeping. Finally, the sequence returns to newsreel shots of celebrating crowds and a switch via a title to the 'equally mad' celebrations in Sheffingham. This represents a skilful collaging of popular imagery, fiction and newsreel, representations of the metropolis and the county, around a symbolic working-class everywoman of the war and a fictional heroine moving towards a consensual middle-class marriage with her father's heroic tailor. Out of geographically demarcated social locations is created an image of English society as a local community.[215] As I will discuss further in Chapter 4, is not accidental that a distinctive form of 'collage-as-montage' emerges out of English popular culture, nor that this technique will come into its own for the home-front film of the Second World War.

Nell Gwynne, directed by Herbert Wilcox, starring Dorothy Gish, photographed by an American cameraman and a success in the American market, was, according to Iris Barry, 'an enjoyable, lively picture, of a scrappy and plotless variety, but rich in character and humanity'.[216] The story's focus on pictorial and theatrical practices produces in the body of the film a series of parodic performances that I discuss in Chapter 5. However, the opening and closing sequences emphasise picture and performance as cultural documents, interweaving entertainment and social discourse, exploiting Nell's familiarity as the subject of many theatrical and pictorial representations. Thus the opening four titles favour the oral storyteller's voice against historical authority: 'So the legend of "Pretty, Witty Nell Gwynne" has come down to us – alive and warm – the tale of the ragged, tender-hearted orange pedlar, who loved and laughed her way through triumph and disaster.' The scene opens on a domestic set, theatrically dressed and lit like a realised genre picture's domestic interior. A sailor and 'war-broken soldier' playing a pipe watch indulgently frame right – family friends, but also representatives of the People. Nell's mother, bowed and careworn, sits disgruntled left frame. In the centre Nell/Gish dances and juggles oranges, self-consciously performing to both diegetic spectators and cinema audience, followed about by a look-alike HMV terrier, one ear cocked. Nell's prologue complete, a title shifts us to 'a corner of Whitehall Palace . . . the most brilliant and dissolute court in Europe'. Here, 'The Merry Monarch, King Charles II' (Randle Ayrton), framed between two marble pillars and flanked by his attendants, is seated on a dais before his mirror. In the following shot he gazes into the mirror/camera, his familiar portrait realised before our eyes.

At the end of the film, the King's death leaving her to the mercy of the hypocritical and self-seeking James, Nell rises to a final pictorial finale in which her figure melds legend and document, theatrical performance and picture. The concluding sequence begins with a medium shot taken from behind Nell, framed by the King's bedposts and withdrawing from her final parting from the dead monarch. Slowly she walks across a stage-set bedroom, to stand head bowed in the frame of the doorway. Cut to James standing stock still, staring at her. Following a title declaiming 'The King Is Dead: Long Live the King!', James disdainfully raises his hand for her obeisance. Watched by dumbfounded clerics, she walks in a stately, unswerving horizontal line straight past him. A long shot reveals a bust of Charles between two candle-stands in the distance. Her figure walks between two pillars and sweeps up the steps to the statue, where she kneels, raising her arm in epic pose, while a title announces: 'My King for ever!' In the return shot her hand gestures from her mouth to his and then to her breast. She turns and pauses as the shot fades out. A title follows, commemorating the lasting legacy of a woman 'who had no place in history but a place in every heart' – the palace she begged the King to make into the Chelsea Pensioners' Hospital as reparation for the nation's war-wounded, a reparation which many in the 1920s still waited for. The title fades out and up comes a long shot of the hospital. A final title brings us to the present: 'Whose figures are one of the cherished sights of London: the Chelsea Pensioners', followed by a shot of the pensioners in uniform, standing at its entrance, raising their hats in salute. The film closes with a dissolve into a documentary shot of three white-bearded heads, recalling perhaps the popular painting of the pensioners by Hubert von Herkomer, in a melding of acculturated picture, performance act and document.[217]

Arguably, the circulation of familiar stories, characters and pictures enables a degree of cultural exchange – in Bakhtinian terms, of potential dialogism. For in crossing class or generational boundaries, such images reappear as cultural signs in new juxtapositions. Built into the realisation, with its dependency on familiarity and recognition, is a necessary degree of self-reflexivity. Thus, to end where this chapter began, Maurice Elvey's realisation of John Collier's *A Fallen Idol* (see Fig. 2.6b) inevitably entered into dialogue with Collier's reference to the mid-century triptych by Augustus Egg, *Past and Present* (see Fig. 2.4). Both paintings provoked controversy, raising questions about the consequences of the story unfolding in the pictures. For while Egg's initiating tableau appears uncompromising, it contains the forces – the startled glance of the younger child, the collapsing house of cards, the awed speculation of the diarist accompanying the triptych ('what a fall hers has been') that in the companion pictures demand our compassion for the consequences. Some sixty-odd years later, Elvey seizes on the narrative openings in Collier's more private and anecdotal picture by concluding his film with the question, 'Will he forgive her?' *The Bioscope* reviewer implicitly recognises the role of such picturised documents in sustaining social debate:

> *The Fallen Idol* has been dealt with in a sincere and painstaking manner, and the reconstruction at the finish of Mr Collier's popular painting is naturally brought about, and accurately accomplished . . . The 'problem,' which worried the half-penny papers so much . . . seems less mystifying than ever when one has seen the events which are made to lead up to it . . . however, the producers . . . finish their play on the reconstructed painting, and sow seeds of doubt in our hearts anew . . . So the mission of *The Fallen Idol* as a provoker of argument will continue its good work, unimpaired, throughout the country.[218]

In this respect, the well-known painting not only provides potential plot material and aesthetic satisfactions but cultural reference points. In particular, the shift in address from Egg, to Collier, to Elvey's film exemplifies a discursive circuit in which the moral values attached to marriage, heterosexuality and class become available for debate and the slow processes of change. Continuing the process, similar circuits can be traced, working their way through films as different a *General Post* and *Nell Gwynne*.

3 Performing British Cinema

If the pictorial theatre creates a public arena for the staging of cultural identities and boundary encounters, the performer is the site where private and public meet. Moreover, with increasing emphasis on the individual and personal life as sources of authenticity, the actor becomes the focus of demands for modernisation in line with changing conceptions of the 'natural' and of realism. Rejection of melodrama is most strident concerning its expressive rhetoric for projecting emotions. However, reform works out differently in different cultural contexts. In America the transformation effected in film acting, combined with the rise of modern publicity, changed the nature of theatrical stardom. Crucially, the micro-perception offered by the camera's attention to the actor's body produced an entirely different kind of performer who, trading off personality, appeared simply to 'be' rather than to 'act'.

However, in British culture such transparency was difficult to achieve. The cultural significance of theatre, emphasising locations as sites for public enactment and acting as role-playing, led to considerable critical ambivalence about film acting. This chapter traces some of the twists and turns of these debates, arguing that if the theatrical stage provides a public space for acting out private dilemmas, and pictorial framing, a mode of visual articulation, the consequent foregrounding of acting as public presentation makes British cinema above all a 'performed' cinema.

RESTRAINT AND PASSION

The public/private opposition that I have argued underpins the reform of British theatrical practices in conformity to middle-class codes of decorum gave a particular cast to the value of restraint in English culture. For, contrary to increasingly vocal complaints about underplaying and class-bound inhibition in English acting, restraint emerged in the mid-19th century not as negation of feeling, but for the intensity it implied of what is *not* expressed. G. H. Lewes describes the capacity of Charles Mathews 'to be as interesting as if . . . quietness were only the restraint of power, not the absence of individuality'.[1] Some fifty years later, J. T. Grein, reviewing John Martin Harvey in *The Only Way* (1925), describes how, when 'Carton forfeited his life to save her whom he loved, Mr Harvey made a great impression, but now it was by his composure, by the sobriety of his words and the suppression of his emotions'.[2] In *Masks or Faces?*, contributing to an ongoing debate about the value of emotion in acting, William Archer quotes an unnamed critic to the effect that 'it is such emotion as is not expressed by tears and sobs . . . that brings tears to my eyes and sends cold shivers down my spine'.[3] Similarly, J. T. Grein comments that, as in real life, a deeper impression is made 'if by restraint, suppression, indication rather than emphasis, the turmoil within is manifested'.[4] The point here, however, is not lack of emotion but how it is signified. Archer continues: 'of course the effort of repression can be simulated in cold-blood; but . . . it is precisely in such passages that the ear most quickly detects and rejects even the most delicate art of the mechanical performer'.[5]

THE POWER OF RESTRAINT

From the 1920s to this day, restraint remains a widely appreciated dramatic and filmic value, reiterated time and again in trade, critical and fan press. Equally, however, restraint is rarely approved without its contrary, 'power' or 'passion'. So, for example, *The Bioscope* praises David Hawthorne's performance in Guy Newall's *Testimony* (1920) for his 'power of expression and power of restraint'.[6] Similarly, George Arliss in the American *The Green Goddess* (1923) is praised for his 'restrained but powerful acting'.[7] Maurice Elvey's films 'gain in *effect* [my emphasis] by their restraint of methods',[8] a view echoed by the *Westminster Gazette*, declaring that *Mademoiselle d'Armentières* (1926) gains its 'stirring effects by sheer subtlety and restraint'.[9] In the international hit of 1923, *Woman to Woman*, Clive Brook is, according to the *Weekly Dispatch*, the 'stern-faced protagonist of passionate events'[10] – a perception fuelling his speedy rise to film stardom in the early 1920s. *The Motion Picture Studio* praises his 'restrained but potent acting',[11] while *Picture Show* admires his 'mobile face, depicting emotion with gripping restraint'.[12] Of *This Freedom* (1923), it notes in a characteristic oxymoron the 'restrained passion' of Brook's performance as the long-suffering husband of a modern career woman.[13]

This discourse, however, steers a fine line between its oppositional values. Mere restraint brings, as we shall see later, complaints about the repression of the English character, unable to express feeling, particularly now that British audiences are increasingly attuned to the very different kind of performance mode offered by the American films dominating British screens. Indeed, a French critic is quoted by the *Morning Post*, in terms made notorious thirty or so years later by François Truffaut, to the effect that 'There is no race in the world to whom showing their sentiments is so repugnant. The spirit behind the cinema is the very opposite of the characteristic British spirit.' He continues: 'the only role British actors portray realistically is that requiring extreme reserve . . . e.g. the strong silent man type'.[14] But equally significant are the cries of abhorrence echoed across the trade and review press against unbridled feeling. Thus *The Bioscope*, admitting the Frenchman's point about undue restraint, tartly rejects 'the grotesque grimacing and exaggeration of movement which often passes for acting abroad'.[15] The *Western Dispatch* for 5 September 1926, with American films in mind, declares: 'sentimentality and sobstuff . . . are the greatest moral and artistic shortcomings of the modern film'.[16] The *Western Morning News* agrees, claiming that 'kinemagoers are heartily sick of brainless sobstuff . . . highlife . . . and stunts',[17] while a reader writes to *Film Weekly* to warn that Ivor Novello's popularity is waning because since *The Rat* he has been cast in 'soppy love dramas'.[18] Earlier in the decade *The Motion Picture Studio* had asked, 'Do English Actresses Lack Life? Or Is More Restraint Needed in America?'[19] Such contradictory positions suggest that neither restraint nor passion

are acceptable on their own. Restraint provides pleasure only if we see and feel that there is something to restrain. Passion is powerful only if generated against the counterforce of outward control. In his 1920s notebooks George Pearson quotes Lewes's argument that 'as in all art, feeling lies at the root . . . but form and structure derive from the intellect'.[20] Similarly, for William Archer, 'the key is real emotion and control'.[21]

As changing social values challenge the rationale for restraint, Orientalism and Victorianism alike offer the pleasures of repression. Thus Matheson Lang's stage rendering of Mr Wu is 'too impassioned and fanatical merely to kill . . . yet quiet and polite always'.[22] *The Bioscope* notes of Hepworth's remake of *Comin' thro' the Rye* (1923), 'violent passions blare fiercely beneath prim Victorian exteriors'.[23] It is not surprising that American critics condemned Hepworth's film, for the power of the restraint/passion coupling is a translation of an aristocratic authority into charismatic performance.[24] The British film industry made a number of attempts to tap into this class-inflected magnetism, while titled sons and daughters were drawn to the stage or film as a means of escaping the restrictions of their class, or, alternatively, of playing out the last gasp of their heritage in a democratising age.[25] Thus *The Picturegoer* publishes an interview with the celebrated society beauty, Lady Diana Cooper (née Manners), under the title, 'Filming Lady Di', which plays the aristocratic underpinnings of the restraint/passion paradox to the full:

'Simplicity in acting appeals strongly to me. Repression in one's movements without exaggerated gestures I feel represents the highest plane of screen art.'

For three hours and a-half one afternoon Blackton worked on the vivid personality of Lady Di, and taught her the art of registering the emotions of horror, surprise, and sorrow. Always she was the confident, self-possessed aristocrat. There was no temperament here. She clenched her slender bejewelled hands and mirrored fear in the depths of her expressive blue eyes with an assurance which told of her descent from a line of fighting ancestors who for centuries faced the world with courage and self-reliance . . . Yet when the cameras finally ceased to operate, the fresh girlishness of her nature which flashes out, despite the inherent restraint which rules the true-born aristocrat, came to the surface.[26]

A DISTINCTLY ENGLISH STYLE OF UNDERPLAYING

Highlighted here is the tension between performance, understood as the registration of melodrama's
primary emotions through gesture and facial expression – surprise, horror, sorrow – and a class-defined
sense of what is socially and aesthetically appropriate.
As Lewes, quoted in Chapter 1, comments, 'there are
scoundrels in high life, but they are perfectly well
bred'.[27] Under the pressure of democratisation and
the extending social reach of representation, the definition of 'well-bred' behaviour and its claim on 'naturalness' becomes a stake in a struggle for cultural
hegemony. For theatrical managements in pursuit of
middle-class audiences, behaving 'naturally' means
avoiding the showy and pretentious, relegating theatricality as 'artificial' or 'false' and reinforcing the
value of restraint. Thus leading actor-managers such
as Charles Hawtrey, George Alexander and Gerald
du Maurier developed a laid-back style of performance that sought to realise their characters by appearing simply to behave rather than act.

The refusal of self-projection translates restraint
into a 'distinctly English style of underplaying'[28] – a
style that, according to Michael Sanderson, came to
a head in the 1920s.[29] A. E. Matthews, a noted
exponent of underplaying in both theatre and film,
recounts his version of how the style hit the London
theatrical world of the 1890s when Charles Hawtrey,
noted as an actor of drawing-room comedy and well-
made drama, was goaded by criticisms of his 'flamboyant, declamatory manner'. Advised to 'be
himself', apparently he did just that and as Matthews
says, 'became talk of the Town'.[30] However,
Matthews questions the designation 'natural':

> He was described by such terms as 'imperturbable' and
> 'easygoing' – to imply that he never 'acted'. The simple
> truth is that he acquired the art of concealing the fact
> that he was acting. This he did with such perfection that
> it amounted to genius – his influence on his contem-
> poraries was immense, and . . . is felt to this day
> throughout the English-speaking stage.[31]

Maurice Elvey describes directing Charles Hawtrey
in *A Honeymoon for Three* (1915):

> Hawtrey took to films like a duck to water. His style of
> comedy was always the dead-pan, do-nothing style,
> which was not very common in that period . . . This

quiet method established a fashion which was peculiarly
English – not even British – and Hawtrey was the chief
exponent. This made it very easy to film him. He didn't
want to gesticulate, or act. He wanted to do nothing.
You were able to get right up to this expressive face.[32]

Michael Sanderson cites Ramond Massey as credit-
ing the initiation of the 'art that conceals art' to
Gerald du Maurier, an actor who, according to Hugh
Hunt,[33] dominated the postwar acting profession
into the mid-1920s:

> Although it was thought that he made acting look easy
> – merely playing one's self and reproducing one's trivial
> drawing-room behaviour – for Du Maurier it was art
> disguising art. He worked hard at it – 'the smooth natu-
> ralness of his performances came from laborious
> preparation' – practising 'business' with drinks and ciga-
> rettes in front of a mirror for hours at a time. 'Little
> things like that don't come easily to me' he told Massey.[34]

Henry Edwards was one of several actors, including
Guy Newall, Ivy Duke and Kenelm Foss, who,
moving spasmodically between stage and screen in
the teens and 1920s, took this performance mode
into British cinema, developing it in different ways
discussed below.

The modulation of restraint into underplaying
contributed to democratising class performance
signs, aristocratic sang-froid translating into good
manners or middle-class tact, and supporting a naturalness of behaviour that could communicate without embarrassment across social differences while
sustaining social boundaries. Nevertheless, in the
appreciations quoted above, underplaying is still
valued as an *acting* skill where acting serves to separate the role performed as public communication
from the private, not-to-be-disclosed self, which
might threaten to overplay. In *The Passionate Adventure* (1924) the aristocratic hauteur underpinning the
'do-nothing' style of Charles Hawtrey or Gerald du
Maurier is taken to self-conscious extremes by Clive
Brook. As Lord Adrian St Clair, his most energetic
move is to examine his nails, puff laconically on a
cigarette or make a sardonic little twitch of his head.
Brook plays both literally and metaphorically the
'buttoned-up' Englishman (Fig. 3.1). Adrian's most
common gestures – all precisely calculated and timed
– are those that enact masculinity as the power to

Fig. 3.1. Clive Brook, 'stern-faced protagonist of passionate events', in military guise in *The Passionate Adventure* (1924)

repel or discard human contact in an objectifying, impersonal way. He flicks an imaginary speck of dust from his lapel after Pamela, his sister-in-law, jauntily kisses him in an attempt to make him unbend. In contrast, Drusilla, his wife, is played by the American, Alice Joyce, who was noted for her transparent naturalistic acting.[35] But in the British context of this film, her mask of world-weariness does not quite capture the duality of the 'doing-nothing style' that, demonstrating simultaneously the skills of public performance, hints at a self lurking beneath.

MASTERLY INACTIVITY OR UNNATURAL RESTRAINT? THE PROBLEM OF THE ACTRESS

A fear, however, that performance was an endangered skill is registered in the increasing number of complaints that British actors are incapable of expressing emotion, echoing William Archer's warning that restraint could become a mere mannerism, making claims to hidden passion under false pretences. So at the beginning of the decade the visiting American director, Hugh Ford, writes in *Kinematograph Weekly* that 'the tradition of restraint featured to such an extent in English theatre has become a menace. The greater part of present day players look with horror on the idea of portraying strong emotions.'[36] In 1923 P. L. Mannock confronts 'the difference between repose and woodenness', arguing that the reaction against 'exaggerated action and "mugging" ' enables some actors to stroll 'through [their] pictures with the steadfast expression of a weighing-machine and the gestures of a somnambulist'.[37] Later in the 1920s

a fan writes to the *Northern Mail and Newcastle Clarion*, complaining that British actors refuse 'to let go'.[38] If theatrical reforms had at their best taken the restraint/passion coupling to piquantly nuanced heights, mechanical application could reduce it to the bare bones of its class origins. At its extreme, as Clive Brook describes in his unpublished autobiography, emerged the 'furniture actor', who not knowing what to do with his hands, and terrified of putting them in his pockets, clung to any available piece of furniture the set afforded.[39]

Nowhere are such complaints so prominent, however, than in the debate that ran through the 1920s on the British actress, highlighting in its sometimes overdetermined vehemence the role played by femininity in the generalisation of restraint into a cultural dominant. For if the repression that produces underplaying was a much admired source of authority in male actors, the impact of restraint on female acting was far more problematic. Writing at the end of the decade in *Film Weekly*, Monty Banks pinpoints the contradiction in which British femininity is caught. Associating women with melodrama, he notes that Western culture expects from the represented woman 'emotional sympathy and temperament'. However, the 'British code of reserve . . . is so pronounced in women . . . that it requires much skill to make them unbend – to lose their coldness'.[40] What Banks complains of arises from the role of 'woman' in the fifty-year-long process of reorganising the class cultural codes of melodrama discussed in Chapter 1, which involved not only its refinement in line with a middle-class verisimilitude but a realignment of masculinity. William Archer, pondering in 1888 the new unease 'we Anglo-Saxons of this generation' exhibit when confronted by tears, goes on to suggest:

> As a general rule, however, unrestrained weeping is a mark of passivity whereas it is activity in one form or another that most deeply interests or moves us. One of the most touching of all phases of activity is the successful repression of tears.[41]

This revealing version of the restraint/passion coupling suggests not only a reversal in the gendered division of emotional labour, whereby male repression opposes female melodrama, but also an attempt to let the hero have it both ways. What this might mean for the shifting role of woman in modern drama becomes clear in his complaint against Wilde's *A Woman of No Importance* (1893):

> The young man's crude sense of the need for some immediate and heroic action is . . . entirely right; but how much better . . . would the scene be if the mother met his Quixoticism with sad, half-smiling dignity and wisdom, instead of with passionate outcries of unreasoning horror . . . What is all this melodrama about?[42]

As the representative of virtue, the nineteenth-century melodramatic heroine had to be quick-witted and robust in order to withstand the malevolent machinations of the villain, who frequently would not only engineer her misrecognition but enfeeble the hero. However, in shifting the action to the drawing room and making it conform to middle-class expectations, 'virtue' frequently becomes a matter of long-suffering self-suppression in the interest of maintaining social and personal boundaries, rather than the defiant innocence of the traditional heroine. By the 20th century, the colonisation of the 'ordinary' by a middle-class value system is ensured by control as the mark of the postwar modern woman. Charged, in the absence of servants, with efficient household management, she carries responsibility for her family's psychic health and so for general social stability.[43] Thus in February 1922, *The Motion Picture Studio* argues that

> British girls are not normally and naturally temperamental. Our national social system has been directed to repressing the exhibition of real emotion, with the result that expression is naturally and instinctively checked until the power of soul expression – emotion-expression – becomes paralysed by disuse . . . The facility for giving rein to one's emotions must be cultivated.[44]

Dora Lennox follows this idea up later in the year when she argues that, whereas Americans look for 'pep' and 'vim' in their stars, the potential vivacity of the English is 'stifled, smothered at birth' by social conventions that it is the job of the female in particular to uphold. Consequently, neither actress nor producer is willing to risk going beyond them.[45]

St John Ervine, playwright and drama critic for *The Morning Post*, pens a far less sympathetic critique of the British actress, specifically linking the practice of restraint with class in a 1926 article on 'English Actresses and the Film . . . the Craze of Immobility'. Entranced with the performance of the French Yvonne Printemps in a recent London production, Ervine blames the failure of English women to become successful film actresses on

> the immobility of feature so fashionable among nicely-bred girls. The practice of what is called 'good form' has resulted in a host of persons from whose faces expression has almost been eliminated: imperturbability has been carried to the point of nullity and what was formerly an exercise in self-control has become a standardised and an empty appearance. Our young ladies betray so few of their feelings in their faces that one is tempted to believe they are wearing masks.[46]

Recalling the vivacity of Ellen Terry and Marie Tempest, Ervine argues that 'this dead, dull manner is a modern invention . . . what biologists call an acquired character which can and must be abandoned'.[47] As part of an ongoing debate, he appends a letter from a reader recommending that 'our dreadful little cold, common film actress should get other employment'. Ervine's response reveals the class-informed knife-edge that the aspiring actress must negotiate: 'When we invite . . . [our young actresses] . . . to be vivacious in their manner, we are not asking them to behave like low-class barmaids: we are asking them not to look like mummies or funeral mutes.'[48] And the debate continues in the next week's *Morning Post* with a stream of letters summarised by Ervine under the heading, 'The Inexpressive English Face'. Here the influence of music academies and acting schools are held to blame, with Dickens and Hardy cited for an earlier generation's embrace of what can only be 'melodramatic' emotion: 'in what orgies of emotion they indulged: in what orgies of repression do we'.[49] This familiar oxymoron underlines the ambivalence that runs through this debate, which once again tries to square the circle of decorum: 'An artist is superior to fashions in manners, though that does not imply he should behave as if . . . ill-bred.'[50] When this debate is reported in *The Bioscope* a couple of days later, it appears under the unrepentant heading, 'Magnificently Immobile English Actresses'. At the same time, the journal emphasises more forthright conclusions:

Mr Ervine believes that so long as we rear people in the belief that it is bad form to show their feelings in their faces, so long will we be unable to produce a film-actress from the class which now predominates on the stage. It may be, he maintains, that the English film-actress will come from the working class, where immobility of expression is not practised.[51]

Outlining the dilemma of the film actress, who is 'either accused of over-acting or of being consistently wooden', the writer suggests that since complaints of overacting prove the capacity for emotion, the answer lies in 'control of emotion which can only come through the joint effort of actress and producer'. Thus we return to the familiar oxymoron of passion in restraint.[52]

ACTING FROM THE HEART

This contrasts with the historico-cultural context of American acting. Rejecting both rhetorical display and repressive control, American naturalism cultivated what the actor and playwright, William Gillette, termed 'the illusion of the first time'.[53] What the audience witnesses is not the result of repeated performance but the very first utterance of a character's thoughts and feelings. Here, an underpinning egalitarianism asserts 'the heart' against the constraints of class-bound conventions. For it was acting from the heart that made the American yeoman sturdy, independent and true, enabling the stalwart frontiersman to project a future across space and time, and, conquering geography, to make nature carry the signs of his life story. Thus America's egalitarian ideology, and the melodramatic aesthetic it adapted, reconciled instinctive feeling and masculinity now expressed in action, while femininity threatened to reimpose the social manners and constraints ensuring a patina of European 'civilisation'.

In American cinema 'acting from the heart' supports a biographical narrative, projected into *mise en scène* and action, conquering social as well as geographic barriers. At the same time, melodrama's emphasis on bodily gesture and vocal intonation as external signs of inner emotion and moral feeling supports the identification between performer and character. This context welcomes the naturalism of the Stanislavsky system introduced in the 1920s, which, fostering identification between actor and part, maintained 'the illusion of the first time'. Con-

trariwise, in Britain, the campaigns of Archer, Grein and Shaw slowly pushed the boundaries of representation to absorb Ibsen and the Ibsenites. But whereas Ibsen's social vision found little favour in America, neither Stanislavsky's precepts, nor their later American adaptation as the Method, were particularly welcomed in Britain, where acting remains a potent and necessarily visible cultural signifier.

SELF AND ROLE

Richard Dyer suggests that the rise of the social sciences, Marxism and Freudian psychoanalysis threw increasing doubt on the trustworthiness of public or self-conscious behaviour. In this context, countervailing discourses of personality and stardom emerge to ensure the authenticity of the individual person so crucial to social organisation in Western capitalism.[54] The persistence and vociferousness of the debates about acting in Britain offer a specifically national twist to this process, highlighting its significance for a culture that centres on demarcation between persons socially defined. Thus, if 'acting from the heart' and the 'illusion of the first time' presume identification of actor, role and audience, the aesthetic of restraint and passion depends on our perceiving a gap between performer and performance, self and role, instituting a division between personal and public expression. On one level, then, visible acting produces the bounded roles and personae through which dramatic interchange between socially demarcated protagonists can take place. However, the very nature of acting as a publicly legitimated form of expression opens up the existence of the more problematic space behind the act. Matheson Lang defends Henry Irving against the accusation of personality acting by emphasising not Irving's 'mannerisms' and 'marvellous features', which were seldom disguised, but the '*mental* effect of his impersonations':

> It has always seemed to me that in great acting the *mental* picture conveyed by the actor to his audience is far more important than the mere external effects of his characterization; just as in painting, a great artist will show the *mind* shining through the actual portrait of the features of his subject (original emphasis).[55]

Both character acting and the understated performance produced by the exercise of socially coded restraint emphasise the public, external persona; but the great actor, the lead roles, must aim to indicate by indirection another space in which resides the inner self. At the end of the 19th century, Dion Boucicault offers a solution to this tension between personal identity and public persona, foreshadowing the categories of social psychology, in a conception of multiple character:

> First there is the man by himself – as he is to himself – as he is to his God . . . the inner man . . . the unclothed man. Then there is the native man, the domestic man, as he is to his family . . . Then there is the man as he stands before the world at large; as he is outside in society. Those are the three characters. They are all in the one man, and the dramatist does not know his business unless he puts them into one character . . . They are as necessary to the great picture as they are to the life they represent.[56]

Paradoxically, then, if the 'theatrical' is required for the production of stages for action, the visibility of 'acting' is required as witness to a secreted, private self.

For his 1888 study, *Masks or Faces?*, William Archer conducted a survey among actors (repeated by J. T. Grein in 1923) to discover whether actors do or should feel the emotions called for by their roles. The answer in almost all cases was that, while it is necessary to have felt or at least to understand the emotions to be performed, for an actor actually to feel them while performing would entail a retrograde loss of control over the part and over the audience. As noted in Chapter 2, G. H. Lewes insists that performance as an art of representation (not illusion) depends on the selection of the typifying, articulating gesture and the suppression of the incidental detail that supports the 'illusion of the first time'. Distance between self and role and a capacity for self-restraint are necessary to this process. 'The actor', Lewes argues, 'is a spectator of his own tumult, and, though moved by it, can yet so master it as to select from it only these elements which suit his purpose.'[57] It is an aesthetic driven to representation, not 'acting from the heart' so prized in American theatre. For Lewes, the actor's 'passion must be ideal, sympathetic, not personal',[58] while William Archer, in *Masks or Faces?*, declares that there is 'no absolute illusion about the identity of character and actor on either the actor's or the audience's side'.[59]

This gap between self and role appears in different forms: between the actor and character; between the character's outward performance and imputed inner self; or between the actor's inner self and the role to be played. Lang's answer to J. T. Grein's questionnaire as to whether actors really feel the emotions they act, echoing Lewes's precepts of seventy years earlier, is circumspect: 'We must not confuse feeling with being. The actor can feel the part and keep his mind, as it were, "looking on", controlling and guiding his emotions.'[60] This suggests an internalisation of the gap between observer and observed, a kind of fracturing of performance, which supports the oxymoronic value promoted by Lewes, Archer and Grein of combined passion and control. This process of 'looking on' at a characterisation as it is being produced parallels that of the actor as documentarist, looking outwards to observe real-life behaviour in order to secure an objective foundation for a performance. Thus 'losing oneself in the part' is less an abrogation of control than the result of a highly constructive and technical process. For the role of Pete in Hall Caine's play adaptation of *The Manxman*, Pete (1908), Matheson Lang travels to the Isle of Man to learn the dialect.[61] For the play, *Mr Wu* (1913) he is inspired by the mannerisms of an adviser from the Chinese legation:

> The way he sat with his hands spread out on his knees, the funny little trick he had of putting his head on one side and laughing in a queer, high-pitched voice, the slow deliberation of his movements, and queer effect of his walk . . . I set myself to watch and listen to him and reproduce his mannerisms in the part . . . plagiarising . . . his personality.[62]

The tension here between subjective immersion in, and objective construction of, the role suggests the compromise effected in British acting between personal authentication of roles required by demand for 'the natural' and maintenance of the objectively documented character.

MATHESON LANG IN *OTHELLO* AND *CARNIVAL*

Matheson Lang's film version of his stage success, *Carnival* (1922), explicitly plays with such issues. The stage play was adapted from the Italian *Sirocco* by H. M. C. Hardinge, assisted by Lang, who developed for himself the role of a premier Italian actor,

Silvio Steno, about to open the new Venetian season as the Moor in *Othello*, with his actress wife, Simonetta playing Desdemona (Hilda Bayley, also in the film version). What Silvio does not yet know is that his best friend, Count Andrea Scipione (in the film, Ivor Novello), is, off stage, romancing Simonetta. Lang's theatrical performance of *Carnival* was preceded by Shakespeare's *Othello* as a matinee offering. In this, according to J. T. Grein, he gave the definitive Othello of the century. In Desdemona's death scene, 'Matheson Lang is so real, there is such an absence of theatrical effort, that, although we shudder in awe, we do not avert our faces in repellence . . . the Othello of Matheson Lang is a powerful illustration of the duality of our mind'.[63] Grein understands this duality in various ways: not only theatricality versus reality, but nature versus culture, and Othello's 'childlike character' versus 'the real man' he potentially was. Playing Othello in the afternoon, and then Silvio Steno playing Othello in the evening, must have emphasised for audiences who attended both – as for Lang himself – the duality of this interpretation, suggesting a further duality: that of the actor caught between self and role, life and performance (Fig. 3.2). Where, particularly in British culture, does the one begin and the other end? When *Picture Show* came to review Lang's film performance, its critic lamented: 'Oh why doesn't Matheson Lang revive *Carnival* with Hilda Bayley . . . in the theatre to follow the film.'[64]

In this respect, the film *Carnival* opens – as will, twenty years later, Olivier's *Henry V* (1944) – by documenting its own work as a performance. A title declaims, 'Venice, city of silence and shadows, romance and tragedy . . . decay speaks of splendour . . . chosen by the immortal bard for Othello.' There follow pictorial documents of the tourist imaginary – the Doge's palace, St Mark's Square, gondolas – and then the bald statement: 'Silvio Steno, Italy's greatest Shakespearean actor, prepares for Othello', accompanied by the credit 'Matheson Lang', in which the famous actor is as much a documented 'character' as the fictional protagonist. The next shot presents Lang seated at a table in the foreground, facing the camera, framed between two draped velvet curtains and a high mullioned window filling in what can be seen of the background under a rouched pelmet. Lang's dignified square face and eyes, enlarged by make-up to represent the actor, are deep in thought as he slowly passes

Fig. 3.2. Matheson Lang playing Silvio Steno, playing Othello in *Carnival* (1921)

his hand over his face, to dissolve into a close-up of Othello, then, breathing deeply, back into Silvio giving a self-satisfied nod. The film opens, then, with an acknowledgment of theatre as the condition of the film, a strategy recognised and welcomed by *The Bioscope* reviewer: 'Theatrical in subject, theatrical in treatment, it is also theatrically effective.'[65] Such theatricality did not inhibit the film's success in Britain either, where it received a Royal Command Performance, nor, apparently, in America.[66]

The clash between theatricality and modernity is set up as a clash between rhetorical and colloquial performance styles and outlooks. Silvio, realised in Lang's generous bodily presence and expansive gestures, his hair sleeked back to emphasise a distinguished face, discourses with the younger Count Andrea Scipione, played with appropriate nervous tension by Ivor Novello (appearing in his third film), slightly hunched, hands clasped. He is insisting that Shakespeare's psychology is wrong: Othello should have separated from Desdemona, not murdered her. Silvio's reply to such banal literalism is to launch into Othello's speech of self-justification: 'Let me not name it to you, you chaste stars, it is the cause' – rendered, as if to point up the opposition between romanticism and modernity, in gothic script. Cut to a shot of Silvio, his eyes upturned, his arms momentarily held out capaciously and easily at rhetorical shoulder level, palms towards us, and slowly lowering. At this point, Andrea's bathos is inadvertently supported by the entrance of Silvio's small son, imitating his father's gestures with little arms held stiffly out before him, followed by the title, 'You chase the stars, it is because . . .'. From his childish intensity, the film cuts to Silvio, who, momentarily disoriented and frowning at the interruption, drops his arms from rhetorical to colloquial position. Then, good-humouredly lifting the child onto the table, he instructs his son how to avoid 'arm flinging' by moving in rhythmic stages from rhetorical into the epic, a lesson in the subtlety of gesture for the audience as much as for the fictional child. These opening scenes document a series of ambivalences – between life and acting, self and role, truth and performance, subjective apprehension and external objectivity, adulthood and child's play. Eliding such binaries makes acting a potent trope for identity and social exchange in a culture caught between passion and restraint, private self and public role.

If the first shot of Silvio 'thinking the part' via a dissolve seems to endorse the filmic identification of actor and role, the narrative focuses on the dangers of such confusion. In the process it dramatises the duality that Grein attributes to Lang's Othello. In the final quarter of the film, which concerns Silvio's mistaken perception of Simonetta's infidelity and growing jealousy, the alternation between private and public enacted through cross-cutting between performance on stage and green room backstage dramatises the dangerous slippage between self and role. At the same time, we are switched alternately between the viewing position of the audience *for* the film to that of the theatre audience *in* the film. From here we observe Silvio as performer of Othello – and, incidentally, something of Lang's electrifying performance in this role. Then, positioned in the wings, we observe Silvio as both public performer before an audience and private actor struggling to get a grip on both self and role as he comes backstage into the green room between his scenes.

A title documents the point at which the film's drama has now arrived – 'The Premiere of Othello. Silvio lives the part he now assays to play' – and in so doing underscores the importance of distinguishing acting from being. The camera then irises-out to disclose a high-angle shot of the audience, gently craning to see, followed by a shot of the stage from the stalls, where Othello, Iago and Desdemona are enacting the handkerchief scene. Two low-angle shots of boxes highlight the rapt anticipation of their occupants as they await the tragic outcome. Having established the context, the camera takes up position behind Othello and Desdemona, the proscenium reverse framing the audience beyond the stage. As she departs, Lang/Silvio lets his cloak fall, the purpose of which is clearly to reveal the expressive way Lang acts with his muscles. Switching back to the stalls, we find Lang/Silvio/Othello shrinking and squirming, his shoulders and thighs contracting in a gesture of profound irritation and nausea, as Iago bends over him, whispering his poisonous insinuations. The camera is behind him again, when, the pressure too great, Silvio/Othello leaps up – 'I'll tear her all to pieces!' – his hands clenched, arms stretched out in rhetorical gesture, the watching audience again caught in frame. A temporary cut to off stage via the title, 'The Green Room: Silvio is terrifying – almost living the part', is followed by a return to the view from the stalls, with Iago bent over Silvio, shrinking away as if from some noxious force. He leaps up, seizing Iago's throat. The shot cuts again to a position behind the actors, Othello's back in shadow as he hurls Iago to the floor and then swings in a lurching movement off through the left wing. Applause from the audience brings Iago to the wings to call for his return and, his broad silhouetted shoulders momentarily blocking the frame, Silvio/Othello staggers back onto the stage, clapping his arm across Iago's shoulders as they bow to the applauding audience. Thus the film frame cuts into the stage actor's space and across the proscenium, constructing a private within a public space. The film audience gains privileged knowledge of a personal drama erupting within a public performance for an unknowing theatre audience applauding at the back of the film frame. They, separated from the action, appear as if themselves projected on a screen framed by wings and proscenium – cast as extras in the players' story.

Simonetta takes the stage, while in the green room Silvio is handed an incriminating note sent to his wife by Andrea, who is immediately summoned. The action now switches between Simonetta and

Silvio on stage, delaying impending 'real life' confrontation by the equally real demand that the show go on. Finally, while the action cross-cuts to Simonetta performing Desdemona's willow song, Silvio, dangerously relaxed and 'natural' in his Othello costume, sets up a second backstage drama, begging Andrea to help him find Simonetta's secret lover. As the two roles begin to merge – Othello with the jealous actor-husband, public performance with private self – Lang's body gives a little shiver and a title snarls: 'Somewhere a villain is smiling and I can't get at him!' Andrea/Novello, awkward in his formal dinner jacket and as stiff as a mannequin, is at a total loss how to play the part Silvio has handed him. The return of Simonetta to the green room (missing from the NFA print, since she is suddenly there in mid-action) and a confession that she went to the Carnival Ball with Andrea temporarily lowers the rising temperature. Silvio nodding, pulls himself together in a dignified movement, momentarily restoring decorum while the information sinks in and lining up with the others in an effective farewell as Simonetta is called back to the stage for the start of Desdemona's final bedroom scene. As Silvio recomposes himself for Othello, he makes the link 'my best friend' with Shakespeare's 'it is the cause'. Gradually, back on stage the confusion of role and self is completed as Silvio's identification with the part of Othello threatens real-life murder and the drama enacts the danger of closing the gap between self and role.

George Pearson, in his notebook, quotes approvingly from G. H. Lewes: 'if the actor were really in a passion . . . he would present a painful, not an aesthetic spectacle'.[67] This is what Lang/Silvio now enacts, as the wildness of his utterances breaks not only with Shakespeare's lines but with the restraint that gives passion the effect of art. As Silvio substitutes Simonetta for Desdemona, Andrea for Cassio, his hand circles Simonetta's throat. A frontal shot shows Simonetta cringing back in fear. Cut to a frontal close-up on Lang/Silvio staring into the camera, speaking angrily as his face moves closer, his eyes filling the frame. A title sounds the murder threat: 'And now Simonetta thou diest'. Silvio turns from profile to look again frontally into the camera, shifting us into Simonetta's place, as we look into his eyes. The next shot reveals the diegetic audience turning to each other and jumping up in dismay.

Carnival as film, then, intensifies, through the interaction between stage play and cinema, the bina-ries caught up in the significance of theatricality, role and performance in English culture. Arguably, in assessing the relations between British theatrical practice and film, the most significant division is less between stage and screen, than in the tension shared by both between acting on the one hand and 'non-performance' – being oneself – on the other. For film performance, the pressure towards 'being' rather than acting devolved in two contrary directions: the production of stars and the use of the non-actor. But before pursuing these alternatives, I want to look at an equally dominant mode of performance representing a corrective to the extremes of the restraint and passion coupling.

CHARACTER ACTING

Emerging out of a mode of perception and expression that underpins a reforming middle-class theatrical hegemony, the aesthetic of restraint and passion is practised largely by the lead or 'straight' characters, who are associated with a middle- or upper-middle-class station. However, as many acting manuals acknowledged, in concert with the evidence provided by natural historians and anthropologists, codes of expression vary with class, gender, ethnicity and age.[68] The question posed by extending representation, but uneasily glossed over, was whether such differences represent nature or culture. The elision of the natural with the true and therefore the aesthetically pleasing stems from a middle-class ethos. Henry Neville's handbook, combining acting with the social skills of elocution, deportment and public speaking, stresses the need for grace, harmony, balance, while avoiding rigidity, 'ridiculous contortions' and affectation.[69] The beginner should start with

> the ordinary walk which belongs to the person of sanguine temperament . . . The foundation of all good style is a natural, easy carriage; firm, erect, manly and free from the hips . . . The bent, or flexed leg gracefully loose and ready; walk straight, feeling the first impulse in the thigh. No rolling, bobbing, strutting, or peculiarity belonging to character.[70]

Neville here is drawing on a thread that runs from an earlier psychology of humours, through the codification of gestures of the actor's handbooks, to the definition of actors' 'lines' as a casting device. All claim a basis in nature but produce categorisable semiotic codes contributing to the cultural work of social differentiation. The 'type', however, is naturalised in the actor's own body. Thus Dion Boucicault advises: 'Nature knows best. If you happen to have a short, sharp face, a hard voice, an angular figure, you are suited for the intellectual characters of the drama.'[71]

However, as democratisation demanded increasing social inclusion, a class-based verisimilitude must open out to encompass those who formerly took the stage as 'the helpless and unfriended' − not just 'ordinary' people but the working class, conceived threateningly *as* a class rather than the poor, or lower orders. In this context, the documentarists discussed earlier played a significant role in forming a cultural perception of the city and regions of Britain as a set of socially abutting but demarcated spaces, peopled by socially differentiated inhabitants. Their accounts and illustrations of social types and lifestyles reinforced the development of character-drawing and character acting as a refinement on the dramatic 'lines' of the stock company. So William Archer welcomes a shift from the older, broader and affective skills of comic or tragic actor to the 'exquisite fidelity' of 'the character-actor, the man who finds his models in the drawing-room, the counting house, the workshop, the cottage and the street'.[72] The 'ideal', then, is increasingly redefined as the 'typical'. Thus Neville's handbook, focusing on the practices of the 'straight' actor now defined as 'ordinary', provides a middle-class and apparently characterless norm against which the 'peculiarities' of class, gender, age and ethnicity produce the eccentrically distinctive character types beloved by British audiences down the decades.

NATIONALISING NATURALISM: *HINDLE WAKES*

Character acting, emerging out of a theatre conceived as a space for public stagings and public recognitions, represents a key mechanism for the social extension that Raymond Williams associates with the emergence of naturalism and realism as dominant modes.[73] This symbiosis of characterisation and the documentarist impulse towards objective observation and social mapping coloured the British response to Continental naturalism when it arrived in the last quarter of the 19th century to stimulate the emergence of the independent theatre movements, and the rise of 'new drama'. Jan McDonald argues that

the long years of acting reform initiated by the Vestris/Mathews and Bancroft managements (discussed in Chapter 1) meant that the British embrace of naturalism in the 'new drama' was less concerned than their various Continental counterparts with formal innovations of stage design and performance style.[74] If naturalism sought to represent life as it is lived,[75] the documentarist emphasis encouraged a controlling observational stance. The new dramatists, then, bent on winning back to the theatre a middle-class intelligentsia, produced a cautious rethinking of the grounds of verisimilitude towards a wider inclusion of social and moral issues explored through the interactions of a socially representative ensemble of characters. The public/private split and an investment in socially defined identities is not breached; rather, the new arenas of dramatic action remain socially and psychologically bounded, and British claims to increased naturalism or realism continue the systematising work of social mapping begun by the documentarists. Thus Jan McDonald notes how the new dramatists detail 'the clothes [characters] wear, the rooms they inhabit, the food they eat'. Harley Granville-Barker, for example, habitually provided 'his actors with a closely documented personal history on which to build their performance'.[76]

This extension of the social and psychological subject matter of a minority intellectual theatre through close observation of British life brought into view a set of new encounters, as protagonists, differentiated by gender, class and age, set about readjusting rather than overthrowing the boundaries of previous generations. Stanley Houghton's benchmark *Hindle Wakes*, first performed in 1912 and made into films in 1918, 1927 and 1931, has Fanny Hawthorne refusing the respectability offered by marriage to Alan Jeffcoate, the scion of a new-rich family with whom she has disgraced herself. In refusing the female role of class mediator − and her aggrieved mother's desire for upward mobility − Fanny challenges both social and gender boundaries (Fig. 3.3). If the class and gender assumptions underpinning Alan's behaviour are exposed by Fanny's bid for female autonomy and refusal of a social facade, nevertheless the film's ending offers only a Monday-morning return to the factory. There is no classless space for Fanny to progress to. Elvey's 1927 film version opens with a deliberately constructed montage sequence, juxtaposing the terraced Cotton Street

Fig. 3.3. British character actors at the boundaries of class and gender: Marie Ault, Gladys Jennings, Norman McKinnel and Humberston Wright respond to Canadian-born star Estelle Brody's challenge as Fanny in *Hindle Wakes* (1927)

homes of the mill workers with the mansion of their self-made employer, Nathaniel Jeffcoate, lying off Midas Street. Carefully documented images contrast domestic interiors, waking and breakfast rituals, to identify precisely the social and cultural location of protagonists whose destinies will bring them into fateful encounter. The careworn face of Mrs Hawthorn is contrasted to the pampered dithering of Mrs Jeffcoate; Fanny's single pair of best shoes to the stacked pairs Alan chooses from. These represent carefully selected and acculturated signs of a recognisable verisimilitude, rather than redundant, proliferating details caught because they happen to be there. But if marrying into upward mobility does not represent a liberating choice for the working-class heroine, it is possible for the film to reposition its visual documents to suggest the possibility of negotiating or shifting boundaries. If the two mothers are used to represent typifying and oppositional class identities, Nathaniel Jeffcoate is a self-made industrialist who has himself crossed social boundaries – as

we are reminded when he cools his breakfast tea in his saucer. He can countenance breaking his son's society engagement to protect Fanny's honour because he and his foreman, Chris Hawthorne, shared boyhood backgrounds. Such visual documents and dramatised exchanges between the two men recalling the past introduce signs of a new social fluidity. It is with this possibility that the film ends as, jauntily walking away from the camera towards the mill, Fanny nods non-commitally to the factory-hand who would like to take Alan's place, maintaining her freedom – as far as marrying is concerned – to do as she, rather than the narrative, pleases. Class verisimilitude is maintained but the future is open.

British responses to naturalism, then, refine rather than displace the craft of character acting rooted in categorisation of social types. Indeed, in the context of a class-stratified culture – in which, as Michael Sanderson's statistics show, the legitimate theatre draws actors largely from the ranks of the middle and upper middle classes[77] – the actor's preparation may echo the boundary-crossing adventures of the nineteenth-century documentarists. So Violet Hopson advises:

> If you are cast for, say, a slum girl's part, get down into the slums for the 'atmosphere,' don't wait round a West End Restaurant, you will never find what you are seeking there. Do not rely on what you have read about the slum folk. It is only when you have come into direct contact with the actual types that you will be able to successfully represent them before the camera.[78]

This perspective conceives the 'type' not as a reductive limitation but as a cultural manifestation to be collected by the actor and stored for future use. Thus in 1921, a hapless reporter tries in vain to commandeer the director-star, Henry Edwards, for an interview:

> 'Look!' cried Henry Edwards. 'There's a Type! Come on, we must follow him!'
>   'The troops are starving,' I protested.
>   'No matter,' said Henry Edwards. 'Lunch must wait. Did you notice his nose? Magnificent. And his ears are well worth a close-up.'[79]

As noted above, the connection between physique and social or psychological type had a long theatrical and pictorial history, deploying body shape, mannerisms, dress and accoutrements associated with home and work as signs of gender, class, age. Thus Stewart Rome enumerates different types of maid available to the female character actor: 'from the dainty little Parisienne "femme de chambre" who dresses madame's hair, to the slatternly maid-of-all-work who scrubs the boarding-house passage way, with her hair in curling papers, at four o'clock in the afternoon'.[80] He goes on to compile a socially variegated list of male types defined by profession: 'butlers, waiters, clergymen, policemen, sailormen, smart City men, well-tailored society men, bookmakers, solicitors, judges, flunkeys, doctors'.[81] Rome notes that while certain types belong to particular genres, the 'continued demand for "something new" calls for representation on the screen of every type of humanity, which indirectly utilises every class and description of motion picture player'.[82]

Character actors, then, combine social document, based on recognisable details of gesture, gait, mannerism and dress – Rome notes that his list of char-

acter types requires the actor to provide appropriate clothes – with eccentricity associated with individual 'touches' provided by the actor's own quirks of physique and personality. These are important in order to revitalise, through a touch of difference, the 'type', who it is clear from trade and fan press discussions it is the audience's pleasure to recognise. Character acting at its best is singular but categorisable. Marie Ault, for example, used her middle-aged rotundity to specialise in an abrasive if essentially soft-hearted maternity, sometimes dignified by pathos. She turned this quality to various effects – as bar-lady at the White Coffin in *The Rat* or lower-class mother looking for social advancement, benignly in *The Lodger* (1926) and vindictively in *Hindle Wakes*. Gordon Harker used his large lower lip, ambling gait, bloodhound eyes and numerous tics and shrugs for a variety of lower-class serving or support roles, always slightly out of key with what is going on around him. These ranged from boxing second in *The Ring* (1927), farm-hand in *The Farmer's Wife* (1928), to, unusually, self-made millionaire and an American – the only way, perhaps, to make the role credible – trying to rein in his wayward daughter in *Champagne* (1928). Miles Mander's wiry, slightly ungainly body and public schoolboyish facial features, sporting a toothbrush moustache, appeared repeatedly in the roles of somewhat louche lovers, or Englishmen gone to seed in the colonies, as in *The Pleasure Garden* (1926) and his self-directed *The First Born* (1928). Humberstone Wright produced white-haired, paternally wise and slightly eccentric elder statesmen, commanders and father figures in *The Garden of Resurrection* (1919), *Boadicea* (1926), *The Flag Lieutenant* (1926), *Hindle Wakes* and *High Treason* (1929).

MOORE MARRIOTT – 'OUR BEST CHARACTER ACTOR'

The most feted and versatile character actor of the period was Moore Marriott – claimed in reviews and readers' letters over and again as 'our best character actor', whose tour de force in *Sweeney Todd* (1928) I discuss in Chapter 5.[83] Not much remains of his pre-sound film work, but his capacity to disappear into a range of character studies is evident in the two surviving reels from the much celebrated *Monkey's Paw* (1923), adapted by Lydia Hayward from the W. W. Jacobs short story. Here Marriott plays an elderly, paternally benevolent husband and father, James White, whose fate-tempting wish on a reputedly magic monkey's paw brings only the hubris of his son's death. Marriott produces characterisations embodied in the loving care by which each gesture, glance and movement is formed. The father listens good-humouredly for escaping air as he mends a bicycle puncture for his son. He throws a confidential glance to his wife as the colonial visitor who has brought the monkey's paw knocks back their whisky – communicating a shared understanding based on years of comfortable cohabitation. He gives closely competitive attention to an evening chess game, during which he is gradually drawn by his son's curiosity to test the magic paw. Such treasurable moments emerge from Marriott's apparently long habitation of the protagonist's body and personality, sketching a character with deft strokes that bring the person to life before our eyes in a way that attests both to the actor's skill and the lifelike quality of the creation. The unspectacular nature of such qualities received a surprised and warm response in America from Louella Parsons writing in the *New York Morning Telegraph*: 'we found a picture with an excellent story, beautifully done . . . The acting was in keeping with the story. The parts were all so well played that the tale unfolded with the smoothness of a well-oiled machine.' Astutely, Velona Pilcher, in the American *Christian Science Monitor*, argues that without stars or front-rank screen actors, the W. W. Jacobs series of films are not exactly 'artistic . . . they are too realistic; the acting in them is not distinguished, but is the result of very clever type casting'.[84]

TECHNOLOGIES OF PERFORMANCE

Character acting, however, based on acculturated types confronted the very different kind of naturalism introduced by the camera in its capacity seemingly to break into the player's interiority, capturing inflections beyond the conscious control of the actor. Thus a major argument ran through the 1920s over the necessity or not of acting skill to the film performer. It was, for instance, frequently argued that while stage actors were able by long training to adapt to the demands of the camera, it was less possible for the film actor to move in reverse direction. For the success or otherwise of the acting lay less with the performer than with director and cameraman.[85] Albert Chevalier, for example, finds it impossible to

conceal his disdain for film acting: 'I have yet to hear of the studio-cooked player who has made a hit in spoken drama.'[86]

Just as photography interacted with Pre-Raphaelitism to re-articulate the revealing gesture and dramatic situation, so film also 'upped the ante' for naturalism. Thus *Kinematograph Weekly* says of Joyce Dearsley in *General Post* (1920) that she displays a 'tendency to over-act and lapse into slightly theatrical attitudes when she should be just natural'.[87] *The Bioscope* criticises the performance of George Arliss (a noted British stage actor of the period) in the American *The Devil* (1921), because 'Every glance and gesture is that of an experienced actor, but one sees exactly how and why every glance and gesture is made. The performance is drowned in the noise of the machinery.'[88] Conversely, the *Northern Weekly Telegraph* declares the acting in *Woman to Woman* was 'so good as to be almost completely natural'.[89] Similarly, *Kinematograph Weekly* writes of the comedy, *Four Men in a Van* (1921), that it offers 'the type of acting that charms by its very lack of acting. The four men simply live, and they create an atmosphere that is irresistible.'[90]

Between being 'almost natural' and 'acting that charms by lack of acting' a new concept of the 'natural' is emerging, reinforced by the experience of very different performance styles in Continental and American films, which demands unselfconscious presence before the camera rather than the studied underplaying associated with restraint. For the equation of the 'natural' with 'underplaying' still suggests a holding back of expression that threatens to 'overplay'. Those championing the cinema as a distinctively different kind of performing art valued what seemed like direct access to inner being through the scrutiny by the close-up on face, eyes and hands, offering revelations that bypassed verbal language and the traditional gestural codes of melodrama, now seeming old-fashioned by comparison. Thus the *Glasgow Evening News* reports the 'extraordinary method of conveying emotion' used by Alice Joyce, the American actress, whose 'features are completely immobile, yet she expresses any feeling with the merest inflection of the facial muscles. The effect is amazing, and obviates the use of sub-titles and pantomimic gesticulation.'[91] 'W.L.A.', in the *Leeds Mercury*, fearing the threat of synchronised speech, invokes cinema's 'really impressive improvements . . .

tend[ing] away from the art of the legitimate theatre
... for example the facial play that show[s] the
thoughts passing through the mind of the character
without the intervention of words'.[92] Similarly, the
Leicester Mercury, commenting on the greater closeness cinema permits to the actor, admires Emil Jannings in *Vaudeville* (1925). 'How much suffering and
elation he expresses by the mere poise of his massive
shoulders, how we can read his thoughts by the mere
flicker of an eyelid or the curling of the lip.'[93]

ACTING OR BEING?

Such intense scrutiny by the camera shifts attention
from the work of performance to the existential presence of the actor, pressuring performance towards
'being' rather than 'acting'. In this sense, the actor
functions as 'raw material', putting at the film-
maker's disposal body, self, emotions, mind and personality. According to Lilian Bamburg, the essential
requirements for the aspirant film actor are 'a good
screen appearance', 'an expressive face' and 'personality'.[94] Kenelm Foss, who enjoyed making controversially radical pronouncements, declared of theatrical
stars: 'I have seen with enthusiasm every British and
Continental star existing during the period, and not
one of them, male or female, has ever done more
than play sublime melodies upon the lute of his or
her own personality.'[95] Therefore, he concludes, the
medium of film, lacking colour and voice and rendering disguise transparent, makes 'any elaborate
attempt at impersonation ... quite futile'.[96] If film
can dispense with acting, neither, suggests Michael
Orme, does it need words. Responding to the revelations of German cinematic practice, he writes in *The
Illustrated London News* that 'the Art of Kinema has
its own methods for revealing the realm of the mind,
the sphere of the soul'. In *Vaudeville*, filmed 'through
the eyes of the central character, we see – actually see
– his thoughts, his dread ... with not a word on
screen'.[97] This further undermines the control of the
actor, as Anna May Wong warns: 'You may think you
are acting well ... but there is one thing that will
give you away. That is your eyes. The eyes have
rightly been referred to as 'the windows of the soul'
and the film camera will unerringly detect any false
expression in them.'[98]

Arguably, however, for all the talk of soul, cinematographic vision in British culture rarely dissolves
the barriers of socially coded physiognomy, gesture

and expression in the illusion of unmediated contact
with the inner self celebrated in Continental film
acting and in a different way in American stardom.
Rather, the British actor's body is used to authenticate a social type. Under the camera the film actor
produces less intimations of the soul than signs of
social position and identity. The difference is highlighted in *Blighty* (1927), which fields a typically
mixed cast of performers. This includes experienced
stage players, Ellaline Terris and Seymour Hicks;
Jameson Thomas, rising film actor and creator of a
series of magnificently laid-back Englishmen; the
Houston Sisters (comedy and variety entertainers),
who contribute small pantomimic caricatures to the
Armistice scenes; and Nadia Sibirskaia, an actress
'imported from France'.[99] In the role of a French
single mother bringing her baby to meet the English
upper-middle-class parents of its now dead father,
Sibirskaia offers up her face and being to the camera
with a stillness and transparency quite unlike anything produced by British performers. However, if
the function of the theatrical in British cinema is to
provide a legitimising public space for socially
defined performances, film does not simply reproduce theatricality – it threatens, as Anna May Wong
suggests, to expose it, to press behind the role, to
demand the real thing. George Arliss, for example, in
answer to J. T. Grein's questionnaire about actors and
emotion, points out:

> An actor who ever played in the 'movies' will have discov-
> ered that the camera registers thought in the eyes; the
> most fleeting emotion is recorded and the camera has
> no mercy on the actor who is thinking of other things
> or is incapable of imagination; and what the camera sees
> the audience sees ... the [eyes] cannot truly register an
> emotion that is not behind them.[100]

Ivor Novello registers similar discomfort at the intrusive closeness of the camera: 'the cold, calculating
camera, made of glass and steel, will not give the public
anything that the artist has not supplied'.[101] Out of
this perceived symbiosis of camera and performer
emerges two contrary forms of playing. On the one
hand, the existential self-revelation offered by many
Continental players – such as Nadia Sibirskaia or Emil
Jannings – and on the other, the Hollywood star
system, which lifted the performer beyond the film fiction, promising access to the very person of the star.

STARS AND BRITISH CINEMA

Although Rachael Low is dismissive of Matheson Lang's 'theatricality'[102], he nevertheless appears repeatedly in various polls taken through the 1920s in an attempt to identify British stars to rival Hollywood's. This seemingly paradoxical fact, discussed further in Chapter 5, should be borne in mind when examining the arguments running through the 1920s about the absence of a British star system, so frequently targeted as a major cause for the failure of British cinema to out-compete American films. Only two figures consistently appear in the terms applied to Hollywood stardom – Ivor Novello and Betty Balfour.[103] However, as was continually pointed out, plenty of British actors (men in particular) emigrated to become stars in Hollywood,[104] while the unprecedented furore of the Pickford/Fairbanks visit in 1920 demonstrated the appeal of Hollywood stars to British audiences. However, resistance to the star system is also vocal, and it is therefore not surprising to find the trade press of the 1920s in a quandary about how to approach the new phenomenon as it clashes with indigenous values. So we find in articles and letters by actors, producers, critics and fans a contradictory mix of opinion. This includes outright resistance to stars for economic and high cultural reasons, equally vocal laments at the lack of investment in stars and reliance on the draw of West End stage names,[105] combined with advice on how to produce and nurture stars.[106]

Exemplifying this quandary, *The Motion Picture Studio* announces in February 1922: 'We are convinced that the star system is one of the contributory causes to the present dearth of real screen talent.'[107] Then in August the journal partially retracts: 'we are convinced that the star-system is the right system for the moment'. This recommendation, however, is geared to marketing interests in the face of considerable cultural discomfort:

> There are many, with us, who would desire to see a more educated Public with a more refined taste in film matters, just as we would like to see a more refined taste in literature and the drama. But it is a commercially unsound policy to snap fingers in the face of the Public and say 'You think you like jazz tunes – we think you ought to like opera and opera we're going to give you'.[108]

Despite this apparent capitulation, the editorial ends with a sting in its tail: 'America is star-mad. Star-gazing is not merely a mania out there – it's a disease.' Similar ambivalence is expressed later in the decade in *Film Weekly*. Josie Lederer, blaming the British public for dependency on American audiences to make stars, concludes ambivalently: 'They are like that . . . in America, sudden in their likes and dislikes, more easily moved than ourselves, and more prone to welcome anyone new.'[109]

However, intermixed in this babble of conflicting opinion run discourses that inadvertently suggest why the ambition of reproducing American stardom in British culture was largely doomed. So in 1919 this message appears in *The Bioscope* from the ex-patriot Tom Terris, who warns against the 'cancerous growth' represented by the star system, arguing, 'the one great remedy . . . is the director – backed by a good story'.[110] In 1924, under the heading 'Stars and the Public', *Kinematograph Weekly* declares, somewhat optimistically: 'it becomes more and more evident that neither star nor all-star cast has great appeal to the public . . . the one thing that attracts . . . is the best-seller novel and the popular stage plays. These . . . are the real stars.'[111] *The Bioscope* declares towards the end of 1926 that 'the bogey of the "star" system has been well and truly laid . . . merit in the film, literary and technical, is what is wanted, and wanted in America more than some of the chiefs in the business imagine'.[112] Taking a different tack, *The Motion Picture Studio*'s 1922 complaint against stars quoted above concerned their depressive effect on the 'crowd of clever artistes, with potential or latent talent' for whom there is no room at the top and therefore no chance of development.[113] Maurice Elvey, writing in August 1920 for the house organ of his production company, *Stoll's Editorial News*, replies bluntly to a running argument about the problem: 'why we have no male stars, crudely stated, is simply that we don't want them'. For Elvey stardom threatens acting: 'the process of starring is also the process of cramping . . . [the star] has to specialise in one type of character . . . so continuously that at last his acting becomes a kind of mechanical second nature'.[114] Thus it is the star system that turns the valued character 'type' into its negation – the stereotype. Ivy Duke warns in *The Picturegoer*:

> They find young players who fill the requirements of certain parts . . . and then never give them a chance to play anything which calls for the depicting of another

kind of personality . . . The stars and the players of the screen should also have their opportunities of learning what acting really is . . . to extend our knowledge of character work . . . and to give us a chance of portraying personalities entirely different from our own.[115]

At the end of the decade a reader writing to *Film Weekly* similarly complains of the dominance of the 'fixed screen personality'. She argues that not only is this deadening to the players, but 'it is boring to a good part of the audience, who must never find out anything new about their artist's abilities'.[116] The magazine's 'Studio Correspondent' contrasts celebrity and acting rather more bluntly:

As a community . . . [our actors] . . . haven't the ways of Hollywood. They have not yet learnt the virtues of a seasonable divorce. In short, they are at present too busy acting – and training to act well – to learn the most important art of throwing about 'big money'.[117]

Together with the value of 'story' explored in Chapter 6, the particular values associated with 'acting' and 'character' represent a British cultural mind-set that worked to undermine the fervent wish to create British stars.

THE NON-ACTOR AND STARDOM

If the combined revelatory power of cinematography and stardom threatens the distinction between self and role so crucial for visible acting, some British film-makers, drawing on the documentarist vein in British culture, proposed alternative means of exploiting the camera in a campaign for the non-actor. Thus Kenelm Foss notes, 'Fortunately, on the screen, unlike the stage, experience as an actor is not a *sine qua non* for any but prominent parts . . . each scene is so short that the amateur has no time to give himself away.'[118] Like Henry Edwards, Foss looks for 'types' found on the street among 'real' people. But whereas Edwards seeks such types as material for his own character constructions, Foss, emphasising the greater 'spontaneity' of the amateur, wants them to replace the professional actor. In similar vein, F. Martin Thornton recommends producers to select

prototypes of the characters . . . people who, in actual life, [are] the living replicas of those described in the scenario. . . types so cast invariably register what is

required of them far better than stage actors . . . because they know nothing about acting as acting and portray the character to life by the simple process of being themselves.[119]

However, 'being oneself' in the documentarist perspective is less about displaying personality than mapping protagonists by social position and role. Thus the following year in *The Motion Picture Studio*, Foss continues his argument on behalf of the non-actor: 'in my experience, it is absolutely impossible to make an actor look like a policeman, and *if* (and I emphasise *if*) I had my choice I would engage the real policeman'.[120] In this sense, the culturally prized 'type' shifts from the textually constructed character, realised via character acting, to the socially constructed person found in a 'real-life' role. 'Being oneself' is elided with fulfilling one's social position. So Foss continues: 'A real policeman looks like a policeman, no matter how much he is disguised! But it takes more than a uniform to make . . . [the actor] convincing.'[121] For Foss, at least, it seemed that social players might take the place of character actors, although his emphatic 'if' suggests the unrealisability of this ambition within the prevailing production context.

The presumed spontaneity of the non-acting protagonist drawn from 'real' life suggests a link between documentary and stardom as different routes to modernisation taken by British and American film performance. Lilian Bamburg, with her eye on the ultimate goal of many an aspiring film actor, argues: 'Naturalness, without theatricality or any impression of acting, must be the aim of every film aspirant, and this is where those early Stars made their niches.'[122] This connection between being natural and stardom suggests the irresistible advantage Hollywood gained from American naturalist practices, which support the elision between the private person of the star and his or her roles within films through the 'illusion of the first time'. Frederick J. Allen, defending 'Stars as Box Office Attractions', highlights stardom's promise of access to the person: 'there is nothing more attractive than the human personality, and the public appears to pay more attention to the stars than to the pictures themselves'.[123] In this respect, 'acting from the heart' modernised the empathic and emblematic identities of melodrama's protagonists. For its emphasis on spontaneous expression of personality, coupled with the unprecedented access that film allows to the body of the performer, guarantees the authenticity of melodrama's values personified by the star, further authenticated by reference to the actor's life.[124] In this sense, the hero's projection of his or her life story across social boundaries coalesces with the rise of the star as a shining emblem of democratic opportunity.

The radical democracy of the American star system made a powerful contrary appeal to the British popular audience, one scarcely understood at the time, in the social mobility it permitted for both stars and their characters, and in the equality of audience/star identification. For stariness may make stars extraordinary in their personae and lifestyle. But in giving audiences access to their selves through the commitment of their bodies and personalities to their roles and making available through publicity their personal habits, loves, dislikes and losses, they prove to be much like us – ordinary. However, if enormously appealing, such obliteration of the boundaries between persons was problematic for a cultural imaginary invested in social location and demarcation, closing the gap between self and role that I have suggested is crucial to performance in British culture. In an article entitled 'Should Stars Specialise?' for *The Motion Picture Studio*, Fred Wright struggles with this dilemma, as the older notion of character 'type' gives way to star 'personality'. While recognising the asset of stars who 'by reason of an attractive personality have "got over" ', the culture's investment in acting brings Wright down on the side of versatility. Pauline Frederick, for example, is 'an artiste who will hold . . . interest by reason of her talent, no matter in what part she is appearing'.[125]

The frequently used notion of 'getting over' implies recognition of a second gap – that between performer and audience, which must be crossed in order to produce the identification implied in stardom. If the ethos of restraint made this difficult at the level of performance, it also impacted on the publicist's approach to the all-important production of fan discourse. In these early days of star-making, British journalists are diffident about pressing personal questions, reporting, rather, publicly shared lifestyle practices of home-decorating, cooking and hobbies but respecting the boundary that fronts the intimate recesses of personality. Thus in 1925 *The Bioscope* announces a new series by Geoffrey Ben-

stead Films featuring *Stage Stars Off Stage*. Purporting to offer 'intimate pictures, in their own homes and places of amusement, of many of our most popular entertainers', the review makes it clear that the series focuses on entertainers 'keeping up the act' and 'staying in character' even off the stage. 'It is', claims the reviewer, 'delightful to find that our favourite players are not too anxious to throw off the cares of business as soon as they leave the stage door, but seem to thoroughly enjoy acting with as much zest at home as they do in the theatre.'[126] Comparable series put out by *Pathé Pictorial* and Pathé's *Eve's Film Review* feed fan interest in stars with character constructions, derived from dress, home decor, hobbies and performed roles. Such fan-writing practices are a source of bitter-sweet irony in Anthony Asquith's *Shooting Stars* (1928) when rising star, Mae Feather (Annette Benson), is interviewed by Asphodel Smythe – byline *Flicker* – of *The Film Fan*. Hints of Mae's attraction to the comedian, Andy Wilks, and discomfort at the unwelcome attentions of her co-starring husband, Julian (Brian Aherne), are intercut with her effusive, publicity-seeking responses to the interviewer. Close-ups of Mae, making various gestures of high-flown sentiment, and of Julian's half-amused, half-disconsolate glances at her are juxtaposed with the words the reporter speedily scribbles on her pad, noting such clichés as 'Beauty the very Breath of Life', 'Adores all furry and feathery things'. Cross-cutting between Mae's dressing room and technicians on the lighting rig exposes the superficiality of the star interview. Exchanging sardonic looks, the men attach a hastily contrived iron cross, inscribed 'for valour', to the pigeon that in a previous scene had pecked Mae, throwing her into hysterics and creating mayhem in the studio. In the meantime, Mae, having run through 'Art', 'Poetry', 'Roses', 'Shakespeare' and 'Children', and finding Julian now leaning with his arm across the back of her chair, tops the list with 'Has found ideal mate'. Cut to a shot of Andy Wilks removing his clown's wig and sighing at his reflection.

Pen-portraits of stars focus on clothes and hobbies as public signs of a created character. 'Betty Balfour was wearing a quaint little black dress, with a turquoise blue apache scarf around her shoulders, and on her golden curls sat one of those marvellous creations which give such a "Bettyish" touch to all her films.'[127] Or:

He spoke with the utmost simplicity and charm yet he gave me the impression that he was a prince in disguise. ... Milton Rosmer was pensively drinking China tea. My impression of Royalty incognito deepened. I decided that he was Monsieur Beaucaire, and proceeded to mentally attire him in brocade and ruffles in lieu of the exceedingly well-cut clothes he was wearing, substituting a slender rapier for the tea-spoon balanced in one hand.[128]

The 'prince in disguise' trope suggests a perception of stardom that chimes with the restraint/passion, private/public coupling. Towards the end of the decade, the actor, Donald Stuart, describes the life of British actors in Hollywood in precisely these terms for a fanzine article, 'Private Life in Hollywood':

> In Hollywood there is a British section ... Ronny Colman in private life is one of the most charming and simple humans I know. His acting has rated him the Gerald du Maurier of the films; his shyness has made him my greatest friend. He hides his light under a positive bushel of British reserve.[129]

SINCERITY VERSUS SPONTANEITY

If 'the illusion of the first time' generates the value of spontaneity in performance, the closest British criticism comes to this is 'sincerity'. This quality is invoked time and again as a counter to the imputed 'artificiality' of the theatrical, and one which, in its opposition to 'exaggerated' feeling and personal display, emphasises not self-expression but the familiar virtue of restraint. Thus *The Bioscope* praises *The Lure of Crooning Water* (1920) as 'notable for the sincerity and the restraint of its acting'.[130] *The Film Renter* writes of *Duke's Son* (1920): 'Guy Newall is so extraordinarily natural that one is held spellbound by the sincerity of his art. There is nothing exaggerated in his work.'[131] Sincerity, moreover, distingishes *acting* from American stardom. Thus Lionel Collier, review editor for *Kinematograph Weekly*, looks for 'a sincerity that is rarely seen in American Pictures'.[132] Donald Stuart, already quoted above, goes on to comment: 'Next in line comes Clive Brook. The secret of his phenomenal success is undoubtedly that same British restraint, the shy sincerity of acting, that characterises Ronald Colman.'[133] For *Around the Town*, Clive Brook also figures as the quintessence of sincerity:

If the grimaces of the low-necked 'vamp' and the antics of an unattractive Russian woman had any charm previously, it fades into nothingness before the sincere and finely-restrained acting of Fay Compton, Clive Brook and Robert English.[134]

In suggesting the projection of the actor's self across the gap between performer and audience, spontaneity, it seems, not only disturbs the aesthetics of restraint but threatens social and sexual excess. Thus, in 'every day life ... [Brook] is not seen with the "vulgar crowd", preferring peace and quiet to the much circularised joys of "loose parties" '.[135] Against this disturbance, sincerity, designating the actor's attitude to the role, reinstates professional skill and control, and in supporting the distance between performer and part ensures that what we get is 'acting' and the production of 'character'. For this gap demands of the actor objective evaluation of, and 'sincere' belief in, the role, rather than the fusion that obliterates the performance. Thus Chili Bouchier advises in *Film Weekly*:

> Many amateurs could improve their acting and give a more sincere performance by 'getting to know' the character they are playing. It is not difficult to act just what the director tells you, but such a performance often lacks sincerity. If you know the character well you will be able to feel his or her emotions and introduce many little actions or mannerisms which will produce a real person instead of a mere puppet.[136]

In similar vein, a reader writes to *Film Weekly* at the end of the decade to note an improvement in British films − 'an indescribable "something": perhaps it is the freshness and sincerity with which the characters are portrayed'.[137]

STARS AS CHARACTERS

If the admiration of acting and production of character types rules out the style of spontaneous acting that lays bare the actor's personality, the sincerity that respects the role can offer the compensatory virtue of 'living the part'. Rather than exploiting the role to promote the actor, this frequent demand of film acting suggests a movement in the reverse direction: suppression of self for the sake of the role. It is the character who has the personality rather than the performer, whose life the character absorbs. 'Living the part' in this sense represents a British take on star acting. Thus Maurice Elvey, like Fred Wright and *The Picturegoer*'s correspondent above, admires in very English terms the American Pauline Frederick for her 'natural ability' to submit self to role: 'Her triumph lies in the fact that she has made herself the perfect medium for the delineation of certain character types . . . In these roles she *lives*.'[138] Similarly, the *Daily News* analyses the performance skills of Clive Brook under the heading, 'A Gifted British Actor', in *The Reverse of the Medal* (1923):

> to appear real the General must never abandon his military character. The slightest touch of the stage or film actor telling us how much he feels would destroy the whole tragedy. And that is where Clive Brook is so good. We are made to understand all the father has to face but the actor is always the soldier with a soldier's idea of duty.[139]

As Violet Hopson advises, 'don't think of yourself; picture in your mind what a maid would do, how she would walk, etc. . . . Do not try and act your part – be a maid, live her life for the time you are in the studio.'[140] Rather than role delivering a star, then, the actor, performing at one remove from both character and fan, must deliver a character.

The determining aesthetic of restraint and emphasis on the culturally constructed character produce a form of acting celebrity very different from that of the Hollywood star. Thus Wynham Standing, debating with Hugh Croise in *Kinematograph Weekly*, declares that the work of the actor is to establish a character with the first fade-in, for, he argues, 'all acting is character acting: there is no such thing as a straight part'.[141] And Alma Taylor, for all her starriness for British audiences, tells a *Picturegoer* interviewer, 'I always feel that personal appearances must be such a disappointment to the audience.' The article goes on to explain: 'she liked best to be enshrined in the hearts of picturegoers as a favourite character in which they had seen her upon the screen'.[142] For some fans, too, character was more important than the star. In January 1928 *The Bioscope* gave a whole page over to 'The Complaints of a Film Fan', in which, among other things, 'John Picturegoer' declares his views on acting: 'I am more interested in the *character* than in the artist, and I would much rather see a fine performance by an unknown player

than a weak performance by a star. The stars, in fact, chiefly mean characters to me' (my emphasis).[143] A reader who writes to *Film Weekly* in November 1928 to enter a 'plea for character actors' against an earlier issue's line-up of up-and-coming star talent draws together the two strands of influence on British cinema, theatrical and documentary:

> I do not discern one likely to be a great character artist, like (say) Irving, Tree, Wyndham, Hare, Ellen Terry, Fanny Brough, Lottie Venne were on the stage . . . Pretty faces and fine looking men soon weary one, but great artists are always intensely interesting. Most of the people one meets in real life are character or comedy people; the pretty girls and handsome men are in the minority. Depict life on the films as in real life, and British films will be more successful.[144]

CONTRA THE NON-ACTOR

Thus a marked critical current, in decrying underplaying and restraint, looks not to the spontaneity of the 'first time', nor the naturalism of the non-performer, but rather for a renewal of the skills of character acting, and of gestural pantomime. A 1922 editorial in *The Motion Picture Studio* condemns the 'policy . . . of choosing "types" [i.e. non-actors – ed.] instead of artistes'. The use of, for example, a real bank clerk robs not only actors of work but audiences of the pleasure of acting skills:

> That is the function of an artiste: to clothe himself with the personality of the character and *live it*. We have among our artistes men and women who can transform their face and transfigure their personality at a moment's notice: in the old London days [that is of the London Film Company – ed.], artistes would be clergymen one day, old crossing-sweepers the next, and young subalterns the next – triumphs of make-up and characterisation.[145]

The journal returns to the theme later in the year with a vehement rejection of the notion that 'types' found in real life improve realism: 'Drama will die and the screen become a silver-sheet of fitful shadows if acting is allowed to resolve itself down to mechanical processes, unintelligent gestures, and unthinking facial expressions.'[146]

Seemingly in answer to this problem, in May and June 1922 *The Motion Picture Studio* reprinted a five-part series, 'The Science of Histrionic Acting' by Col. Netterville Barron, a doctor of physiology and a lecturer on acting already mentioned in Chapter 2.[147] These were first published in *The Actor* and subject to a four-part explanation as the 'Barron method' in *Kinematograph Weekly* two years later (May–June 1924). Writing for the stage actor, and clearly drawing on earlier actor's handbooks, his concern was to provide a physiological account of how emotions are registered in the whole body not only the face, in order to get British actors moving again. This return to the significance of gesture arises in part from new scientific ideas. For by the 1920s the body figures less as mediator of inner feelings or thoughts than their source. Thus, drawing on the science of reflexology, Colden Lore shifts the relation between bodily sign and emotion: 'paradoxical as it may seem, we do not weep because we are sorry . . . we are sorry *because we weep*; we feel joy *because we laugh*; we are angry *because we strike*' (original emphasis).[148] George Pearson echoes similar sentiments in a RADA lecture, when he quotes William James: 'emotion is not the *cause* but the *result* of action'.[149] Such arguments underpinned the crusade of those who, like Netterville Barron, reject the impassive, 'do-nothing' style of underplaying, demanding that actors revive the kinetic and pictorial art of gestural movement: 'movement is the cause, emotion is the effect'.[150] But they also contribute to rethinking gesture for the movement-based medium of film.

Equally significant, however, is Barron's attempt, based on William MacDougall's *An Introduction to Social Psychology*, to naturalise the cultural sources of gesture as signifying socially demarcated identities. Thus, operating within the same middle-class norms noted of Henry Neville above, what Barron categorises as 'relaxing movements' – changing one's position or supporting the head with hand – 'are the alphabet of good manners', while what is often complained of as 'overacting' draws from the category of 'convulsive movements'. These, he argues, are the result of incoherent thought or inarticulacy and 'consequently most frequently seen among the uneducated and . . . less civilised peoples'.[151] This perspective rationalises both the relationship between gesture and character and the shift from highborn villains – who, as Lewes says, are 'perfectly well bred' – to the histrionic menace of sub-criminal proletari-ans of the kind embodied by Victor McLaglen and Cyril McLaglen in, respectively, *The Passionate Adventure* and *Underground* (1927).

The unmediated access to the inner self promised by stardom also threatens the boundaries, so important in British culture, that separate the amorphous, non-signifying material of private subjectivity from public acts and significations. In contrast, pictorial gesture and character acting function as formal signs and documents, providing cues to narrative meaning. Violet Hopson attempts to bring the two sides of the process together under the neologism, 'kinemavation' – by which she means close observation of the gestures and facial expressions employed by people in the street or travelling by tube. Taking as her example the seated man who bows his head over his paper to avoid seeing a standing woman, she moves from interpreting gesture to constructing story: 'Imagine how all this would come out in a picture . . . Let your imagination weave a little story, think that you are the lady who is standing and that the man who is sitting is an admirer hitherto unsuccessful.'[152] In this context, the character-based, picturised gesture provides an external carapace, both visual and narrative, within which the authentic can be put into play, but also contained within its frame and thereby submitted to signification.

NATIONALISING STARDOM

In an essay on 1930s British film culture, Annette Kuhn demonstrates that if film stardom is a major source of Hollywood's global appeal, reception of stars is nationally inflected.[153] It is, perhaps, significant that Pauline Frederick's versatility as a character actor appears so often in this examination of British responses to the phenomenon of stardom. Also, that American stars such as Florence Turner, Mae Marsh and Dorothy Gish found a compatible niche in British films from the mid-teens into the 1920s as actresses noted for the performance skills of impersonation and mimicry. Dorothy Gish's difference (see Fig. 5.4) in this respect from the more inwardly luminous style of her sister is perfectly showcased in Herbert Wilcox's *Nell Gwynne* (1926) (discussed in Chapters 2 and 5) and *Madame Pompadour* (1928), illuminating the distinction between British and American stardom. A defender of British cinema writes to *Film Weekly* to point out: 'British films are different, and people think that because they are different, they are inferior. Britain . . . [has] artists who are very natural, and who have the solid traditions of their country written on their faces.'[154] In this respect many British actors arguably succeeded in Hollywood precisely for the dramatic and aesthetic potential of their culturally different performance styles and acting personae – for example, the English reserve, refined charm, cool attractions of Clive Brook, Ronald Colman and Madeleine Carroll. If this is the case, it is hardly surprising that Hollywood stars, representing modes of identity attuned to the loosening of social and economic relations of American capitalism, exercised a powerful reverse fascination. Attractions of a different mode of body language and interpersonal relations offered by Hollywood work as powerfully on the imaginations of British audiences as they do for the British encountering foreign nationals at home or abroad. This does not, however, represent mutually exclusive appeals, as shown by the contradictory ways in which fandom was articulated in the press, magazines and readers' letters. It is perfectly possible both to be enamoured of the exotic and democratic personalities circulated in the Hollywood star system and to respond with a certain relief of recognition to the character types and performance skills of home-grown talent.

In the New Year of 1929 *Film Weekly* issued a correspondant's challenge to its readers to name 'twenty artists of any nationality . . . as good looking or as talented as the twenty American stars cited (some actually of English birth) . . . named'. According to *Film Weekly*'s analysis, the majority of respondents championed British artists. It publishes a letter from Miss G. Edwards of Cheam, Surrey, who, despite admitting her favourite star is American, finds British actors to pair favourably with each of the American stars named:

(9) *John Barrymore* . . . leaves me cold. We can produce as fine a character actor – Matheson Lang.

(5) *Janet Gaynor*, youth and a great personality. Our 'Tessa' can equal her in every way – Mabel Poulton.

(7) *Laura La Plante*, quite sweet, but not so clever as our own Lillian Hall-Davis can be.

Interestingly, she pairs against Clive Brook the English actor in Hollywood, Carlyle Blackwell, the American taken up in British films.[155]

TWO BRITISH STARS

Significantly, Ivor Novello and Betty Balfour continued to top the list in terms of popular mention. Arguably, these two actors, who achieved unquestionable stardom in British cinema, did so because of the degree to which their particular personae and performance styles worked productive variations on British norms. Thus Betty Balfour's stardom, fulfilling the prediction that reinvigoration would emerge from working-class performance traditions (see above), is founded on her identification with the chirpy cockney skivvy, Squibs. The character of Squibs was derived from a music-hall sketch and brought to life on film through Balfour's capacity to employ the music-hall performer's direct address across the footlights, reaching from the screen to engage the reactions of the audience (see Chapters 5 and 6). Significantly, however, try as she and some of her producers might, she was unable to realise a stardom outside variations on the character. Her film-acting career died as the Victorian context that produced Squibs was displaced by the more potentially fissured 1930s, from which emerged the acerbic, Depression-resistant Gracie Fields.

Novello, on the other hand, who came closest to developing a mode of star performance divorced from the discrete boundedness of a character, had a far more problematic relationship to cinema. He ardently desired against all advice to go on the stage, something he did not achieve until he was approaching thirty, and on the back of the success of his films, *The Rat* in particular.[156] Novello's definitive status as a film star, while still identifying with the theatre, dramatises some of the tensions that mark British performance style in cinema. As a star, Novello does indeed offer his body and persona to the camera in a way that promises access to the person as if 'for the first time' and so denies the performance skills that are prized by the British theatre. The unusualness of Novello's performance presence is registered in the uncharacteristically intimate and sexualised writing of critics who responded to his persona, for example Edith Nepean writing about *The Rat* films:

> I have just seen two amazing Ivor Novello films . . . Ivor Novello is proving that he is not a screen star worshipped by thousands because his hair is black satin, his eyes slumbering fires, his skin pale, his lips passionate, but he has the temperament of genius.[157]

Or James Agate describing his stage role in *Liliom* (1926), in which, cast against type, Novello is required to 'act'. Novello offers 'beautiful profile and baby grace . . . his body . . . a river of grace, his thighs a cascade of loveliness, and his soul [shining] with a glow like that of a fountain lit up by coloured electric lights . . . a public school Adonis . . . modish wistfulness' – all, Agate concludes, inappropriate for the part.[158]

However, despite seeming to offer the accessibility of film stardom, Novello aspired to the romantic theatre of melodramatic expression and rhetorical flourishes – which tends to alienate current tastes. In the context of the 1920s a unique solution to these contradictory tendencies was found, encouraged, perhaps, by a gay identity that could not be publicly expressed.[159] Novello does not provide a socially coded performance – his ambivalent class identity, treating both street urchin and upper-class scion as theatrical disguises, bears no relation to the social graces of Henry Edwards's underplaying, at ease across the social spectrum. Rather, Novello makes a performance out of *not performing* by throwing away in camply flamboyant manner gestures that belong to romantic-melodramatic rhetoric. Alternatively, he retreats into passivity before the camera, putting himself on display, draping his body across table corners or over sofa backs (Fig. 3.4). This pictorial practice is taken to macabre extremes in *The Man Without Desire* (1923) when his face appears serenely framed in the glass panel of a coffin lid, or in *The Rat* when, as described in Chapter 2, he poses picturesquely for the crowd in the coffin-shaped arches of the White Coffin. Novello's performance style,

Fig. 3.4. Ivor Novello, indisputable star, 'body draping' in *The Rat* (1925), with Isabel Jeans as Zelie de Chaumet

then, plays on the tension between movement in theatricalised space and the containment of public presentation within pictorial posing and framing. In this way he both indulges theatrical expressiveness, promising transgression of the boundaries and constraints of middle-class decorum, while at the same time exercising restraint and passive underplaying with camp knowingness and irony. This performance of a non-performance as a compromise with theatricality depends less on gesture than on cinematic devices – framing, the close-up and lighting – which serve to present the star performer as himself a gestural figure, a projection, exemplified literally in the celebrated Novello profile.

In the British context, then, 'starring' emphasises the production of character, type or performed role. Understatement as a gesture towards naturalism nevertheless retains visible acting skill not only in the construction of a character but in making visible the performativity of the character's role and social position. It is the necessity of emphasising the 'part' *as a* part that prevents the loss of role in the being of the performer.

AN ACTOR'S ART CINEMA?

What, then, did Britain's actors bring to a cinema seeking to re-establish its position in the postwar years? The absence of an art cinema movement was, then and since, frequently attributed to a lack of interest among British writers and artists in the potentialities of film. However, in the late 1910s and early 1920s a small group of stage actors moved into cinema with artistic – if not avant-garde – intentions. Henry Edwards was one of several, including Guy Newall and Kenelm Foss, who, moving spasmodically between stage and screen in the teens and 1920s, seem to belong to an incipient generation of cinematic actor-managers, since they acted in, scripted and eventually directed films, seeking greater control of the production process and a space for artistic expression. Edwards worked in the shadow of Hepworth as director of a subsidiary company, while benefiting from the relatively independent stability of the Walton studios. Guy Newall, after a chance meeting with George Clark during the war, set up a film company, George Clark Productions, with Clark and the actress who was to become his wife, Ivy Duke, which remained active until 1923. Henry Edwards and the Newall/Duke team were recognised in the trade press as innovative film-makers working at the quality end of the industry. Kenelm Foss, an actor, trained painter, a poet and novelist, had less success in consolidating his work, moving from company to company. Yet he writes passionately if ambivalently about the art of film, struggling with the need to conform to commercial dictates and mass appeal, and was involved in cinema throughout the 1920s. Edwards and Newall frequently wrote, acted in and directed their films, working with small stock companies, while Foss often combined two of these three functions. All three eventually returned to the theatre, while Newall and Foss turned also to literary writing. Alongside these three, Adrian Brunel, who trained as an opera singer, played small acting roles in cottage-industry burlesques that he both scripted and directed (see Chapter 6). Ivor Novello might also tangentially be placed in this group. Initially, Novello had written *The Rat* with Constance Collier for a film to be directed by Brunel, but the project failed to find a backer, while *Downhill* (1927), his second Hitchcock film, was also a Novello/Collier collaboration. However, while attaining a unique stardom in British cinema, he showed little interest in film-making, his sights always firmly set on the theatre. Alongside Novello, the work of Edwards, Newall and Foss, functioning variously as actors, scriptwriters and directors, highlights the different ways in which acting is preserved as acting while accommodating to the naturalistic scrutiny of camera, modernising performance and characterisation within material based on romantic or melodramatic premises.

HENRY EDWARDS: DEBONAIR NATURALIST
Henry Edwards combines the range and touches of the character actor with the laid-back ease of an underplaying Hawtrey or Du Maurier. For Edwards, this style serves to authenticate or 'naturalise' what remains an essentially romantic and extrovert theatricality that instills his characterisations with an infectious exuberance. Thus in *East Is East* (1916) – which he both directed and, partnering Florence Turner, starred in – Edwards plays an out-at-knee, jauntily cloth-capped garage hand, Bert Grummet. Playfully flirting with Victoria Vickers, he follows her family to the hop-picking fields in Kent, but unselfishly retreats when she comes into an unexpected fortune. Anonymous financial help from Vicky and silent loyalty to his lost love leads Bert to

rise in the fish and chip business, and so to purchase the country cottage from which Vicky once prevented him stealing chickens. Drawn back to this district, Vicky re-encounters Bert, and, after the inhibiting formalities of afternoon tea, finally reunites with her upwardly mobile East End boy in the kind of nostalgic rural retreat now emerging as the normative dream of postwar English society. Edwards provides a 'picturesque' rendition of Bert. Lending his twinkling eyes, infectious smile and mobile body to project playful cockney cheekiness, he exercises manful restraint as Vicky moves West, allowing Bert eventually to mature through a mix of bumbling awkwardness and boyish underplaying charm still popular in actors such as Hugh Grant. Thus Edwards's performance plays class-inflected performance codes against each other to recast the passion-restraint dynamic for specific dramatic purposes. Maurice Elvey draws on Edwards's combination of romantic panache and underplaying for the part of Dick Lascelles in a second, and highly successful, film adaptation of *The Flag Lieutenant*. Edwards's approach to performance as play-acting juxtaposes gestures of mock romantic bravado – enthusiastically cheering his lads on in a rowing race or miming a request to marry the Admiral's daughter – with efficient heroics when he single-handedly saves a beleaguered British fort. Later, winsome appeals to said Admiral's daughter, whom he has little hope of marrying, are followed by stoic self-suppression. He refuses to take credit for action mistakenly attributed to his friend, the lack-lustre Major Thesiger, bringing about his own public humiliation when branded as a coward before gathered officers, their wives and daughters.

GUY NEWALL: BRITISH CINEMA'S FINEST ACTOR
If Moore Marriott is evoked as Britain's best character actor, Guy Newall is characterised almost as frequently as 'Britain's finest actor', largely, as noted above, for the sincerity of his naturalism. Starting out with Ivy Duke as a light comedian in the Lucky Cat series, Newall, in contrast to Edwards, took the 'do-nothing' style to melancholic extremes, in the George Clark films that followed. 'He worked so slow he seemed becalmed,' says *Variety* scornfully of *The Lure of Crooning Water*.[160] For *The Cinema*, however, his portrayal of Lord Francis in *Duke's Son* is 'a work of art', while *The Film Renter* declares, 'There

is nothing exaggerated in his work . . . throughout the production he dominates every scene.'[161]

How does an 'almost becalmed' mode of underplaying dominate? One answer lies in the romantic and melodramatic fantasy material Newall adapts for himself, which both sustains and is sustained by his stylistic minimalism. In this respect, the plots of his films posed problems for some critics in their predilection for 'immoral', 'sentimental' or, as the *Daily News* says of *Duke's Son*, 'very foolish, unreal' storylines.[162] In almost all cases, however, Guy Newall's and Ivy Duke's performances overcome these reservations. Thus *Kinematograph Weekly* argues of *Fox Farm* (1922) that despite offering 'a picture of a man whom Fate dogs, loveless and lonely, with no companion to confide in but a dog which gets killed', Newall's acting avoids the 'false note' that 'would have turned pathos into bathos'. He is 'natural without being commonplace, dramatic without being unnatural'.[163] *Fox Farm*, his fourth directorial credit in this series, was scripted by Newall from a Warwick Deeping novel. The scenario uses a melodramatised, Hardyesque landscape, peopled with sharply caricatured rural types. These support a domestic drama between the three lead characters, which, to adapt Desmond MacCarthy's comments, seeks to tell the story of average, largely inarticulate characters, showing 'what is usually hidden and mute – perhaps even unspoken to themselves'.[164] In an early scene, Jesse Falconer, a debt-ridden farmer, comes under attack from his discontented wife, Kate, played sympathetically by Barbara Everest enacting the irritation of a woman long oppressed by a husband given to philosophical fatalism. As Kate harangues him, Newall performs the emotional withdrawal that so irritates her, his spirit seeming to retreat into the depths of his being. Leaning back heavily at full-length in his chair, he draws thoughtfully on his pipe, while with slow deliberation lifting one leg to balance the heel of his boot on the toe-tip of the other. The gesture is 'natural' in that it derives from observing such common, almost instinctive movements, but its timing and performance within this emotionally heavily laden exchange is calculated as a clearly articulated sign of the character's indifference to unpaid bills.

Newall's immobile performance style is based on a shortish, heavyish body, square face, high forehead, receding hairline, long upper lip and slightly protruding ears. He is not unhandsome, however, and *The Bioscope* doubts his suitability for the part of Bellairs in *The Garden of Resurrection*, the lonely man obsessed with a feeling of ugliness (see Chapter 6).[165] Nevertheless, he renders the weight of his body almost palpable, sinking into chairs, leaning on mantlepieces or forward across a table, standing foursquare, unmoving, in the centre of a room, at the foot of stairs or in a landscape (see Fig. 6.3). Such poses and bodily movements make statements of emotional stasis, of plumbing the depths or of foreboding. With this immobile body, Newall looms, sways, leans and, as *The Film Renter* says, 'dominates'.[166] Meaning is generated by slight stretchings and tensions that run through his body and deft facial muscle retractions caught on film. As *The Times* notes, his 'concentration on the screen enables him to study the requirements of the camera'.[167] Thus he develops a repertoire of miniscule signs: a ripple across his somewhat saturnine, mournful face; a drag on his pipe; a slight play of muscles around the mouth to produce a flinch; a tightening of the brow or round the eyes to indicate vulnerability. More theatrical in scale are his hunched back and hands clapped to the head during moments of melodramatic outburst. Mainly, however, Newall superimposes on a naturalist non-performance – frequently anticipating rather than fulfilling emotional climax – a play of minute gestural detail that belongs to what William Archer and others recognised as a Pre-Raphaelite touch. This also applies to his characters' pursuit of the beautiful, the soulful and the idealised (see Chapter 2). In this respect, Newall shares with Novello, Edwards and Foss a somewhat wistful aesthetic of romantic beauty, fey fantasy, lightened and ironised by – all important for a culture infused with a notion of performance – a sense of 'play' (see Chapter 6). Thus in a *Bioscope* interview accompanied by his portrait, debonair in bowler hat and leaning on a walking cane, he declares, 'I like being associated with beautiful plays . . . it is much nicer to do the things one likes doing than just turn out the stuff . . . for popular demand.'[168]

At the centre of the films that survive, Guy Newall figures as the oddball: lonely, unloved or misunderstood, obsessed with his sense of ugliness, a dreamer after better things – things playful (*Duke's Son*), philosophical and poetic (*Fox Farm*), beautiful (*The Garden of Resurrection*), fatally passionate (*The*

Lure of Crooning Water). In these films Newall constructs his character as outsider, spinning out of an inner fantasy life a drama in which his dreams clash with people content to live by the custom and practice of the 'ordinary' world. So, for example, in *The Garden of Resurrection*, the theatricalisation of Newall's non-performance occurs through the projection of his character's loneliness into a fantasised melodrama built around an overheard restaurant conversation (see Chapter 6). In *The Lure of Crooning Water*, theatricality invades his rural backwater when Georgette (Ivy Duke), a society actress, is sent to his farm for a rest cure and he succumbs to her seduction. As playboy and penniless younger son, Lord Francis Delamere, in *Duke's Son*, Newall's character embarks on the dubious performance profession of card-sharper. This results in a melodramatic *coup de théâtre* with his exposure before a high-society assembly, to which he responds with nonchalant admission and a shrug, concluding at the end of the film in melodramatic pathos as he and his wife (Ivy Duke) prepare suicide by charcoal-burning asphyxiation. Finally, in *Fox Farm* Newall exploits a melodramatic plot device when a misfiring fuse explodes in his face. Blinding him, the accident enables his estranged wife to start an affair, on the discovery of which his character fills his knapsack and, followed at a distance by the faithful Ivy Duke, walks off into a Hardyesque landscape. All these films explore through shifting social performances a tentative re-mapping of social and sexual relations, resolved either in the reconfirmation of rural harmony or in an unimaginable future, which, if unknown and threatening, is not without hope. Newall's return to film acting in Geza Von Bolvary's version of *The Ghost Train* after a three-year absence (1927) marks a distance between the wistful, often fey fantasies of these and other early 1920s films and the more socially targeted realism that emerged with the onset of the 1930s. Newall playing Teddy Deakin creates a caricature that appears to delight in satirising and destroying the soulful character of his earlier films by realising in his body the ugly, alienated, irritating figure that character always feared to be.

THE ART OF CASTING: KENELM FOSS

Regrettably, as far as I know, none of Foss's film performances has been preserved. However, his contribution to debates about performance has already been noted in his polemic concerning the use of the non-actor to provide the all-important type. In this regard, Foss mounted something of a crusade for casting as an art. Casting was indeed a cause for discussion and complaint throughout the 1920s, a concomitant of the focus on character acting.[169] Foss himself devoted a whole chapter to it in *The Work of the Film Producer* (*c.* 1919), as well as contributing articles to the trade press and fan magazines. For him, 'one of the secrets of the successful film is in the casting of the characters', and he stresses the importance of assessing 'the potentialities, dramatic and photographic, of each new type' offered by the prospective performer.[170] The importance of the character type underpins Foss's rejection of the stock company, so important to others such as Maurice Elvey. Taking the adaptation of novelistic sources as an example, he argues that 'each new character is so widely different in every respect that the stock company to fill those numerous roles would have to be enormous'.[171] A fan writing to *The Picturegoer* lends support in complaining that 'most filmed novels are hopelessly miscast'.[172]

For Foss, then, the character type combines both the social and aesthetic: 'Types! That is what casting comes to, first and last – the selection of proper types.'[173] Thus his approach to casting is both pictorial and dramatic, arguing that 'selection and proportion are as necessary to composing one's cast as to composing one's scenario'. For the sake of narrative clarity and aesthetic appeal, cast members must be distinguishable through 'contrast(s) of physique and temperament'.[174] *The House of Peril* (1922) exhibits his delight in the potential of casting to construct a creative play-off between different character types, with their associated performance styles. From a play based on a novel by Mrs Belloc Lowndes, the story negotiates the types of True, New and Fatal Woman in two contrasting female figures. Fay Compton as Sylvia Bailey – cool, independent-minded but innocent English widow abroad, seeking to extend domestic moral virtues to the world at large – and Madeleine Seymour's flighty Anna Wolsky, a decadent, worldly-wise cynic and gambler, who introduces Sylvia to the casino at Deauville. A division in Sylvia's affections extends character contrast to the male leads, Foss's scenario playing off the staid, prosaically practical and repressed English lawyer, Bill Chester, against the romantic, horse-riding and, moreover, Continental Compte de Virieu, whose addiction to the casino Sylvia thinks she can cure (see Chapter 2). Both men, however, prove woefully inept when, instead of rushing to Sylvia's rescue, they bicker over who will propose to her. The play-off between types involves similarly contrasting performance styles to realise them, while differentiating national types. Thus English underplaying and the restrained grace of romantic drawing-room comedy intersect with the full-blown pantomimic malevolence of the Wachners, a German couple who prey on the successful gamblers of Deauville. Lured by the fascination of a promised seance, Anna and then Sylvia become their victims.

The skills of casting for which Foss campaigned were recognised by *Kinematograph Weekly* in its production note on his *The Wonderful Year* (1921): 'A feature of the film is the unanimous satisfaction of all the artistes with their respective roles, thus complimenting the casting capability of this hustling producer.'[175] Clearly, skilled casting also involved creating enjoyable and therefore productive working relationships that provide some of the zest with which *The House of Peril* is enacted.

CODA: COMING HOME TO BRITISH CINEMA

Neither the effort to find stars nor recourse to non-actors proved capable of eliminating 'acting' as a force in the British cultural imaginary. For the kind of 'non-performance' associated with 'being' rather than acting is alien to a mode of perception that identifies persons by their social location and utilises differentiated performance styles drawing on socially defined cultural codes. One pleasure of acting, then, lies in newly recognising – and perhaps seeing challenged – such codes at work in the situations invented by film fiction. However, it is necessary to such pleasures that we recognise the performance of the codes *as* a performance. And this requires the maintenance of a gap between performer and role. A key mechanism for achieving this awareness, I have suggested, is the construction of protagonists who are themselves performers. But underpinning this strategy is the documentarist's perception that, like pictures in a print-shop window, any cultural practice is both constructed performance and social signifier. Thus much of British fictional practice works in quotation marks: the cultural forms of one social group circulating through media constructions and popular imagery function dialogically as quotations or documents drawn from a national cultural formation. For example, Violet Hopson's list of types an observant actress might find on the streets are familiar cultural constructions found in popular genre paintings, music-hall sketches and films:

> There is always some new character to be studied – the old man with the organ on the corner of the street, the flower girl with the buoyant spirits, the tiny girl who mothers five or six diminutive children, the old lady in the train who looks with disgust at the flapper and her male escort, the fussy old lady in the draper's shop who has handled every yard of lace and has still not decided which she will have, the expression of the poor assistant, as she wearily starts to replace the cards of lace – they are all absorbing types, with a special mission in life. Study them.[176]

The vein of humorous, knowing recognition that greets such types makes them precious, if largely safe, creations – creations that, nevertheless, carry a national trademark. Trade critics, journalists, audience members and writers of actor's handbooks take much satisfaction in pointing out the mistakes the Americans make when trying to construct English characters. For example, *Lloyds Weekly News* mocks an American film's placement of 'cuspidors' (spitoons) in an English drawing room, while allowing spats to be worn with evening dress is a frequently remarked upon howler.[177] Complaints about American slang littered through subtitles abound throughout the decade, becoming stronger as the prospect of the talkies came nearer. Thus a letter to *Film Weekly* complains of the American producer: 'he peoples the whole of Europe with Americans dressed up to look like the various natives but not to act like them . . . They cannot even imagine a country where American slang is not spoken. Oh for a picture that would screen us as we really are.' Significantly, the writer's conception of 'how we are' is based not on street observation but on literary types: 'There were not the likes of Captain MacHeath and Polly Peachum in their country, and they failed to see that it was possible for some other country to produce them.'[178]

THE ACCULTURATION OF RECOGNITION
This chapter, then, has suggested how the slow democratisation of British culture led to a search for

the recognition of audiences attuned to social division, generating a range of different, intermingling performance practices. British film-makers utilised a far more flexible and adaptable range of pictorial practices and gestural codes through which to tell their stories than historiographic accounts of the linear march to modernity allows. While underplaying supports the class confidence and easy authority of drawing-room or romantic characters, verisimilitude extended to wider social inclusion resolves into character acting, articulated through a socially coded gestural lexicon. In this context, the character actor provides differentiated and more colourful substance and vitality across a range of socially demarcated bodies, through signs of personal life elaborated in individual touches and eccentricities. In particular, character acting can move outside middle-class rectitude and reserve to realise representations of working-class and marginalised characters. If, on the one hand, character drawing continues the process of class identification and social mapping, on the other, the democratising direction of naturalism brings hitherto excluded vernacular codes into play. Thus a wider range of performances, gestures and tonalities become available for extended recognition, enlarging the number of social types that appear, and, perhaps, broadening the meaning of 'home'. In September 1927, E. Raven, under the title, 'Clogs and Shawls', waxes lyrical, despite enumerating its shortcomings, about Elvey's second version of *Hindle Wakes*:

> Not the greatest film ever made. Not an epoch in the history of screen development . . . But in spite of all this a great day for England. It might have had a thousand more faults and still it would have been for me, London born and bred as I am, a home-coming. *Hindle Wakes*, Stanley Houghton's story of the Lancashire cotton mills, at long last gave my own country to me, where I had given up hope of finding it – on the screen.
>
> It wasn't only the clogs and the shawls and the band playing 'The Lancashire Lass'. The whole tone of the thing made it inconceivable as the product of America or Germany or any country but our own.
>
> Something was due to Norman McKinnel as the self-made mill-owner. By a thousand shades of subtlety he was a Briton and a Northcountryman and no American Cotton King. Marie Ault, too, was a mother who had no connection with roses round the door, She was hard, but terribly and pathetically real.[179]

Thus the figures produced by skilled character actors are a delight to film critics and fans because so clearly distinguished, identifiable and bounded – by age, gender, ethnicity, nationality, and particularly by class. Character types and their actors provide appropriate figures to inhabit the socially demarcated stages created by the theatricalised *mise en scène* of British cinema. In providing the pleasure of recognition, they offer a democratising function and respond to an increasing demand for 'credibility' as against the emotional frisson of the restraint/passion scenario. Such character types, often produced in semi-comic mode, bring down to earth the high-flown because repressed emotional stances of the 'straight' or lead parts, enabling different verisimilar perspectives to coexist in the same fiction and producing a set of dialogic relations between types, modes of characterisation and performance styles. Home, then, is where we both recognise and are ourselves recognised. The acculturated bodily and gestural images of Lancashire cotton weavers and new-rich mill owners can equally perform this task, so long as sufficient gap is maintained to enable us to perceive the outlines of the type and the labour of performance as an articulation of identity:

> to see *Hindle Wakes* was to come back to the fireside and to friends with whom one could speak one's mind without fear or favour. I enjoyed myself thoroughly, and half hoped the American citizen continued at a loss. It was England for the English and too good to be shared.[180]

In the process of recognition rather than identification, the private spectator may finally encounter at the boundaries of social and cultural differences a sense of shared community that makes a nation a home.

PART TWO

CONJUNCTIONS

4 Directors' Picture Stories

Imagining film stories in terms of theatrical stages and pictures posed a challenge to a modernising film industry seeking the capacity for narrative fiction now established by Hollywood. In particular, pictorial framing and frontal shooting inhibited the scene dissection facilitated by analytic editing, on which depended the illusion of a seamless fictional world that was fast becoming the norm. However, out of the culturally conditioned mode of perception sketched in Part One, British film-makers developed a variety of strategies to handle the challenge of adapting theatrical staging and pictorial seeing to the needs of narrative cinema. In this chapter, then, I examine some of these pictorial-narrative solutions in the work of Cecil Hepworth, Maurice Elvey and Graham Cutts. I conclude with an analysis of *The Manxman* (1929), which suggests how, at the end of the decade, this pictorial-theatrical-narrative mode underpinned the work of an undisputed master of the cinematic – Alfred Hitchcock.

CECIL HEPWORTH: PICTORIAL POET OF BRITISH CINEMA

Hepworth is, as Rachael Low points out, unusual among early British film-makers in not having a theatrical background.[1] One of the early pioneers of filmic storytelling, he came to cinema via experience as magic-lanternist, photographer and some art training.[2] It is not, however, entirely accurate to dissociate Hepworth from the theatrical, for the lanternist, in order to build up a satisfying entertainment out of a heterogeneous collection of materials, needed both to think as a showman and be attuned to the responses of a live audience. Moreover, as Jon Burrows shows, it was the policy of the Hepworth Company in the teens to work with distinguished stage actors, adapting their plays to the screen.[3] However, as noted in Chapter 2, Hepworth's films were valued at the time for their 'beautiful screen pic-

tures'.[4] And Hepworth's retrospective valuation of his films stresses – in similar vein to the pictorial photographer, H. P. Robinson – his desire to produce aesthetic effect as beauty: 'Much of my success, I am sure, is in the aesthetic pleasure conveyed, but not recognised, by the beauty of the scene and generally mistaken for some unknown other quality in the film.'[5]

The magic lantern had a formative impact on Hepworth's capacity to combine pictorial sensibility, popular entertainment and film. In his autobiography he declares, 'A kinematograph projector is in essence nothing but an ordinary optical or magic lantern with a mechanism fitted in front in place of the slide carrier.' And he proceeds to describe how he bought his first 'experimental film-projector', adapting it so that he 'could at any moment change over in a second from lantern slides to "living pictures" or vice versa by merely sliding the platform across'.[6] The 'living pictures' referred to 'throw-outs' purchased from R. W. Paul's junk basket. In Hepworth's memory, his development of the dual projector enabled the various pieces of the 'mosaic' of his childhood to fall into place:

> Remember my early life: photography–limelight–lantern shows–lectures. The next step was obvious and inevitable. What more natural than that they should be grouped in a few short series having a 'story content', be fertilised by suitable films from the said junk basket, built up with lecture and music and taken all over the country.[7]

Hepworth registers the consequent tension between picture and narrative in an anecdote about his experimental use in the late 1890s of multiple projectors. One threw a 'brightly coloured proscenium' frame round a film projected by a second machine, combined with another to project a title beneath and a fourth ready to dissolve the next film fragment into the end of the first. This small aesthetic triumph, however, was put down by Alfred Moul, impresario of the Alhambra, who insisted that 'the only thing that really matters is the subject; that is the story'.[8] Although Hepworth professes always to have remembered this dictum, he later records advice given him in the teens by Pinero concerning 'preparation' in play-writing, the meaning of which he confesses he had not 'the faintest idea'.[9] At the same time he acknowledges his debt to his chief scriptwriter, Blanche MacIntosh, 'whose writing I scarcely ever altered', partly, perhaps, because he had little interest in narrative structure as opposed to pictorial situation and was happy to have others deal with the process of its construction.[10] Similarly, he leaves 'acting' to the actors, although he is strict about banning make-up in the belief that facial expression is not a matter of the eye but of minute movements in the 'tiny interstices in the skin around the eyes' – the detailed perception of the Pre-Raphaelite.[11] And, most controversially for later critics, Hepworth disclaims in distinctly pictorial terms any interest in viewing rushes, or in editing as a constructive process: 'Only the direst need will form an excuse for lifting an audience up by the scruff of its neck and carrying it round to the other side' – of the picture.[12]

While Andrew Higson's study of Comin' thro' the Rye (1923) suggests that Hepworth was quite capable of analytic editing when it suited him,[13] Hepworth defends his pictorial practices in the terms of the painter: 'When an artist starts to paint a picture he does not select a canvas twice the area he wants for the finished work.'[14] Pre-production is the time of pictorial organisation, involving 'a kind of misty mosaic for which I had to construct the various little pieces'.[15] Thus Hepworth's conception of film as 'living pictures', grouped serially to illustrate 'story content', emphasises the composite organisation of the painter's canvas or illustrator's plates rather than the linear development of a narrative trajectory. Through the process of 'cutting out and rearranging the pieces . . . and forcing myself to visualise every little scene as it would appear on the screen',[16] Hepworth creates 'an imaginary picture'.[17] Perhaps there is more to link Hepworth and Hitchcock than seems at first likely, Hepworth's conception of the entire film as a 'mosaic', made up of finely balanced pictorial fragments, suggesting a kaleidoscopic compositional approach close to montage.

THE PASTORAL CONTEXT

Hepworth's pictorial concept of beauty is also bound up with pastoralism. The 'pastoral imaginary' has a long history in British culture. While stereotypical images such as 'sheep' and 'running water' make easy targets for knowing satire both at the time and since,[18] at its most productive the pastoral represents a cultural and aesthetic site of negotiation between transformational economic forces, shifting mental frameworks and reconfiguring desires.[19] Its ambivalent position between regressive and conservationist values is often acknowledged through overt fantasy and self-conscious nostalgia.

The establishment of the National Trust (1895) and the Society for Checking the Abuses of Public Advertising (SCAPA) figure in recent 'heritage' critiques as exemplars of middle-class values serving commodification.[20] But at the beginning of the 21st century it is possible to take a longer view. The English country house filled with 'heritage properties' and the landscape protected as a source of pastoral or picturesque middlebrow aesthetic experience of the kind advocated by The Picturegoer participate in the democratisation of 'art' and 'culture' (see Chapter 2).[21] If middle-class inspired, the interest in cultural heritage spread its net very wide. It was supported by Victorian antiquarianism, worldwide travel and the rise of anthropology, paralleled at home by the work of the documentarists and major photo-journalist projects investigating urban and dying rural cultures. It embraced a renewed interest in folklore, fairy tales, folk song, country dancing and harlequinade (see Chapter 5), alongside movements to preserve historic buildings and landscapes, and the foundation of national museums and art galleries. This heterogeneous mix of ideas, values and practices underpins the persistence of pastoralism into twentieth-century mass-produced art, facilitated by the advent of the railway, the motorcar, photography and the illustrated press. Pastoral and 'heritage' imagery served commercial enterprises – including the growth of advertising – aimed at high-paying middle-class consumers as well as the cultural embourgeoisement of the respectable working and lower middle classes.[22] But cinema itself is a part of this rising commodity culture. It is hardly consistent to point to British cinema's failings to achieve American standards of capitalist-financed, mass-produced film entertainment, while at the same time rejecting its engagement with a key area of native cultural production. As Andrew Higson points out, recourse to English landscape and historical sites was a major way of distinguishing British from American film-making.[23]

Pictorialism and the pastoral feed each other. For newly urbanised markets arising on the back of industrialisation, the pastoral narrative generated new affects and meanings. The potential for rapid rise and fall and dramatic reversals of fortune made the relation of past and present one of acute disjuncture. As Martin Meisel argues, narrative caught in a picture – in which geography clashes with biography and significance arises from the future consequences of past actions – turns the imagination back to a prelapsarian age. There, before the crisis or expulsion into the 'real' world, time stands still. In narrative paintings, Meisel suggests, the future is bleak, and, while the imagination is caught in awe of what will happen, it is also invited to retrospection, to the memory of how things were, rooted pictorially *in place*. The temporal dimension of the narrative picture 'makes the most immediate action recollection while the presence of a narrative voice is to turn recollection into reportage' – equally a form of rooting through articulation.[24] If the narrative picture both dramatises and offers some measure of control over the juxtaposition of past, present and future, photography intensifies the picture's temporal burden. As past and future meet in the located present of the photograph – its here and now – its pictorial composition provides both evidence of and a bulwark against personal, social and cultural change.

This materialisation of memory and the past informs the opposition of city and country. The identification of the country with a time of innocence, stability, childhood, and feminised moral values now largely foregone, made the combination of pictorialism and pastoralism a potent source of pathos that poses what we know now against what we didn't know then, evoking the ambivalences of nostalgia. Moreover, the very fact that rural ways of life, in contact with landscape, and the cyclical rhythms of the seasons are beyond modern, largely urban experience makes the pastoral even more available to imagination, retrospection, recuperation. 'Home', in industrial and urban societies, is no longer the site of daily endeavour (except for an enforced female labour force maintaining its myth), but the place we set out from and hope to come back to. Thus the pastoral, in

its evocation of a place of origin, offers potent images of a return, combining the personal and social. This use of the pastoral was particularly prevalent in the aftermath of the Great War, which revealed starkly the destructive forces of capital combined with the machine.[25] However, the countryside represents not only nostalgia for what is lost. As its agricultural productivity declines, it becomes a site of fantasy in which desires are reformed, for retreat but also for self-discovery and re-energising connection with different rhythms. I will explore this dimension of the pastoral in the following discussion of Hepworth's pictorial approach to film-making in two films of the 1920s: *Tansy* (1921) and *Pipes of Pan* (1923).

Pastoral Moves: *Tansy*

In Hepworth the pictorial and pastoral intertwine, but neither as simple decoration nor as pure nostalgia. As argued of *Tansy* in Chapter 2, if pictorial cinema shares with photography the power of the picture to halt and locate time, its theatricalisation utilises the dynamic of the tableau, which throws the figures of the arrested moment into life. Hepworth's frontal camera and pictorial framing, while inhibiting immersion in the three-dimensional space of a narrativised world, fosters our relationship with a picture, which is rarely encountered in isolation and exists as a kind of public statement. In film, 'living' pictures means 'moving' figures, and frames that are composed, as it were, by the shake of the kaleidoscope that scatters the figures, breaking and reconfiguring pictorial patterns. While shots may be 'framed' by an opening and closing fade, and the spectator may be positioned behind or to the side of the frontal camera, Hepworth puts no constraint on actors moving to the camera, entering or exiting in a virtual brush with its lens, or from left and right bottom corners of the frame. This continual breaking of the frame by figure or animal movement and the attention-seeking fades function as rhetorical picture presentation. The spectator is thus distanced and at the same time continually made present, evoked as a spectator. Hence the pleasure often noted by sympathetic reviewers in the gaze at the picture. Gazing is an act of exploration, an encounter with re-articulated signifiers, inviting cultural readings.[26] Thus *Tansy*, adapted by George Dewhurst from a story by Tickner Edwards, effectively illustrates its story, organised in a pattern of tableaux constructed for aesthetic effects and emotional significance and anchored by captions, through which the narrative is moved from one stage to the next. In these 'moving pictures', familiar figures and situations form a mosaic that resonates with signs of a disappearing past and presages, both negative and positive, of change. The socio-cultural movements caught in these shifting pictures emerge in dialogue titles as emotional undercurrents, anxieties and desires.[27]

A prologue to the story sets out its pictorial-narrative co-ordinates. The opening credits are superimposed over a skyline shot silhouetting a horse-drawn plough. A title situates the next picture: 'On the gentle slopes of Devon an old shepherd passes his days.' A high-angle shot follows of sheep streaming up the hillside past the camera, which, turning to track them, draws past the viewer a moving panoramic landscape. A second caption introduces Tansy as a figure of continuity with passing tradition: 'His grand-daughter inherited his firm and loving control of the flock.' As Tansy jumps up, surveying the downs, a tracking camera identifies her with the movement of sheep across the landscape. If her grandfather represents the rural past, industrialised modernity intrudes in the next sequence with the appearance of Clem (Gerald Ames), the itinerant harvester, clothed in shiny leather cap and boiler suit, who travels with the threshing machine from farm to farm. Cross-cutting between Clem's leap over a farm gate and Tansy's approach, tracked through the corn, effects their encounter. Meanwhile, the farmer waiting by the threshing machine and checking his watch opposes the picture of rural dalliance made by Clem and Tansy as they walk hand in hand down a tree-lined lane towards the camera to pose at a gate – a key prop for rural seduction.

A title introduces a third co-ordinate – the all-male Wilverley household who have worked Fairmile Farm 'from way back', consisting of a widowed father and two brothers, the elder, Joad (James Carew), also widowed. A familiar graveyard picture finds Joad 'embittered by memory of the loss of his wife', brooding over her grave. Humorous rural portraits familiarly associated with village life complete the rural mosaic: women energetically pulling on bell ropes; the vicar out fishing; Joad and his younger brother, Will, meeting at the field stile. While the Wilverleys search their district for a new shepherd,

the farmer uses Tansy's escapade with Clem as an excuse to evict her along with her grandfather from their tithe cottage. Thus an encounter with Joad on the road to Goldringham in search of new work brings Tansy and her now dying grandfather to Fairmile Farm, where she becomes the object of rivalry between the two brothers.

Within this mosaic, Tansy offers a symbolic figure on the cusp of change, working within shifting social systems, in whom past and future values meet and whose 'placement' is crucial to the revitalisation of social values.[28] On one level, Tansy refigures melodrama's 'sign of virtue', her instinctive innocence making her unable to anticipate Clem's trap but vigorously resistant once it is sprung.[29] On another, as *The Bioscope* reviewer notes, Tansy presents 'a very up-to-date shepherdess'.[30] The images of Tansy/Alma Taylor working with her dog rounding up the sheep, pitch-forking hay, guiding sheep through dipping-troughs and striding through the landscape must have recalled for the film's audiences documentary photographs of land girls working the farms, challenging illusions of feminine fragility during the First World War.[31] This resonance is strengthened by the dysfunctional Wilverley family with its variously 'wounded men', of whom only the youngest, Will, shows any signs, with the coming of Tansy, of liveliness.

As a symbolic figure, then, Tansy mediates between past and future, caught between two articulations of lived time. The cyclical time of rural life (imaged in dalliance at the trysting gate, the routines of village life and the seasonal tasks of the farm) registers the rhythms of the body and the seasons. It opposes the encroaching experience of linear time, running to the rules of capitalist production imaged in the clock-watching farmer, who evicts Tansy as a troublemaker, and in Clem, the uprooted itinerant servant of the threshing machine and unscrupulous sexual exploiter. Tansy, like Thomas Hardy's Tess, is a living, moving woman in a landscape fraught with the struggles of a patriarchal society in the throes of modernisation and threatened with moribund stasis. This is not to suggest the feminism of either Hardy or Hepworth, but the vitality of the symbolic figure represented by woman who has investment neither in a fossilised past nor the mechanised future.

It is through her relationship with her dead grandfather that the past is both let go and rediscovered.[32] Thus overhearing the Wilverleys lament their lack of a shepherd, Tansy declares: 'Give the flock to me and old Airybella here and you'll ne'er rue it.' Joad is scornful: 'A woman for a shepherd and a woman-critter for a dog!' There follows Tansy's long, lyrical and unedited sheep roundup, a noted cinematic tour de force by cameraman, Geoffrey Faithful.[33] A collage of moments in the farming annals follows that records the impact on the brothers of images of Tansy walking among the sheep, pitchforking hay, handling lambs. Again Tansy is caught between two temporal zones represented by a constraining domestic tableau and exterior free-ranging movement. The widower, Joad, sits at the table, tapping his boot with his crop, expressing menacing male power. With a grim little smile he announces to the consternation of his father and perceptive retainer, Robert, his decision to wed Tansy, without as yet having asked her and apparently unaware of her growing attachment to Will. The scene cuts from the claustrophobic inertia of the domestic interior to a shot of sheep streaming uphill, Tansy and Will following. The pastoral domain embodies freely flowing momentum, filling out rather than fragmenting the experience of time, integrating the temporal into the spatial.

It is within this flow of pastoral imagery, which documents as it pictorialises the sheep-rearing calendar, that later Tansy effectively courts Will. Out on the Downs and at the sheep-dipping troughs, she moves seductively in and out of shot, breaking the frame and inducing frequently off-balance compositions. With Will she guides the sheep through the dips, lightly touching him as he works, unaware of the brooding Joad, watching, a disconsolate figure of dangerous emotions. He turns away from them – a movement repeated through a quick fade down and up – sharply completing the turn, mouth open, brows knit, arms flung wide. This conflict between the stasis of a patriarchal order – represented in different ways by Joad and by Clem – and the regenerative contact with the freely flowing energy of the pastoral promised by Tansy comes to a head in the scene of climactic fraternal confrontation already discussed in Chapter 2. Tansy's worth and the nature of the fraternal conflict now acknowledged, the film concludes with the familiar coda of melodrama. What has at last been recognised is again almost lost as Will rushes into the landscape to rescue her from the clutches of Clem. He reunites with Tansy in a back-lit, hilltop silhouette, dappled by sun shining through leaves.

Hepworth's pictorialism, then, emphasises the aesthetic and emotional effects of situation – what is happening in the shifting composition, when events hang in delicate balance or are brought to a climactic head – rather than in the way one thing leads logically to another. Notoriously, he preferred the fade out and back again between shots as a solution to sequencing images composed for the sake of their pictorial effect and hence likely to be of different-scale or organised within different sized vignettes. And it is the lanternist's voice or illustrator's caption that realises the narrative thread in picture-titles: 'And so, Tansy came to Fairmile Farm'; 'Another day and still Joad has not put his fortune to the test'; 'It was not until Sheep Washing time that the two brothers realised what was between them'. However, if Hepworth's focus was the picture, nevertheless he could handle pictures through which figures move. And in responding to the aesthetic and cultural values of popular, middlebrow pictures, he took a showman's pleasure in reconfiguring 'found' images and cultural signifiers in kaleidoscopic mosaics, dynamised by the tensions of conflicting values.

PICTURE STORIES: *PIPES OF PAN*

Hepworth's approach to picture-making as the construction of a mosaic or collage has a number of effects. As 'found' material, the picture becomes effectively a document, capable of self-conscious cultural reference. Of *Tansy*, for example, *The Bioscope* commented: 'The sheep which figure so prominently in the story provide many beautiful pictures. Incidentally the life of a shepherd is illustrated very fully.'[34] As collage, the mosaic brings different emotional effects into juxtaposition. Thus the pressbook for *The Pipes of Pan* promises 'a story of sweet dreams and bitter realities . . . a strange mosaic . . . of pathos, comedy and beauty'. The result, according to *The Bioscope*, is an 'attractive blend of beautiful screen pictures with robust humour and conventional sentiment'.[35] This piquant mixture of contraries opens up the ambivalences at the heart of the pastoral imagination, negotiating in both *Tansy* and *Pipes of Pan* loss and rejuvenation.

In the process of pictorial and emotional collage, *Pipes of Pan* – like the earlier *Alf's Button*

(1920) – generates a discursive critique. For the film is structured as a series of quoted pictures and stories, much like a Victorian scrapbook or, nearer to Hepworth's practice, a magic-lantern show. Thus the credit sequence appears superimposed on the turning pages of a photograph album, revealing a picture of a sylvan scene of silver birches encircling a pond. The album – a record of collected images – renders the pastoral as culture. A narrator's title – 'Down a little Surrey Lane one morning an old Tinker, Miles Bunning, was mending his pots and pans' – introduces a rural itinerant, plying his fast dying trade. A medium shot centres the tinker, his cart and horse behind him, the road curving off to the left, while the picture-making camera pans to the right, to include his daughter, Polly (Alma Taylor), intently polishing a pan, against a background of minutely defined willow herb. As in *Tansy*, it is the daughter who represents continuity, the title highlighting her pride in 'the Metal Polish her father has invented'. A slow pan to the left pauses on Polly's father, pipe in mouth, smiling indulgently, and then swings on to reveal a young urban tourist, backlit, leaning on his bike, watching them. Realising he's been spotted, 'Cyril Farman . . . suddenly develops artistic tendencies', hastily parking his bike and pulling out his camera. Miles's scowl softens, as looking at his daughter he sees the picture Cyril wants to take. While Cyril sets up his camera, Miles brings out her hat, to be waved away by the young man, a joke recalling H. P. Robinson's complaints against country folk who, not understanding his rustic aesthetic, insisted on turning out in their Sunday best for his pastoral photographs.[36] Cyril snaps Polly gazing at her reflection in the burnished pan (Fig. 4.1).

The next episode introduces the source of the story, devised by George Dewhurst from 'a pretty fanciful little picture or picture postcard which was popular in the shops at the time'.[37] Following the postcard's title, 'The Piper of Dreams', a medium shot opens on a woodland scene, echoing the credit image. A small child enters carrying a pipe and sits on a mossy mound. He pulls out a scroll depicting in an oval frame an elfin figure, topped with a peacock-feathered hat, playing a pipe in a similar sylvan setting. So we have a partial 'realisation' of a popular picture that incorporates the reproduced 'original' in its re-enactment. Both photographic copy and the filmic realisation are reproduced

Fig. 4.1. Cyril's picture of Polly, which becomes an advertising gimmick for 'Bunning's Metal Polish' (*The Pipes of Pan*, 1923)

in sharp pictorial detail, picking out the art-nouveau tracery of ferns and entangled roots among which picture-postcard and filmic children sit. Polly is drawn to the scene, where the child, showing her his scroll, explains that he too is attempting to pipe up the fairies that in the picture fly bird-like around the piper's hat. At the wave of Polly's hand, numerous fairies appear skimming, like *Les Sylphides*, across the pond's surface – a sequence of which Hepworth was technically very proud.[38] Both picture postcard and this sequence tap into the popularity of Victorian fairy painting, which had inspired romantic ballets and survived in children's illustrated fiction. Fairy lore had recently revived with the publicity surrounding the Cottingley fairies, supposedly photographed by two children and enthusiastically publicised by Conan Doyle in *The Coming of the Fairies*, published in 1922.[39]

Lionel Lambourne and Christopher Wood both suggest the rich and ambivalent significance of the fairy, transformed in later decades into the extraterrestial being of science fiction. On one level, Lambourne suggests, fairy fantasy aestheticises the effects made available by the microscope and the camera, delighting in 'obsessive detail'.[40] On another, as

Wood argues, fairy painting provided 'a fantasy world for forbidden subjects; sex, nudity, violence, dreams, nightmares', all under cover of the 'respectable aura of art'.[41] Both impulses cross over into pastoral via the child, whose link with Arcadia and Pan legitimates access to a fantasy world combining covert sexuality and innocence which could be taken variously towards the fey or nightmare. I shall return to the role of the child in 1920s storytelling in Chapter 6. Here, his significance lies in Tinkerbell's question: 'Do You Believe in Fairies?' The film's pressbook comments hopefully, 'There is much in this mundane world that is evil, particularly for those who are looking for evil. But there is much more that is beautiful for those with eyes to see it.' The link between the eyes of the child and classical myth returns the pastoral to an earlier domain where nature is deified, alive with spirits, acknowledging the connectedness of the human body to the earth. It is the power of the child's belief that confirms the possibility of fulfilling adult desire to realise this connection anew.[42]

However, in attempting to realise the imaginary, the child needs the support of the pastoral maiden, for he is burdened by a disbelieving father. In the sequence that (in the truncated NFTVA print) follows, we find another wounded man, Anthony Helme, who 'when his young wife died at the commencement of his career . . . lost all interest in his work'. He now arrives with picnic basket and kettle to entertain the fairy his son has found in the woods. The whimsical nostalgia of this sentiment is countered by the robust burlesque of the following scenes, beginning with the introduction of Cyril's father, Irwin Farman, 'The Managing Director of Universal World Wide Enterprises'. His secretary, James Flaxman, Dickensian with stiff wing collar and crabbed gestures, peers over his glasses into the camera before joining his boss to hear of Cyril's idea for a much needed advertising 'stunt'. This involves Cyril's photograph of Polly, gazing into her polished pan, woman and product melded in an advertising gimmick. 'Why, Sir, it's a great idea! With a new metal polish to exploit we can get fresh capital and make a good thing out of Miles Bunning.'

Making 'a good thing out of Miles Bunning' becomes the object of two 'quoted' pictures that follow. Captioned by the satirical title, 'The Result of a Chance Photograph in a Surrey Lane', a shot of a poster bearing the words BUNNINGS METAL POLISH is

superimposed over trees. Miles leans cross-legged against a pedestal topped by a gleaming bottle, rakishly smoking a cigar and sporting huge hoof-like shoes – a bacchanalian image contrasted to the fairy ballet summoned by his daughter. This cartoon-like image fades to the Farman premises where a contract is signed, and Miles excitedly anticipates 'turkey and jam roll' for tea. From this we flip to the next picture, captioned with SCAPA-conscious irony, 'Sweet Are the Uses of Advertising'. Miles, sat on the arm of his caravan trailer, calls Polly to view the news story now woven out of her photograph, headlined: 'Romance of the Roadside: Chance Discovery of Wonderful New Metal Polish: Travelling Tinker's Invention'. But Polly is distracted as she catches a sound from the woods, followed by an image of the child piping, while a narrator's title intones: 'Her first Intimation that when you climb, someone must be left behind.'

After a restrained, pathos-filled leave-taking, in which the child's father predicts that the Pipes of Pan will call her back, Polly, Miles and an uproarious Aunty Maggie arrive at the Farman premises. There they cavort through a series of comic turns engineered out of a clash of class manners and expectations, largely directed at nouveau-riche snobbery and inauthenticity – including a burlesque courtship in which Aunty Maggie pursues James Flaxman. This combination, played with the taboo-breaking delight that made *Alf's Button* and George Pearson's Squibs series so popular, is here rendered bitter-sweet in Alma Taylor's performance, much admired by P. L. Mannock for its 'nervous perplexity and social gaucherie'.[43] Although Miles gradually gets the feeling 'we was in the way in there', he is willing to contemplate an engagement between Polly and Cyril, which cues her flashback to the child in the woods. However, Polly's potentially fairy-tale rise is interrupted by the news that Aunty Maggie has absconded with James Flaxman. A switch to the woods finds Anthony Helme telling a fairy story to his son, who asks, 'Didn't the Princess ever come back to the Pedlar?' His father replies, 'The old witch, "Pride", kept them apart.' The tale is continued in a sequence of pantomime or magic-lantern-like images. With the castle as background, the pedlar moves along the front of the frame, craning to look over its walls, while a bent old crone pursues him from behind. A dissolve brings in the Princess at her window and the story of thwarted desire is enacted in dumb show, concluding in a close-up of the father clutching his child while dialogue titles articulate the problem of belief. In real fairy tales, the child says, they always live happily ever after. 'That wasn't a fairy tale', replies the father, and desperately hugs his son.

But, as it turns out, a comic fairy tale is all that the putative upward mobility of Miles Bunning and his daughter can realise. Aunty Maggie has not only eloped with James Flaxman but the latter has defrauded the company of its capital. By this time, however, both Miles and Polly are thoroughly disillusioned with the Farmans. Polly is allowed a dignified riposte to Cyril's clumsy attempts to end their engagement: 'You think the game has gone far enough. I am afraid I was tired of it when it began,' while Miles in his anger tears up the poster advertising his polish. Laughing at the impending fate of James Flaxman at the hands of Aunty Maggie, her father forewarns Polly: 'I suppose you know, Polly, this'll be the finish of us?' – to which she replies: 'Isn't it really the beginning of us?' Together they sneak out of the house to their caravan and the woods. According to the reviews, it is the child's death (in an ending missing from the NFTVA print) that brings Polly and the widower together again, something they found unnecessarily troubling. However, in terms of the trope of the piping child – who recalls a lost past as source of originary happiness and magically facilitates belief – his disappearance once his work is done is quite appropriate.

The infusion of pastoralism into 1920s British films created a space for the exploration of shifting values as the past is slowly and uncomfortably reconstituted. If industrialisation and urban development in the grip of capitalist expansion represents an aggressive, acquisitive future, it is in the countryside, with all the mixed values it represents, that the future is brought to a certain account. At the same time, the past must loosen its grip in an accommodation to change – the child dies, the widower must overcome his mourning. The powerfully resonant images collaged together here – as also in *Alf's Button* – are drawn from the popular circulation of pictures, magic-lantern stories and music-hall turns. Hepworth's mosaic mixes Dickensian caricature and picturesque figures of pastoral fantasy in a mutual critique of what urbanising, industrial society lacks, thereby easing the uncertainties and losses of change and 'progress'.

MAURICE ELVEY AND PICTORIAL NARRATION

In 1927 a rather sad little exchange takes place when *The Bioscope* replies to a complaint by Cecil Hepworth in the *Daily Mail* against the uptake of new, younger film-makers at the expense of an older, experienced generation. The writer points out that whereas ' "Experience" proved unable to provide a remedy' for one of the 'gravest slumps' in British cinema's history, 'the rehabilitation of the British film has been due, fundamentally, to new *methods* rather than to new *men*' (my emphasis).[44] The director named as exemplary is Maurice Elvey, whose remarkable film-making career spanned four decades from 1913 to 1957, claiming credit for over 300 titles. And yet in this period Elvey's films were no less pictorial than Hepworth's. The differences in their approach and practices is therefore instructive, particularly since Elvey was successful in reconciling a cinema of pictures to the needs of storytelling in a manner capable of competing with the American standard. In this respect, it is also notable that Elvey escaped the 1924 slump by signing a three-year contract with Fox to make films in Hollywood, but returned early, seemingly unable to accommodate either to Hollywood's studio methods or to its culturally determined narrational mode.

Unlike Hepworth, Elvey's pictorialism was born of the theatre and, rather than 'beauteous pictures to gaze on', his reviewers emphasise his production of 'staged pictures', which excel in terms of their picturesque mounting, with detailed interiors and furnishings, atmospheric exteriors and control of lighting, figure grouping and crowd management.[45] Equally noted is his skill in casting, discovering screen types with current appeal and encouraging subsequent stars.[46] As opposed to Hepworth's lack of interest in actor direction, Elvey speaks repeatedly of the importance of theatrical training for the film performer. He advocates collective, actor-led ensemble work over the producer-dominated system now emerging in the theatre, and, he implies, over the compartmentalised division of labour required by Hollywood.[47] Studio profiles and interviews make clear that his professionalism and energetic leadership of the ensemble extended to careful choice of and involvement by skilled cameramen (e.g. John Cox, Paul and Germain Burger), scenarists (e.g. Eliot Stannard) and editors (e.g. Alma Reville).[48]

Elvey did not, like Hepworth, grow up in an art-orientated, intellectual family context. Reputedly unhappy at home, he left at the earliest opportunity for London's theatreland, eventually joining Fred Terry and Julia Nielson's company, with whom he toured between 1908 and 1911. During this period, as well as founding the Adelphi Play Society (see Chapter 1), he also joined the Fabian Society, writing political articles, and developing a love of music, opera and ballet.[49] According to Elvey, the film that converted him to cinema while in New York was a four-minute version of *The Flying Dutchman*. The sight of 'a *real* ocean with a *ghost* ship' promised the possibility of reconciling costume romance and contemporary realism, populist appeal and experiment (my emphasis).[50] The late teens and 1920s provided a fertile context in which Elvey moved from filming realisations of famous paintings (see Chapter 2) to the pictorial elaboration of the screen biography. This included *Florence Nightingale* (1915), *Nelson* (1918) and, most ambitiously (and, as it turned out, problematically), the contemporary *The Life Story of David Lloyd George* (1918), which was mysteriously suppressed and never screened until recently rediscovered and restored.[51] Shortly afterwards Elvey became chief director for Stoll, for whom he undertook an ambitious programme of literary adaptation, to which I will return in Chapter 6. Elvey thus differs from Hepworth in his conception of filmmaking in his regard first for acting and second for story. Arguably, these concerns contributed to a third differentiating feature, an emphasis on editing that underpinned his accommodation to the changed cinematic environment of the mid-1920s, when Hollywood had consolidated its grip over British screens.

In Elvey's commercial success, however, lay his subsequent critical downfall, for he shamelessly mixed what the filmic intelligentsia sought to keep separate – the artistic and experimental with the commercially popular – colonising the cultural no man's land of the middlebrow. His interviews and articles express a characteristic ambivalence about art and culture: 'Around the late twenties films improved enormously. They became, to use a horrible expression, an "art form".'[52] When John Sharp in a radio interview asks if Hollywood's lack of 'culture' drove him back to England, he replies, 'Well, it's a horrible word, but that is true really.'[53] At the same time, Elvey remained committed to a populist conception

of the audience, answering a 1927 *Picturegoer* questionnaire with the comment: 'nor must we forget that we are, in the end, the servants of the public, and that we must provide first-class entertainment or cease to exist'.[54] To address this public, Elvey employed a range of culturally differentiated materials, motifs and practices, drawing on a notion of Englishness as a storehouse of histories, landscapes, pictures, class types, actors, stories, documents and landmarks. Thus he describes to Denis Gifford how in *The Great Gold Robbery* (1913) the 'great detective' dived off Westminster Bridge to waylay robbers absconding with a cargo of gold. This 'enabled you to have the Houses of Parliament in the background . . . if you could get a landmark in this was a great selling-point'.[55] Such a combination of document, picture and drama, deriving from the long-standing practice of nineteenth-century sensation scenes, is used again in *The Sign of the Four* (1923), which involves pursuits through London streets and down the Thames in shots featuring familiar city sights. In a similar vein, Elvey's touring experience with the Terry/Nielson company developed his feeling for romantic nuances. In 1923 he tells a *Motion Picture Studio* interviewer, 'I have a firm faith in the public appeal of real history, which has, as a rule, a definite romantic value besides.'[56] Reviewers noted the mixed-class appeals of such heterogeneous practices. Thus, *The Bioscope*, reviewing *Don Quixote* (1923), declares that, in combining the pictorial effects of the Andalusian mountains – which bestow 'a romantic interest to the figures of the knight and his humble squire' – with the comic turns of the popular George Robey, 'Mr Elvey has catered for every possible taste'.[57] Elvey, then, constructs his films out of an eclectic amalgam of different class-inflected aesthetic practices and materials – including melodrama and documentary, history and romance, artistic pictorial effects and narrative suspense, restrained acting, sincere characterisation, authentic Englishness and 'well produced . . . punch'.[58] Arguably, in pioneering the historical biographical film Elvey found a way of reconciling the American heroic trajectory to a geographically class-located history.

The pictorialism of the romantic stage and theatrical use of popular painting supported the 'picturesque effects' for which Elvey's films were so often praised. In his early films Elvey displayed a fondness for different-shaped frames, the pictorialising effect of

which is more marked and fragmentary because frequently lacking the fade used by Hepworth to smooth
transitions between shots. Noting that many photographers gravitated into cinema, Elvey claims that he
was taught film-making techniques by the photographer, Charlie Raymond.[59] However, photographic
pictures are interchanged with staged pictures,
emphasising deep staging for narrative action. Unlike
Hepworth's practice, Elvey's actors rarely cross the
frame in a near brush with the viewer that emphasises
the arbitrary, two-dimensional nature of the picture
frame. Moreover, he doesn't confine his camera to
frontal shooting. Thus, in the absence of fades, and in
his heavy use of the vignette, Elvey's pictures are both
more clearly 'cut' out from their diegetic canvas while
moving towards the status of filmic shots. In Elvey's
early films, then, collage is the means of linking pictures. In the process he develops a technique capable
of shifting from the narrative pictures of the decade's
early years to a form of adapted pictorial narration in
the latter half of the 1920s that was dependent on
editing for its effects. In the following analyses of sections from three of his films – *Comradeship* (1919),
Mademoiselle d'Armentières (1926) and *High Treason*
(1929) – I explore the nature of Elvey's pictorialism
and the system of montage that he developed to rec-
oncile the picture to storytelling.

HEART-READING PICTURES: *COMRADESHIP*

Henry Edwards, addressing the problem of wresting
narrative progression from shots conceived as pictures, writes in 1920 of 'the difficulties that confront
the scenario writer when he sets out to tell a story in
the language of actions, which the heart must read
from pictures on the screen'.[60] *Comradeship*, among
the first films to deal with the Great War, is exemplary in its management of pictures for the complex-
ities of 'heart-reading'. This is not only a matter of
audience reading but, crucial to Elvey's method of
pictorial storytelling, of the interaction between characters who must learn, with the help of pictorial gesture and iconography, to read each other. The film
weaves a cross-class love story together with a tale of
cross-class comradeship born of the trenches, contex-
tualised by competing images of opposing national
identities and political values. It opens with pictorial
credits announcing the themes of Love and War. The
first picture is of Lily Elsie as Betty Mortimer, framed
in a heart-shaped mask, within which her tripled

reflection is centred in a white-rimmed oval mirror,
flanked by two side mirrors. With her back to us, she
adjusts her hair under a nurse's cap – the sign of shifting class as well as female identity. Following a title
relaying a quotation from the King expressing his
hope that 'the splendid spirit of comradeship on the
battle field will be kept alive in peace', a second warns
of the dangers of political agitation, 'even in peaceful
England'. Such warnings give way to a prewar image
of a picturesque row of cottages that dissolves into the
deserted high street of the small rural town of Melcombe, disturbed only by one pedestrian and a dog.
Emblematic shots establish the orphaned hero, John
Armstrong (Gerald Ames), 'proprietor of Melcombe's
most flourishing trading concern' (a drapery business), who has taken up his now deceased guardian
uncle's zealous politics, making public speeches in
favour of rational-scientific social and economic policies. A soft-edged circular mask reveals an idealistic
young man with dark curly hair and moustache – not
unlike Elvey's own photographic portrait that he used
to accompany his directorial credit (Fig. 4.2).[61]

Armstrong's drapery store, where we meet
German cutter, Otto Liebman, and counter assistant,

Fig. 4.2. Elvey the intellectual in a portrait he used to introduce his
films, a 'foible' forgiven by *Kinematograph Weekly*

Peggy Matthews, is juxtaposed in the next sequence with Fanshawe Hall, a picturesque country mansion framed within an iris shot and surrounding trees. An orange-tinted, rectangular shot of a stage-set-like sitting room follows, in which Betty's uncle is posed before the fireplace with his newspaper. A title, 'Rumours of War', and a date – 'Saturday pm, August 1st, 1914' – begin the countdown. Following brown-tinted shots of a rowdy public meeting where John argues against war with Germany, a blue-tinted sequence opens with Otto and Peggy posed in silhouette on a wooded hillside, framed by tree trunks. While she tweaks his coat collar, Otto looks severely into the distance over her shoulder, intimating to the audience a more final parting than she anticipates. A close-up of her uplifted face, looking questioningly into his and framed by luxuriantly Pre-Raphaelite hair bursting from under her straw boater, is balanced by his profile, ominously shadowed by his large black hat, cut in half by the left frame.

This private moment is interrupted by a return to the sitting room at Fanshawe Hall, where Betty's cousin, Lieutenant Baring (Guy Newall), points to his newspaper, reinforcing a discourse of war that counters Peggy's attempts to read Otto's conciliatory gestures as signs of a normal holiday parting. A return to the lovers discloses a farewell picture. Framed by tree trunks, Peggy now stands, her back to us, centre foreground, while Otto canters downhill, turning at mid-frame to wave light-heartedly up to her. Tentatively, she raises her hand in reply, then turns to us, hand to her mouth, pondering his meaning. A dissolve takes the picture into a big close-up for the full impact of emotion, her hand pressed over her mouth, her eyes large, staring off screen right. At this point we leave Peggy's story for a parallel tale of blocked perception and impending enlightenment, as John Armstrong is 'called to Fanshawe Hall'. Boxed within a wavy-edged oblong frame producing a widescreen effect, the sitting room is now explicitly constructed as a public arena, into which Baring brings John to join his uncle. However, with the entry of Betty, another thread is interwoven. The medium shots that show her observing while she moves towards their space – 'A woman's instinct attracted by his masterful intellect in spite of their difference socially' – contrast to the widescreen frame reserved for male debate about the imminence of war. At last Betty, breaks into their frame and their

lively argument. In the next mid-shot, John is kneeling on the sofa, leaning into her space. Each rests a hand on the sofa back, eyes meeting, at which point she speaks: 'If war comes, we shall convert Fanshawe into a hospital and wish to ask you to subscribe.' He draws back, questioning the likelihood of war. But the moment of implied recognition between man and woman is held across two interpolated shots of the Colonel, pacing up and down and waving his newspaper, asking indignantly, 'Good sir – would you leave our women folk to the mercy of the invading enemy?' This piece of caricaturish business is juxtaposed with shots of Betty and John in suspended animation, while a personal dimension to the politics of war sinks in: 'AND HIS THEORIES SEEMED FUTILE: he had not thought of harm to her.'

Elvey has now established a pictorial iconography and method of juxtaposition that creates an emotional switchback from picture to picture, supporting character and narrative development. Otto Liebman's treachery is confirmed for the audience by brief shots as he boards a German gunboat, to be immediately followed by the illustrative title, 'All Alone', and a low-angle long shot of Peggy's figure, walking in silhouette against the same tree-lined skyline where she bade him farewell. Marrying together popular images of deserted girlhood with those of ravaged English womanhood familiar from war propaganda, she leans with arms stretched horizontally against a tree trunk, her body swaying. Then, turning, she throws her arms to heaven and collapses. Back at work, Peggy nervously informs her employer, 'Liebman has not turned up this morning.' Peering over Armstrong's shoulder, she reads the note he has left: 'When you open this I shall be in my own country. I intend returning to Melcombe as your master.' A number of big close-ups, sometimes frontal to camera, render Peggy's choked-back horror, juxtaposed with Armstrong's impatient failure to guess her situation. Cut to the familiar skyline, now fiery red, where Peggy leans against a tree, hands over her bowed head, swaying from side to side. Finally she turns her face to its trunk, an icon of despair.

The following sequences that develop in parallel the stories of Peggy's abandonment and John's shifting state of mind demonstrate just what can be done in the way of 'heart-reading' pictures to open up the mingling of politics, both personal and national. First, Betty, 'her interest in the masterful firebrand' leading her 'to purchase goods at his emporium', finds herself embroiled in an argument with John about his failure to volunteer. He argues, 'The most efficient side will win. I have my business to attend to.' With a sweeping gesture, Betty speaks: 'It may be efficient to molest Belgium, but we want merciful efficiency.' Staring him fiercely in the face, her arm and cupped hand swinging to the left, motivates a cut to a propaganda image of Germans bullying Belgian women. A quick fade returns to Betty in full flood, he poised to reply, tense eyes fixed on her, their bodies leaning across the counter towards each other, their right hands crossing but not touching, cupped in the expository appeal of politically antagonistic lovers. Before he can reply, yellow-tinted newsreel footage cuts in to document a street parade of troops led by a brass band with bystanders waving from the pavements. Betty leaves and, back in his office, John stands, hands in his pockets, staring slightly off camera, brooding. Then with a fleeting smile, he shakes his head: 'My business. I can't throw up my life's work, even for her.'

It is the emotional sympathies between women that break Armstrong. Peggy has finally told him of her pregnancy, and is collapsed in tears at his office desk when her stepmother arrives. Coincidentally, Betty also comes to the shop. Attracted by raised voices, she opens Armstrong's office door to be greeted with a dramatic tableau, the stepmother glaring grimly at John, who hovers helplessly over the grief-stricken girl. Heart reading of pictures now goes on apace, as Elvey, finding the emotional rhythm of the situation, flicks between medium close-ups of Peggy weeping, the shouting stepmother, Armstrong hovering distressed at the door and the astonished Betty looking in, trying to fathom what is going on. The climax is reached in the stepmother's pronouncement: 'As she has made her bed so she must lie on it, I've done with her.' Shocked at this cruelty and gathering herself into a picture of compassion, Betty glides into the scene, past the helpless John still hanging onto the doorframe, as the stepmother sweeps out. A two-shot pictures Betty comforting Peggy, while in a medium close-up John watches, followed by the polemical title: 'The survival of the fittest?' This exchange between a tableau of emotional enactment and a heart-reading spectator is repeated several times, until a three-shot unites the trio, in which Betty, turning to John, announces, 'I'll

look after her.' Following his somewhat guilty look to camera, and a pictorialising title – 'The crumbling of the walls of selfishness' – the sequence closes on John, suggesting the power of an enacted picture to change heart and mind.

One more picture is required to complete his conversion, not to warmongering but to collective responsibility. The following episode opens with a title announcing the consequence of the previous one: 'An offering from a full heart.' Betty, now a nurse, is seated at her desk in the entrance of Fanshawe Hall, when John enters. A close-up displays a cheque for a £100 made out to the hospital, followed by his declaration: 'Is there no thought in your life for one who . . .'. Slowly Betty turns into profile to meet his gaze and then back to her work. He continues, 'I have always worshipped you . . .', but she raises both hands cupped in a sign of deprecation and, gracefully gesturing to the left, crosses in front of him, as he holds his hat disconsolately. Cut to a long shot from inside the hospital ward looking down the aisle between two rows of beds. A door at the back of this view opens to reveal Betty holding it wide for John, who, poised as it were on the threshold of the picture displayed to us, is reluctant to step in. A high-angle close-up of a soldier in one of the beds is followed by a mid-shot of the pair, framed in the doorway, mullioned windows behind throwing a religious cast over the scene, as Betty indicates with her gracefully cupped fingers the vista of the ward. A close-up of another patient is followed by her question: 'You will not speak a word to those who have suffered that your business may continue?' A mid-shot registers his embarrassment, and in the following shot they have returned to the desk in the hall. Now Lily Elsie appropriates the gestural language of recruitment to assert feminine independence. Raising her cupped right hand to indicate the ward, and slowly turning her wrist, she extends her index finger to point up the meaning of the picture she has created – 'So you see my life is dedicated.'

These sequences exemplify Elvey's amalgamation of performance and picture for narrative and thematic development. His collage pulls familiar pictorial gestures and iconography, including images circulating in wartime propaganda, into a distinctively unmilitaristic set of relationships. While anxieties about political extremism are aired, particularly in the titles, pictorialism supports neither unthinking patriotism nor regressive pastoralism based on class hierarchies. The Colonel uncle enacts this aspect of wartime propaganda but in an affectionately mocking, Blimp-like caricature. The emotional centre, however, concerns community and human charity. Female compassion and practicality express, through the language of Lily Elsie's beautiful and eloquent hands, values relegated by self-interested rationalist politics based on the scientific Darwinism and racial supremacy. Such theories are associated with the male characters and enacted in a body language of cramped movement and ineffectual positioning in relation to the women. After John leaves the scene just described, Betty is left for a few seconds, her arm and hand still held in the mould of their farewell handshake. Slowly her fingers close over her palm, drawing it up to her breast, as if to enclose and protect his touch.

Emphasising the slow process of feminisation necessary to reforming militaristic masculinity, John is next located walking through the blue-tinted tree-lined landscape associated with Peggy's agony, the camera tracking behind him as he nears the hill. With the camera still positioned behind him, he looks up, to project into the night sky a personal version of many a frontline lantern slide and postcard: Betty, her arms reaching out to him. He kneels, his hat falling off as he leans back, his arms stretched out on either side of his body as he opens himself to her influence. The female appeal, of course, draws on familiar propaganda imagery. But his remaking through occupying Peggy's position in the picture and Betty's interpretation of the call to war in terms of identification with humanitarian and collective needs shift the terms away from militarism and triumphalism. Jay Winter suggests that the popular imagery produced during and after the Great War represents a return to traditional motifs of sympathetic community needed to anneal the monstrosity and overwhelming losses it entailed. Here the religious cast of the image reinforces the search for human significance in what was widely experienced as an inhuman and incomprehensible event.[62] Betty later receives news of John's enlistment in a letter that asks for her 'comradeship', a relation that displaces heterosexual passion by equalising gender relations. She replies, 'I'll be your comrade but you'll find plenty where you are if you'll only look for human kindness.' Thus the collage of pictures across differ-

ent characters' stories produces new resonances, images of the fallen woman and Florence Nightingale combining, as Peggy gives birth, but also becomes a nurse, at Fanshawe Hall.

John's introduction to camp life introduces a new set of pictures that explicitly construct comradeship across class boundaries. An illustrative title, 'In Camp', opens on an almost abstract yellow-tinted image of rows of tents receding into the picture, glowing in the night, where the shadowy figures of soldiers squat at open tent doors or are projected in silhouette on the canvas. A slow track to the left opens the view past the ranked tents, revealing an officer, accompanied by John, checking each one, until arriving at the nearest tent. Signalled to enter, John responds, 'I fear this tent is full', to be bluffly answered – 'Room for dozens me lad . . . anyway it's your lordship's baronial 'all. 'OP IN!' Cut to an interior shot, where John's need to squash himself into the circle opposite the camera produces a vignette of social interactions, as he looks round smiling nervously under the curious examination of the others. After a joke at the expense of John's 'perjamers', the sequence concludes with a magic-lantern-like finale. Outside, two sentries come into shot, followed by the title, 'Put that blinkin light out!' A silhouette thrown on the tent wall thumbs its nose at us, while others make animal shapes with their hands.

John's introduction to camp life concludes with yet another blue-tinted tree-bordered skyline, as he goes outside to smoke a cigarette to escape the raucous gathering inside the mess hut. Cuts between Ginger, playing the squeeze-box, and John outside, now seated on a fallen tree trunk, connect the two as prelude to a sequence that contemporary reviewers found particularly moving. Leaving the hut, Ginger comes into John's shot, leaning to light his cigarette from his pipe. Sitting shoulder to shoulder beside him, backs to camera, he comments: 'I've heard we're next draft for France.' Raising clenched fists, John leans towards Ginger, whose next line names rather than enacts emotion: 'Mate – I'm afraid.' John's hand touches his shoulder: 'So am I, chum – afraid of being afraid.' Ginger swivels away and then back, putting his arm across John's back: 'You'll stick to me, mate, if I feel like – you know . . .' John, turning into profile, nods and they shake hands. Ginger, back to camera, leans away from John to rub his eyes, while

John hesitantly pats his back. The passage of emotion from Peggy's desertion through John's conversion has now come full circle via the circuit of picturesque iconography. Class differences are recorded according to performance and verbal codes: John is restrained, Ginger emotional, and their names position them differently in the fictional hierarchy – it is John's story, not Ginger's. But John, as middle-class businessman, is purposely isolated in a temporarily de-classed company of men among whom it is possible to picture working-class traditions of support and comradeship as the source of a new community. A title closes the circle: 'And so Betty was right – the new and more human Armstrong finds his first comrade.' Cross-gender and cross-class 'comradeship' emerges as the only meaningful thing to be wrested from the task of imagining the trenches.

Having introduced John and Ginger to the front, the film brings them quickly home on leave, partly to initiate complications in their personal narratives. Ginger encounters and falls for Peggy, while John, hoping to see Betty, observes her giving a locket to Baring, intended to be passed to him, but which John misconstrues as a sign of their involvement. Crucially, these sequences stress the social dislocations of war, offering pictorial documents, including documentary-style shots of WMCA canteens and tourist images of London, to reinforce the desired comradeship that will link home and war fronts, and begin, tentatively, to re-imagine social relationships. Thus the Armistice is represented by newsreel footage of fireworks and crowds outside Buckingham Palace. Armstrong, however, returns at the war's end blinded, and, although he now knows the misrecognised locket given to Baring was meant for him, he refuses to tie Betty to a blind man. Ginger has also rejected Peggy, having discovered her former attachment to Liebman in a melodramatic encounter in the trenches with the German. Back in Melcombe, a pastoral scene brings the men together. Seated once again on a fallen tree trunk, Armstrong recalls their first conversation and asks what in 1919 must have been a crucial question for thousands of returning wounded men and their families: 'Do you remember, ages ago, sitting on a log like this? – You told me you were afraid of War – well, I'm afraid of Peace. What's a blind, helpless man to make of his life?' The language of hands now images the comradeship that might heal the peace. Seeing Peggy approaching,

Ginger stiffens, while Armstrong grabs his hand, preventing his departure, and with his other reaches for Peggy's. After initial resistance, their hands clasp across his body.

Ginger and Peggy seal their personal story with a kiss, but John's rapprochement with Betty is given the public enactment due central protagonists who also represent social authority. Armstrong, in an echo of the film's opening images, is found addressing the inauguration of the ex-servicemen's club he has founded. At the back of the frame a banner announces that Melcombe Comrades Club has been 'Founded to organise in United Comradeship all those who have served in combat in the War so that neither [they nor] their interests shall be forgotten'. After the speeches, Betty approaches Armstrong, who, initially taking her hand, struggles for control and pulls away. Sighing, Betty takes the initiative: 'Your organising ability has done so much for others. Won't you do something for me?' A shot of audience members waiting, as it were, for the curtain close, is followed by the completion of Betty's whispered question: 'Won't you marry me, my dear?' He stands transfixed, while a high-angle close-up focuses on his clenched hands resting on the table edge. Her hands move into the shot. Cut to a close-up of their faces, he still dumbstruck. In a repeat close-up, his hands are caressed by hers, while his fingers open and, initially moving away along the table edge, finally close over hers. Cut to his face as he briefly smiles and nods. In medium shot Ginger and Peggy cheer, followed by a long shot from the back of the hall, recording a cheering ovation as the audience stand, waving their hats.

PICTORIALISM MODERNISED

If *Comradeship* dextrously weaves iconographic pictures and performance signs to mix story and contemporary issues, its prevalent use of masks and vignetted shots in order to frame and thereby pictorially present pictures and documents inevitably disrupts the seamlessness of narrative causality. Following the disastrous downturn in the British film industry of 1924 and an unhappy spell with Fox in Hollywood, Elvey eventually linked up with Victor Saville (producer) and Gareth Gundrey (scenario editor), in a winning team that enabled Gaumont to claim one of British cinema's frequently heralded revivals.[63] Their first film, *Mademoiselle d'Armentières*, based on a story of romance in the trenches spun by Saville from a popular song, proved a huge box-office hit, despite provoking some controversy about its relation to King Vidor's *The Big Parade* (1926) which it shortly followed.[64] Both films entered sensitive territory. In a 1926 review, James Agate registers what was at stake when, after a lull of several years, film-makers tackled the 'war's tragedy and the imaginative disengaging of its meaning'.[65] The repeated outrage of reviewers confronted with the American *The Unknown Soldier* (1926) has already been noted in Chapter 3. Although some would prefer to do without the love plot in Elvey's film, it is largely preferred to Vidor's for its capacity to 'realise the human aspects of soldiering', 'the soldier's view'[66] and its 'British spirit'.[67] The *Westminster Gazette* praised 'its realistic atmosphere, blended with humour, pathos, drama, without excessive sentiment . . . [but] . . . depicting little human emotions'.[68]

Sadly, only the last quarter of the film survives, but it suggests Elvey's distinctive solution to the problem of marrying a cinema of pictures with the demands of continuity editing. The film, like *Comradeship*, links love and war, but this time drawing on mythical images circulated in wartime France, combined, according to the *Daily Telegraph*, with 'scenes extracted from the official war records of the Allies'.[69] The French *estaminet* or café, which provided the comfort of female company for soldiers far from home, had given rise to the figure of 'Mademoiselle'. According to Saville, she represented 'a bit of a soldier's la-de-da', but Armentières provoked for him the grim memory of the town from which he, along with so many thousands, set out for the front.[70] The *Yorkshire Observer* refers to Mademoiselle as 'that gracious lady whose memory is perpetuated in song',[71] while the *Evening News* claims that she had become as famous a myth as the Angel of Mons.[72] This suggests a potent image enshrining and mythologising the shared experiences of British soldiers marooned in France. The figure reappears in Brunel's *Blighty* (1927), commissioned by Balcon the following year. Both films end by bringing her back to England, claiming her as the maternal centre of the postwar national home.

Elvey starts, then, with certain iconographic images already available to the public imaginary in pictorial format, some of which appeared in *Comradeship*. However, picturising the image through iris shots or masks is no longer an option, such practices now displaced by the demands of continuity cinema. Pictorial presentation, however, is naturalised through the internal framing and compositional effects practised by a pictorial-theatrical *mise en scène* discussed in Part One. For example, the second shot of the surviving reel presents a stage picture of soldiers marching towards us through the proscenium-like stone arch, supported on wing-like walls, that leads into Armentières, revealing the houses and towers of the city as a backdrop. A shot picking up on Mademoiselle's movement from the street into the *estaminet* cuts to reframe her between the dark curtains that separate café from the lit-up kitchen beyond, to which she runs to join her aunt in a domestic interior. The film's closing shots, countering as it were the picture of troops leaving Armentières for the horrors of the trenches, show its now bowler-hatted hero walking with a limp towards the camera, down a street of suburban villas, talking to a small boy. At the garden gate, his father pauses, and, smiling down to the child, says: 'That's the story, my little man . . . and how Mademoiselle d'Armentières became your mummy.' Cut to a view past father and child to Mademoiselle, standing framed between porch curtains, woman-as-sign, captured for English peacetime.

If framing is naturalised within a theatricalised *mise en scène*, the light show offered by the battlefield enables a similar naturalisation of the practice of fading and wiping, lighting up and closing down on views fleetingly glimpsed through the brilliance of explosions or mists of smoke and producing the pictorialised effects of silhouetted figures and skyline shots. This play of dark and light is used to realise the iconic, mythological status of Mademoiselle, both legitimating her otherwise unlikely presence in the trenches and making her a symbolic and mediating witness to the horrors of trench encounters. At the same time, Elvey exploits the capacity of film to release the trapped movement of the picture. So, following Mademoiselle's frantic search for her lover among the soldiers marching to the front (see below), a long shot of heavy cloud hanging over the night-time battlefield singles out her lone figure running across the skyline, followed by an ambulance. An interior shot from behind the driver picks up her figure as the ambulance swerves to overtake her. Cut to the exterior, its passing lights catching her up-thrown arm. She runs after it as it drives into the darkness, and we glimpse her jumping onto the tailboard just before it swings her out of shot. In the next sequence the ambulance arrives at the trenches. A long shot revealing hurried troop movements across a pool of light at the back of the frame is temporarily blacked out as the ambulance crosses in front of the camera in a naturalised wipe. As the vehicle turns into the lighted area, we glimpse the girl clinging to the tailboard, only to see her slipping away into the darkness as the ambulance comes to a halt. Later, in moments of battle, clouds of smoke following gunfire serve to fade out the screen every now and then, while a long shot across no man's land reveals a soldier running along the skyline, lit up by explosions in the night sky. This use of light and darkness naturalises a magic-lantern-like flicker effect, revealing the discontinuity of perception in the front line and producing the perspectives and fleeting visions experienced by men in the trenches discussed by Paul Fussell.[73]

The elusive image of Mademoiselle is picked up shortly by a shot taken at a crossroads in the trenches that pinpoints in the darkness the white-dressed figure of the girl slithering down their earthen sides, and heading off down one of the passageways. Shrinking back into a cutting, she watches a soldier leading a wounded comrade, his eyes bandaged, along the trench. In fearful anticipation she desperately asks after her lover. The sequence ends with a medium close-up, in which she stands transfixed, her arms held out in a parting gesture. James Agate, noting a recent clutch of war films, suggests 'there is obviously a growing inclination on the part of the public for the graphic representation of war scenes', one reason for which is 'the passing of time which makes bearable that which earlier was unbearable'.[74] Agate is one of those who find the mingling of love stories and the war trivialising. But his recognition of the need for images that make the war bearable chimes with Paul Fussell and Jay Winter on the wartime and postwar production of mythologising symbols.[75] Drawing on the available iconography and word-of-mouth rumours, such images realised – rendered sensible – in ways both bearable and understandable what is ultimately senseless and unbearable. In the sequence I have just outlined there is little narrative as such; only a collage of pictures in which the presence of the camera and therefore the

viewer is made materially evident, picking up fleeting glimpses of trench warfare. At the same time, these sights are mediated by the presence of Mademoiselle – 'that gracious lady whose memory is perpetuated in song' – as feeling and compassionate witness.

FROM PICTURE STORIES TO FLICKER-BOOK MONTAGE

More remarkable are the strategies Elvey has developed by the mid-1920s for collaging images to progress narrative in a distinctive 'flicker-book' approach to editing, closely resembling the constructive principles of Soviet montage – a point returned to below. Not loath to take the viewer by the scruff of the neck to the other side of the picture, Elvey's technique both joins together different angles and 'views' of the same set-up and cross-cuts between parallel actions. The first sequence I examine opens the surviving reel of *Mademoiselle d'Armentières*:

1. SHOT 1   H/A MS on soldiers' legs marching from right to left. Cut.
2. SHOT 2   LS of soldiers leaving Armentières, marching from left to right under the proscenium-like arch described above. Cut.
3. SHOT 1   Repeat.
4. SHOT 3   MS of the street, soldiers marching from left to right, past the *estaminet* at the back of the frame, in front of which stand three onlookers, including Mademoiselle. Cut on her movement as she turns to go in.
5. SHOT 4   MLS between dark curtains that frame Mademoiselle as she moves from café to the domestic interior visible beyond, and runs to her aunt (Marie Ault), working at the kitchen table; both peer back through the curtains towards the street.
6. SHOT 1   Repeat.
7. SHOT 5   Mid-shot of Mademoiselle chattering with her aunt. The aunt looks serious, her arms folded, shaking her head. They glance every now and then back through curtains, across the café to street. Cut.
8. SHOT 3   Repeat.
9. SHOT 5   Repeat: the girl questions her aunt, who grimly nods, apparently confirming that this march represents the awaited 'big

push'; the girl runs to the door and off camera. Cut.

10. SHOT 3   Repeat, but the girl appears in the door-way of the *estaminet*. Cut.

11. SHOT 6   Mid-shot: a male bystander in French farmer's clothes stands idly smoking a cigarette as she appears beside him, turn-ing from gazing off left to the right. Cut.

12. SHOT 1   Repeat.

13. SHOT 6   Repeat, but she swivels from left across the camera to look anxiously to the right then to the left. He watches her amused. She glances at him briefly, then back to the soldiers. Cut.

14. SHOT 1   Repeat.

15. SHOT 6   Repeat: she turns again from right to left, then to him. He looks darkly at her from under his hat. Cut.

    TITLE   Eh! bien quoi? . . . C'est le 15 demain . . . Avez-vous oublié qu'ils vont tenter le 'grand coup'?

16. SHOT 6   Repeat: he's laughing maliciously, she continues scanning the marching soldiers, her gaze appearing more inward as she breathes heavily.

17. SHOT 1   Repeat.

18. SHOT 6   Repeat: her gaze is frontal, and only her eyes flick right and back to the front; her hand moves up to touch her cheek; she starts forward to the left, almost running off.

19. SHOT 1   Repeat.

20. SHOT 6   Repeat: her hands wring the kitchen towel she is holding.

21. SHOT 1   Repeat.

22. SHOT 6   Repeat: she is craning right, then swivels back to the man, the back of her hand to her mouth, her fingers curled into her palm; he says something to her and she tosses her head, clapping her hand to the side of her head and looking back anxiously right.

23. SHOT 3   Repeat, but slightly reframed: soldiers marching past the *estaminet*, but the girl is gone; the camera now tracks with the soldiers marching in rows of four, their heads turned to the back of the frame. As they pass the *estaminet*, her figure is seen between them running alongside;

then she runs between the rows to the camera on the other side of the street. Cut.

24. SHOT 7   The camera picks her up with a slight jolt, as her body twists round to face the soldiers again; then she turns to run alongside them, her arms bent at right angles to her sides, her fingers splayed in a little fluttering movement, as she falters and stops. Cut.

25. SHOT 2   Repeat: soldiers leaving Armentières under the arch, she among them.

26. SHOT 8   H/A MLS on soldiers marching right, she running alongside them but to the left, and looking up to one particular soldier – her lover, Johnny (John Stuart).

27. SHOT 3   Repeat, reframed as in (23) and with a static camera: running alongside her lover, she pleads with him as the soldiers march past the *estaminet*, until they and she are out of shot.

28. SHOT 9   H/A MLS over the column marching towards the camera, her figure clinging to Johnny, then dropping her arms, and coming to a standstill, as they carry on marching towards the camera.

29. SHOT 1   Repeat.

30. SHOT 10 MCU track on Johnny and his older comrade, Fred (Alf Goddard), who remonstrates with him as he gazes obdurately forward.

This sequence is composed of thirty shots plus one title, but only ten basic set-ups, or 'pictures'. Narra-tive drive here depends on flicking between pictures in a way that ignores the spatial logic necessary to the illusion of a three-dimensional world. The sol-diers' feet are first viewed from Mademoiselle's side of the street and march from right to left. But the camera crosses the line to view the whole procession from the opposite side of the street as it passes the *estaminet*, so that they march from left to right. Thus the collage, flicking between pictures and forcibly transporting the viewer between recto and verso, suggests lines of contrary emotional force – the march to war, familial control, a girl's desires – which, intersecting, materialise as aesthetic sensation as much as they act out or narrate a story. Through intensifying cutting between her desiring figure and the soldiers' marching feet, Mademoiselle is drawn both emotionally and physically into the movement of the soldiers.

On the battlefield this approach to pictorial montage offers a series of graphic pictures of the trenches, of the war-torn landscape, of comradeship between soldiers. Montage then juxtaposes these shots rhythmically and pictorially, ringing the changes through reordering repeated images in different sequences. At the same time, contrasts of camera angle, shot scale and lighting pattern emphasise the distinctness of each image, thereby creating a rapid flicker-book effect. Contrasting views of different sides of the same set-up – a bit like flicking round the sides of a house of cards – produces a kaleidoscopic perception of the fictional terrain rather than a sense of seamless space. This technique evolves into a distinctive method of marrying picture and narrative progression, building a story through overlapping series. As one series unfolds, a new image belonging to the second is inserted, so that, as the first gradually dies out, the second takes over. The following table of shots from the political science fiction film, *High Treason*, exemplifies this method of narrational montage. As war is about to break out between the Confederated States of Europe and the Atlantic States, the sequence constructs a face-off between Evelyn Seymour, leading a band of women committed to peace, and her erstwhile boyfriend, Captain Michael Deane, who has orders to protect the aerodrome:

1. SHOT 1 H/A LS of a line of male, black-leather-clad soldiers across the front of the frame confronting a line of white boiler-suited women across the back of the frame within the aerodrome compound.

2. SHOT 2 H/A LS of soldiers running to the planes parked outside to the left of the compound.

3. SHOT 3 MS along a line of soldiers with their backs to the aerodrome compound exit, the women pushing against them, some breaking through.

4. SHOT 2 Repeat: Evelyn is seen breaking through and running out onto the tarmac.

5. SHOT 3 Repeat: One soldier moves from the line to the exit looking off frame left. Michael joins him.

6. SHOT 4 MS of a soldier guarding a plane.

Evelyn runs in from frame right, showing her peace badge and pleading with him, but is denied.

7. SHOT 3 Repeat, but split by a title in which Michael orders the compound to be cleared. Some women escape out onto the tarmac; the soldiers respond indecisively, some firing, others looking to Michael, who walks out of frame left.

8. SHOT 5 H/A shot of women at the front of the frame struggling with the soldiers who are attempting to guard the planes.

9. SHOT 4 Repeat: Michael enters, and Evelyn turns, flustered, to face him, interrupted by a title in which he orders her removal, after which she is dragged away.

10. SHOT 5 Repeat.

11. SHOT 4 Repeat.

12. SHOT 6 BCU of Michael, followed by a title in which he orders the soldiers to form ranks.

13. SHOT 7 MS of Evelyn standing, wide-eyed and breast heaving, in front of a line of waiting women. One of the women passes her a flame-thrower as they back away. A title carries Michael's order to stay clear.

14. SHOT 5 Repeat: Evelyn moves away from the camera, one arm raised, the other swinging the flame-thrower. Michael moves forward to confront her.

15. SHOT 8 MS of three soldiers looking nervously at each other, as they raise their guns.

16. SHOT 9 MS of the women shrinking back as Evelyn, in front, faces the camera and leans back to hurl the flame thrower.

17. SHOT 10 MS of Michael as he takes one step back, and his soldiers behind him retreat.

18. SHOT 8 Repeat: the middle soldier raises his gun.

19. SHOT 9 Repeat: Evelyn breathing heavily.

20. SHOT 10 Mid-shot of Michael standing in profile, his soldiers fleeing off frame right.

21. SHOT 5 Repeat: Evelyn and the women now run forward to the planes, surrounding and passing Michael, who is rooted to the spot.

22. SHOT 11 MLS from behind the planes as the women surround them.

The result is a pictorial collage that builds up a concrete sense of impending conflict. At the same time, cross-cutting – between men and women, heroine and hero and the different political camps each represents – evokes the contrary desire to bind together the two sides of the cut, the two sides of the narrative opposition.

Elvey's method, then, does not deny the status of the shot as picture, but develops collage into a form of construction approaching Soviet montage.[76] Charles Barr has attributed such methods to Eliot Stannard, one of the most prolific scriptwriters of British cinema, and a frequent scenarist for Elvey's early films, whose work Barr analyses in relation to his later collaboration with Hitchcock.[77] Although none of the three films considered above were scripted by Stannard, it seems likely that he and Elvey drew from similar nineteenth-century pictorial-narrational practices: episodic theatrical entertainments and the accumulation of graphic detail, combined with switches in spatially located points of view to build character and incident in the popular nineteenth-century novel. Eisenstein, indeed, analyses passages from Dickens's novels to demonstrate the work of montage.[78] In contrast, Stannard's discussion of his adaptation of Galsworthy's *Justice* (1917) suggests the accommodation of collage to geographic narration:

> I showed in rapid succession Falder locked in his cell, a dog chained to his kennel, a small bird imprisoned in a tiny cage; then in equally quick succession happy children free from care romping in a sun-lit garden, a dog racing happily after a tennis-ball, a lark soaring up to the heavens.[79]

The effects here arise from the cumulative juxtaposition of images forcibly divided by their separate spatial locations. In another article Stannard develops the meaning of such contrasts:

> In order that you may more fully realise the horrors of solitary confinement I have shown a wild bird at liberty soaring upwards into the sky; the mental agony of the guilty is contrasted by the mental innocence of children playing in the sunshine.[80]

The prisoner and the bird, the mental states of prisoner and child represent spatial renderings of past and present – once he was free and innocent but now guilty and confined. Juxtaposing shots treated as pictures spatialises time, evoking loss and nostalgia.

The degree to which Stannard and Elvey, in the context of a British cultural poetics, were developing a constructional system antagonistic to the norm established by Hollywood is registered in contradictory responses to the film's 'restless' style. While *Kinematograph and Lantern Weekly* praised 'the sudden flash from the horrors of solitary confinement to a vision of freedom',[81] *The Bioscope* complains that 'sudden flashing from one subject to another has too much the effect of a mechanical trick' – a complaint frequently made against Eisenstein's practice.[82] The journal makes similar criticisms of *The Elusive Pimpernel* (1920), made without Stannard: 'Mr Elvey is inclined to dissipate the dramatic value of a situation by his restless, rather disjointed style, and by his fondness for developing two separate themes simultaneously.'[83] By the mid-1920s Stannard was collaborating with Hitchcock, contributing at the end of the decade to the most pictorial of montage films, *The Manxman*, to which I will return. Elvey's flicker-book approach, meanwhile, had moved beyond the collage of symbols to inhabit the image itself, which was cut up into various angles and points of view and recombined as in a kaleidoscope of continually shifting and differentiating perceptions. Years later, in a 1963 radio interview, Elvey repeats his conviction that film is a 'restless medium', demanding multiple rather than singular points of view.[84]

JACK GRAHAM CUTTS AND CINEMATIC VISION

The heart-reading of pictures and perceptual fragmentation exploited in Elvey's films is underpinned by the peculiar dialectic between documentary objectivity and subjective vision that Charles Barr sees as characteristic of British cinema.[85] As suggested in Chapter 2, pictorialism renders both cultural practices and social activities as documents. The problem, then, for British film-making is how to realise subjective identities and desires in a public world that is socially defined and demarcated. The distinction between objective document and the inner processes of personal life overlaps the distinction between geography and biography discussed in Part One as distinguishing British and American cinematic

styles. The egalitarian possibility of biographic hegemony over geographic location in American cinema
facilitates the construction of a coherent and continuous three-dimensional world tailored to the narrative trajectory of a hero. Continuity editing and *mise
en scène* subordinate this world to the expression of
the protagonists' desires and subjective impulses.
However, in so far as pictorialism – supporting a theatricalised staging of socially demarcated locations
and the production of culturally referential images –
serves to define and constrain its protagonists, *mise en
scène* in British film-making does not easily provide
correlatives for the projection of their desires and
antagonisms. Rather, it retains a quasi-autonomous
function, controlling biography and narrative development. Moments of spectacle or pictorial effect
remain semi-detached from narrative progression,
pressing in on rather than expressing the protagonists' motivations or feelings. The rapturous praise
that greeted Graham Cutts and Michael Balcon's
Woman to Woman in 1923 implicitly recognises this
difference. Reviewers repeatedly comment on the
control of spectacular effect that, while 'imposing and
dazzling, never swamps or clogs the unfolding of
narrative'.[86] Rather, it is 'an intrinsic part of the story
. . . logical and inevitable'.[87] Nevertheless, this is
recognised as an *American* virtue – the *Daily Express*
declares it 'the best American film made in England',[88] while another reviewer refers to 'that correct
Hollywood touch'.[89] Nevertheless, *The Film Renter*
regrets that despite a cabaret scene worthy of De
Mille, 'what one misses . . . is that particular touch
which marks out the British picture'.[90] Regrettably,
what that 'touch' is remains undefined.

'WE TOUCH EACH OTHER WITH THE SENSE OF SIGHT'

The problem of expressing subjective apprehension in
a publicly defined world was not new. Pre-Raphaelitism, in particular, had not only set about refining the
externalised rhetoric of bodily gestures used in the
melodramatic tableau to command public space but,
by emphasising incidental and private gesture, had
shifted attention to the face and eyes as sources of
inner perception and subjectivity within public scenarios. In this sense, the Pre-Raphaelite drama of perception refines the external practices of melodrama
that physically place characters in a position to over-
hear, observe or spy on others' lives and secrets (see

Fig. 1 – frontispiece). Effectively, as argued in Chapter 3, the boundaries that demarcate social space are
internalised to divide subjective from public worlds.
Film, as was so often remarked, offered a medium that
played on this boundary. Thus, constraints of social
location and codes of behaviour stimulate covert looking and internalised perceptions for the creation of
drama – what George Pearson referred to as 'eye
play'.[91] Heart-reading the pictures and performances
out of which these films are made demands a viewer,
not only in the cinema but, as suggested in Chapter 1,
within the film's fictional world. For, if a *mise en scène*
of socially separated locations requires clearly defined
and demarcated bodies, nevertheless eyes can and do
cross these boundaries, reaching into another's personal space. Pictures and performances are constructed for someone; they are intended to be seen;
they seek a look. If bodies should not touch, we may,
in the words of Henry Neville, 'touch each other with
the sense of sight'.[92] The work of Graham Cutts is
exemplary in fathoming and developing this potential
in ways sometimes recognised as peculiarly British.

CUTTS: MASTER SHOWMAN

As far as I have been able to tell, apart from partisan
personal gossip that circulates about his relationship
to Hitchcock, what we know of Graham Cutts as a
film-maker must be gleaned from the trade press and
is scant. Nevertheless, he is briefly acknowledged by
Herbert Wilcox in his autobiography as the 'master
showman of the North', who threw up his job as
exhibitor to direct *The Wonderful Story* (1922) for the
company they formed, Graham-Wilcox Productions.
He went on to become 'one of the top British directors of his time'.[93] While, not surprisingly, Wilcox
writes their story with himself as lead player, Rachael
Low ponders why he suppresses mention of their
successful second production, *Paddy-the-Next-Best-
Thing* (1923).[94] According to Iris Barry, in a feature
article on Cutts for the *Daily Mail*, he took *The Wonderful Story* to Wilcox rather than the other way
around.[95] Similarly, Michael Balcon, acknowledging
Cutts's offer of the film rights to *Woman to Woman*,
gives him little credit for the film, moving swiftly on
to retail the story (still prominently in circulation
today), of his allegedly jealous attempt to sabotage
The Lodger (1926), showpiece of Balcon's up-and-
coming star director, Hitchcock.[96] Rachael Low
argues that Wilcox's success was founded on Cutts's

work and quotes A. V. Bramble, who asserted the same of both Wilcox and Balcon's Gainsborough Studios.[97] The trade press offers plentiful evidence of the industry's regard. *Kinematograph Weekly* is uncharacteristically ecstatic about *The Wonderful Story* – 'It is wonderful, and the wonder is multiplied by the fact that it is British.'[98] It later names Cutts as 'an energetic and enterprising director' on his joining Gainsborough[99] and, following the success of *The Rat* (1925), a 'sure-fire maker of box-office attractions', all of whose 'productions have found a market in America'.[100] An unidentifiable clipping in Clive Brook's scrapbook names him as 'Britain's leading and most entertaining screen director',[101] while the *Westminster Gazette* claims his place at 'the forefront of imaginative and artistic film directors'.[102] Announcing what in fact never transpired – *Easy Virtue* (1927) to be made by a 'Coward–Cutts combo' (Balcon gave the project to Hitchcock) – the *Evening Standard* quotes Balcon as saying that 'the future of cinema lies in the hands of the young men and that Mr Cutts, as one of the most brilliant, is a notable newcomer to British films'.[103]

By 1926 Cutts is hardly a newcomer, and possibly Balcon is taking the opportunity afforded by an enthusiastic journalist to give Cutts some of the recognition he deserved. Certainly, his later reputation has been dimmed by the role Hitchcock played in many of his productions, ensuring that revivals of these films are presented as the apprentice work of Hitchcock, together with the recirculation of gossip to the detriment of Cutts as a film-maker.[104] His best-known films made without Hitchcock, the Rat trilogy, are dominated by their star, Ivor Novello, revived enthusiasm for whom also diverts attention from Cutts. Furthermore, his film reviews show little of the concern with artistic quality bestowed, for example, on the work of Hepworth and Elvey. Cutts's films accrue respect because they provide much of the bezazz of Hollywood and broke into the American market. Although Cutts received offers from Hollywood, it appears that he pinned his faith on Gainsborough and a revival of the British film industry.[105] But while reviewers take pleasure in his capacity to beat the Americans at their own game, unease is also hinted at the nature of the game he plays. His first film, *Cocaine* (1922), which features nightclubs, a fearsome Apache dance and juvenile drug-taking, was banned and, retitled *While London*

Sleeps for a second trade show,[106] mentioned only in guarded terms by *Kinematograph Weekly* in its reviewing of *The Wonderful Story*: 'we believe Graham Cutts has one mediocre melodrama to his credit'.[107] Despite praise for the latter film, the paper expresses similar sentiments about *Flames of Passion* (1922), which it viewed as 'a crude, sordid melodrama'.[108] As late as 1927, *The Picturegoer* found it 'an extremely sordid film'.[109]

It seems that a fascination with show business reported by Iris Barry led Cutts to seek out the incipient sexuality and violence of theatrical spectacle.[110] Apache dancing features in at least four of his films. Indeed the *Westminster Gazette* welcomed *The Return of the Rat* (1929) as a 'vigorous and full-blooded' film that 'out apaches all the apaches imported from America'.[111] *The Bioscope* announces as one of the pleasures of *The Rat* that 'the Follies Bergère, the greatest spectacular show in Paris, has never been so thoroughly filmed'. Spectacle melds with document: 'Not only will you see scenes on the stage . . . but also the even more famous promenade and bar.' For 'Britishers', the main attraction is the 'forty-eight little English dancers known as the Tiller Girls'. The paper also reports that Cutts hired Gabiel Rosca, 'the most expert knife fighter in Paris', for the fight with Novello as the Rat.[112] Nearly every review of *The Triumph of the Rat* (1926) mentions the entrancing set piece in which Cutts appropriates the – then unusual – aerial view for the release of hundreds of balloons above the heads of 250 extras hired for the ballroom sequence.[113] Cutts, then, is perceived as a director who goes for the visceral, sensational effects of theatrical performance. He is perhaps the only director of this period whose work suggests an excess that gets 'under the skin' of both his characters and reviewers. For example, in February 1925, *Theatre World* rejects Ivor Novello and Constance Collier's play of *The Rat* as a 'succession of stale, sex-sensation-seeking stage tricks'.[114] In October, however, it greets Cutts's film as the 'best British production since *Carnival*' and Ivor Novello as providing 'the best acting of his screen career', adding that 'Cutts has excelled himself', especially in the White Coffin scenes, 'for the atmosphere created is almost uncanny'.[115] 'Uncanny' – the familiar made strange – is a Freudian's 'give-away'. As if to cover what has just been revealed, the reviewer goes on to assert: 'this is not a hasty or morbid film but good clean entertainment'. Iris Barry, making a case for Cutts to be taken seriously, similarly attempts, none too convincingly, to counter accusations of overemphasising 'cabaret scenes' and the 'sexual element' by citing pressure from Wardour Street.[116] Nevertheless, that a sense of the uncanny hovers around Cutts's work is evident in other veiled statements about the attractions of his films. Despite his apparent modernising and Americanising impact on British film-making, like Elvey, he refused the chance of Hollywood, and for some reviewers his work projects something peculiarly British. The ambivalence in *The Star*'s review of *The Rat* is revealing:

> It is hoped that eventually Graham Cutts will find a story to match his powers. The Rat films . . . [give us] . . . a half-view of a style that may be described and welcomed as British but American influence always seems to get the upper hand. If given a full chance these British methods . . . would pay.[117]

Typically, what 'these British methods' are and what precisely is revealed by the 'half-view of a style' are not explained.

In fact, beyond acknowledging the capacity of his films to compete with Hollywood, few critics were able to define their aesthetic qualities, not even Rachael Low, who is careful to distinguish his non-Hitchcockian collaborations from the later master's work.[118] This is perhaps because, apart from *The Wonderful Story* – which *Kinematograph Weekly* praises as 'a masterpiece in a setting of country lanes and cottage homes . . . [with] . . . lighting beyond praise'[119] – Cutts's films do not offer scope for pictorial evaluation in the terms lavished on Elvey's output. It is, rather, a certain intense and unpredictable energy that is noted both of his working methods on the studio floor and in his *mise en scène*. As the *Westminster Gazette* declares of *Triumph of the Rat*, 'Mr Cutts seems to delight in grandiose ballrooms and scenes photographed at unexpected angles'.[120] It is his passionate protagonists, inventive cinematographic techniques and visceral *mise en scène* that are most frequently noted as qualities that define a certain sensational excitement, if no one quite dares to put their finger on the precise source of the drama. However, despite an apparently early grasp of American continuity displayed in *Woman to Woman* (scripted, it must be said, by Hitchcock) and a canny

knowledge of 'what the picture-going public wants', noted by the *Birmingham Dispatch* among others,[121] Rachael Low suggests he had 'only a sketchy interest in film structure'. His inventiveness was focused on 'the big drama' and 'tricky camerawork'.[122]

In terms of pictorialism, Cutts's particular contribution lay in an instinctive sense of the power of the look, not only as a means of controlling others but as generator of projected internalised visions. His development through the 1920s shifts from narrative picture to theatricalised stage, for which he mobilised the camera to release movement not only of characters within a fiction but of the protagonists' looks at each other. In the end he found the means – to be taken up later by both Hitchcock and Anthony Asquith – to release the look, detached from the body, into pure movement through space. Through such cinematic looks and seeings, Cutts's films engage the audience in 'sight as touch' across the socially maintained divisions between private and public. This use of camera movement, combined with a protagonist's look and a predilection for 'the sexual element', goes some way to explaining the ambivalence of reviewers' praise. In this respect his films' insinuation under the skin of the public personae of British fiction anticipates and opens up the terrain Hitchcock would claim as his own.

EYE POWER IN *THE WONDERFUL STORY*
Following the attempt to deal directly with taboo social material in *Cocaine*, Cutts's second film, *The Wonderful Story*, initiates a shift from the picture as object of a protagonist's reading (see discussion of Elvey above) to the picture as projection of a protagonist's look, as object of a desiring investigation. Thus the story of Robert Martin (Herbert Langley) – crippled on the eve of his wedding to Kate and forced to watch her growing attachment and eventual marriage to his brother, Jimmy – opens up the psychosexual dynamic inherent in the relation between picture, character and viewer. Robert's desiring look is 'picturised' through collage juxtapositions rather than set loose into spatial mobility. This dynamic is foreshadowed before the fatal accident. An oval frame encloses a fecund pastoral image in which Kate is feeding piglets and chickens surrounded by abundant foliage. A mid-shot brings Jimmy to ask her about her engagement to Robert. A return to the oval frame contains and centres the pair chatting in a

pastoral scene that suggests they make an ideal match. This symmetry is disturbed, however, when Robert enters their picture at the back of the frame, puffing laconically on his pipe, pausing to rest his hand on a plough to observe them. A close-up focuses attention on Robert seeing, introducing a discordant note into an otherwise Edenic scene. After his accident and loss of Kate, Robert's look becomes a powerful agent, capable of penetrating the surface of the pictures Kate and Jimmy present, not only 'touching' them but, by locking into their return gaze, entering into their subjectivities. A title introduces the danger: 'Came the day Robert began to hate his brother.' Kate arrives with apples for Robert, but is reluctant to stay by the bedside. As she rises, Robert seizes her wrist. Two close-ups focus his grip and her pain. In the following two-shot, Jimmy enters and a series of looks between the characters registers a new and threatening dynamic between them as Robert's jealousy erupts. A close-up focuses on Kate's pained expression, and her eyes turn frontally to look just over the camera to where Jimmy stands. In an answering close-up Jimmy's eyes turn to fix on her, their expression growing troubled. In a reverse shot her return look suggests sensed danger, and in the next, Jimmy's eyes pick up her message and swivel in the direction of Robert. Cut to Robert frowning grimly, observing this exchange of looks, his hand still gripping Kate's wrist tightly. In the next shot Jimmy glances back at Kate, then meets Robert's eyes with a look of warning. In the reverse shot Robert, glaring back at Jimmy, finally lets go. As if to cover over what has potentially been made visible through this exchange of looks, Jimmy offers Robert the basket of herbs and flowers he has brought home. Robert smashes it from his hands.

Robert's jealousy and despair now increasingly fuels his 'eye power'. When Kate admits her engagement to Jimmy, this power overcomes his paralysis as he strives to reach her in the kitchen, where she has retreated to make tea. A title explains: 'Instinct, which there is no gainsaying, a slow unreasoning force moving to its appointed end.' Turning his head to watch her departure, a collage of shots records his struggle to move his inert body towards the kitchen. He reaches the fireplace, where, his white shirt shining in an arch of light from the stove and his hands hanging onto the mantelpiece rail, his body strains to follow his gaze towards the kitchen. Cut to a view framed by the kitchen door where Kate, unaware, prepares tea. In the next shot, his arms twisted across his back, Robert hauls himself hand over hand along the rail, falling clumsily onto a fireside settle that blocks his passage. Cut to another shot of Kate at her tea-making. Return to a mid-shot of Robert, framed in the arch of the fireplace, towering up over the settle back, straining towards the kitchen. The camera has not moved, but in alternating a straining gaze and body struggling across space with the unaware object of that gaze, Cutts is putting in place a structure of subjective and objective shots that Hitchcock will develop.

The next shot is positioned behind Robert as he looks through the open kitchen door at Kate. Hearing his movement, she turns, a series of fleeting expressions crossing her face: startled surprise, a smile of welcome, her mouth opening to cry out. Initial pleasure and hope as they reach out to each other, his arm encircling her, fades as a big close-up over his shoulder into her face, looking into the camera, catches the dying light in her eyes. Fear enters her look, and, her smile faltering, she pulls back, frowning apprehensively. An equally large close-up captures Robert in half-profile, shadows playing over the left side of his face, as he searches her face with growing menace, the muscles round his eyes working heavily, his frown intensifying. In a reverse shot her mouth opens speechlessly, as she tries similarly to fathom the meaning of his expression. His hand grips her shoulder, shaking her, and her face contorts. As if in answer to the picture of horror he presents, a cut-away offers an alternative picturisation of masculinity – Jimmy, distracted from mending the roof by a playful kitten.

None of the shots in this sequence deploys the mask or oval frames that make pictures of the earlier courtship scenes. It is as if two discursive threads interweave in the film. A chain of serial pictures represents the objects of the characters' desires, endowed by the distancing effect of self-conscious presentation with aesthetic significance. And a second thread, making much use of close-ups and frontal or angled shot/reverse shot, focuses on the active process of desiring through a look that struggles to call up or control the meaning of the picture, or, more dialectically, another's look – implicitly evoking an answering desire. It was perhaps the need to dramatise a protagonist whose paralysis confines him to a fixed spot that encouraged Cutts to develop the capacity of the look summoned by a picture to traverse an otherwise proscribed space.

FORBIDDEN LOOKS

As I have already suggested in relation to *The Rat*, the look, combined with moving performers and a tracking camera, introduces a mobility of perception capable of countering the socially demarcated boundaries of the geographic imaginary. In two further stunning examples – from *The Sea Urchin* (1926) and *The Queen Was in the Parlour* (1927) – Cutts's unbinding of the camera and use of the dissolve produce a fluidity in which the dissolution and merging of pictures, identities and desires opens onto a perverse, sado-masochistic sub-terrain lying beyond the boundaries that demarcate and define. These images, however, never lose their material, socially determined specificity, and thus they avoid the expressionist distortion or the surreality of the unconscious found in German or French film-making of the teens and 1920s. Rather, in the combination of picture as cultural document and the look as signifier of an occluded subjectivity, Cutts establishes a distinctive pictorial dynamic. Hitchcock would develop this into a powerful art that, in its worldwide recognition, eclipsed both his own British context and the inventive, fertile imagination of his mentor and competitor.

The Sea Urchin – Cutts's excursion into comedy for his first, eagerly awaited film with Betty Balfour – nevertheless opens on a collage of objects precisely chosen and placed to create an arrangement that is both pictorially dynamic and psychosexually perverse. A table top crosses the bottom right corner of the frame, and scattered across it at various angles lie two dolls, a ball, a jar of paint on its side spilling its contents towards the camera, backed by a mouse's cage and doll's house. A birch rod lies diagonally across the image, making a disturbing conjunction between childhood and punishment. The left frame is broken as a black silk-sleeved hand comes in to grasp the rod; the camera pans left as the rod is withdrawn and the image dissolves into a big close-up of a child in a nightgown, sobbing. Cut from the woman's arm to the back of a shirt-sleeved man bent down at a door, while barred panelling lies superimposed across the child's face. As the camera tracks closer to the man and travels over his shoulder, the

child's face looks up and fades out. The camera now tracks past the man's ear towards the door; he moves aside to reveal a peephole. An almost invisible cut leads into a second tracking shot through the peephole, blurring the focus, and passing into an interior mid-shot to reveal an uproarious pillow fight in progress in the dormitory of a girls' orphanage. Having taken in the 'view', the camera tracks out, dissolving through the peephole and back over the man's shoulder. Cut to a medium shot in which a portly woman in voluminous polka-dot skirt and shiny black blouse comes up behind him and whacks his rear with the birch rod. The camera repeats its movements as she replaces him at the peephole, after which she hauls her companion off to another door, where, invoking aural as well as visual sensation, she bends to listen at the keyhole. Cut to the interior, where a series of shots show the girls, led by an ebullient Betty Balfour, turning pillows into accordions and banjos, while a diminutive child dances a wonderful shimmy on her bed. Images of orphanage and punishment, evoking Victorian sentiment and its prurient underside, are contrarily mixed with a lyrical performance of childhood energies, Betty Balfour's ebullient music-hall turns obscuring for contemporary reviewers the underlying perversity of these scenes. Thus *The Bioscope* explains that Betty Balfour 'goes through all in so light-hearted a manner, and is so obviously capable of looking after herself, that one never feels the slightest anxiety as to her ultimate fate'.[123] At a subsequent meeting of the orphanage governors – a set of Dickensian caricatures exuding both punitive vengeance and paternalist sentiment – Balfour's parodic, knockabout antics expose their pantomimic, but nevertheless insidious, villainy. The film uses Betty Balfour's heart-warming camaraderie to resist both the cruelties meted out to the 'poor and unfriended' and, later, the exploitation of the emerging sex industry represented by the Parisian cabaret to which she is consigned. However, in this virtuoso prologue Cutts has tapped into and implicated the spectator in the voyeuristic appeals of the image, which, beneath a pictorial veneer, play on the ambivalent fantasies of the onlooker.

The Queen Was in the Parlour is an adaptation for Gainsborough's Anglo-German programme of Noel Coward's Ruritanian romance both scripted and directed by Cutts. Here, he takes advantage of UFA's production facilities to mount a spectacle that excels in combining picture and theatricalised setting to suggest the activity of subjective desires and fears both constrained by and transgressing gendered demarcations. In the royal castle the birthday of Princess Nadya (Lili Damita) is in progress, celebrated in two contrasting ways. The surviving print opens on a high-angle big close-up of a birthday cake, graced with nineteen candles, the camera panning up to a pert feminine face.[124] Cut to a medium long shot of a bevy of little girls seated at a round table surrounded by feminine decor. A title switches to Prince Alex who stands before an overbearing fireplace in an austere art-deco smoking room, looking down at his four male military-uniformed companions seated at a rectangular table. A close-up focuses on the monocled Prince pouring champagne, and in a long shot the men stand for a toast, the lighting creating a circle around them, leaving the corners of the frame in an ominous darkness. Having established two contrasting pictures, crosscutting flicks twice between the two gendered parties, before they turn to their respective games. Nadya tells a story to a circle of little girls, while the men get progressively drunk. The mood becomes darker as a new picture introduces the castle exterior: a rain-swept, gothic mansion, sporadically illuminated by lightning, with a lighted window gleaming against the storm.

Nadya has now retreated to her bedroom. A high-angle shot of the great hall focuses on a pair of painted doors, which burst open to reveal the carousing men emerging, framed under an arch resting on ornately decorated pillars. Cut to a long shot from the far side of the hall, across to a gallery resting on huge rounded pillars, under which stands a gong. The Prince marches across and swings violently at it, thus evoking sound rather than the look as an invasive threat. A close-up rests on Nadya's face, deep in thought. With a start her face dissolves into the gong, framed in its circle, her hands to her ears, crying out for her maid, Zana. Close-ups flick between Nadya cowering in terror, the drunken Prince wielding gong hammer and whip, and his terrified servants. Alex finally hurls the hammer at a servant, smashing a nearby mirror. The sequence climaxes as the Prince, wielding his whip, ascends to Nadya's bedroom through an architectural complex of twisting horizontal stairs and vertical supports. A high-angle shot of Alex's dark figure on the stairs is intercut with a

close-up on Nadya in bed, the space between them closing. Return to a shot tracking Alex's leather boots through the banisters, then craning vertically up as he ascends and finally dissolving into a close-up of Nadya. Following the pattern developed in *The Sea Urchin*, the camera now travels up over her shoulder and into her ear, projecting Alex's impending invasion of her body and subjectivity.

Thus Cutts exploits the Ruritanian fantasy of Noel Coward's sketch to elaborate the psychosexual dimension of a visual-aural dramaturgy. If the body of the protagonist represents a public carapace – demarcated, singular, discrete – Cutts uses the penetrative capacity of the mobile camera to explore its vulnerability to another's aural presence and 'eye power'.

VISIONS AND SCREENS

The look that crosses otherwise proscribed public spaces is only one manifestation of eye power. When the look is registered as 'seeing', the emphasis is on internal sight – the force of vision. In his analysis of Holman Hunt's *The Awakening Conscience* (1852), Martin Meisel suggests a double process that registers not only the internalised gaze of the conscience-stricken mistress but also its effects in her perception of the outer world. While rendering her parlour with all the vivid, photographic detail of an objective reality, Hunt's detailed *mise en scène* materialises the heightened clarity and estrangement of a subjective vision. The protagonist's 'sightless' look – enacting the process of seeing itself – becomes the centre of attention, activated as a source of drama, while also, Meisel suggests, offering a 'scientific report on a state of consciousness'.[125]

This doubleness of seeing and the seen maintains the boundary between private subjectivity and the external public world, leaving the inner vision to the spectator's imagination. However, the capacity of combination printing and double exposure to render such 'double vision' in literal fashion enables inner subjectivities to be symbolically represented as projected pictures. Such 'visions' were a key element of Victorian photographic entertainments, and the 'spirit' photography that became popular during and after the Great War exploited these technologies. Projected visions through dissolves and superimpositions were common in the late teens and early 1920s. But the relationship between the eye, the close-up and the increasingly mobile camera released looking and seeing from their fixed positions, documenting, as Charles Barr argues of *Brief Encounter* (1945), perceiving and fantasising subjectivities.[126] Crucial to this exchange between subjective perception and external reality is the capacity of the proscenium-picture frame to become a screen.

Cutts's fascination with the look begins to develop these potentials in *The Wonderful Story* by realising the active desires of a paralysed man. The shot following the title, 'The Wedding Day', introduces not Kate and Jimmy's wedding ceremony, but Robert lying rigid on his couch. A further title, 'A strong mind warped by narrowness of an outlook confined to the ceiling', suggests the elision of subjective and objective vision, materialising not only Robert's seeing but the picture he summons up. A close-up replicates Robert's view of four 'screens' between the beams of the ceiling, blank but for cracks in the plaster. An answering medium close-up registers Robert's wild eyes, staring up at the ceiling. As shots flick between the cracked ceiling and Robert's increasingly intense stare, a dissolve brings up the image of the wedding pair at the altar, their backs to us, framed by side wings. In a high-angle close-up, Robert's eyes close. The shot flicks back to the vision which increases in objective reality, as Jimmy puts a ring on Kate's finger, before dissolving back into the empty ceiling screen. The next shot offers the conventional wedding picture with an exterior oval long shot, internally framed by the church porch gate, as we see the wedding party emerge and walk through the churchyard to the camera.

Just as the masks and iris shots, which literally frame a cinematic picture, eventually give way to the production of naturalised frames within filmic compositions, so the materialised 'vision' imposed on a documented reality is displaced by strategies that naturalise visionary seeing, playing on the screen as a place of projected imaginings. In this sense, British cinema stays in touch with its origins in Victorian visual entertainments, and the pleasure that distance from a created image offers to a viewer seeking visual sensations. Significantly, the cinema is a public space for the projection and communal consumption of private obsessions. The triple exchange between proscenium, picture and screen invokes, as suggested in Chapter 1, the on-screen presence of a picture viewer or theatrical audience, whether literal or implied. Thus in the multi-level set of the White Coffin, the camera, positioned behind Zelie and her entourage, picks up the scene below through the frame of a coffin-shaped arch. What was initially a theatrical space now appears as a two-dimensional screen, on which is played out the voyeuristic fantasy of the upper-class sensation seekers. Here, the pleasures of one class are derived from the life-acts of another.

The potential aggression of this viewing position is played out in an early film by George Pearson, *Nothing Else Matters* (1920). Jimmy Daw has been given a new chance by a theatrical impresario who is also a friend of his wife, of whom he is increasingly jealous. Filming in a Huddersfield theatre, Pearson takes his camera up into the gods to a position – recalling Sickert's theatrical paintings – behind the broad back of a spectator, silhouetted in the darkness. As he leans forward, the stage appears as a lit rectangle framed by black wings and blocked by darkened boxes to the right. On this exposed, brightly lit screen-like space, Jimmy performs a dance routine. This is sandwiched between shots of his apprehensive wife, of performers watching from the wings and of audience members looking at each other, whispering. Finally, in a low-angle shot, Jimmy, tilting slightly while fingering his bowler, begins to crumple. The series returns to the high-angle shot from the gods, positioned again behind the silhouetted figure, who now leans to hurl missiles at the stage, into which is cut a close-up of Jimmy's wife, shrinking as if she has been hit. In a shot from the wings Jimmy looks despairingly to the camera, just over the head of the stage manager, while figures in the opposite wings gesticulate frantically and the manager calls down the curtain. A final high-angle shot from the gods, the silhouette now vanished, has the film (rather than theatrical) audience gazing down on Jimmy's small, lonely figure, trapped within the screen-like proscenium as the curtain falls.

The tension between looking and projected vision, refracted through on-screen surrogates for the film-viewer, invokes the reflexivity that Charles Barr notes of British cinema. For George Pearson, such reflexive moments feed into a meditation on the relation of art and life, rather than rebounding back on the viewing process itself. However, as we have seen, Graham Cutts's imagination takes the potentially perverse pleasures of viewing into the realms of voyeuristic, sado-masochistic fantasy. While the theatrical settings of Parisian dive and Ruritanian palace cushion these implications, the cottage-bound domestic violence of the early *Flames of Passion* reveals this structure more explicitly, thereby exposing the viewer's position and accounting perhaps for stronger critical discomfort. An angry scene takes place between the now unemployed chauffeur, Watson, and his wife, Kate. Perhaps to produce the space and viewing distance necessary to theaticalise a violent row within the confines of a workman's cottage, Cutts switches from alternating close-ups between the faces of husband and wife to exterior shots of neighbours looking down through the basement windows. As the alternation grows more intense, and Watson's leering eyes move closer to the camera, the spectator is first positioned to experience the full force of his deranged hatred and then switched outside to observe the responses of the watching neighbours. This structure suggests the ambivalence of a spectatorship that demands murder and rape to satisfy curious desires – a process Hitchcock will make his speciality. The inclusion of watching neighbours is repeated during the later build-up to Watson's murder of the baby while Kate is absent. With her frantic return accompanied by his brother, the neighbours are joined by a policeman. In the concluding series of close-ups on the violent emotions of the three inside, the watching neighbours are displaced, perhaps as a tacit recognition of the morally ambivalent emotions in play, by a huge close-up of a policeman's hand knocking at the door.

CODA: HITCHCOCK, *THE MANXMAN* AND THE POETICS OF BRITISH CINEMA

Drawing on the compendium of pictorial-theatrical devices explored so far, Hitchcock creates in *The Manxman* the ultimate picture story of British cinema, one that exploits the processes of picture-making and viewing as the switching-point between subjective desires and public language. The drama is enacted through a series of frontally shot picture portraits and group tableaux, the pace quickened when necessary through an Elveyesque flicker-book style of montage, homing in on and activating the emotional turning point of a pictorially realised situation, provoking its dissolution and reconfiguration. Eliot Stannard's script from Hall Caine's popular novel

provides a stock plot line of rivalry between childhood friends – Pete Quilliam, the fisherman, and Philip Christian, the lawyer – for the love of the same woman, Kate Cregeen. The outcome involves the disappearance of Pete to seek his fortune, while Philip becomes entangled with Kate, who had promised to wait. The familiar if illogical plot twists generate emotionally piquant situations between the trio, orchestrated into telling pictures and scenes, framed by windows, doorways and arches. The protagonists, divided socially and temperamentally, view each other as if across the space of picture gallery or theatrical stalls, striving to read each other's hearts and to impose on each other their own desires. Flicker-book montage between frontal close-ups sandwiches the spectator between demanding or heart-reading protagonists, whose glances meets ours as they direct their gaze to the other behind the camera and the viewing audience. As Michael Allen has suggested of Griffith's later films, such strategies emphasise the screen as site of cross-projected fantasies and the position of the spectator as receptor of the desires, fears and antagonisms they generate.[127]

Pete and Philip are monopathic figures, created by diametrically contrasting performances, with only a few emblematic expressions and body gestures as clearly legible indices of character. Pete, the fisherman, played by the Danish star, Carl Brisson, represents the natural man, clad in a black wool jersey, with broad shoulders and capacious arm gestures, a wide smile, displaying gleaming white teeth, and shining, exuberant wide eyes, apparently glimpsing the Kingdom of Heaven just beyond the horizon. However, in his childlike innocence he is also vulnerable, prefiguring the 'maternal' or 'new' man and generating pathos as he sails home unknowingly into the tangled web that awaits his return from abroad. His childhood friend, Philip (Malcolm Keene), brought up in the local manse by his aunt to succeed to the position of deemster or judge, is a rising young lawyer, a true Britisher, with a stiff, upright, suited body, rigid gestures and immobile face. His fixed gaze registers only two expressions: a hungry, repressed longing and a vision of horror, as his desires conflict with the bonds of male friendship, his own ambitions and public honour. Drawing these two men together while also separating them is Kate (Anny Ondra), barmaid in, and in many ways embodiment of, the Manx Fairy, run by her father,

Caesar (Randle Ayrton), a fundamentalist and grasping patriarch. Anny Ondra's mobile features – switching between sexy flirtation, wistful longing and practical determination, and capable equally of facial stoniness or far-away gaze expressing unfathomable loss – make Kate the enigmatic, unknowable object of all three men's desires. But she also struggles to write her own story in discourses that cut across their attempts to fashion her image.

The need of her would-be lovers to cross the distance imposed by frontal pictorial framing and theatrical staging is first enacted in the Manx Fairy, where Pete and Philip have gathered with the local fishermen to sign a petition against encroaching steam trawlers. They linger with Kate, leaning flirtatiously across the bar, turning from one to the other. However, Philip is pulled away by fishermen eager to progress the petition. Two pictures are now set up opposite each other: Pete at the bar in intimate chat with Kate, and Philip, taking the public position at the other end of the room, discoursing with the fishermen. Flicker-book editing sets in motion an intensifying interaction between pictures, emotionally dynamising the space that separates them, and eventually triggering their reconfiguration into new arrangements. In Shot 1 a frontal medium close-up centres on Philip, flanked by three fishermen's heads. As he turns from one to the other, his eyes passing across the camera become abstracted and his speech slows. A reverse medium long shot (Shot 2) looks with Philip past the out-of-focus faces pressing in on the sides of the frame, across the crowded room of dark-jerseyed bodies to a lighted gap focusing on the bar. Here, Pete leans at ease looking down on Kate, who, eyes lowered, laughs, while Pete lightly touches her hair. Flick back to Shot 1, where Philip's eyes lower and he continues speaking more slowly, glancing from side to side, trying to avoid the frontal look, until his gaze is again arrested, caught looking into the camera. Return to Shot 2, where Kate looks up at Pete, replying to his banter. Cut back to Shot 1, Philip's anxiety becoming more palpable as he stops talking, and then, pulling himself together, calls out to Pete. Now the first movement to recompose the picture is made as the men also turn, creating more space to focus on Pete, who looks across the space, light-heartedly waving away Philip's call, and turning back to Kate. It takes six of these alternations – twelve frontal shots in all – before Philip's increasing

anxiety and urgency drag Pete away from his semi-private space with Kate across the room to the public arena in which the fishermen await him.

The following sequence centres on the tableau or peep show that carries both projected desires and requires social reading. The bar has emptied except for Philip, seated in a dark corner bent over paperwork in the left front corner of the frame, and Pete's dark-clothed body straining taut against the bar, gazing intently through a window-framed partition into Caesar's living room. The next shot shows what Pete sees framed in the glass panes: a family tableau with Kate seated at a table beside her father going over the accounts, her mother back right, dozing over some sewing by the fire. Indicating to Philip his intentions, Pete approaches the living-room door. The next shot shows in dumb show the impact of Pete's off-screen presence on the tableau. Caesar, his self-satisfied expression falling, lays down the notes he has been counting, and bringing his hands to his lapels, slowly rises. A dissolve takes us into the emotional threat he represents as he leers grimly into the camera, driving Pete back. In his unwitting innocence, Pete now asks Philip to speak to Caesar on his behalf. Again we are positioned behind Pete as he cranes from the bar to see the little drama enacted behind the glass panes, carrying the burden of his projected desires. From his mimed gestures we see that Caesar is at first pleased when he thinks that Philip is asking to court Kate himself and then thunderstruck to learn his true mission. A flicker-book exchange between the two set-ups leaves the audience in the public bar. We either watch the tableau framed behind glass panes – subjected with Pete to Caesar's reverse gaze as he peers horrified back through the dividing window – or we become recipients of Pete's frontal, close-up looks into camera, projecting at first optimistic, then fading, hopes and eventually fear as he attempts to read what is going on in the peep show beyond.

The characters' 'heart reading of pictures', as Henry Edwards puts it, is complicated by the enigmatic pictures offered by Kate and by her equally ambivalent readings of those she views. Frequently centred as the object of three men's desires and ambitions, her volatile and changing emotions nevertheless drive their fates. She is projected image and object of desire, frequently pictured in a window frame. But in seeking her own desires through the outlets and identities offered by theirs, she binds the men ever more closely together, bringing them all to ruin. The turning pages of Kate's diary, recording a growing intimacy as her encounters with Mr Christian change to assignations with Philip – briefly pictured in some of the most picturesque landscape images caught in British cinema (Fig. 4.3) – provides a segue into the next picture drama, which racks up the emotional situation a notch further.

Philip has set out determinedly from the manse to the Manx Fairy, possibly with the intention of cooling relations with Kate, but this founders when Caesar, clutching a telegram, tells him 'Pete's dead!' A medium long shot over the heads of Caesar and two other men present Philip with the anticipated picture: Kate, slightly hunched, standing stock-still, her back to us in a room beyond the bar and doubly framed by the doorway and the curtained window behind her. Caesar tells Philip that Kate has not spoken a word since the news arrived. A tableau of stasis, of locked emotion, follows, until Philip breaks purposefully into motion, pausing only on the threshold of the room where Kate still stands. A flicker-book montage constructs his cautious approach as he enters her picture, willing her to turn into frontal close-up, her lips pursed, looking into the camera, breathing heavily. The viewer is again caught in the exchange of the close-ups that realise their intensifying reconnection, becoming the recipient of an astonishing emotional reconfiguration – 'Philip we're free!' This unexpected interpretation of a scene of tragic loss demands of both Philip and audience a retrospective rereading of the pictures that have gone

Fig. 4.3. Hitchcock's picturesquely framed landscape in *The Manxman* (1929)

before. The shock is worked through a continuing flicker between frontal close-ups of each of the protagonists, as, raising her clenched fists, Kate moves towards Philip. The sequence comes to a close with a picture of the newly formed couple framed in the doorway to the pub, her head bowed on Philip's protective shoulder, to be followed abruptly by a big close-up of Pete, smiling into the camera, telegramming his return.

Before this happens, however, theatrical picture staging is given over to Kate, as she leads Philip into an old mill house, their prospective home. Out of the architecture of the upper floor, Hitchcock and Norman Arnold, his art director, construct two pictorial stages at either end, utilising framing beams, gantries and heaped corn bags, and at Kate's end, a raised stage-like platform. A two-shot of the pair, standing side by side, a prospective bridal couple, is followed by their view of the length of the mill loft. Kate runs to the far end, where she turns with a little pirouette, as if performing on stage, framed within a proscenium created by sloping crossbeams, with steps leading up to a platform behind her. Her glance is caught by the grinding stones and laughingly she heaves them into action, at the same time releasing movement trapped not only in the stones but in their own bodies, prefigured in the kissing country couple they pass on their way into the mill. Philip stands tensely by a coiled rope, his arms flexed as if braced for action, yet locked in the frame at the far end of the loft, watching her. In an answering frontal shot she is poised, bent, her arm on the winding mechanism, looking back intensely, the stones revolving by her side. She straightens up, her fingers curled in anticipation, and giving a little shudder, she glances once more at the revolving stones and then back to Philip, still stock-still. Deliberately she walks out of her staged picture and into his, framed by a low rafter and corn sacks. He remains rigid, until she raises her arms towards him and he seizes her in a passionate kiss, the unleashed movement completed in a dissolve of the two mill stones sliding over each other.

Pete returns, having established his earning credentials, Philip retreats out of honour, and Caesar impresses on Kate her duty to keep her promise. The sequences of betrothal and her wedding reduce Kate to a cipher – an image – in a patriarchal scenario. But her pregnancy by Philip, and the latter's refusal to let her tell Pete, releases her repressed desire to escape the picture in which she is confined. When Pete interrupts her scene with Philip, Kate begins her intended confession. Philip walks away to stand at the open porch door. A mid-shot lines up Pete, who stands facing the camera, back to back with Philip and framed by the open door, the men seemingly conjoined at their right and left shoulders. The next mid-shot frames Kate, her fingers twisting nervously, within the heavy arch of the kitchen range, two confrontational pictures echoing the stage pictures constructed between Kate and Philip in the mill loft. Here, however, Pete in his innocence is the only moving figure, crossing into her picture and begging to be told what is amiss. She only retails half her message before Pete, in a series of ecstatic shots, is thanking heaven for the joyful news and calling the reluctant Philip back into the picture. In mid-shot Philip turns and looks to the camera with frozen horror. The return shot pictures Pete cuddling Kate, she gazing back in defeat at the camera, the audience and Philip off screen. Pete turns away, swinging his arms up from his elbows in epic triumph, then stretching out to Kate and Philip on either side, who turn to the front staring grimly into the camera, configured in a tableau of ritual crucifixion.

Kate's suicide attempt brings her to court on the day of Philip's inauguration as deemster. The court-room provides the tightly regulated public place where intimate truths become official statements. The key to the trapped momentum locked in the protagonists' inner desires is turned by the woman's voice. To the deemster's decree that she can return home, Kate announces deliberately and expressionlessly: 'I am not going back.' This triggers Pete's acknowledgment of her earlier love – to whom he does not yet know – and, in turn, Caesar's climactic revelation of Philip's guilt. This turning point breaks up a mosaic of frozen pictures: Caesar's arm pointing in accusation at Philip; Philip stood on a knife-edge of momentous decision; Kate rigid with shock, staring into the camera; Pete looking bewildered from

one to the other, while all is chaos around them. As in a kaleidoscope, these elements are reconfigured in movements of astonishment, scandal and the pained recognition of the chief protagonists. The crux of the scene is the retrospective reconfiguration and rereading of the significance of the pictures that have gone before. In medium close-up, Pete turns to the camera, his eyes unfocused, to be met by Caesar's line: 'Can't you see Pete? Can't you see?' Finally, Philip makes a public confession, resigns his position as deemster and sets out to make amends to Kate. The final curtain tableau, however, does not suggest that anyone has gained from this conclusion. Back in the mill-house kitchen, the scene fades up on Pete standing upright in the centre of the room facing the camera, his back to the kitchen table, Kate stooped miserably over the cradle framed by the mantle over the hearth, and Philip, standing, hanging his head at the open doorway. Slowly Kate lifts the baby, turning to look across the room to Philip. Cut to the shot Graham Cutts used for *Flames of Passion*, the window panes filled with the vindictive faces of neighbours gazing in. As Kate moves to go, Pete bends to kiss the baby, then draws himself up, staring into the camera, as she passes behind the table at the back of the frame, and out past Philip at the door. This is the theatrical conclusion. Cinema, seeking out and realising the incipient movement trapped in the picture, offers a low-angle long shot as Kate and Philip progress slowly uphill with the baby under a stormy sky. This dissolves into a big close-up of Pete's face at the mast of his boat, hair blowing in the breeze, his eyes softly grazing the camera lens: a mirror shot of the opening, except that now his boat is not coming home but setting out to sea.

The Manxman is a product of the poetics of British cinema, demonstrating both the rootedness of Hitchcock's techniques in its pictorial-theatrical practices and the powerful and distinctive cinematic language they can generate. This very excellence has served to obscure Hitchcock's aesthetic allegiances.

5 Class Acts: Genres, Modes and Performers

The aesthetic success of Hollywood cinema rests on the capacity of two interlocking systems – the star system and the genre system – to bind the manufacture of film narratives together with marketing aimed at audiences. The gradual emergence of a genre system functioned to transform a range of inherited materials – literary and dramatic forms, popular entertainment traditions, topical events – into stabilising production categories. By the end of the 1920s Hollywood offered a roster of film types that knitted together into a system capable of both stimulating and supervising production, defining markets and reviewing categories. At the same time, flexible boundaries between genres facilitate crossovers, ensuring broad appeal and the capacity to track shifting audiences.

If the emergence of genre categories is associated with a stabilising industry, the conditions of postwar British film-making were, as Rachael Low's study documents, extremely *un*stable.[1] Needing to abandon the practices of artisanal manufacture for those of a full-blown industrial system, the British film industry was in constant flux. At the same time, producers struggled to gauge the market for British films and to define a national voice in competition with, or accommodation to, the dominance of Hollywood, while also looking to Film Europe for co-production deals and the possibility of strengthening an identity to counter America.[2] British film-makers, then, sought to found stable categories of production on contradictory and shifting cultural terrain.

Denis Gifford, in his herculean task of cataloguing British film production, undertakes to place each film in a one-word category defined by content according to trade-press terms and plot summaries.[3] Throughout the decade four categories dominate: comedy, romance, crime, drama. Others with lower numerical entries include adventure, war and sport while a sprinkling fall into the categories of history,

fantasy, horror, trick and 'act' (i.e. recorded variety acts). By 1928 two categories dominate: comedy and, with the coming of sound, the musical. Gifford's categories vary in their degree of elasticity. Comedy, for example, covers a wide range of subject matter, while romance is narrowed from its association with adventure to a focus on love. Noticeably, Gifford avoids the category 'melodrama'. However, the plot lines for drama, distinguished as 'serious', suggest domestic melodrama, while crime is almost inevitably melodramatic in mode. In this respect, comedy, romance and drama/melodrama, while implying certain motifs and strategies, represent cross-generic modes, capable of treating a range of material and indeed drawing on each other's practices. Only 'crime', defined by a content that necessitates a certain set of protagonists and narrative moves, comes close to constituting a coherent genre. While Gifford seeks precision with single-word designations, his one-sentence plots, together with the evidence of the films themselves, suggest a broad content that may be treated within a variety of modes, whether romance, melodrama or comedy.

Contributing to such fluidity is British cinema's ambivalent location which is not only geographical – positioned between Hollywood and Europe – but historical. The moment of industrial consolidation takes place within a stratified society whose sense of continuity between past and future had been dislocated by the traumatic experience of modern technological warfare. If this trauma failed to yield the imaginative rupture sought by latter-day modernists, the films of the 1920s are indirectly marked by what Michael Williams, following columnist, Edith Nepean, has identified as the 'war touch' – the registration of the widespread experience of bereavement and the upheavals of the Great War.[4] These films offer imaginary spaces of fantasy and nostalgia, even while the future beckons from an America exporting to Britain a new, vigorous popular culture via the dance hall, jazz, Hollywood, the motor car and other consumer experiences. If these fantasies appeared to some whimsical and regressive, the vivid presence of American films, articulating through different aesthetic and generic practices alternative socio-cultural values, reinforced debates in the press and trade journals about the worth of different kinds of film and modes of film-making.

Such debates are reflexes of cultural encounters facilitated by the processes of modal and generic production. For while production categories serve to manage cultural and aesthetic diversity in the interests of stabilisation, they also appropriate and remix generic elements, producing new combinations in search of new markets. In the process the boundaries that divide and assign social status and function to different cultural and aesthetic practices are contested. As this chapter will show, critics have much at stake in such boundaries. Since generic forms exist within so active a condition of intertextual mutation and discursive ferment, they both contribute to and reveal clues about the shifting parameters of cultural identity working through at an imaginary level in mass-produced fictions and fantasies.[5] In the transitional state of 1920s British society, materials belonging to different generic forms and cultural practices represent potent social signifiers. Drawing these into the emerging forms of filmic storytelling, therefore, often produces 'telling' aesthetic and cultural encounters.

In this context, then, this chapter traces less fully formed genres than the clustering of modal tropes and generic elements to form loose generic constellations. In particular, I focus on the modalities of romance and melodrama – and their associated cycles such as the costume romance, crime melodrama and domestic melodrama – while closing with an alternative, more explicitly parodic, constellation, drawing on music-hall practices.

CULTURAL MODALITIES

Melodrama is inextricably linked to the emergence of a popular mass-mediated sphere organised in different generic kinds, the shifts between which trace changing processes of aesthetic and social perception at work. For example, out of the highly flexible aesthetic of melodrama, organising its materials into emotionally and visually spectacular confrontations

between ethically opposed antagonists, a range of sub-generic forms and cycles proliferated. Many of these provided the underpinnings of familiar American film genres of the 20th century: cape-and-sword melodrama surviving as the swashbuckler or Ruritanian romance; domestic melodrama as the family melodrama; gothic melodrama as gothic romance or gaslight melodrama; blood-and-thunder melodrama as crime melodrama; and so on. Hollywood's distinctive, interlocking genre system drew on a national imaginary bent on pulling diverse cultural identities and traditions into a new overarching, egalitarian American identity. For, melodrama's figures of villainy and virtue can appear in a variety of social positions and embodiments. Starting from an American identity conceived as the source of unclassed virtue, Hollywood transformed the class oppositions of European melodrama into new configurations: for example, the new country pitted against the old; the Westerner against the Easterner; the pioneers against the indigenous nations, and so on. In time, such oppositions reverse across the line of villainy and virtue to reformulate moral struggle anew as the conditions of ideological recognition change. British culture, however, was unable to deny by homogenising social difference in a national 'melting pot'. Thus melodrama's reform led to a number of splittings. In Chapter 3, I suggested how the aesthetic of restraint and passion appropriate to the middle-class drawing room subjected 'straight' roles to a psychological fissure between the outer public persona and an occluded inner self. Below, I examine a differently inflected melodrama that combines with romance to transform the aristocratic villain into a twentieth-century anti-hero of romantic or costume melodrama, less as a class exploiter than a figure capable of activating female sexuality. Conversely, broader, 'rhetorical' performance and confrontational address are retained for the now proletarianised villains of crime melodramas or for music-hall style comedy. Thus aesthetic practices diverge along class-inflected modal lines. Such critical and cultural fractures consolidate the fault line between the highbrow intelligentsia and popular mass audience.[6] Broad appeal in the British context depends less on a homogenising convergence of materials into classifiable genres, than the production of fictional arenas in which a range of culturally differentiated forms and styles can mingle. British production, then, largely favours modal categories such as romance, comedy, melodrama and social realism, which are less dependent on thematic or iconographic definition and more able to shift between a range of social protagonists and locations.

Within these constellations the cultural-aesthetic practices discussed in Part One of this study evolve a set of stratagems that work around the tension between socially differentiated identities and the official egalitarianism of modern democracy. For romance, melodrama and comedy are constellations that support role-playing, disguise and the staging of alter egos. Such stratagems enact fissured imaginings, whether internal – public persona fronting inner feeling – or external, through cross-class or gender dressing and adventuring. It is no accident that these modal types and generic constellations involve performers, since entertainment practices function as cultural markers and merge into social acts. Thus this exploration examines, along with typical films, the players who particularly lent themselves to play-acting, dressing up, disguise and doubling of characters as a means of crossing boundaries and switching back and forth between repression and release. Through such mechanisms drama is generated from encounters between socially demarcated protagonists and cultural types, while maintaining the boundaries of social difference.

Revivals and Reinventions

The reform of melodrama effected in mainstream theatre proved something of a pyrrhic victory for middle-class culture. As the idea of the 'natural' continues its democratising slide into identification with the 'ordinary', British theatre confronted the problem posed by Desmond MacCarthy in a 1930 BBC talk on Galsworthy and realism. According to his argument, since 'external life has become less violent, exciting, picturesque . . . the drama that stands for reality is of necessity less demonstrative'.[7]

Hugh Ford, whose complaints about the 'menace of restraint' were noted in Chapter 3, recommended as countermeasure reviving the 'art of pantomime'.[8] Netterville Barron – the doctor with an interest in acting, discussed in the same context – had himself written several 'wordless plays'.[9] His activities linked a new interest in physical culture with a revival by the artistic intelligentsia of earlier folk and urban entertainment traditions, which were seized on at the turn of the century as a source of authentic theatricality

just as they appeared to be dying out. The link between the 'pantomime' recommended by Hugh Ford and Barron's 'wordless plays' lies in the renewed interest in the art of mime (as distinct from the Christmas pantomime). According to Jon Burrows, this was stimulated by the visits of Continental mime companies to Britain and the United States.[10] As an art form, mime promised the intelligentsia access to an expressive medium less contaminated than melodrama by the commercial production of mass entertainment, while at the same time authenticated through derivation from a traditional folk culture that no longer posed the threat of vulgarity because it was fast disappearing. In 1899 the *Journal of the Folk Song Society* is established and in 1907 Cecil Sharp publishes the results of his cycling forays into rural England in *English Folk Song*. Pageants retailing the history of local communities, starting in 1905 with Louis N. Parker's Sherborne pageant, spread throughout the country in the 1900s, mounted with a patriotic twist during the war and in 1918 leading to a showpiece of theatrical historicity, *The Pageant of Drury Lane*. The figure of Pierrot, deriving from the fast disappearing harlequinade, makes a comeback through the seaside Pierrot shows popular through the 1900s, taking London by storm in a successful revival by the Co-Optimists over several seasons in the 1920s.[11] The figure inspires a 1922 advertisement in *Pictures* for a breath sweetener, 'Sweet Lips', featuring Pierrot and Pierrette and the following verse:

> Though the Carnival is over, dear Pierrette,
> That night of wild delight I'll ne'er forget,
> For you squeezed my fingers slily
> And your 'Sweet Lips' whispered shyly
> That you'd dance with me through life, my own
> Pierrette.[12]

Working across film-making, theatre and poetry, Kenelm Foss brought out a book of illustrated verse in 1920, *Pierrot Speaks*, dedicated to a litany of Pierrot's lost loves. Intertwined with such revivalism is renewed interest, noted in the last chapter, in fairy tales and classical myth. In 1922, J. G. Frazer's *The Golden Bough: A Study in Magic and Religion* is published.

While these revivals both serve a middle-class antiquarian interest in a past popular culture and permit an escape from mundane naturalism, they offer film-makers a relatively 'high-toned' artistic dimension with broad, democratising middlebrow appeal. As discussed in Chapter 4, Hepworth's *Pipes of Pan* (1923) combines the revival of fairy and classical motifs. George Pearson shares this interest in traditional entertainment forms. The prologue for *Nothing Else Matters* (1920) features a dance between Pierrot and Columbine, interrupted by Harlequin, while *The Little People* (1926) turns on the conflict between folk tradition represented by the puppet shows Pearson encountered in Italy and modern commercial entertainment represented by the Mayfair nightclub (see Chapter 6). Such antiquarian research and self-conscious revivals feed a wider set of cultural practices among the middle classes, providing material for amateur theatricals, charades and fancy-dress parties, which find their counterpart in the frequent episodes already noted featuring carnivals, country-house parties and masked balls.

The Beloved Vagabond (1923), adapted from a novel and long-running play by W. J. Locke, combines many of these features in a picaresque romance that involves cultural boundary encounters in an 'out-of-class' romance fantasy. A prologue features the Pied Piper, while a masque staged at the fancy-dress ball involves Pan, danced by a young Jessie Matthews in her film debut. Such mythic figures are used to suggest retreat from the hierarchical order of the adult world into the anarchic fantasy of a prelapsarian time. The film centres on the picaresque adventures of Gaston de Nerac (Carlyle Blackwell). He is cheated of his bride, Joanna Rushworth, by the villainous Compte de Verneuil, who is threatening her father with bankruptcy and criminal prosecution. In order to protect her family from ruin, Gaston slips out of her life and society, becoming the layabout President of the London-based Lotus Club.[13] He adopts his washerwoman's young son, who has a penchant for secret reading – *Paradise Lost* – and latent artistic talent. Renaming the boy Asticot and taking to the road in Brittany – 'the Country of Vagabondia [where] . . . every man may be king' – Gaston, now known as the minstrel, Paragot, completes his family romance by adding Blanquette, a young orphan girl, to his troupe. One day Joanna appears among the café clientele. After a passionate violin solo, Gaston smashes his instrument, sends Asticot off to an art master and Blanquette to friends in the country, while

he himself sinks into drink. However, Asticot keeps secret watch over him, while the Count on his deathbed confesses to Joanna the reason for Gaston's disappearance. Joanna and Gaston meet again, and he attempts to cast off his identity as Paragot. But the film follows the original story in casting its lot with the fantasy. Refusing the socially respectable happy ending, Gaston leaves Joanna and her upper-class world behind for pastoral retreat with his family of waifs and strays. Thus dressing up and identity switches negotiate in fantasy symbolic class relations, privileging more democratic imaginings. As an intertitle comments, Asticot's 'Paradise Found' lies in the kitchens of the Lotus Club, where he is surrounded by the tantalising smells and cheerful bustle of cooking. While Gaston/Paragot disintegrates, the Child, Asticot, is endorsed as guide into the new century. Developing his powers as an artist, Asticot takes control of the Beloved Vagabond's story. For if Gaston's encounters with Joanna deal either in the tragedy of loss or a possible conventional happy ending, Asticot effectively creates an alternative to both, engineering Gaston's reunion with Blanquette, the classless figure of folk tale who secretly loves him. She, unlike the Child in Hepworth's *Pipes of Pan*, survives.

Revivalist practices and motifs, then, encouraged an endemic penchant for dressing up and disguise as a kind of cultural transvestism, through which imaginary figures try on others' identities and engage in cross-class encounters. The fantasising modality permitted by devices such as the masked ball, charades, fairy ballets and harlequinade found another, more flamboyant, outlet in the romantic costume melodrama, which, combining picaresque adventure in picturesque historical settings with heterosexual romance, was by 1923 experiencing cinematic growth rather than decline.

ACTING ROMANTIC

In the theatre, as noted in Chapter 1, romantic costume melodrama had never disappeared. It was perpetuated in the repertoires of actor-managers such as Fred Terry or Sir John Martin-Harvey. They built careers on the popularity of roles such as Terry's Sir Percy Blakeney, hero of *The Scarlet Pimpernel*, or Martin-Harvey's Sidney Carton in *The Only Way*, a stage adaptation of Dickens's *A Tale of Two Cities*. At the age of sixty-two Sir Martin-Harvey recorded his performance for posterity in Herbert Wilcox's film version of 1925. For British cinema, one of the strongest links with this romantic theatrical tradition was forged through Matheson Lang, already discussed in Chapter 3 for his role in *Carnival* (1921). Although from cinema's teen years into the 1920s, numerous star actors made guest appearances in film records and recreations of their theatrical successes,[14] Matheson Lang, like Ivor Novello, pursued a considerable film career from 1916 into the 1930s. In 1919 he succumbed to pressure from Stoll to sign a twelve-film contract, where he came under the direction of Maurice Elvey. After an apprenticeship with Frank Benson's touring Shakespearian company, Lang, like Elvey, had spent his early years alternating between romantic dramas, Shakespeare and the new drama of Ibsen and Shaw. While signed up for the Vedrenne/Barker seasons at the Royal Court (1904) and later at the Savoy (1907), Lang achieved his first notable theatrical success as John Storm in Hall Caine's modern romantic drama, *The Christian* (1907) at the Lyceum. A virtual national theatre under Irving, but, following his departure in 1902, operating unsuccessfully as a music hall, the Lyceum had now, Lang notes in his autobiography, reopened as a 'People's theatre', offering 'a popular home for romantic drama' as well as 'Shakespeare for the People'.[15]

Through the contract with Stoll, Lang took this strand of popular theatre into the cinema of the 1920s, by preference adapting his already practised stage roles to what he experienced as the unsympathetic conditions of the studio. Rachael Low notes that Lang was 'one of the many actors particularly fond of the element of disguise and dressing-up in the theatre . . . specialis[ing] in elaborate make-ups, which he brought virtually unchanged to the screen'. Low sees make-up as 'no substitute, on the screen, for casting a suitable person in the first place'.[16] Lang's popularity in star polls, however, suggests that dressing up and disguise did not constitute a problem for his followers but were part of the appeal of the romantic melodramas that he favoured and the style of acting they required.[17] J. C. Trewin, characterising his theatrical persona, comments: 'Lang, handsome and sonorous, was . . . an actor who never seemed really at ease in a lounge suit.'[18] Although, as Lang makes plain in his autobiography, he undertook film-making largely to provide a means of financing his elaborate stage productions,

he was nevertheless committed to professionalism as an actor whether on stage or in the studio. Against those who regarded Lang as a Shakespearian lost to romantic drama (for example, his *Manchester Guardian* obituary writer),[19] stands J. C. Trewin's comment:

> Lang . . . was the most consistent romantic player of the Twenties . . . [who] never patronised his characters. He enjoyed them and presented them sincerely in the broad romantic method . . . *Carnival* was a florid play but he believed in it in the theatre, almost as much as in *Othello* itself.[20]

As Trewin implies, theatricality is central to this belief. In this respect, dressing up is not only a part of 'acting romantic' but a key element in a cultural aesthetic that depends on performance and the production of public identities. Both Elvey and Lang resisted the division of the arts into 'high' and 'lowbrow', preferring to stake out a populist middle ground that combined unpretentiousness with assurance of a broad audience, high-quality entertainment and the financial success that would support further production. This led to a good working partnership between them and the creation of a formula that clearly appealed to one segment of the film audience.[21]

DRESSING UP: THE COSTUME ROMANCE

Several trade and fan papers comment on the apparent surge in romantic costume drama in the mid-1920s. In December 1921 the American scenarist, Jeanie McPherson, writing in *Kinematograph Weekly*, warns would-be screenplay writers against costume stories, despite a revival appearing imminent.[22] By January 1923 Martin Lane comments that 'the recent spate of historical and romantic films' suggests an end to the 'taboo' against 'the despised costume drama based on actual historical fact' or 'the romantic type of picture set in scenes of the past'.[23] *The Motion Picture Studio* analyses the underlying production considerations. Companies such as Ideal, Hepworth, Stoll, Davidson, Samuelson and Gaumont, who had formerly resisted costume pictures on grounds of expense, were now forced by American competition in the sphere of the contemporary picture to look elsewhere for novelty. Once the breakthrough in costume drama had been made, it became clear that 'screen versions of countless great and appealing subjects' now offered 'greater chance of popular approval and a firmer likelihood of a foreign market to recoup . . . the additional outlay'.[24] Lane details these likely appeals: 'the whole book of English history teems with film stories, tragic, humorous, romantic, thrilling, adventurous, picturesque'.[25] Although conceding the 'great deal of labour, attention to detail, accuracy of costume and incident and much research work' required, it is emotional effects and visceral sensations – the core appeals of the melodramatic mode – that he stresses. *Pictures and the Picturegoer*, exploring twenty costume plays of 1923, focuses on the thrills of fencing – 'the most gallant fashion of all', in which the screen affords 'a close view, and clear insight into a fascinating if deadly occupation'.[26]

There is, nevertheless, a tension in this welcome for the romantic costume drama, between the values of historical accuracy and realism and the cavalier romancing of costume drama. S. R. Littlewood, critic for *The Sphere*, claims that film possesses 'an entirely new technique, unknown to the stage, which allows of romance and realism being blended', as a result 'abolish[ing] the division between tale and history'.[27] The realism of film backgrounds, he suggests, misleads by apparently authenticating romance, which flies in the face of accuracy. Similarly, an *Evening News* critic argues in 1926; 'Film art is applied romance. While the filmmaker must build on romance, he must also build towards reality.'[28] Given this prevailing concern, even the *Pictures and the Picturegoer* commentator, cited above, feels compelled to suggest that, fascinating though watching male bodies in the cut and thrust of a sword fight may be, there is something educational to be learned.

This concern with verisimilitude is perhaps to be expected when cultural practices serve also as cultural documents. Conversely, if the document is also a product of culture, it is available for the imaginary work of melodrama and romance. Martin Lane, in *Kinematograph Weekly*, suggests 'that, though we live in democratic times, there is in all of us an inherent love of pageantry'.[29] Kathleen Mason, in her column for *Kinematograph Weekly*, 'Through Women's Eyes', puts a gendered twist on this claim, asserting the appeal 'of romance and adventure to women to whom nothing of the kind happens'.[30] In this respect, romance provides a pivot between the differentially gendered spheres of adventure and love. At the same time, these comments suggest that the continuing appeal of melodrama and costume romance arises partly from their dramatic exploitation of the class and gender boundaries necessary to a class-differentiated verisimilitude but which are increasingly open to the excitements of transgression in 'democratic times'.

There are a number of ways in which romance gives back what is increasingly rejected in traditional melodrama and proscribed by the equation of realism with the mundane. Historical settings legitimate the retention of expansive and expressive performance styles and dramatic encounters. Lilian Bamburg, in *Film Acting As a Career*, advises that 'if you are called upon to fill a "crowd" in a Costume play, your gestures must be more elaborately courteous and picturesque, while, at the same time, slower than those of a modern man or woman'.[31] At the same time, as is clear from Bamburg's reference to 'courtesy', romantic costume drama justifies aristocratic settings and protagonists capable of expressive power based on class control while still emphatically different from ordinary behaviour. Costume, setting and musical accompaniment enlarge the impact of refined underplaying, while historicised class settings provide a certain high-toned verisimilitude. The sweep of a gown or sleeve, the angle of a hat or wig, the shine and rustle of brocades gliding across gilded sitting rooms, checkered halls or down curving staircases render large and important movements that appear 'natural' because small-scale – a turn of the head or wrist, a wave of the arm or twist of the body. Part of the success of Herbert Wilcox's *Madame Pompadour* (1928) lies in the grandiloquence lent by its elaborate costuming and sets – including royal court rooms, grand staircases, decorative boudoirs and garden parterres – to relatively underplayed and, in the case of Gish, unpremeditated, throwaway gestures.

Aristocratic and country-house settings contribute something of these effects to contemporary stories. In *The Passionate Adventure* (1924) Hitchcock's grand country-house sets leave Clive Brook and Alice Joyce little acting to do. Sweeping staircase, elegant dressing rooms, reflecting mirrors, overbearing carved marble mantelpiece – combined with the elegant evening dress through which the protagonists live up to their surroundings – enable the actors to minimise body movements and facial expressions, while still projecting inner turmoil and passions on a grand, rather than domestic, scale. For a culture dependent on public arenas for action and codes of behaviour, such use of set and costume is crucial. A fashion artist, writing to *The Picturegoer* in January 1929, makes a telling point against the identification of realism with the ordinary:

> The American star is clothed . . . to make her exotic and accentuate her charm . . . some of the gowns [British] stars wear are probably what they would use in private life, quiet, good taste, etc. but on the screen they appear ordinary. They should be daring, brilliant costumes that could tell a story themselves and that express the scene portrayed.[32]

As I shall discuss below, *The Passionate Adventure* uses class-differentiated costumes and settings as contemporary disguises to tell the stories of characters enmeshed in cross-class and gender encounters.

If, then, the body tells a double story through underplaying offset by scenery and dress, the historical costume drama exploits a further tension. For the romantic protagonist crosses the border between contemporary reality and history, conceived in Sue Harper's terms as an imaginary country – a place of refuge from common sense.[33] Matheson Lang, the actor ill at ease in contemporary dress, reflects on his early acting experience, commenting that he found himself leading a 'double existence'. From the daytime ordinary world, night-time took him into 'the completely different realm of the imagination . . . the hours in the theatre seemed the most real in my life'.[34] *The Bioscope*'s response to *Mr Wu* (1919), in which Matheson Lang re-created his popular stage role of 1913–14, responds to the replaying of this tension as theatre passes into cinema:

> Intrinsically, the play is not especially good material for cinema treatment. Its story is lurid and theatrical, and . . . to have transplanted its drama from the artificial atmosphere of the stage to the coldly naturalistic conditions of the screen without destroying its weirdly thrilling qualities is therefore a considerable achievement.[35]

Such achievement calls on visible acting and theatricality to support romance threatened with de-realisation by the screen:

> The fact that the whole production belongs primarily to the theatre rather than to the cinema lessens one's

sense of the unreality of Matheson Lang's performance which clever and thrilling as it is, is essentially a piece of acting and not a piece of nature.[36]

ETHNIC TRANSVESTISM

The distance that makes history an imaginary country is doubled in those films set in the Celtic kingdoms, such as *Rob Roy* (1922) and *Young Lochinvar* (1923), or in foreign and colonial territories, such as *Mr Wu* or *A Romance of Old Baghdad* (1922), both of which starred Matheson Lang, Here dressing up and romantic embodiment enter into imaginary encounter not only with class but with ethnic difference. Of *Mr Wu*, Rachael Low complains that 'never for a moment did [Lang] look Chinese'.[37] But for *The Bioscope* critic, literal impersonation was not the point, nor perhaps for Lang. Creating this figure was for him an initial step towards dismantling the stage Chinaman through a re-inscription of the aesthetic of restraint. In his autobiography Lang describes how, when in Shanghai playing *Macbeth*, he was fascinated by his back stage visitors:

> As they sat in my dressing room, large bland men most of them, with charming manners and an extraordinary sense of dominant personality, the idea came . . . 'what a wonderful thing it would be to get up a play for London about a real Chinese of the type of these men'. Up to then the usual stage Chinaman . . . [was] . . . a rather exaggerated monster of villainy in melodrama, the exact antithesis of these quiet, dignified, cultured people. I became obsessed with the idea and used to watch these men with this in view.[38]

Lang's terms are exactly those of G. H. Lewes observing the shift in stage practice worked on the villain by Madame Vestris and Charles Mathews (see Chapter 3). And trade-press reviews suggest that for Lang's admirers the doubling involved in oriental impersonations taps into the neuralgic conjuncture of restraint and passion through ethnic rather than high-society personae, generating overdetermined and sexualised encounters at the boundaries of racial, cultural and gender difference. In both play and film, Lillah McCarthy plays an English matron marooned in the Far East, whose son has an illicit affair with the daughter of a Chinese overlord, Mr Wu. The disgraced daughter is killed and the son imprisoned by Mr Wu, while his mother is entrapped when she comes to plead for his release. In a period when British imperialism is coming into question, the art of disguise opens up the imaginary identity of a racial 'other' within the limited but expanding terms of a shifting colonial imaginary. *Stoll's Editorial News* comments as the film goes into production: 'Wu never loses his dignity, but there is something more impressive – the Eastern mystery that constantly allures the matter-of-fact Englishman.'[39] *The Cinema* notes: 'the story is based on a poignant theme that cannot fail to be instantaneously popular, contrasting, as it does, the ethics of the two stratospheres'.[40] Thus Lang appropriates from his culturally determined observations of Chinese mannerisms a performance characteristic capable of rekindling the frisson of drawing-room melodrama, while reconstructing the colonised 'other' through the dynamic of external restraint masking internal passion. Thus we have *Kinematograph Weekly*'s oxymoronic delight in Wu's 'burning desire for revenge hidden beneath an icy reserve'.[41] Harold Wimbury's description of Wu's proposal to trade Mrs Gregory's sexual submission for the release of her son details how Lang played this role and just what he could do with a fan:

> The whole interview, with its gorgeous setting, is real and tense. The woman had no excuse. She is here an animal encaged, shut from the world in the grasp of this man, who is immovable in his consuming hatred – too impassioned and fanatical merely to kill. Yet he is quiet and polite always, smiling, bowing, shooting to or snapping open his fan.[42]

Lang's predilection for doubled roles and ethnic impersonation realised in *Carnival* and *Mr Wu* is given full reign in *The Wandering Jew* (1923). J. C. Trewin describes E. Temple Thurston's play as a 'sad piece of tushery', which Lang 'staged and performed with as much care as if it had been *Lear*'.[43] However, it gave Lang multiple scope for disguise as Matathias, the Jewish aristocrat condemned to wander through the centuries until his accusation against Christ as an imposter is redeemed. Time is turned into a 'romantic scenic-railway excursion' from 'Jerusalem to Antioch, Palermo and Seville'.[44] At the same time, this story suggests the ultimate nightmare of the geographic imagination as the Wandering Jew attempts to locate a home, a woman he can possess, a child he can protect. All are destroyed by a literal and metaphoric leprosy that drives Matathias on to a new country and century. For Lang, the plot affords serial opportunities for disguise and dressing up, and for the theatrical exposition of the overreaching, cultural performer he makes of the Wandering Jew. His melodramatic appearance at the feast of a drunken Crusader King as the darkly mysterious Black Knight, invisible in his deadly looking armour yet a seducer at heart, is followed by his transmutation into a worldly Italian Renaissance merchant, alienated from his wife's affections by her attraction to Christianity. Finally, he takes the stage in Seville against the Spanish Inquisition as the world-worn, saddened but now wiser doctor of medical science whose combined knowledge and prayer enables him to cure rather than inflict the curse of leprosy.

Lang's larger-than-life presence dominates sets, crowd scenes and landscapes. In the early personae of the Wandering Jew, he play-acts his various impersonations – including responding to the ray of light that symbolises Christ – presenting the character to the audience. Feeding audience anticipation of impending hubris, he invites appreciation of the energy of his egotistical desires and corresponding nervous irritation when he is thwarted by the counter-demands of Christian conscience in those he wants to love. In the process he offers pleasure in the skill of the actor who can manipulate facial features, musculature and limbs as materialisation of desire and its thwarting in the twists, tilts and shudders of the body. If no history of the Judaic diaspora, the film produces at the level of fantasy a tragic counterpart to the figure of the Beloved Vagabond (also filmed in 1923). Both Gaston and Matathias are uprooted protagonists in search of a stage for action, for a role commensurate with desires that look beyond what their respective – imaginary – societies offer. Whereas Gaston is allowed to run away into the fantasy, Matathias confronts reality in Seville in the form of the Spanish Inquisition, from which he protects a Jewish couple while apparently miraculously curing their child. When the forces of the Inquisition close in, Lang's performance as Matathias, aided by Elvey's dramatic use of space, shadowy lighting and the menacing opposition of the hooded and villainous Chief Inquisitor, gains in intensity and moral stature, as he draws himself upright, solemn and statuesque. In this respect,

Lang's adaptation of the pictorial gestures of melodramatic performance and characterisation make the body of the Wandering Jew the site and sign of moral growth. The repetition of events – the separation of mother from child, the appearance or infiltration of the cross into Matathias's space, the cure of leprosy – and repeated images – the cross, the religious procession, the leper, the bell – enact the working of destiny through history via pictorial illustration rather than causal development. This sense of historical forces working across the spaces, cultures and generations of the world is intensified through a pattern of cross-cutting typical of Elvey's films, creating schematic relations of necessity between contingent events separated by time and location. Matathias curses the Nazarene, Judith collapses; the leprous child recovers, Matathias is taken to the stake. And if the Jew is redeemed by implicit conversion, in Lang's performance Matathias, declaring himself a truer Christian than his inquisitors, takes on the role of Christ himself, exposing anti-Semitism and dying at the stake – a final collapse of the doubled character in identification.

Against the demand for cinematographic transparency of performance, the romantic costume film emphasises impersonation and dressing up – the visibility of acting. Visible acting in its turn maintains the gap between actor and role, threatened by American stardom, which, based on spontaneity rather than sincerity of performance, collapses film role into the 'private' self of the star. For British cinema, then, romantic costume drama justifies the theatrical potential of film that maintains the visibility of the actor and underpins the popularity of Matheson Lang among film fans.

FROM PANTOMIME TO TANGO

If middle-class revivals of traditional popular entertainments signal a search for aesthetic appeal lacking in the mundane behaviour associated with everyday life, another source of energy was perceived in those working-class cultures that were not subject to the ethos of restraint.[45] Here, more anarchic and potentially confrontational forms survived in less respectable locales of entertainment: the music hall, pub entertainments and the provincial and outer-city venues that were still home to 'barnstorming' melodrama. While country houses hosted masked balls, ballets, charades and fancy-dress parties, the cities offered more proletarianised and democratising venues, open to class mingling and explicit sexualisation: the nightclub, dance hall and cabaret. Responding to a 1927 questionnaire from *The Picturegoer* on future talent for British film-making, Sinclair Hill comments:

> The cabaret is an excellent 'breaking ground', because the performer is in the same relation to the audience as the film player to the camera. The typical cabaret girl has grace, verve, personality and youth. That, rather than West End 'names', is what we need.[46]

Different performance styles and performer/audience relations intensify the frisson of dramatic encounters and narrative negotiations. In *Palais de Danse* (1928), for example, Lady King and her family intend to employ a 'West End name' for their *Cinderella* tableaux to be staged as a charity fundraising event in Tottenham's Palais de Danse, thereby instigating an ironically nuanced cross-class romance between the nightwatchman's daughter and Lady King's son (see Chapter 6). Conversely, in *The Rat* (1925), the high-class courtesan, Zelie, bored with the theatrical offerings of the Champs Elysee, is taken to a low-class haunt of the Parisian underworld in search of more frenetic excitements: a knife-fight and apache tango. This juxtaposing of social venues with their corresponding social actors and performance styles allows the theatrical to slide into the social act, mapping while dramatising the boundaries of social difference and rendering fiction as cultural document.

The apache tango occurs frequently as a subcultural form that romanticises and sexualises subcriminal working-class protagonists within a formal dance routine. 1925 saw another film based on its folk-hero, *The Apache*, directed by Adelqui Millar (Fig. 5.1), now unfortunately lost. Apache dances are frequently featured in nightclub scenes, for example in Cutts's first film, *Cocaine* (1922), his later *The Sea Urchin* (1926), where the tango ends with the female dancer's death, and in Henry Edward's *A Girl of London* (1925). While centred on the spectacle of working-class masculinity, the dance requires collaboration from a female partner, calling up an expressive female sexuality – often threating a poor but respectable heroine who has strayed onto the scene. Cabaret similarly brings female sexuality into the

Fig. 5.1. The apache, folk heroes for the 1920s: here in *The Apache* (1925) directed by Adelqui Millar

MELODRAMA AT THE THRESHOLD OF MODERNITY

While Netterville Barron's articles in *The Motion Picture Studio* explaining his system of 'histrionic movement' never mention melodrama, the editor includes in one of them a boxed inset containing a few brief paragraphs by William De Mille entitled, 'What Is Melodrama?'[47] The question is necessary because by the 1920s the 'name' of melodrama is enough to divide audiences along class lines. De Mille argues that the core appeal of melodrama is 'a human character in an acute situation' and that achieving this end is more important than causal logic. As suggested in earlier chapters, what counts as 'logical' or 'natural' differs between American and British perceptual frameworks. Hollywood's success lay in the means it found to maintain a degree of causal plotting, while projecting melodramatic emotion and moral conflict into a cinematic *mise en scène*.

In Britain, as 'natural' becomes defined in terms of a class-inflected undemonstrativeness, melodrama increasingly carries a working-class or feminised attribution. Thus the rejection of melodrama is also a relegation of its audience. 'Crude', 'primitive', 'absurd', 'lurid', 'cheap', 'rubbishy' and 'sordid' are just some of the terms applied to sensation-driven melodramatic serials and action films laced with a hint of sex and associated with 'lower-class' audiences, 'cheap halls', the 'uneducated or 'unsophisticated' *and*, importantly, with American culture. The *Evening Standard*'s review of *London Love* (1926) suggests that underlying this hostility runs an unease provoked by the master opposition that drives 'old-fashioned' melodrama – class. 'It is no doubt good showmanship to symbolise evil in the person of a West End man of title . . . while virtue radiates in the East End. We protest when the Americans do this sort of thing.'[48]

The Americans, as noted in Chapter 3, are also criticised by English reviewers for 'sob stuff', the feminising sentiment now associated with the female audience for domestic melodrama. Hollywood's *The Unknown Soldier* (1926) produced cries of outrage not only against what was felt to travesty a solemn British ritual but against its 'quite unlimited sob stuff' or, as the *Daily News* put it, 'obvious sob stuff which appeals to Americans'.[49] Miles Mander's contribution to *The Motion Picture Studio* recalls the terms under which melodrama was reformed:

public eye, with an ambivalent allure that may front covert or explicit sexual exploitation as, for example, in *Piccadilly* (1929), *The Sea Urchin* and *Champagne* (1928).

The eponymous Rat stages a tango as a sexual challenge to Zelie's class dominance, previously registered by her control over the waiter's attention and her provocative amusement at the Rat's responses. Seizing an adoring habituée of the White Coffin, the Rat swings her onto the dance floor, ripping her skirt and forcing her to match his frenetic movements. The game concludes as Zelie sends the waiter over to him with payment for his entertaining 'act', which he promptly affects to burn as a lighter for his cigarette. In this way performance is both theatrical and instrumental to a drama of contesting class and gendered rituals. At the same time, the camera, tracking in on the upper-class sensation-seekers, both documents the excitement of their voyeuristic position above the crowd and records through their eyes the haunts and pastimes of an imaginary underclass.

Underlying the average American character is a partiality for what we English call 'sloppy' sentiment. Sentiment may be sloppy; it may be anything you like to call it. It is, nevertheless founded on heart lure, which is present in the composition of most of the peoples of the world, although perhaps less markedly so in the stoical Anglo-Saxon. Cut out Melvillian sentimentality, but let us have refined sentiment.[50]

In the same issue, Challis Sanderson, production manager for Stoll, suggests the difficulty of establishing broad, cross-class popular appeal: 'Most popular genres are melodramas and good comedies, but . . . the public will not admit it.'[51]

Conversely, the democratising appeal of melodrama is still recognised, as *The Referee*'s review of Dinah Shurey's *Second to None* (1926) suggests, drawing reference points from nineteenth-century examples: 'After all the lower deck must have its turn. The best of Dibdin's songs were written, not of admirals and captains, but of plain bluejackets and the hero of *Black Ey'd Susan* became immortal without any noticeable advance in rank.'[52] The terms that welcome – or excuse – melodrama suggest its down-to-earth democratic appeal: 'good honest melodrama' or 'frankly, melodrama, but . . .'. The *Bioscope*'s response to a 1917 Fox film, *The Victim*, illustrates under the heading 'Who Likes Melodrama?' this frequent ambivalent twist between rejection and appreciation: 'Not a convincing story, frankly melodrama, but as such, on conventional lines, may prove popular with a certain class of audience who like their sensations highly coloured . . . unconvincing to the logical but sound melodrama for those who like it.'[53] And the *Evening News*, contrary to the *Evening Standard*, is rather cheerful about the class appeals of *London Love*, which it declares to be a 'highly successful melodrama for the unsophisticated', including 'a wicked Sir' and a 'shifty chauffeur'.[54]

Although often ambivalent, such accounts chime with comments by Shaw and Agate on the theatre's loss of the broader expressive means of 'the good ship melodrama',[55] suggesting that pleasures and meanings have been sidelined in the process of reform. Thus the reviewer of Wilfred Noy's film version of 'a famous melodrama', *The Face at the Window* (1920), writes:

By naturalising the characters, and softening the exaggerations of the actions, he has made a drama of a

melodrama. Although, in this process, the play may have lost some of its fiercer transpontine thrill, it has certainly gained in many respects as a work of art.[56]

Ivor Novello, quizzed by the *New York Telegraph* about his play, *The Rat*, has no doubt about the covert pleasures of a class-migrating audience:

Of course *The Rat* is good old-fashioned melodrama, but the characters in it talk and act as you or I would if suddenly confronted with such situations . . . People love melodrama. They always will . . . Actually many of them are bored and tired from trying to be too intellectual.[57]

The qualification 'old-fashioned', so frequently combined with 'good' or 'honest', recognises that as modern sophisticates we are not supposed to enjoy melodrama, but nevertheless we – or at least some of us – do, while 'honest' evokes the straightforwardness and lack of pretension of entertainments associated with the pleasures of ordinary working people. The *Yorkshire Post* describes *Mademoiselle d'Armentières* (1926) – which 'commanded the ungrudging applause of a Yorkshire audience not easily conjured to enthusiasm' – as:

good honest melodrama. It pretends to be nothing else . . . it is not to be judged in the same category as *Mons*. Love at first sight between a British Tommy and a girl in an *estaminet*, spies, German intelligence officers, an attack . . . 'a ruddy massacre' . . . a happy ending . . . these are some of the thrilling ingredients.[58]

This mix of ingredients that both thrill and offer 'heart interest' clearly aims to attract as wide an audience as possible. But beyond this, the terms of approbation suggest not only melodrama's 'elemental appeal' but the necessity of the working-class audience to the critical imagination both to sustain and legitimate melodramatic appeals for the pleasure of all:

As a writer of melodrama, pure and simple, Mr Charles Darrell has few superiors. With a skill born of long and varied experiences of many classes of audiences, he weaves round an unsophisticated and conventional tale of love and villainy all manner of dark deeds . . . Such dramas are, of course, as elementary as they possibly could be, but they appeal very forcibly to a large section of the public which desires nothing better than to have its meat hot and strong . . . It is, of course, a full-blooded, 'heavy' story, in which much has to be taken for granted, but, once that is done, one can settle oneself down to enjoy an interesting and skilfully arranged drama, and quite cheerfully join in the applause which awaits all heroes and heroines and the jeers that are the villain's portion.[59]

Such 'full-blooded' actions and 'flesh and blood' performances in their very theatricality counter the anaemic grey shadows of the screen, compensating metaphorically not only for the absent body and voice but also for the restraint associated with the good-mannered behaviour demanded of serious drama.

BRINGING HOLLYWOOD HOME: THE CRIME MELODRAMA

Ideal Films was founded by Harry Rowson initially to distribute American films.[60] But on entering production, Rowson's ambition to raise the quality of British cinema focused on British nineteenth-century novels and stage melodramas such as *Lady Audley's Secret* (1920). This gained the studio its subsequent reputation for 'old-fashioned production', deploying 'a visual concept . . . entirely theatrical' and fostering a 'hired fancy-dress appearance'.[61] However, Rowson's unpublished autobiography suggests a shrewd understanding both of the populist and modernist appeals of American cinema and of the native culture in which Ideal would successfully establish itself in the late teens to the mid-1920s. Two Ideal films – *Out to Win* (1923) and *Through Fire and Water* (1923) – clearly found a way of injecting American 'pep' and 'vim' into the emergence of crime melodrama as a central genre of popular British cinema.[62] Both *Kinematograph Weekly* and the *Grimsby Telegraph* identify the influence of American 'crook melodrama'.[63] *The Film Renter*, under the headline, 'Back to MELODRAMA', declares of *Out to Win* that for exhibitors who like 'good, honest, exciting drama', Ideal has 'brought back kinemagoers to what, after all, they most prefer'.[64] *The Cinema*, describing the fire and water effects of an elaborate prologue for *Through Fire and Water* that mixed film, sound and live action, continues: 'To this stirring strain the picture develops with amazing force and rapidity . . . Christine escapes from a locked bed-

room, swims from the mainland to the island, arriving in the nick of time to rescue the man she loves.'[65] Even *The Studio*, a magazine devoted to art and design, is drawn to review the film:

> Flora Le Breton and Clive Brook in quite conventional roles are equally excellent. From the moment seen, one knows the final embrace is a mere matter of footage; yet they are really alive, brimful of personality, youth and know not fear, without any recklessness. They look extremely nice people, and act naturally and easily. What more does anyone want?[66]

Indeed! Several reviews suggest considerable critical footwork as they renegotiate aesthetic values under the pressure of shifting class, gender and national values circulated through the new medium of film. The *Westminster Gazette* is explicit about its move to recuperate melodrama for the educated, when, under the sub-heads of 'Flight in a Flaming Airship' and 'Thrills of Film Melodrama', it begins a review of *Out to Win*: 'Film melodrama is anything that the producer cares to make it. That it need not be a mere photographically animated penny dreadful was demonstrated by Mr Denison Clift in *Out to Win*.'[67] According to *Kinematograph Weekly*, while constructed 'on the frank lines of American crook drama', the film fulfils the demands of a British middle-class intelligentsia: 'there is a tone which lifts it up above the ordinary screen melodrama . . . with characters that are people not puppets'.[68] But absorption of American influence is also apparent in the 'quickfire lines' of its production and conformity to demands of continuity, which is 'remarkably brisk', with 'the big scenes – the blazing airship and car chases – [arising] naturally without evidence of gratuitous interpolation'. The review concludes, negotiating these cultural cross-currents, that 'the highbrow may smile . . . but it is a first-rate British picture'.[69] These films, then, are seen as successful because not only do they mix class-cultural traditions but they combine the pleasures of American and British filmmaking: 'First-class showman's proposition . . . thrills galore, love interest, exteriors such as only the English countryside can show, good interiors and splendid acting'.[70]

This reconciliation of contrary values is fostered by crime melodrama's openness to modernisation through spectacular use of technology – itself associated with American popular culture – instilling excitement while preserving the decorum of British performance style. Significantly, Clive Brook is central to the success of both films. *The Film Renter* speaks of his 'fine, virile and convincing performance' in *Out to Win*,[71] while *The Motion Picture Studio* responds to his 'assured briskness, subtlety and attractive personality' which no American actor could match'.[72] 'Virile', 'manly' and 'restrained' are the qualities most frequently attributed to him. *The Motion Picture Studio* speaks of his 'essentially British masculinity' and his 'restrained but potent acting'.[73] If Matheson Lang found an outlet for passionate restraint by donning the mask of ethnic otherness, Brook's combination of virile masculinity and class reserve is energised by association with technology. Whereas his early career suggested the refinement of melodramatic villainy in aristocratic mode, in these films the thrills of criminal action mediate between class-inflected sub-genres. Cars, airships, guns, demanding a virile impassivity to match their mechanical power, displace the 'full-blooded' performances associated with the dire deeds of the 'penny dreadfuls'. The technologically equipped hero, combining restraint and passion in a modern form, is thus capable of crossing between class arenas in a manner less culturally threatening to middle-class audiences. Thus the crime melodrama combines adventure, thrills and stunts, provoked by a proletarianised underworld, with the sang-froid of the class authority wielded by the hero detective. In this sense Brook's position on the class boundary of melodrama, combining upper-middle-class authority with the thrills and sensations of technological combat and the chase, points to a reconciliation with the machine and modernity not available to Britain's war-torn painters and poets. That his persona was amenable to the renegotiation of masculinity that followed the Great War is suggested by the praise that greeted his roles in *Woman to Woman* (1922), *The Reverse of the Medal* (1923) and *The Passionate Adventure*, the last of which is explored in more detail below.

GENERIC STRATAGEMS: CROSS-DRESSING, DISGUISE AND DOUBLES

The ambivalences and contradictions in these critical responses to a reforming melodramatic mode across British and American cultures suggest the degree to which its practices and values are bound up in the shifting contours of class, gender and ethnicity in this period. Central to the clarifying dramaturgical schema of melodrama are the social, moral and psychic polarities embodied in the figures of villain, hero and heroine. As suggested above, this structure is highly flexible, since any *body* can fill the positions of the protagonists, any topical or cultural material can provide sources for plot complications, and any set of social, economic or political forces can be played through melodrama's fateful encounters and familial agonies. Moreover, the role of this schema in producing a range of sub-generic forms supports the mixing of fictional sources and generic motifs so central to British cinematic poetics. Thus transgressive villainy may stem from the power of a corrupt aristocracy – a 'wicked sir' – but equally, and perhaps increasingly as middle-class hegemony becomes more assured, the villain emerges from a brutalised, sub-criminal, working-class masculinity. Such figures call on different performance styles. The romantic but decadent aristocrat exploits the muted authority of the gestural range of the upper-class character: ramrod back, fixed and commanding eye contact, slight turn of head, condescending bow or hand gesture, subtle inclination or twist of the body, arched eyebrow, dilation of nostril – for example, the vampiric Herman Stetz in *The Rat*. In contrast, the villain from the lumpenproletariat uses melodrama's larger bodily gestures of brute force and uncontrolled passion: broad, hunched shoulders and looming back, raised clenched fist, snarling lips, bared teeth, darkened brows, blank stare and violent body jerks. These are the 'convulsive gestures' that Netterville Barron associated with the inarticulacy of the uneducated, lower classes and primitive peoples. While the decadent aristocrat introduces a frisson around female sexuality in romantic melodrama – for example, in *If Youth But Knew* (1926) and *The Rat* – the sub-criminal, lower-class villain threatens social order, class privilege, the sanctity of the family and rule of law. He is a deeply disruptive and transgressive figure, whom we meet, for example, in *Flames of Passion* (1922), *The Bargain* (1921), *The Passionate Adventure* and *Underground* (1928).

A key mechanism for orchestrating this mix of types, performance styles and generic motifs is the use of doubles, disguise and cross-dressing. This section, then, explores such practices through a number of films that play variations on the theme of oppositional, doubled and switching identities.

VILLAINY DOUBLED: *SWEENEY TODD*

A 1927 report in *The Bioscope* suggests that melodrama's 'transpontine thrill'[74] was still a draw at the end of the decade: 'On Monday of this week *Maria Marten* reached its hundredth perfomance at the Elephant Theatre – the latest achievement of a season which has drawn all the West End to the South Side.' At the same time, it announces that Walter West was 'putting the finishing touches to the screen version of the famous old melodrama'.[75] This was an independent production, followed quickly by *Sweeney Todd* (1928), for Harry Rowson on behalf of Ideal – by this time confined once more to distribution. Although judged by Rachael Low 'a curious choice for West, and out of keeping with the times',[76] Daniel Gerould shows that theatrical interest in Todd has a long and sustained history. His 'Toddography' traces the repeated recycling of this tale from its appearance as a magazine story, 'The String of Pearls', in 1825 to Stephen Sondheim's musical version in 1979, along with three London stage versions in the 1920s.[77] Aside from West's version, also missing from Gerould's list is an amateur film made for charity in 1926 by British film critics, eager to prove their credentials. E. A. Baughan, drama and film critic for the *Daily News*, is remembered two years later in *Kinematograph Weekly* for his impressive performance as Todd.[78] The choice of *Sweeney Todd*, then, was not so odd.[79]

However, realising *Sweeney Todd* on film was not all plain sailing. *Kinematograph Weekly* reports that there had been much debate as to which source text to use, the George Dibdin Pitt (1847) and Fred Hazleton (1865) versions differing widely,[80] while Gerould's Toddography suggests the variety of staging approaches available. George Dare's 1925 production took Todd seriously 'as an embodiment of evil'.[81] Conversely, the revival at the Elephant and Castle that proved so popular starred Tod Slaughter, whose series of 1930s film revivals would reinvent with some relish Victorian 'blood and thunder' melodrama. For their part, the Rowson/West team developed inventive strategies for enabling 1920s audiences to re-experience the excitements of melodrama while retaining their sense of modern sophistication. Crucial among these was the mechanism of doubling narratives, characters and performance modes.

The film is introduced through a neat 'bookend' structure, opening within a carefully denoted petit-bourgeois household of the 1920s. A stiff and humourless husband returns home from the office less than pleased to find an empty house and no dinner awaiting him. Knowing titles warm up a potentially supercilious audience with a joke about modern families: 'For men must work and women must wait, Except the wife who's always late'. His wife returns in a flurry from shopping and hurries the kitchen maid, while the petulant husband retires to the fireside with his newspaper. Taken by the headline, 'The Death Chair: A Powerful New Story of the Infamous Barber of Fleet Street, Sweeney Todd', he settles back to read. A jokey narrator prompts audience expectation: 'Look at this fellow . . . He's so wrapped up in the tale of Todd, the dirtiest dog ever, that he fancies he is Sweeney!. . . Don't disturb him . . . What does he see?' The newspaper is now pierced by a barber's pole as the tale bursts through the print into screen reality, with images of Todd, played, a title informs us, by Moore Marriott.[82] A refrain recalling the ballads in which such stories used to circulate – 'Gold, Gold, Gold, Bright and Yellow' – is juxtaposed with an affable, brawny-looking Todd in a wig, playing with a black cat. However, putting the cat down, Todd sinks into a fixed, unfocused stare and a further title speculates: 'All day long . . . and at night too we wager his mind only ran on filthy lucre.'

A second doubling strategy gives Todd a 'maniac brother, Nick . . . an 'orrible criminal hiding from justice' at the barber's shop, played by Harry Lorraine in full bood-and-thunder manner. It is this brother who devises the idea of the trap door connected to a concealed lever that will swing the occupant of the

Fig. 5.2. Sweeney Todd and his 'maniac brother, Nick ... an 'orrible criminal,' rendered by two contrasting performance modes in the 1928 film version by Walter West

barber's chair into the stone cellar below. However, when Nick collapses with maniacal laughter into the chair, Todd seizes the moment to pull the lever and exploit its gruesome benefits for himself. This splitting of Todd enables the film to exploit two modes of performance and their contrasting appeals (Fig. 5.2). If Harry Lorraine's barnstorming pastiche on villainy cushions disbelief and plays up to the knowing amusement of the audience, it also effectively reinforces the deadly seriousness of Marriott's playing, his eloquent and shifting expressions and movements contrasting Todd's chilling fratricidal calculation with Nick's mere mania. Thus when Marriott is alone, he dispenses with schematic gesturing (often along with his wig), relying on a fixated distant stare, a cold, inward smile, eyes glancing askance, lips pursed, a slight hunch of the shoulders, arms folded stiffly across his chest – gestures that indicate tortuous inner passions kept under calculating, rational control.

In the scenes that follow, Todd builds up his business as he courts Mrs Lovett (Iris Darbyshire), widowed owner of the pie shop next door that provides a solution to the diminishing burial space in his cellar. Todd's calculating innuendo, his lust for accumulated wealth elided with sex as a lure, is met by Amelia Lovett's equally intense excitement of displaced passion. Louis James's comment that 'an ingenious critic might say Todd was living by capitalist principles, eating people is right' suggests the underlying force of this macabre and enduring tale.[83] The intensity of interaction between Marriott and Darbyshire takes this premise to so logical a conclusion that they sometimes come close to exposing the true – as opposed to Nick's pantomime – mania driving the logic of finance capitalism, turning desire into nightmare. In the cellar Todd gloats over the bodies he has buried, calling them up one by one, their images dissolving in and out to his command.

Todd's downfall begins when his story intersects with a costume romance between Mark Ingestrie and Joanna Oakley, daughter of a rich merchant. After Mark's return, enriched from trading in the West Indies, their courtship looks set for success, were it not for his visit to the barber's. But Todd is thwarted by Amelia Lovett's jealous desire for Mark and the bold intervention of Joanna, who, cross-dressing as a young man-about-town, decides to investigate Mark's disappearance. Pretending to need a shave,

she jumps out of the barber's chair and hides when Todd leaves to pull the lever in an adjacent room. The disappearance of his victim, as he slithers, snake-like and increasingly dumbfounded, round the edges of the trap door, peering into the gloom for the body, accelerates a mental disintegration already suggested by his growing rapaciousness. However, unlike the dementia registered in the contorted histrionics of Lorraine, Todd's disintegration is carried not only by the intensity of Marriott's performance but by his projection of mental images that return to haunt him. Alerted by Joanna, the beadles arrive and corner Todd, while a vengeful crowd gather to watch through the window. Trapped, he now falls back into the barber's chair. A cut to the cellar stairs dissolves into Nick's ghostly apparition, staggering up, laughing and grimacing, until, reaching the lever, he ejects Todd into the cellar below. Todd's body destroyed along with his mind, we return to the present. Roused from his sleep by his wife, the husband, still fending off the vengeful Nick, drags her to an oval mirror, where to his relief and his wife's amusement he finds it was all a dream. We are back in the stuffy parlour of a petit-bourgeois couple, now overlaid with graphic images of human faculties distorted by accumulation-driven desires.

West's version, then, offers a paradigmatic example of doubling strategies used to renegotiate the excitements of melodrama by drawing on opposing performance signifiers while benefiting from the appeals of a range of entertainment practices. The force embodied in the Demon Barber is modernised not only in the contemporary framing of the petit-bourgeois marriage. Marriott's skilful modulation between burning resentment, simmering under a public front of calculating control, and delight in a knowing villainy revealed 'to the side', as it were, of outward subservience and bonhomie reanimates the socio-economic resonances of the story.

DOMESTICATING MELODRAMA: DOUBLING FOR THE FAMILY ROMANCE

The pairing of doubled or split characters in *Sweeney Todd* effectively externalises the growing complexity of villainy, drawing from the developing field of psychology and psychoanalysis. As David Mayer argues of Leopold Lewis's play, *The Bells*, the psychologising of the villain tends towards a dissolution of the boundaries between good and evil, between melodramatic monopathy and the tragically divided hero of tragedy.[84] Even Sweeney Todd, as Daniel Gerould's 'Toddography' shows, may attain tragic dimensions in the 20th century. However, the geographic framework of British cultural imagination made the more literal doubling or pairing of protagonists – particularly male brothers, as in *Sweeney Todd*, or companions – a prevalent device for revising and realigning moral schema and polar identities across the range of modes and genres of the 1920s.

In Henry Edwards's family melodrama, *The Bargain* (adapted in 1921 from a play he co-wrote with Edward Irwin), Rex McDougall plays Richard Wentworth, the unmanageable son of a prosperous family, who runs away to Australia. There, he degenerates further as he fails to find gold, drinks away what he earns and browbeats Bella (Mary Dibley), the woman with whom he lives in a poverty-stricken shack. Wandering from the outback into their lives comes Dennis Trevor, played by Henry Edwards, who, slipping into a raging torrent as he scrambles over rocks, is saved only because Richard breaks off from beating Bella in a row over rent money and dashes to rescue him. Despite *Kinematograph Weekly*'s complaint that McDougall is unconvincing in his 'too stereotyped role',[85] his dark-browed, moody and embittered body movements and heavy gestural mode of performance are clearly intended to contrast his brutalised masculinity with the smooth urbanity of Edwards. Bella and Richard are products of the harsh conditions of the prospector's life, and violence seems to be the currency of their relationship. Dennis Trevor, on the other hand, is the natural gentleman, realised in Edwards's almost gesture-less projection of outgoing but undefined personality, conforming to the criteria of middle-class performance. Declaring himself 'no one in particular, floating through life', he is capable of fitting into any social situation, and exhibits a respect for women, fine manners and seeming trustworthiness that will enable him successfully to impersonate an apparently reformed Richard, winning the credence of his father and relatives.

Removal to the colonies permits a distanced perspective on changing class relations at home. Richard is the social product of a late, self-made Victorian widower, Grosvenor Wentworth, who had earlier moved his family from the nostalgically remembered 'Woodlands' to the nouveau-riche surroundings of 'Bewley Court'. But unable to fit in, Richard took the downward path of the wayward son, now turned proletarianised villain. The arrival of a letter from England is used to reveal the bitterness and cynicism with which Richard, and through him Bella, regards his 'loving father'. A photograph that he shows to Dennis ('taken the last time I saw my father') reveals a patriarchal head of family, upright beside a slouching boy with dishevelled hair. The contrast suggests the social and emotional distance between father and son, now echoed in the different performance styles of Dennis and Richard. A second letter arrives from Richard's now sick father, who is concerned to reconnect with his heir. However, this is opened by Bella at the very moment that Richard gets involved in a fateful brawl in a neighbouring town saloon. During his arrest the photograph functions as a device to enact an unspoken and therefore inexplicit 'bargain' between him and Dennis, who will go to England in his place. As a chameleon-like protagonist, able to fit into almost any situation, Henry Edwards's Dennis slips equally imperceptibly into the part of repentant prodigal, an identity offered by Wentworth's question, 'Is that you Richard?', as Dennis enters the sickroom. Remaining silent, Dennis supplies a visual sign: his hand clasping the father's. Thus the 'nobody' floating through life is fixed into position by familial desires, confirmed by the acceptance of those gathered in the sickroom. Playing this role, Dennis begins to enact the 'true' son by managing the property and by falling for Mary, Grosvenor Wentworth's ward.

These distinctions between players and social arenas are supported by contrasting photographic styles, the Australian sequences shot with a harsh documentary quality, compared to the pastoralism of the family melodrama enacted in England where Edwards dominates. In this respect the scene of Dennis's nemesis is also a scene of nostalgic reconstruction of the old days of benevolent land-ownership. A pictorialising camera looks down from behind Wentworth, now conveniently recovered from his terminal illness, seated at the head of a trestle table, surveying the dining tenantry under swinging Chinese lanterns, surrounded by a marquee and overarching trees. It is the values embedded in this pastoral image, rather than the brutalising outback of the gold prospector, that the realignments of the film's 'family romance' seek to preserve. Grosvenor's toast to his 'son' is cut without mediating fade to Richard, who, now released from prison, has returned to England and hovers at the gate. Dennis's inward response – 'This is the unhappiest and most uncomfortable moment of my life' – is juxtaposed with Richard's dark form lurking in the shadows of the tent. The fete is brought to a close by a lyrically filmed dance silhouetted against a bonfire, undercut by the brooding figure of Richard into whose path Dennis almost walks when he breaks away to ponder his duplicitous position under the trees.

Now impersonating Dennis, Richard wins an invitation to stay as the man who saved Grosvenor's son. The climax of the film is staged as a clash of performance styles, when in a fit of drunkenness Richard reveals his identity, laying belligerent claim to his birthright against the favoured position of Dennis Trevor. While in a gesture of high-minded and underplayed stoicism Dennis prepares to leave, Richard, realising he has blown his chances, dismisses the family with an insolent thrust of clenched fists to heaven. In a clear move of social reorganisation, Wentworth bribes Richard to return to Australia, adopting his impersonator as his 'true' son. As Dennis and Mary embrace in their first kiss, Wentworth steals out of their closing, self-consciously constructed 'picture' – a scene of picturesque domesticity set in a pastoral garden.

The reorganisation of social and familial relations through the device of doubling and the crossing of continents by legitimate/duplicitous, good/bad sons exemplifies an alternative strategy to the democratising trajectory of the American hero, able to cross social boundaries in an effort to forge a New World identity. Through the clash between pictorial nostalgia and documentary realism and the contrasted characterisations of two 'sons', *The Bargain* raises unresolvable questions about class, family relations and social change. However, in the role of a social shifter, Edwards appears to be staking out a classless middle ground for a new meritocratic masculinity that is gradually detaching from entrenched class location. The ailing new-rich Grosvenor, who makes such a remarkable recovery, functions as manipulating narrator, orchestrating behind the scenes a family romance in which the future of the next generation is imaged in terms of a remembered past that, the narrative suggests, is fast being lost.

THE ARISTOCRATIC VILLAIN AND FEMALE-ORIENTED ROMANCE: *IF YOUTH BUT KNEW*

If proletarianised masculinity now produces melodrama's villain, the aristocratic villain is not entirely lost. Rather, he becomes the anti-hero of female-centred romantic melodrama, his combination of class power and aristocratic masculinity weaving fantasies around women's sexuality. Alternatively, he transmutes into the degenerate English colonial who first exploits and then is destroyed by the outer reaches of Empire.[86]

If Youth But Knew (1926), one of the few surviving films by the much respected director George Cooper, starts out as a low-key comedy of modernity played through generational change. But as in *The Bargain*, change is forestalled by displacements across continents, the future taken over by geography and held in a colonial past. Beginning, 'Yesterday, as the great Victorian era was drawing to a close,' in the rural Home Counties, we find Dr Martin Summers (Godfrey Tearle) in the character of modern man, wrestling with the mechanics of a home-engineered motor car. Asked to attend to the sprained ankle of the film's ingénue heroine, Dora (Lillian Hall-Davis), he invites her to accompany him on the London–Brighton race, her widowed mother acting as chaperone. Needless to say, the car breaks down, mother is not amused and deserts her duties for a passing pony cart to the nearest station, leaving the young people to stay with the car. This gives the earnest doctor his opportunity and a long engagement is promised, while he goes off to the Colonies to earn the means to set up home. All this is conducted in a fairly pleasant, low-key, humorous manner. The emotional temperature rises when the heroine is spotted at the hunt ball by a local landowner, Sir Ormsby Ledger. He comes visiting not in a car but rides in – as it were from another age – on a thoroughbred hunter. With his aristocratic assumptions and seductive leer, he represents an alluring if dangerous attraction from the past. Mother, however, impressed by the opportunity to move in higher social circles, remains oblivious to the threat, welcoming Ormsby's offer of riding lessons for Dora (contrasting with the driving lessons used by the working-class seducer in *Flames of Passion*). Predictable consequences follow, when, her horse refusing to jump, Dora falls. Dismissing her engagement to Martin as the promise of a child, Sir Ormsby lays claim to Dora's womanhood.

The ultimate crisis is enacted in the hours before she is due to marry Martin, following his return after several years' absence, his earning power assured. Dora's vigil through the night, illumined by shafts of moonlight, ends with Ormsby's early morning arrival on his stallion. As she leans in her wedding dress before the dressing-table mirror, his hands appear at her window. She turns to find him, in backlit profile sweeping off his hat, an aristocratic infiltrator from the past, intruding into middle-class domestic space. Their profiles are held in a fixed gaze, and then as she turns away, he moves to clasp her, his arms wrapping round her from behind, pulling her white, taut body into his clutches. Cut to Martin waiting at the church, framed within a soft oval mask, and in the next shot her mother finds her in a dead faint on the floor, her sexualisation implicitly complete but the intruder gone. Cross-cutting between anxious mothers, gossiping bridesmaids and Martin's dash back to Dora's house brings the couple together, where she makes her refusal as he kneels at her feet. A close-up focuses on his eyes as they register swiftly changing emotions, and, after clasping her hand intensely, he departs, a title commenting: 'The church bells fell silent.'

The tale recommences eighteen years later in the Nigerian jungle, with a reprise and a set of reversals. Martin has returned to Nigeria, where he regresses into imperial degeneracy as a 'big white chief', stretched out under a photograph of George V. He is cynically indifferent to the attentions of his devoted black maid, Lolanda. Crossing continents to stage the action in the African jungle enables an intensification of the play of oppositional doubles in two ways. Seizing a whip when Lolanda is attacked as she tries to warn him of an uprising, Martin's face dissolves into and so obliterates that of the black insurgent, Anlifa, suggesting a telling identity between these figures of the imperial imaginary. Meanwhile, Ormsby, leading a big-game hunting party – which includes his and Dora's now mother-less daughter, Doreen – provokes an uprising from which Martin temporarily rescues them. Martin attempts a blood transfusion between himself and the wounded Ormsby. It fails, but his dying rival entrusts Martin with the care of Doreen. Back in England Doreen gets engaged to her young tennis partner and a second wedding is planned. Doreen is donning her mother's wedding clothes, when she is

told her mother's story. As the tale cross-cuts to wedding guests arriving in their cars, Doreen prepares to repeat history, her pity for Martin awakening conscience rather than sexuality. Despite substituting the word 'ring' in reference to his missing gloves, thereby revealing his desire for Doreen, Martin releases her to marry into a modern if solidly normative partnership. Thus the film forecloses on the more ambiguous fantasies embodied in the figure of the seductive horse-born aristocrat or the liminally incestuous cross-generational romance.

THE PASSIONATE ADVENTURE: DOUBLING AND CROSS-CLASS DRESSING

Paradoxically, the animation of colonial space as cinematic imaginary territory for a nation moving towards decolonisation had to await the input of non-British nationals – from the Kordas in the 1930s and Pressburger with Powell in the 1940s. However, as already discussed, the shared perceptual framework of nineteenth-century melodramatists and social investigators found sufficiently exotic and dangerous territory closer to home, already formulated in visual traditions ripe for cinematic realisation. In 1883 George R. Sims introduced *How the Poor Live* by declaring the need to travel 'into a dark continent that is within easy walking distance of the General Post Office', a vision that Robert Colls and Philip Dodd point out is echoed fifty-odd years later by John Grierson, who, in promoting documentary, aimed to 'travel dangerously into the jungles of Middlesborough and the Clyde'.[87] Document and the imaginary feed each other.

Such a conception of the nation space as mapped into different social and class territories offers a twist on the devices of dressing up and doubling through the mechanism of cross-class dressing. In *No. 5 John Street* (1921) the encounter between a titled factory owner and a tramp pursued by the law leads to their switching clothes, enabling the tramp to walk away unnoticed by a passing policeman. Meanwhile, the factory owner observes at close quarters the conditions of his workers and joins a strike meeting outside his factory gates at which Communist Party literature is circulating. The theme is played out with poignant irony in *Champagne*, where the heroine attempts to rebut her estranged fiancé's disapproval of her sartorial extravagance by swapping costumes with her maid. The joke rebounds to her discomfort, however.

Throwing open the double doors of her dressing room to appear before the assembled company as 'little orphan Annie' – aided by a handful of torn-paper snowflakes – it is not her fiancé who is shamed, but her own blindness to the disparity between her pampered existence and that of her penurious maid.

Graham Cutts's *The Passionate Adventure* suggests the powerful resonances of dress and location for such cross-class adventuring in a domestic melodrama that turns on class and gender exchanges. The film opens on two intertitles that (translated back from the German print) explicitly shift melodramatic polarisation from a nineteenth-century world riven by externalised moral forces to the psychosomatic drama of love and hate staged in the soul: 'Two forces live in every human heart, one clear, divine and one dark, bestial . . . both forces lie dormant in the heart of Lord Adrian St Clair.' The 'heart' in British cinema, however, is no existential space, exposed to the probe of the camera. Our introduction to the hero – performed with a bravura exhibition of sangfroid by Clive Brook in a role he delayed his departure to America to play[88] – emphasises less 'soul' than physical embodiment and dressing up as material keys to character. Adrian sits at a twisted angle to the camera, while his valet grooms his hair. A mask shot highlights the locked door that separates his room from that of his wife in-name-only, Drusilla (Alice Joyce), who sits in her boudoir, idly reading a magazine, while her maid fits her shoes. Valet and maid have more intimate access to the bodies of their upper-class employers than the latter do to each other. Dressing up not only entails putting on a public persona but involves class relationships.[89]

It is, then, no accident that *The Passionate Adventure* opens with the act of dressing for dinner. This sartorial introduction establishes a couple fascinating in their skilful execution of unpleasantness. As they leave their respective rooms to encounter each other on the landing, they perform with mechanical precision the rituals of marital sociality. As in so many upper-class scenarios, the apparent privacy of the home is structurally organised for public view by servants, family and the camera. Adrian saunters languidly into frame from the left, as Drusilla exits from her boudoir; he makes a sharp right-angled turn to plant a kiss on her forehead. In mid-shot they turn frontally to the camera, eyes downcast and sullen-faced as it tracks back while they walk towards us,

talking but with eyes averted. The shot cuts to a rear view as they complete their measured walk to the head of the sweeping marble staircase that will take them to dinner with Pamela (Lillian Hall-Davis) and her fiancé, Inspector Stewart Sladen. Thus estrangement within marriage permits the 'acting out' of the social codes of restraint as repression, now foregrounded through self-conscious class-based underplaying.

Idle after-dinner chat, however, introduces the prospect of war, stirring in Drusilla a certain excitement as she immediately commits Adrian to enlist. A new theatrical arena opens up that promises to realign the psychic oppositions of the private couple with cataclysmic forces released in the wider world. The night before Adrian leaves is registered in an unsettling shot past Pam's backside as she sits on the billiard table to pot a ball. At the back of the frame sits Adrian in a new costume (see Fig. 3.1) – the military uniform of an officer, a distant, distorted figure gazing blankly into a huge marble fireplace. That evening makes explicit the drama of the locked door connecting their bedrooms, as a repeated series of dissolves from door to lock and handle finds first Drusilla, then Adrian, contemplating a move neither is willing to make before the other.

If the codes of repression and restraint have brought the upper-class couple a to complete impasse, the war challenges a static class system, through a pictorial, magic-lantern-like show of symbolic transmutation. A montage of documentary, painterly and theatrical images creates a shadow play of clashing bayonets, overlaid by a crucifix, projected on the walls of a shattered French town. A fan of billowing smoke spreads over the scene, and when it clears, two figures, Adrian and an unnamed cockney private, fall into a shell hole. Their encounter, like the exchanges of Armstrong and Ginger in *Comradeship* (1919), explores the boundaries of class, beginning with the soldier's remarks on the hardship for 'such a fine man as you to endure such a life'. From here the dialogue titles slip into parallel trains of thought that fail to meet. For Adrian, war summons up the image of a locked door and his own repressed violence, while the soldier recalls the underworld of London's East End.

Adrian returns home, arriving at Waterloo to a pageant of multiple reunions.[90] The scene renders brief images of a new class and gendered democracy as Adrian mills among the crowds and shakes hands companionably with uniformed women, searching in vain for Drusilla, whom he eventually finds in the back of her chauffeur-driven car, parked at a distance from the throng. Despite such images of shifting social relations, nothing has changed for these protagonists, caught within the codes of an upper-middle-class decorum based on self-repression. Disconsolately languid in his dressing gown and idly opening a book, Adrian reads, in an echo of his war-front encounter: 'Most nervous diseases develop through the patient having nothing to do; such people should take themselves to darkest London, to see how wretchedly other people actually live!' The polarised oppositions of melodrama are required to reinvest life with significance.

Making the excuse of a golfing trip to a dismayed Drusilla, Adrian is next found exiting the left luggage room at Waterloo Station, cross-dressed in worker's cap and jacket. Intervening in the violent ejection of a young woman, Vicky (Marjorie Daw), from an East End tenement, Adrian is knocked out by her assailant, Harris (Victor McLaglen). Harris disappears to be arrested later by the police, and Vicky takes her unconscious rescuer into her shabby bedsit, where he spends the next few days recovering. Now, Adrian slips into another's class identity as, switching between English lord and East End bank robber, he embarks on further life adventures. During these episodes, he does indeed learn something of the struggles of other lives, and crucially of other modes of social and sexual relationships. While Drusilla wears a mask of frigidity to front a fugitive sexuality as befits her class position, Vicky – played with engaging sympathy by Marjorie Daw – offers an open smile into the camera, frankly declaring her desire for the stranger whose manners are considerate and respectful rather than bullying and belligerent. Vicky, however, is merely a catalyst in Adrian's life journey, a title declaring that, his interest in his wife rekindled, he is ready to leave his East End foray. However, the melodrama, once started, must be played out. Bill, a local lad who is soft on Vicky, bursts in with news that Harris has escaped. Ironically, Adrian is doubly trapped. Vicky's tenement is under surveillance by the police, led by none other than Inspector Sladen, his future brother-in-law. Rather than dropping out of the adventure, Adrian's cross-class role expands, as Vicky attributes his anx-

iety to avoid the police to a criminal record. To this he responds with a half-amused, self-important nod as he takes on the novel persona of bank robber. Narrowly escaping detection, Adrian slips from the building, promising to return.

Adrian is now operating in two generic scenarios – the sub-criminal and drawing-room melodrama – playing across the boundaries of character type and performance mode, with their oppositional class connotations. If the reform of melodrama in British culture led to a mode of underplaying and a valorisation of repression that threatened moribund stasis, the film's clash of class styles promises to dynamise repression, creating a dialectic between stasis and performance, fixed and transmutable identities, repression and passion. Clive Brook's capacity to perform performance is crucial to this dynamic, as is a dramaturgy capable of constructing different theatrical spaces that call on competing performance styles along with the class and gender identities they bring into play. Hitchcock's exaggeratedly contrasting set designs support this clash of acting styles. Thus, from Vicky's tenement, with decaying plaster, exposed brickwork and torn net curtains, we cut to a long shot interior in Adrian's mansion. Framed by an overpowering marble mantelpiece to the right, we look across a vast lounge to an angular marble staircase, down which Adrian, now attired in evening dress, nonchalantly saunters to face Drusilla's pointed comments on his golfing expedition and family gossip with Stewart Sladen about the Harris case. Acting 'acting' as a front for concealed anxiety, Brook resorts once more to the laid-back naturalist's repertoire of precise but minimalist gestures: an index finger rubbing his lip, a slight tilt or toss of the head, the easing of his collar, the forced casualness of his arm stretched along the back of a sofa.

Returning to Vicky, Adrian drops into the role of hardened criminal, amused at her admiring assumption that the money he provides comes from his 'bank job'. Adrian wants to make his farewell, but his nemesis in the figure of Harris is approaching. As Vicky attempts to prevent his departure, declaring herself ready to die for him, a medium close-up shows Harris looming out of the dark shadows of a nearby street. Cross-cuts between Vicky and Adrian, and a camera track before the approaching Harris, build suspense. While Adrian prevaricates in embarrassment and Harris, preceded by his shadow, moves menacingly into the stairwell, Vicky tearfully recognises her situation: 'You don't love me and have never loved me!' Before Adrian can find the right words, a close iris shot shows the door latch beginning to move. They pull apart, the door slowly opening to reveal Harris, who slides into the room, closing the door behind him, not once taking his eyes off them.

As Vicky shrinks away from Adrian, the scene is played out through the contrasting but equally bravura performances of Brook and McLaglen. Brook, acting on cerebral calculation, strings out a series of impersonating signs, adapting to this sub-criminal scenario the sang-froid of precise underplaying. McLaglen, the proletarianised heavy, draws on the expressive power of a body that spills over into the *mise en scène* (Fig. 5.3), bringing with it threatening shadows. Instinctively he is aware of an impersonator out of his class, betrayed, perhaps, by Adrian's authoritative superiority. Thus Brook drops into a combative posture, mimicking the melodramatic heavy – hands thrust in his pockets, puffed-out chest – gestures compromised by his supercilious smile. Harris, considering his options, looks down at his hand opening and closing into a fist, then back at

Fig. 5.3. Victor McLaglen, the proletarianised heavy, draws on the expressive power of bodily gesture. Here with Marjorie Daw as Vicky in *The Passionate Adventure* (1924)

Adrian, who, in the next shot, adapting his upper-class repertoire, nonchalantly takes out and taps a cigarette, then with affected casualness tosses the packet in the air and onto the table. Puffing on his cigarette, he turns sharply to the table, all the time looking back at Harris, and pointing him to a seat. Nonplussed, Harris watches this performance from the doorway. His shoulders hunched, he slowly moves towards the table, where Adrian sits half-twisted, one arm leaning on the table, one leg crossed over his knee, holding up his cigarette in a show of confident and authoritative possession of Vicky's domestic space. Bemused, Harris sits, bending to finger the unfamiliar tablecloth, and commenting sarcastically, 'Quite cosy here, isn't it?' Adrian, ordering Vicky to bring a bottle, swings round to face Harris from the opposite end of the table, leaning forward to conduct business in a series of alternating shots in which the bottle is passed and glasses filled and emptied, Harris watching the proceedings with growing amusement. During this process, a medium close-up catches Harris as he glances down, lifting the edge of the tablecloth slightly. At floor level, an answering shot shows Adrian, incautiously confident, stretching out his legs and crossing them at the ankles, while Harris's feet line up on either side. In the next shot Harris drops the cloth, leaning back and eyeing Adrian – who is sitting bolt upright, arms folded – with amused satisfaction. Thus the conflict between the respectively cerebral and instinctual performances of Brook and McLaglen is paralleled by the different ritualistic moves played out above and below the table. Knocking back another drink, Harris smacks his lips in anticipation. Eventually, he leans back, his hands grasping the corners of the table, while at floor level we see that his feet are hooked behind Adrian's. Violence finally erupts with the first two-shot of this sequence when Adrian is jerked forward from beneath and assaulted as his head hits the table, Harris leaping on him. In the following fracas, in which Harris pulls a knife, Adrian is saved by Vicky's quick-witted action as she seizes the fallen knife and stabs Harris, apparently killing him.

Pressing his wallet on Vicky and urging her to go into hiding, Adrian remains to make unconvincing excuses to Sladen. In the meantime, Vicky decides to unravel the story of the cross-class impersonator, when following her discovery of both Drusilla's photograph and the key to his left-luggage box in his wallet, she arrives on Drusilla's doorstep to return his case, hoping to see what kind of woman 'could deserve such love'. Melodrama resolves into farce as Adrian steals back in through the library window, Pamela and Drusilla try to hide Vicky, and then Adrian, from Sladen, and Adrian tries to shield Vicky from the law. In the end it is Sladen, the detective, who, announcing 'The Play is over', holds the key to the entangled identities at stake. In a concluding shot Adrian is framed against an archway with Vicky and Drusilla on either side of him. Drusilla's frigidity sent Adrian on a class-boundary-crossing adventure. But if Vicky as a working-class figure can offer a more freely expressive sexuality that unlocks Adrian's capacity to respond to female desire, she recognises the class boundary that divides her from Adrian and sadly hands him back to Drusilla. But in case anyone thinks the process of transmuting identities stops here, the concluding image suggests it will need to start all over again. The final images are shot at floor level at the foot of the stairs, as he takes two steps up, she one back.

Towards the end of the drawing-room melodrama, Drusilla says to Adrian, 'If only I could read your thoughts.' This, of course, is what a combination of camera and naturalist playing was often thought to permit, founding the star in the identity of self and role, giving ultimate and authentic access to the human personality or soul. However, in British culture the 'real' person is what can be differentiated in the externalised signs of costume, behavioural traits, workplace and home, signs that have to be set into play with each other in order to hint at the social, psychic and ethical forces that drive them from within. Hence, in British popular culture – and certainly in its cinema of the 1920s and beyond – play-acting and dressing up allow protagonists to travel forward in time geographically by exploring the located identities of others.

TAKING TURNS: MUSIC HALL'S PARODIC ACTS

Since in melodrama the paths of antagonists, separated by social, temporal and geographic division, must be engineered to cross, the diverse social and cultural elements crucial to verisimilitude in British fiction are bound together by the centripetal drive of its plotting based on the happenstance of coinci-

dence. Far from arbitrary, coincidence provides evidence of moral polarities that work themselves out as personalised economic and social forces in people's apparently random lives. Such an ethically driven structure is open to a degree of ideological control, the happy ending realising in fantasy the desires of a dominant consensus.

Conversely, the ideological significance of music hall lies in the space it opens up for the potential clash of entertainment forms, for, contrary to the centripetal drive of melodramatic structure, music hall tends towards dispersal. Its programme constructs a series of deliberately differentiated acts and turns, opening to a range of heterogeneous materials and practices, potentially anarchic in their juxtaposed effects. If the aim to maximise audiences and bring in the middle classes led to commercialisation and a degree of sanitisation, music hall also drew the legitimate into its own orbit. For example, the dramatic sketch provided versions of theatrical plays, abbreviated initially to eighteen minutes and then, under 1905 licensing laws, to thirty minutes, while famous scenes from the classic repertoire were performed by players from mainstream theatre.[91] In this respect, the music hall was home to players from the legitimate theatre as well as to a range of local and popular entertainers from the circus, fairground and variety – who, according to Michael Sanderson, were more likely to come from working-class backgrounds than legitimate theatre actors.[92]

If commercialisation toned it down, music hall remained important as both a cultural site and cultural signifier, and as such its practices exerted a powerful if less analysed influence on British cinema aesthetics, offering a quite different articulation of class-conscious boundaries and performance modes.[93] 'Turns' and 'acts' – necessarily differentiated in the interest of variety – work against the centripetal drive of melodrama, encouraging narrational serial discontinuity. Mixing protagonists brings social performance modes into tension and contact. The direct address of the music-hall performer and shared familiarity with the audience obliterate the distance imposed by the aesthetic of restraint and boundary maintenance in favour of forced contact and community. In a culture where 'performances' function as social signifiers, the context of music hall and its entertainment practices encourage parody and pastiche, lambasting or foregrounding established cultural forms and representations. However, despite claims that music hall represented a more authentic culture, it is first of all a culture of performance. The turn is itself bounded as a singular act, while the music-hall performer's relation to audience follows a set form. But an emphasis on parody and topical reference creates oppportunities for remixing cultural forms into potentially new formations, reorganising boundaries and infiltrating different social priorities and perspectives.

The influence of music hall on the practices of British cinema in the 1920s can be traced in three main ways. First, it encourages serial discontinuity, producing the experience of filmic time as a collage of episodes and acts rather than a logically unfolding narrative. For example, the plot of *Call of the Road* (1920) is a tenuous concoction, stringing together a number of 'acts' or 'turns' that offer discrete pleasures. Thus we have a hell-fire club brawl, a duel, a magic-lantern joke using the story of the 'miller and his wife', two boxing matches – one parodic, one serious – various cross-class disguises, a pair of country fiddlers as chorus, and two folk songs: 'There were three ravens sat on a tree' and 'There was a jolly miller once'. George Pearson's quartet of Squibs films, based on a character deriving from a music-hall sketch, is similarly structured. The first, *Squibs* (1921), offers a series of comic turns and picaresque adventures, cross-cutting domestic comedy with episodes from East End pub and street life, and drawing on a cast of music-hall types. These include Squibs's drinking, betting, ever hopeful, ever losing-out father, played by Hugh E. Wright, himself an ex-music-hall performer; Squibs's wayward, flirtatious sister, Ivy; her straight policeman boyfriend, Charlie; and a chorus of cockney neighbours. Familiar icons construct a collage of working-class life: Sam's always empty beer bottle, his ever present bowler hat; Squibs's cheerful materialism and robust energy, breaking into a song and dance at the first opportunity.

Second, as suggested above, the self-conscious presentation of the 'act' or 'turn' to an audience invited across the barrier between art and life into complicity with the act contributes to the parodic and self-referential nature of British film-making. For example, the repeatedly thwarted attempts of Squibs and Charlie to enjoy a Sunday outing in London both document popular leisure pursuits – a trip to Epping Forest, the Tower of London, the zoo, the pub, the boating park,

the Bioscope – and send up the obstacles to pleasure posed by officialdom on the one day a cockney flower seller is free to enjoy herself: a coal strike leads to the cancellation of the Epping train; the war has closed the Tower; the zoo is reserved on Sundays for Fellows of the Royal Zoological Society; the pub is subject to early closing; boats are not hired out on Sundays; and to add insult to injury, the Bioscope is in Middlesex, where Sunday screenings are prohibited by the local authority.

Third, if the social performance or 'act' is always a cultural marker – a performance of a performance – music hall's 'turns' may play on conflicting class codes while its collage of acts encourages a clash of class- and gender-inflected performance styles between different entertainers. Such encounters within or between turns open up and play on the doubleness of parody. In *Nell Gwynne* (1926), Wilcox does not attempt a historical reconstruction of Restoration theatre. Rather, he exploits Nell's association with Drury Lane to support the tale's progression through a series of music-hall-like acts that offer alternately piquant stage pictures, comic pastiches of fashionable manners and signs of class-inflected knowingness, often communicating complicity with her doubled audience through an arch look into the camera. Thus Nell, upstaged at court by the King's mistress appearing in a new and extravagant Parisian hat, uses Drury Lane for a very public retort. She sweeps on stage in a hat that envelops her whole body in a grotesque parody of aristocratic femininity, which she flaunts shamelessly at the royal box (Fig. 5.4). Later, Nell shocks the puritan wing of the court surrounding James by appearing in a boy's suit and, after sliding down the banisters, fights a mock duel with one of the King's courtiers. Nell's career is thus performed as one long provocation to the codes of behaviour and cultural prerequisites of the ruling class, through counter-acts and parodic mimicry derived from a different social arena of entertainment based on the music hall.

These practices drew scepticism in some quarters. Taking a realist stance, *The Cinema* found Squibs and her father unconvincing, demanding that 'British producers realise the need for LIFE STUD-IES.[94] Pearson, however, implicitly resisting such naturalist criteria, emphasises the potential for comedy in mixing and contrasting performance types and acts. *Squibs*, he writes, is

Fig. 5.4. Dorothy Gish as Nell Gwynne upstages the King's mistress (*Nell Gwynne*, 1926)

a simple tale of a Piccadilly Flower-Girl madly in love with a stolid policeman, but alas, she was the daughter of a very shady father who earned a precarious living as a street-corner bookie! To bring a policeman into that queer home was the perfect equivocal situation to produce the fun of rich comedy.[95]

As the film develops, further 'turns' are extracted from 'the policeman's parents: father an ex-police Inspector and mother an ex-cook . . . dynamite only awaiting a spark!'.[96] In this way the cultural parody of music-hall turn is built into the film's episodic storyline.

Similarly, in Hepworth's highly popular *Alf's Button* (1920), the First World War squaddie, Alf, acquires by chance a magic button, through which he calls up the service of a genie. The genie, not understanding the English class system, creates a range of hilarious pantomimic transformations, which, at the same time, make acute social points: the country manor house turned into a harem, and the local home guard into a tribe of screaming dervishes. Graham Cutts's *The Sea Urchin* similarly draws on serial turns as its structuring principle, creating juxtapositions that, as discussed in Chapter 4, combine

perverse with farcical effects. The music-hall antics and robust cockney persona of Betty Balfour, playing orphaned Fay Wynchbeck, mock and undermine the combination of economic and sexual power through which children are abused in a Dickensian orphanage and female flesh is sold in a Parisian cabaret, where Fay is effectively enslaved. A picaresque narrative thread strings together a series of knockabout comic turns – including the rescuing hero's two plane crash-landings, two cabaret acts involving a high-class harlequinade and violent tango, and a gustily performed impersonation of the cabaret impresario by W. Cronin Wilson. There are escapades on train and boat as hero and heroine flee their pursuers, and a near drowning close to the shores of Cornwall, where Fay is returned to distant maiden aunts, played by Haidee and Marie Wright as a duo of wittily pantomimic caricatures. Each 'turn' is presented as a staging of performance in which music-hall conventions, resisting both sentiment and melodrama, wind up to hysterical farce.

In contrast, George Pearson uses the clash between performed 'acts', types and cultural documents to draw out a tragic perception of the life underlying such class-ironic resistance. For if Balfour turned Squibs's domestic routines into the dance of a resilient 'comic cuts', at the same time she could equally communicate a powerful sense of empathic pathos through the star/character's feeling for and identification with the grief of others. In the second Squibs film, Pearson exploited generic hybridity to draw out such counter-currents by intertwining a string of comic skits with a dark crime melodrama. The music-hall structure of alternating turns becomes an emotional roller coaster, snapping between moods and jolting our perceptions and sensibilities.

COMMUNITY VERSUS THE BOUNDARY: *SQUIBS WINS THE CALCUTTA SWEEP*

Squibs Wins the Calcutta Sweep (1922) was co-written by George Pearson and Hugh E. Wright, who plays Squibs's incorrigible drunken father, Sam. Since the previous film, sister Ivy has married the criminal Weasel, while Squibs still dreams of marrying her policeman boyfriend, Charlie. The inspiration for this film lay in the potential hilarity of class reversals provided by a winning sweepstake ticket, which Sam buys with Squibs's purloined savings. Before she can make him sell it back, she wins a place in the Calcutta Sweepstake, and eventually £60,000 in the Derby. Out of this situation Pearson and Wright string together a series of slapstick music-hall turns, through which Squibs and Sam play out a comically rumbustious father/daughter relationship, including a series of running gags that turn on the class reversals made possible by their small fortune. Squibs and her father, kitted out in furs and spats, arrive by open-top car to purchase a country mansion (Fig. 5.5). Here, creating uproar among an array of furnishings and fittings, which renders them weird and absurd, they poke fun at upper-class pretensions, oppressive authority and the class-economic exclusion of the working class from material comforts.

The hilarity of music-hall gags intertwines with a second story, diametrically opposed in tone, that engulfs Ivy when the Weasel commits murder during a Park Lane robbery and flees with her to Paris. Thus interleaved with images of Squibs's unshakeable faith and cheerfulness runs a dark crime melodrama that summons up Victorian pictures of careworn and angst-ridden faces in bare attics and shabby hallways. Aiming, he says in his notebooks (citing Griffith), to build dramas, 'not action by action but emotion by emotion', Pearson's intercutting between the two scenarios polarises material and emotional extremes.[97] A carnivalesque East End street party for the neighbours, reckless present giving and country-house buying pulls against the downward spiral of Ivy and the Weasel into penury, destitution and criminal madness as outcasts in Paris. Comic turns and gags clash with moments of climactic emotional and mental reversal or oppositional encounter – for example, when Squibs realises what it means to have £60,000 at her disposal, or Weasel and Ivy realise what it means to have committed murder. Similarly, later, after the hilarity of arriving in Paris, Charlie and Squibs come close to estrangement when his duty as policeman cuts across her family loyalties. A final clash of mental and emotional worlds erupts as Squibs bursts into her sister's hideaway, full of her

Fig. 5.5. Squibs and her father purchase a country mansion, their sense of fun and material pleasure mocking upper-class pretensions (*Squibs Wins the Calcutta Sweep*, 1922)

own success and good fortune, to be confronted by a stony, uncomprehending Ivy.

Threading through both comic turns and dramatic climaxes of sudden wealth and sudden ruin runs a nostalgic discourse on class and community, in which the closeness of the working-class community, its image of robustness, unselfish materialism and cheerful hedonism, are evoked and celebrated. Pearson documents the neighbourhood street party by switching camera position back and forth between inside-home and outside-street, breaking the barriers between private interior and shared public space. Equally, the chaos of Squibs's working-class home is contrasted favourably with Charlie's decorum-ridden, mean-spirited stockbroker-Tudor household. Such strategies feed a national fantasy of an undivided society. Significantly, after the bitter destruction of a devastating world war, it is Squibs's loyalty to Ivy that symbolises uncompromising bonding across social division. After the Weasel's panic-stricken suicide, and the discovery of their hideout by the police, Ivy collapses on Squibs's lap. A close-up focuses on her hand caressing the stricken and outcast Ivy, while a title responds to the implict challenge to any authority that would separate them: 'Ain't we sisters?' Such class-infused fantasy of community invested in the maternal returns in the 1930s in the films of Gracie Fields and in the 1940s in the home-front films celebrating nation as community.

The reflexiveness encouraged by the film's music-hall underpinnings foregrounds the acculturated signs of class carried in the body, dress and symbolic objects. This slippage between theatrical and social act makes failure a breakdown in performance. Thus the unpremeditated act of murder turns the Weasel from a brutal criminal to a shivering wreck, while the resilience of Squibs lies in her capacity to keep the show going. In this respect, an interesting figure is the reporter who haunts Squibs after her win, a menacing reminder of the demand that social life be lived as a public performance. However, the matching of the film's iconoclastic if respectable working-class heroine with a policeman boyfriend, and the image of discrete but menacing police surveillance that haunts the Parisian scenes, introduces a tension into the construction of the resilient flower girl as an icon for the nation. If she succumbs to the policeman, becoming unequivocally middle class – but equally if she disowns him, remaining loyal to her working-class origins – she will destroy her function as a fantasised bridge between classes. Pearson's feel for such emotional and ideological cruxes enables him to keep the tensions in play rather than seeking concluding resolutions. *Squibs Wins the Calcutta Sweep* ends not only with an image of sisterly bonding in a world palpably wrecked by men but with a plea to the audience in the form of a question mark: 'Ain't we sisters?'

MUSIC-HALL PERFORMANCE: ROLE AND STAR
Music hall and related modes of entertainment – pantomime, variety, vaudeville – rework the public/private opposition and codes of restraint that maintain the boundaries of middle-class verisimilitude in legitimate theatre. On one level, parody plays on the borderlines between cultural forms. The skit at its sharpest brings one social perspective to bear on the cultural norms of another, crossing boundaries semantically if not through narrative outcome. But more significantly, in refusing the footlights as a boundary between performer and audience, music hall shares in the practice of early 'transpontine' melodrama, exploiting the aside and direct address to the audience to invite participation. Thus the turns and skits that structure *The Call of the Road* demand an audience presence both within and without the film, addressing the audience directly by a choral commentary or a performer's aside and inviting it to respond – for example, by superimposing musical staves and words over Alfred/Victor McLaglen singing 'There were three ravens sat on a tree'.

Significantly, it was through her ability to make Squibs reach out from the screen metaphorically to touch the audience that Betty Balfour became not only the most popular but perhaps the only female star of the 1920s. As suggested in Chapter 3, the star produced by British culture is a public 'character' and in so far as stardom depends on closing the gap between performer and role, Balfour's career depended on the persona of the cockney skivvy. As much as Balfour struggled to do so, she and her producers were unable to free her from Squibs. But paradoxically, the practices and class-infused values of music hall have facilitated the production of British stars, because they are based on visible performance as the means to cross social and cultural barriers. Moreover, it is the working-class protagonist who has the motivation and cultural resources to cross those barriers.[98] However, Squibs was a creation specific to her period, combining in the Piccadilly flower seller a pathos familiar from many a Victorian painting with the equally iconic resilience of cockney humour and music-hall performance – a combination resonant for the war-touched 1920s. But this image required the harsher, grating edge of Gracie Fields's northern class humour and Lancashire patter in order to transfer to the 1930s. Despite the general view that Betty Balfour had a good recording voice and was an excellent singer, her stardom remained locked in the earlier decade. Squibs and Balfour took each other to stardom on the back of the music-hall turn, overturning social division by mockery and mayhem and in its place creating community through shared misfortune and laughter. In the happiness and exuberance that Balfour as a person appeared to share with her character and, according to publicity, spread to all around her, 'our Betty' broke the barrier between the 'grey shadows' of the screen and the living 'flesh and blood' of the audience.[99] Above all, by refusing offers to follow the stream of talented British actors who left for Hollywood and in standing up for British cinema – for example, making radio broadcasts and writing articles on behalf of British Film Weeks – she appears to stake her identity with 'us'.[100]

However, the fact that Balfour was so inextricably linked with her performed character – rather than absorbing roles into a star persona based on her own personality and private life – highlights the ambivalent nature of stardom in British culture discussed in Chapter 3. It suggests the degree to which stardom depends on particular genres to produce roles for fictional protagonists and on a doubling of role and performer. The sincerity, which I suggested in Chapter 3 is valued above the spontaneity of American stardom, demands that actors sink self in the role. As in the example of Lang and his exotic characters, sincerity commits the actor to belief in the part in order to make it live. But it always remains a *part*, an acted, bounded role. British stars are those who show us both the role and its significance: Balfour's cockney skivvy, Clive Brook's alienated aristocrat, Lang's exuberant, exotic 'other'. In British culture, the role brought to life is, perhaps, a more powerful cultural signifier than the naked personality, access to which is promised by American stars. This may explain why Noel Coward is subject to continuous revivals, and Novello has all but disappeared from mainstream

consciousness. Nevertheless, in their commitment to the reality of the role, British star/actors hint indirectly at the space beyond its boundary of an ineffable selfhood, all the more potent, perhaps, for being unspoken.

SHOOTING STARS AND BRITISH CINEMA CULTURE

The significance, then, of the generic practices favoured by British cinema is their insistence on role-play, and a protagonist's doubled existence – a mode of being fostered in the country-house drama, the picaresque adventure, historical costume romance, music-hall comedy and the crime film. Through such constellations, British film-making is doubly acculturated, building its generic kinds from fragments of existing materials – from the icons, performance styles and narrative motifs generated by the diversity of class-inflected forms circulating in the arena of popular culture. In this context, Anthony Asquith's *Shooting Stars* (1928) – much admired as a brilliant first film, but nonetheless often considered lacking in gravitas – appears paradigmatic as a fabrication woven from the acculturated materials and generic practices of British cinema culture. Set in a multiple-stage film studio, where a Western is in progress alongside a music-hall farce, its husband-and-wife star team are caught up in melodrama that turns illicit romance into tragedy. Mae Feather (Annette Benson) – a would-be British star with her eyes set on Hollywood along with her lover, Andy Wilkes (Donald Calthrop), star of the music-hall comedy – substitutes a real bullet in the stage gun to be fired at her husband, Julian Gordon (Brian Aherne). The guns get swapped between sets, and in a moment of high farce, Andy Wilkes is shot dead while swinging from a chandelier. Through these generic intersections, the film maps out the condition of British cinema culture in the 1920s: its British, American and European intersections; its studio practices, fan magazine writers and audiences; its generic forms and performance styles. Unaware that Mae is not at the theatre but in Andy Wilks's apartment, Julian goes to the cinema to watch their latest release, an 'old-fashioned' melodrama. Here the twin forces of melodrama and music hall play off against each other through the controlling comment of self-conscious parody. In the process, the intersection of Hollywood and British generic forms and performance styles with European expressive lighting, symbol-making

Fig. 5.6. Extras in *Shooting Stars* (1928) ponder 'Whatever happened to Mae Feather?', while she sits alone at back of frame and back to camera

compositions and satirical word/image juxtapositions poses questions about British cinema's past and its future. If the film offers a meaning beyond this reflexive mapping, it is to align the downside of the massification of popular culture with unthinking femininity. Julian is saved for film art, but his mar-

riage is at an end. Mae, forgotten by her audience (Fig. 5.6), returns years later as an extra, unnoticed by her former husband, now installed in the chair of the male 'auteur' in a studio transformed by a cathedral set. But, then, given Brian Aherne's statuesque body and steely blue-eyed gaze, much can be forgiven!

6 The Stories British Cinema Tells

By the 1920s cinema had become a major purveyor of stories. However, pictures, performances and generic constellations provide their materials. British cinema's storytelling is therefore the endpoint for this exploration of its peculiar characteristics. Alongside picture and acting, 'story' is a dominant term in debates about British film-making, gathering to it a range of concerns associated with British cinema from its beginnings to the present day. 'Story' calls up the vexed relations of British films to literary sources, and calls down the standards of 'classic Hollywood narrative'. But arguably, the conception of storytelling running through British cultural poetics offers a countervailing perspective to these strictures. As in previous chapters, then, I am less interested in whether or not British films meet a set of formal rules or aesthetic standards than in understanding the significance of 'story' to the poetics of British film-making and its relation to pictorialism and performance.

In spite of its international context, and a consolidating American standard, this cinema must retain certain indigenous practices and materials in order to gain recognition as British. Moreover, in so far as these practices differentiate social groups, they are essential to the democratising negotiations of a postwar class-based culture confronting the 20th century. Cautious these negotiations may be, and conservative the outcomes allowed in this new mass medium for a newly emerging mass-cultural sphere. Nevertheless, pictures, play-acts and stories, producing signs and documents of cultural difference, are brought into encounter in the shifts between a rapidly modernising present (often figured through the American consumer democracy for which Hollywood stood), an unknown future and an increasingly mythologised past. In examining some of the debated problems of storytelling and cinema, and some of the solutions that emerged in British film-making practice as the decade progressed, this final chapter seeks also to unravel key features of the stories British cinema told during the formative 1920s.

'THE STORY'S THE THING'

Throughout the 1920s the concept of 'story' and 'story value' is wielded as a gold standard of film-making by producers, critics and fans alike. In August 1920 Maurice Elvey launches into a debate about the desirability or not of a British star system to match Hollywood's, arguing, 'here [i.e. at Stoll's], we have made it our habit to film a story, and *not* a personality' (original emphasis).[1] *The Motion Picture Studio* agrees, calling under the sub-head, 'The Story's the Thing', for 'real, true-to-life, honest to goodness stories with a meaning', insisting that 'story vogue should replace star vogue, director vogues, brand vogues'.[2] On behalf of fans, *The Picturegoer* pleads with producers and publicists to stop wasting money on stars and spectacle, fantasising a time when:

> The Press-agent . . . will write about the wonderful pictures, costing 'next-to-nothing' to produce, no elaborate settings, no extravagant dresses to eke out a weak drama, but story, story STORY all the way home . . . After all, the story *is* the thing.[3]

The theme continues throughout the decade. In 1926 a reader writes to 'A Yorkshire Parliament' run by the *Yorkshire Weekly Post* noting the 'poverty of story' shown by Hollywood compared to its investment in 'the popular actor or great spectacle'.[4] G. A. Atkinson sends up the battle cry, 'Cartloads of Novels and No Stories!'[5] In 1927 *The Bioscope* tells film-makers that 'consciously or unconsciously the public appreciates story value, efficient scenarios and capable direction'.[6]

A demand for 'story' may appear to contradict the emphasis on pictorialism or performance in

British film-making. However, story features across the diversity of popular entertainments from which cinema emerges: pictures, songs, melodramas, police reports, music-hall skits all delivered stories. As discussed in Chapter 1, the mid-1920s found British cinema still at something of a crossroads as a developing entertainment industry. The attractive idea of 'Kine-Variety' offered the ultimately unrealised potential for rationalising cinema's mixed-media origins, at the same time that the feature film had become the staple of film exhibition, making story 'the basic material of the film'[7] – its chief commodity form. This brings British film-making under the immediate critical purview not only of Hollywood and its consolidation of the so-called classic narrative system but also of the British literary establishment, with its claims on national cultural tradition. The claim to story is now answerable to specified narrative rules.

However, in the separation of the different arts from their intermixing in nineteenth-century entertainment forms, the 'literary text' distinguishes itself from 'story', which in the reconfiguring sphere of mass-mediated, lowbrow popular culture retains its heterogeneous sources and functions, now expanded by the burgeoning field of mass-produced print fiction (Fig. 6.1).[8] In the common sense of British film-making, then, story represented a value distinct from both the formal properties of high literary production and the tailored format produced in Hollywood's scenario departments as the verbal plan for a film. Consequently, story did not translate easily into the stylistic system now known as 'classic narrative'. *The Motion Picture Studio* quotes approvingly an argument made in *The Stage*:

Fig. 6.1. The burgeoning fields of mass-produced middlebrow print fiction in Stoll's advertisement in *The Bioscope*, 1 July 1920, pp. 66–7

continuity, photography, and a host of technical matters . . . are not worth twopence to people who want a gripping picture . . . the true and final test of a good film is its holding power, and its visualisation of a theme of life presented so strongly that the spectators forget they are looking at a mere reflection on a screen.[9]

Such dismissal of 'technical matters', stressing audience *experience* rather than the requirements of the medium, is consonant with a pictorial-narrative culture in which stories are encountered in a variety of forms. As *Picture Show* points out, 'the public likes a good story . . . told in a simple, straight forward manner, whether in book, stage play or screen'.[10] Story, then, is a cog in a popular-culture machine. Crucially, however, film is not only a story-making medium but a medium for circulating stories made elsewhere.

EMINENT BRITISH AUTHORS

At the beginning of the decade Maurice Elvey, in a fanfare for Stoll's programme of 'Eminent British Authors', declared, 'The holding of the best stories in the world from the film point of view is the stronghold of the British trade.'[11] At its close, Laurence Yglesias counts 'the discovery of stories' among the most important and interesting tasks of film production, recommending neglected authors and titles as yet untapped.[12] If adaptation figures as a perennial criticism of British cinema, the cultural value of story suggests less technical concerns. Elvey speaks not of 'adaptation' but of direct translation of story into film: 'We have made it our habit', he says, 'to film a story' or 'to film a novel'.[13] In his essay, 'A Literary Cinema? British Films and British Novels' (1986), Brian McFarlane draws on the distinction between a cinema that 'captures' its stories and one that 'creates' them.[14] The notion of 'capturing' suggests the continuing practice and pleasure of the 'realisation' – the embodiment of a familiar story in film, offering the delights of rediscovery in repetition, made more real through living enactment. In this respect, cinema, emerging out of a popular culture based on recycling and reproduction, adds to the mass circulation of stories already firmly established as a commercial practice and deeply ingrained as a cultural experience.

This dual process – commercial and aesthetic – is neatly illustrated in Stoll's strip-cartoon advertisement for the Eminent Author Series discussed by

Jane Bryan.[15] In a series of sixteen captioned pictures, a young male writer 'conceives . . . a fine theme for his next novel', which will enter the popular market as both book and film. His publisher leans back satisfied with 'visions of innumerable editions and considerable profits'. Miss Brown 'is attracted by the novel' and buys a copy from a bookstall. Her family is intrigued and follows suit. 'The novel is filmed by Stoll's', and on hearing the news from their daughter, the Browns forgo 'a quiet evening' at home for the more exciting 'prospect of seeing the appealing story and their hero and heroine in pictorial form'. Realisation follows. While the author 'sneaks in at a side door to see the sort of characters he has *really* created', 'the Brown family sit enthralled as the novel they have read and enjoyed is *enacted before their eyes* and the characters in it are *brought to life* (my emphasis)'.[16] The producer of the film appears only in the last picture, a septuagenarian, hovering at the side of the corpulent exhibitor, shaking the hands of the author, who is flatteringly 'congratulated . . . on the masterpiece he has created'. Here, story both gains from and makes room for pictures and acting. The contribution of live performance to story is suggested in Edith Nepean's appreciation of Clive Brook, the 'lucky possessor of a *real* screen face', who, in *Sonia*, 'lives his role in a film so we forget Clive Brook and see the *real* character of the story living before us' (my emphasis).[17]

Realisation seems to have been A. E. Coleby's ambition for a programme of 'filming novels in full', exemplified in 1923 by his mega-production for Stoll of *The Prodigal Son* by the widely popular Victorian Manx writer, Hall Caine. Cut down from an original 30,000 feet (eight hours) to the 17,000 feet tradeshown (five hours), it was eventually released as two films, *The Prodigal Son* and *The Return of the Prodigal* (both 1923).[18] The project was, *The Bioscope* said, 'a sincere and painstaking effort to transfer a lengthy novel to the screen in its entirety', representing 'a literal translation of a novel of the "human document" class'.[19] Coleby, justifying his 'daring' on the grounds that 'people who read books always want to see them screened in complete detail', anticipated the day when films of novels would be released in several parts.[20] *The Motion Picture Studio* complains of such adaptations that 'only 5% or under have ever read the book', and that 'vast numbers would never read a Hall Caine novel without pecuniary inducement'.[21]

More recent criticism places the 'eminence' of such British authors within a commodified 'heritage culture' discussed in Chapter 4. Both arguments simplify the complex processes of circulation. The first misses the degree to which, through circulation across a range of media forms, stories became familiar as part of the cultural ether. One does not need to read *Oliver Twist* to know that he asked for more. *The Prodigal Son* had already been staged in 1905 as well as going through numerous print runs. Stories, characters and their authors, just like famous paintings, circulate as news items, through illustrations, as toy-theatre manikins, china figurines and so on, taking on a cultural reality for many who have never read the books. Indeed, Jon Burrows, noting the emphatic association of Hall Caine, the author, with his film adaptations, has suggested his deliberate involvement with the film industry as a way of circulating his novels.[22] In this sense, films might be seen as taking over the role played by illustrations in the circulation and reception of the nineteenth-century novel. Thus film-makers, assuming audience familiarity, are free to select from their sources. An opening title for *Bleak House* (1920) announces that the novel has material for many dramas, and that this picture takes 'the most dramatic of all the tales . . . the story of the hunting down of Lady Dedlock and the discovery of her secret'.

The heritage critique raises the threat of cultural boundary-crossing to a romantic conception of both working-class culture and high literature as singular forms authenticated by their pure lineage. Against this, *Daniel Deronda* (1921) offered an extraordinary melange of historical and literary allusions. Set 'in the Chelsea of Whistler, of Carlyle, of Rossetti and of George Eliot herself . . . these personages will make their appearance . . . in and about Cheyne Row, not as characters in the story but as casual passersby in the streets that once knew them'.[23] However, this mix of historical figures, novelistic fiction and travelogue is a mark of a culture for which representations and artworks circulate as consumable social signs. In 1925 a London cinema manager, under the heading, 'Lost Opportunities', complains bitterly that English history and English literature provide rich sources of material for successful pictures, which the Americans raid but which are ignored by British film-makers. He then offers a litany of sources, pictorial, literary and photographic: 'History, literature and tradition,

climate, countryside and seaboard, great city and picturesque hamlet, castle, cathedral, mansion and cottage, mountain and valley, fertile plain and rugged
shore, all with their tale to tell.'[24] This exhibitor is
not a member of the literati but a showman who
regards popular entertainment as an active site of
realisation and circulation. He names acculturated
images, the sources of which lie in pictures, history
books, travel guides and novels, providing the material and intertextual opportunity on which British
cultural representation feeds. Novels, then, become
not so much 'touchstones' of literary worth as
Matthew Arnold would have it, but emblems or
signs, which, like pictures and performers, function
as cultural documents and reference points. In an
article headed, 'Filming English Literature', *The Bioscope* comments, 'the American film succeeded by
interpreting America to a curious world'. It recommends, 'not a British imitation of an American film,
but a film which shall be as unashamedly typical of
British everyday life, philosophy and peculiarities as
is the American'.[25] Elvey writes that Marie Corelli's
God's Good Man (1919) infuses his film with 'the very
spirit of the England which the colonist and the
artist sees'. It addresses 'those who have so long
wanted to *realise* old friends, old faces, and the beauty
of England's country places on the screen' (my
emphasis).[26] Here, novel, England and film are sym-
biotically fused, not as a reflection of each other, but
as a cultural landscape, produced from the distance of
the artist, who is, as it were, a colonist of the imaginary, attuned to the resonant signs and icons circulating in national life.

However, the presence in *Daniel Deronda* of
George Eliot haunting the filmic translation of her
own novel points to an increasing concern with
authorial value, acknowledging the changing conditions of novel circulation and reading, including
sought-for cultural prestige and expansion of the
film audience. *The Cinema* declares it a film 'for
exhibitors who cater for lovers of art rather than of
sensationalism'.[27] Literariness is, therefore, a factor
in the search for stories. The literary novel is prized
for its greater complexity, especially in relation to
character. Thus Hepworth writes in *Pictures and the
Picturegoer* that 'the drivel which was good enough
for the short film plots of the old days . . . is supplanted by adaptations of novels and stage plays by
famous authors or dramatists'.[28] Nevertheless, while

Elvey dismisses the 'trash of the kettle-boiling nov-
elists',[29] it is rarely the literary giants of 'the great
tradition' who provide the stories so eagerly sought.
Rather, a raft of middlebrow writers, 'of artistic as
well as popular distinction', are named as Stoll's
'Eminent British Authors': Conan Doyle, H. G.
Wells, A. E. W. Mason, Stanley Weyman, Maurice
Herbert, Jeffrey Farnol, Marie Corelli, Ethel M.
Dell (see Fig. 6.1).[30]

Elvey's arguments against the star system on
behalf of story are both ingenious and symptomatic.
For stars, in encouraging typecasting and star vehicles, wipe out not only the pleasures of acting but of
story, on which character acting depends for roles.
Decrying Hollywood's manufacture of so-called
'original' scenarios based on contracted stars, Elvey
argues: 'If you write stories round one particular
person your artistic limit is very soon reached; but
our well-known novelists do not write their stories
round one particular person, therefore their books
offer the widest possible field for the film.' Thus the
producer is free to cast a variety of character types
from a repertory company of 'useful and versatile
artists, who are capable of filling all sorts of roles'. At
Stoll's he claims, 'we have consistently changed our
casts to suit each separate production . . . to find
artists really capable of portraying the various characters by the great novelists whose work we hold'.[31]
In this respect, realisation by embodiment of character meshes with the significance of character acting
in British film-making. Thus 'Basil Gill's presentation of the Rev. John Walden, "God's Good Man", is
full of the brilliant study he makes of clerical characters'.[32] In its turn, character acting ensures diversity
of protagonists over the singular star hero in order to
key into and manage the social and cultural difference that is the condition of cultural production and
recognition in Britain.

A STORY TOLD IN A SERIES OF PICTURES

Elvey's confidence in Stoll's policy, and apparent dis-
interest in the problems of adaptation, was supported
not only by his experience of realisation but by the
vital role of 'illustration' that functioned as intertext
between print source and film, offering familiar reference points to the audience. Thus Ideal's advertisement in *Kinematograph Weekly* reprints among a
number of complimentary reviews of Elvey's *Bleak
House* a comment from the *Daily Herald* to the effect

that, 'The costumes, make-up and scenic effects are all excellently modelled on Phiz's drawings.'[33] However, the priority as between illustrator and novelist was frequently contested and some feared the reduction of films to mere illustrations of the novels from which they derived. In May 1920, under the heading 'Novels or Original Scenarios – Which?', *Stoll's Editorial News* reports a debate between G. A. Atkinson, critic for the *Daily Express*, and Jeffrey Bernerd, managing director of the Stoll Film Company. To Atkinson's complaint that 'British films are almost wholly devoted to the illustration of popular novels instead of stories especially written for the screen medium', Bernerd argued that Atkinson had 'overlooked the fact that the British public likes to see on the screen "embodiments" of the unsubstantial personalities in a popular novel', citing the success of *At the Villa Rose* (1920) as a case in point. In response, Atkinson raised the problem, noted also by Foss and others, that such attempted embodiments 'seldom come up to the idealised images which one carries away from the book'.[34]

This argument suggests that the contemporary novel, lacking the 'idealised images' formerly supplied by illustrations, brings filmic realisation into problematic tension with the reader's 'mind's eye'. *Pictures and the Picturegoer* raises just such a criticism of the film of the popular novel by W. J. Locke, *The Beloved Vagabond* (1923): 'None of the clever artists quite realise the author's creations', except the child actor playing Asticot, 'who is the character to life'.[35] When Atkinson calls on producers to 'Tell the public that the film is "founded" on the novel and not a "literal" picturisation of it', he effectively recommends a shift in practice from 'realisation' towards a looser form of 'adaptation'.[36] At issue, then, is the accommodation of a culture of pictures and performances to filmic storytelling. This is apparent in the continuing identification of the basic unit of film-making with the 'picture' rather than the shot. For a culture in which pictures relayed 'stories' and were routinely recycled from one medium to another, it appears perfectly feasible for novels to be 'wonderfully presented by a series of pictures'.[37] The resulting elision between picture and shot is evident in the advance notice for *The Passionate Adventure* (1924) which reports a reduction in subtitles resulting from Cutts's conviction 'that the perfect film is one which tells its own story in a series of pictures'.[38]

REAL WRITERS FOR REAL STORIES

However, the growing shift towards a concept of adaptation brings with it recognition of what the realisation denies – the specificity of techniques and material appropriate to different media. The vast expansion of the novel-reading public raises expectations of a story experience engrossing its audience over time, which cinema must meet if it is to claim a position in the market for mass-produced fiction. In this context, where the 'picture' had facilitated exchanges between theatre, fiction and painting, it now threatens to undo the production of story. Thus we find a growing reaction against the cinema of pictures and illustration. *The Motion Picture Studio* hopes for the day when 'real writers' will be employed in constructing 'real stories for the screen. Then we will get real picture-plays instead of merely pictures.'[39] Lionel Collier complains of films that are 'merely a series of incidents strung loosely together with a wonderful array of sub-titling to supply the gaps in the action . . . very often the sub-title is merely illustrated in pictures'.[40] Marjorie Bowen, writing in *The Author*, perceptively notes a shift in the common sense of film-making: 'it is a moving *story* that is required, not a moving *picture*'.[41]

Such discussion increasingly recognises that if a story is not to be directly 'picturised', some kind of articulating process is required for it to be realised in a moving-image medium. Benedict James, a noted scriptwriter who worked for Ideal, Broadwest and Windsor among others, suggests that 'more depends upon the telling of the story than upon the story itself'.[42] The call for 'real writers', moreover, signals a growing awareness that if a story belongs to no particular medium, it nevertheless depends on a linguistic substrate, and that its shaping is in the first instance, even for a visual medium, a verbal process. This awareness of story as a verbalising skill – a branch of literature – drew attention to the work of the scenarist who either adapted or wrote directly for the screen. Thus Benedict James notes the 'dawning recognition that the scenario is the basis of the picture play', a sentiment frequently repeated through the decade.[43]

Much debated in the trade press was the degree to which screenplay writing required literary talent. An unnamed 'author' claims in *The Motion Picture Studio* that 'Scenario Writing' is a form of 'literary work', identifying 'pivotal' incidents and developing plot detail 'as closely as if it were a novel'. In this context the director's work is 'interpretative, not creative, translating the literary word and the artistic thought of the author into "filmable" action'.[44] Similarly, against legal arguments recently confirming the authority of the producer [i.e. director], since it is he who 'has to translate the story into . . . moving pictures', E. A. Baughan insists 'the author [i.e. scenarist] should be the leading man in the making of a film'. Left to himself, the director, even if he 'rigidly follows the "continuity" version of the scenario', is likely to come unstuck, while worst of all is 'the use of the machine made scenario, manufactured by studio experts'.[45] However, commercially aware critics distinguished sharply between the literary skills of storytelling from the production of 'literature'. G. A. Atkinson writes in the *Sunday Express* that 'few eminent authors survive the fierce test of screen dissection', which 'ruthlessly sweeps all this literary integument aside'.[46] He returns to this theme three years later, inveighing against modern novelists and playwrights as 'word-spinners', among whom 'storytelling and plot-making is "not done" '.[47] The novelist, Rafael Sabatini, who had adapted his own work for the screen, argued in 'Why Adaptations Fail' that '*the searching eye of the camera will mercilessly reveal . . . faults*' in a novelist's imagination and story construction, 'piercing the cloak of verbal ambiguities which have dissembled them' (original emphasis). He recommends that the scenarist 'strip the story to the bone and relate it anew in the terms of the other medium to which it is to be transferred'.[48] Rupert Crew in *The Motion Picture Studio*, while claiming the scenarist needs 'literary talent', warns that this is not merely a matter of 'fine phrases'. The writer is required largely for his or her service to story in contributing 'sound plot construction and characterisation'.[49]

In the year of the founding of the London Film Society, Iris Barry also wrestles with the role of the word in the making of a film story. In the *Spectator* she demands new stories for a new medium: 'Few literary men have new tales to tell', while our filmmakers 'want ability to conceive stories at all, however brilliant at translating another man's tale into pictures'.[50] Likening the scenarist to architects whose practice concerns concrete materials but who must formulate their concepts as written plans, 'the words themselves', she argues, 'are nothing save

where they break through the pictures into titles which are still an inherent part of the whole film'.[51] Barry is one of the few in this debate who attempts to specify the skills of the scenarist as a 'new form of artistic expression', mediating between 'the visual conception of the storyteller and that of the director'.[52] Implying a similar distinction between scenarist and director, G. A. Atkinson declares that 'Filmland wants storytelling and plot-making'.[53] For Barry, words are a means of commission to ensure 'different scenes . . . cohere within the film's geography . . . not [as] a disorganised sequence of events, but . . . closely dovetailed'.[54] This produces not a cinema of pictures, but of shots, 'sutured' together through a system of analytic editing as in American continuity, dependent on cut-ins, changing shot scale, matches on movement and eyelines inviting the spectator into a fully substantiated and coherent fictional world.

THE TELLER NOT THE TALE

However, there were frequent complaints among reviewers about close-ups and cut-ins, as well as about the fast editing in American film-making. Thus *The Bioscope* criticises Wilfred Noy's *Face at the Window* (1924) for its use of American-style 'cut-ins', resulting, it argues, in a restless style that detracts from the story and acting.[55] In December 1921 *The Motion Picture Studio* reprinted a letter to the *Toronto Mail* comparing British films favourably with the 'choppy' American style, contributing to a debate that ran through the decade.[56] In this respect, Hepworth was not alone in his distaste for shifting the viewer about. Paradoxically, cut-ins and close-ups belong to the process of scene dissection established by the American 'continuity system' designed to give the viewer direct access to the story. However, by denying the pictorial frame and self-presentation of the actor, this system excludes the significance in British culture of story*telling*. Driven by an aesthetics of social difference that organises action as playacting and images as pictures, British cinema requires a different management of story. In August 1922 *The Motion Picture Studio* reports an 'exceptionally thoughtful and thought provoking article' on British film-making in the *Manchester Guardian* by Caroline Lejeune, in which the young critic suggests the influence of the national tradition of the picaresque exemplified by Fielding, Sterne and Barrie: 'Today the novel's younger sister, the story in pictures, has discovered the charm of the picaresque.' In 'films of the roadside we get some beautiful glimpses of wood and river, some keen sketching of types, not a few tussles and a number of detached scenes of cameo sharpness. What is missing is unity.'[57] In recalling the picaresque tradition, with its emphasis on episodic incident and character type, Lejeune invokes the aesthetic of the geographic imagination. In a culture marked by difference, there is no singular end-point at which a protagonist may arrive – see Pierre Bourcheron's utter destitution that concludes the paradoxically titled *The Triumph of the Rat* (1926). Travelling is the trope of the geographic mode of narration. The journey not only facilitates encounters at numerous boundaries but provides a thread on which to string together incidents, acts, turns and pictures denied by the unity of the causally driven continuity cinema centred on the evolving story of a singular hero. To the traveller's collection of remembered events, pictures and souvenirs must be added the story, not only as architectural structure holding them together but as one among a number of its incorporated components.

Thus while the value of story to film must in the end override that of the picture if the film industry is to compete in the fictional marketplace, it refuses to lose itself entirely in the techniques of cinematic narration. Story retains a social and acculturated dimension in its attachment to an existing fiction, using cinema as a circulator of pre-existing tales. But equally important is its attachment to the author/storyteller, together with the audience for whom it comes into being. This figure, like the painter and the actor, lends significance to the story's circulation. But crucially, the structuring presence of the storyteller ensures the story reaches us as a 'telling' – opposing, thereby, continuity cinema's 'showing'. Thus the self-presentational dimension of the story, which parallels the framing of the picture and the performance of the actor, foregrounds the process of *telling* itself, the work of the story*teller*. It is the articulating role of 'telling' that links the film story to 'literature', while at the same time distinguishing the British approach to film fiction from the American. 'Telling' is a public act, performed equally in the printed book and oral tale. Telling is a public form of exchange between author or storyteller – who may be historical figures or fictional characters, relaying print or oral tales – and a receiving audience.

The storytelling process is itself an object of cultural fascination, recorded in the many popular paintings of viewers visiting art galleries or gazing into print-shop windows; of listeners gathered round an animated teller of tales; or of audiences hanging over balconies at the melodrama or music hall.[58] Elvey's *Nelson* (1918) begins as a naval uncle's tale to his young nephew, whose image reappears at regular intervals. George Pearson captures the power of the story in lovingly held close-ups on children's faces at the puppet show in *The Little People* (1926). The pleasure of the familiar story realised in film, and of the constructive process of storytelling itself, suggests its significance to British cinema culture. It is, then, in the nature of the story as a 'telling' that British cinema poetics produce a literate cinema, one in which, to purloin the phrase used by Iris Barry of film-titles, the verbal dimension of pre-existing literary sources 'breaks through the image onto the screen'. In the following analyses I will suggest different ways this literate telling manages the cultural role of the story and in the process explore the kinds of stories British cinema's intertextual practices retaled for the 1920s.

TELLING TALES AND THE LITERATE IMAGE

THE TRAVELLER'S TALE: *CALL OF THE ROAD*

A. E. Coleby's *Call of the Road* (1920) has already been discussed for its use both of performances and pictures and therefore offers a test case in story management. Based on an 'original' story by Coleby, it combines a picaresque mode of serial discontinuity threading together different pictorial story traditions through a foregrounded process of telling. It does this in two distinctive ways. First, a vocal recitative called up by archaic titles invites us into the ritual of telling/listening. For example, superimposed on a road winding into mountains, the opening title intones: 'Life is as the dust of the road, blown hither and thither. One soul, one speck to rise or fall as the fates decree.' The next image, infected as it were by literary articulation, is a close-up of a goldfinch on a twig – a picture found on the road. Two 'folk' figures appear, identified by Denis Gifford as Paganini Primus and Paganini Secundus, in tall felt hats and greatcoats, with bundles hanging from a stick balanced on their shoulders, itinerant fiddlers featuring as a storytelling chorus.[59]

A dialogue title indicates their tramping status: "'Tis eventide and time we wend our way to gain some cover', followed by a soft-focus iris of the couple to the left of a signpost marked 'Criddingstone – 1 Mile'. The older man, a patch over one eye, takes out his violin, striking up a tune, while the camera pans right, showing the road winding into the back of the frame and thus articulating the theme of the road. An encounter with a rider taking a message to Alfred Truscott begins a process of passing tales from one character to another. This sets up the second story-telling device, linking, in a process of retelling, the various incidents, pictures and acts out of which a skeletal plot is composed.

In this sense, the picaresque enables the geographic imagination to re-tale a life story as a journey charac-terised by boundary encounters, detours, returns and transgressions. Rather than linear biographic progress, triumphing over social obstacles, British cinema's trav-elling protagonists may change places, move up and down the social scale or even effect temporary reorder-ings of the status quo. Storytelling, combined with role-playing, is an effective device by which to achieve this crab-like narrative movement. So gossip about Alfred's doings at the Truscott mansion transports us to the gambling club he runs in his absent uncle's home. After Alfred's expulsion, the curiosity of his niece Rowena provokes Uncle Silas to begin telling her Alfred's life story. But before we hear any of it, the action switches to his encounter with the fiddlers, who have known him from childhood. On hearing of his latest escapade they begin telling him his father's story. Like Alfred, he gambled away his allowance, took to the road and fell in with a band of Romanys, among whom he found a wife. Iris-out and up on Uncle Silas now recounting how he discovered his disgraced brother dying among the gypsies. A flashback re-enacts his reluctant adoption of baby Alfred. Rowena, fascinated with this story, desires to rewrite its ending – 'the story tells of a nature misunderstood' – accord-ing to more feminine principles – 'Even so, dear Uncle, women have been known to have brains.' This facili-tates transition to the next enactment, the duel, which Rowena sneaks out to watch with her maid (see Chap-ter 2). After beating his opponent, Alfred disappears without meeting his cousin, but Rowena's involvement in the story leads her also to go 'underground', chang-ing clothes with her maid and living as a country girl close to the mill where Alfred labours.

Although an 'original' story, the deliberately archaic vocabulary adopted by Coleby for the titles suggests an attempt to introduce into film the artic-ulating, verbalising voice of the storyteller. This 'voice' is both a sign of the teller's immersion in the tale (like the actor lost in the part) and simultane-ously a presentation of storytelling as a performance, to which we contribute by our attention. In this sense, the literariness of the pre-existing written text – the voice of storytelling – distinguishes the crafted tale from the everyday writing of shopping lists, bills, memoranda, etc. The literary construction or turn of phrase cuts the word from everyday discourse – much as pictorial practices cut out a picture from a photo-graphic record – producing the bounded contours that articulate sounds and images as signs. The story-teller's narrating voice and the dialogue exchanges caught within the story are thus crucial components in British cultural aesthetics, and it is no surprise to find British silent films heavily laden with intertitles serving both functions, a predilection that strains against the visual definition of film. Such 'visible audibility' in its turn facilitates the process of inter-textual exchange and circulation: the storytelling voice is socially positioned, sending out its signs to listening/viewing communities. 'Literariness', in this sense, is the aural performance of the shapes, colours, textures, rhythms and significances of the word, the verbal concept that may infect the image. In British culture, in particular, these signs are socially accented. Literary production ingests sounds of everyday loca-tion and difference and, turning them into narration, foregrounds at the same time as controlling the verbal boundaries at which protagonists defined by social position meet.

Nineteenth-century theatrical spectacle and cap-tioned genre paintings, the Pre-Raphaelite marriage of poetic text and picture, the rise of the illustrated press and magic-lantern narratives all depended on their relationship with the articulating word. Martin Meisel, analysing entries to the Royal Academy exhi-bitions, notes, for example, the continuing retention by British painting of the literary, narrating caption or accompanying quotation long after the French had moved towards 'pure' form.[60] Similarly, David Peters Corbett suggests that English modernism was overdetermined by the pressure towards narrative and social representation, even in the work of its most iconoclastic practitioner, Wyndham Lewis.[61] In the context of such widespread union of narrative, word and image, the literariness of British cinema is best understood not simply in reference to its source material but to the 'literateness' of an image seeking its own articulacy as a 'speaking', narrating image.

WIT AND THE IMAGE: THE MINERVA COMEDIES

This process is brought visibly to the surface in an exemplary series of comedies produced by Minerva Films, the company set up in 1920 by Adrian Brunel, A. A. Milne and Leslie Howard. These quirky little films, of which two, *The Bump* (1920) and *Bookworms* (1920), are preserved in the NFTVA, not only make explicit use of the storyteller but, through the verbal-visual comedy of pun and parody, highlight the relation between literary word and image. Declaring their intention to avoid 'the comic picture-postcard type of film which appropriates the trade name of comedy', Minerva comedies shift from the one-off slapstick joke towards a greater emphasis on extended story and verbal wit.[62] Milne had gained his reputation in the teens for his columns in *Punch* featuring 'The Rabbits', members of the twenty-something generation of 'fast-talking hedonists who quip across the croquet lawns and play eccentric games'.[63] In practice, however, Minerva's 'stories' retain a number of features of the slapstick tradition – for example, direct address to the audience, the gag itself – but transposed to a literate level through a storytelling voice, present in the combination of witty intertitle and image.

Both films use the direct address of the oral storyteller, foregrounding the storytelling process as part of their self-conscious wittiness. So *Bookworms* is introduced as 'A Comedy in Two Volumes' superimposed over a drawn illustration of book volumes. It opens with the traditional fairy-tale voice, starting with 'Once Upon a Time', accompanied by sketches of castles, dragons and so on, while both films address a childlike listener. The opening titles of *Bookworms*, for example, invite us self-consciously into a whimsical pastiche of storytelling:

> T: Whom has he seen?
> T: We'll give you three guesses.
> T: 1?
> T: 2?
> T: No, your last chance.
> T: She . . .

Through such titles, the storyteller, like the actor, calls us into the presence of the ritual delivery of the tale as a performance.

This regress to childhood, however, contributes to the ironies of the adult storyteller, both films using story consumption reflexively as an element of their narratives. In *Bookworms* the hero's attempts to gain access to the closely chaperoned girl-next-door mimics the problem of the fairy-tale princess guarded in her castle by a dragon aunt. While setting their bored little niece the task of darning, her henpecked uncle reads risqué books borrowed in plain cover from the local library. *The Bump*'s playful use of storytelling is even more pointed in its mocking ironies. It features the putative romance between bright young twenty-something Lillian and dreamy but ever hopeful, dancing, jazzing Freddie Fane. Freddie's progress, however, is halted by Lillian's longing for a 'real man', personified by John Brice, 'the Great Explorer', in whose book, *Through Trackless Paths*, she is currently engrossed. As it happens, John Brice is a guest at a fancy-dress ball, entrancing Lillian with his tales, and displacing Freddie, who is reduced to playing bridge with her parents.

The arch voice of the storyteller opens the film with a search for the hero, articulated in the following titles:

1. Lillian Montrevor . . . Faith Celli (*the actress bows, smiling to us*).
2. Better take another look at her as she's the heroine.
3. John Brice, the Great Explorer . . . Aubrey Smith (*he gazes sternly in profile off left*).
4. Explanations of John Brice's face (*written on luggage labels attached to different parts of his face*):
   – argument with a leopard
   – battle with a scorpion in Africa
   – shark bite in Red Sea
5. It's just possible he may be the hero. We are not sure yet. Have another look in case.
6. On the other hand, the hero may be Freddie Fane who dances divinely.
7. Now we can begin.

As this transcription suggests, the verbal, articulating voice is not confined to intertitles. In title 4 – which may not strictly constitute a title – the word literally invades the image. Title 6 – 'the hero may be Freddie Fane who dances divinely' – is followed by a transliterating high-angle close-up on Freddie's Charlstoning feet, which pulls out and pans up to focus on his ecstatic smile. Thus two elements are cut from an image, pointed out by the camera, and, in conjunction with the positioning of the adverb 'divinely', become articulate through the transference of literateness from title to image, retaining the gently ironic tone of the story*teller* and direct address to the audience.

The popularity in the early 1920s of the 'art-title' encourages Minerva Films to add 'humorous effects' with intertitles in the form of captioned drawings, which function like illustrations to the skeletal plot. Thus, following his car breakdown, 'Waiting for Freddie' is the title of a line drawing in which an evil genie, cocking a snook at Freddie, emerges out of the car exhaust. This is followed by the transliterating image of Lillian's mother wearily playing Patience. The punning intertitle thus 'points up' the comicality of the following image. By inviting us into collusion with the storyteller, such direct address prevents images slipping past us in a continuous flow. This process turns images, their discreteness reinforced by iris, masks and tableau effects, into props for visual-verbal jokes. Their incongruous juxtapositions, following an absurd or nonsensical logic, perform a kind of literary slapstick. Freddie throws his arms out in a gesture of romantic proposal, only to be handed Lillian's empty teacup. The Great Explorer drops onto one knee to discover through his field-glasses the Piebald Gorilla, while in the next shot a pantomime animal, creeping up behind, discovers him. Thus the literate, reflexive voice of the intertitles articulates images as signs and documents that require reading – quite literally in the case of John Brice's facial scars explained by luggage labels – in order to get the joke.

Foregrounding the storytelling process in this way extends rather than obliterates the picture-postcard or pantomime joke, the music-hall turn or transformations of fairy tale. Moreover, the picaresque traveller of the imagination, collecting pictures, inscriptions, remembered encounters and acts as souvenirs, circulates cultural materials and values from one medium and social arena to another. So if literate titles mediate the anarchic vulgarity of slapstick, nevertheless slapstick is brought to bear on the rituals of an establishment culture faced with social change. When John Brice expands to Lillian on his African travels, a drawn triangular triptych (Fig. 6.2)

shows his arm-waving gestures in the left triangle mimicked by the pantomime gorilla in the right, linked by an inverted triangle, its apex filled by a quarter of the globe under the ironic legend: 'No doubt a similar story was being told in Central Africa.' For all Minerva's ambition to lift up British film comedy, Brunel was thankful to hear the hearty laughter of the first trade show audience.[64] The guffaws were drawn by slapstick with a literate point.

A CINEMA OF INTERTITLES

Literariness, then, is not simply a matter of an external relationship between author or pre-existing literary work and film. Rather, it becomes an element of filmic construction. However, this engagement with the verbal articulation of literariness encouraged British film-making to depend heavily on the written inter- or subtitle, a feature that provoked considerable debate. Those seeking the forward drive of the American cinema complained of British film-making's leaning towards serial incidents 'strung loosely together with a wonderful array of sub-titling to supply gaps in action', particularly when 'the subtitle is merely illustrated in pictures when it could have been dispensed with altogether and the whole scene depicted in action'.[65] However, alternative arguments justified the word as essential to the picture. In 1921 *Kinematograph Weekly* ran a series of four articles by Gertrude M. Allen (admirer of Hepworth's pictorial cinema), the fourth of which considered 'The Function of the Sub-Title'. Claiming the title 'in its rightful place an artistic asset', she

Fig. 6.2. John Brice discovers the piebald gorilla – or does the gorilla discover him? Adrian Brunel's *The Bump* (1920)

describes its absence as lack of pictorial completion, 'like a wonderful box of bonbons without a wonderful ribbon-bow or a statuesque vase robbed of the flowers that were meant to rest there'. Here the 'word' is both content and decoration, suggesting its symbiotic relation with the image. Used appropriately, she argues, the 'sub-title is pregnant with possibilities . . . the chalice of expression from which the screen author should drink deep' for its 'far reaching power of poetic expression'.[66] Despite disliking the 'diffuse and commentary' title, G. A. Atkinson conceives the intertitle's assistance to storytelling in pictorial terms, providing 'a short cut from one pictorial effect to another'.[67] Adrian Brunel emphasises the control offered by the title over the unfolding of the story. Not only do subtitles 'help continuity' but 'fading a title in and out can emphasise changes in tone, mood or direction', while '*telling* explanatory titles and dialogue lines' enable the storyteller to 'make a character stand out' (my emphasis).[68]

The appropriately named *The Wonderful Story* (1922), based on a magazine story by I. A. R. Wylie and scripted by P. L. Mannock, exemplifies both uses of the literary title, illustratively accenting and shaping pictures, while drawing out their narrative links. The film's title is followed by the announcement: 'Played by the oldest cast in the world, one woman and two men.' A photograph across a rising field to an ivy-covered farmhouse and outbuildings carries superimposed the film's fatalistic philosophical premise – 'People die and people are born. They quarrel and make it up. They prosper and flourish and sometimes fall by the wayside, but life goes on.' A low-angled long shot across a ploughed field displays a tableau with horse-drawn plough, one man at its head and a second man and woman behind, taking up their allotted positions on a timeless, pictorial rural stage. They are introduced serially: 'The Woman'; 'One Man'; 'The Other Man'. (Only later are they named as Kate [Ivy Duke], Robert [Herbert Langley] and Jimmy [Olaf Hytten]). It is hard to say, here, whether literary text or image bears the illustrative function; each appears to be competing for narrative control. The development of 'art-titles' in the 1920s – drawn, painted or photographic – introduces the possibility of illustration, not of an external text but of a film's own pictorially produced narrative. Hitchcock, who began learning film craft as a title designer, argued that illustrations accompanying

titles not only contribute colour to the action but help 'space episodes', recommending 'appropriate symbols'.[69] Like the witty title that 'points' to the following image, 'spacing episodes' interpolates a pause, emphasising the process of 'telling' and reading.

The art-titles of *The Wonderful Story* introduce a sequence of rural photographs as illustrations running in tandem with the film's literary-narrative discourse. Thus superimposed over a photograph of grassland and a country lane running past a cottage we are told: 'In this quiet little inarticulate English village, nothing ever happens. You will find the same kind of people everywhere.' Wilcox may have justified his claim to 'realism' for *The Wonderful Story* by this strand of country photography and by the inarticulate ordinariness of his characters. Nevertheless, it is the combination of literary narration with pictorial images that enables the story of the inarticulate to be crafted. A bleeding between titles, pictorial allusions and iconographic images contributes to the literary shaping of a narrative discourse aimed at articulating subjective states. So, as the crisis produced by Robert's paralysis strikes, a storytelling title superimposed over a photographic woodland – 'She had loved this man – but now – were her feelings different?' – guesses at Kate's internal conflict. A shot of Kate in a white shift follows as she goes to her bottom drawer and brings her wedding gown to the moonlit window. She sits before her dressing-table mirror, looking beyond it to the window behind in a familiar Victorian trope of desiring femininity. The void into which she gazes becomes a screen for projected memory and fantasy. First, an idealised image shows Robert as a strong, rippling-muscled man, standing upright against a black backcloth and splitting a log over his bent knee, followed by recall of his current state, stretched horizontal and paralysed on his bed. Finally, Kate summons an image of the future: Robert, pathetic in a wheelchair, reaching out to her in supplication. A fade brings up a backlit image of Kate, the literary-pictorial sequence resolved in a characteristic 'Pre-Raphaelite touch'. Standing with interlaced fingers, palms up, she absently contemplates them, then cupping her hands over her clasped fingers, lets them drop, her opening hands enclosing nothing. She half looks up again, and, with a little 'oh well' shrug, snaps back into her night-time routine, sitting down to remove her slippers. A title comments with a frank allusion to rural sexuality: 'He had swept her off her feet by his strength, his virility, his superb animalism. But now he was not that man any more.' And Kate puts away her trousseau. Then bringing her magic-lantern-like projections to a close, an answering title, superimposed over a country lane, speaks for her: 'The attributes she had worshipped in Robert Martin were dead, and her love for him was dead.' A second title, superimposed over the village green, opens the next chapter: 'The endless book of reality with a fresh page of struggle and growth daily unfolded', and Kate discovers there is another way to cross a stile, this time with Robert's brother, Jimmy (see Chapter 4).

Emphasising the film's 'realism', *Kinematograph Weekly* suggests that the film offers an 'intensely human picturisation of what must be happening in many lives to-day'.[70] Significantly, exactly what is happening is not identified. However, the combination of paralysed bridegroom and frustrated female sexuality suggests an echo of the unspoken psychosexual war wounds of the thousands of crippled and neurasthenic soldiers returning from the Great War, whose physical and mental condition affected directly or indirectly a majority of British families. Herbert Wilcox, for whom Cutts directed the film, claims Rupert Brooke as his inspiration, and the film ends with a verse from 'At Granchester'.[71]

The sequence that Brooke's lines close is something of a tour de force, in which symbolic image calls on literary verse in a process of mutual illustration, of verbal-visual collage. Kate and Jimmy have married, but, as a title points out, cannot afford to set up home on their own, and domestic life is played out under Robert's grim gaze and his verbal curse. While Kate is in childbirth, the parson holds vigil with Jimmy. A title, superimposed over a photograph of the church, tells that 'while they prayed he willed that she should die'. In the following mid-shot Robert lies prone, staring fixedly at the ceiling on which he has previously conjured up the wedding (see Chapter 4). This image is twice intercut with a long shot of a raging storm, collaged with a circular insert displaying a drawn lightning strike. In a high-angle shot the parson reads from the Bible while Jimmy sits distraught and an insert from Genesis speaks of the creation of man and the planting of Eden. A long shot of the village follows and then the storm clouds. Into this fades an image of high-

Victorian kitsch – a baby on a bed of lilies floating closer to the camera and filling the screen as the storm clouds fade out and we cut into a close-up of the newborn. Both baby and mother have survived, but Robert's curse hovers over the household, until the climactic moment when Kate appears some days later and, after hesitating, lays the baby against Robert's side. After a series of anxious looks from Jimmy and Kate to Robert, he finally looks at the baby, his grim stare glimmering into a half-smile. As he curls his arm round the child, Jimmy and Kate kneel down on either side in a tableau of the Holy Family, the wounded man at its centre, symbolically rebirthed and 'illustrated' by Brooke's verse superimposed on an English country lane:

> But Winter's broken and earth has awoken
> And the small birds cry again
> And the hawthorn hedge puts forth its buds
> And the heart puts forth its pain.

STORYTELLING AS CONSTRUCTION

In Chapter 4 I suggested that the power of visionary projection accredited to the protagonists of *The Wonderful Story* is a logical outcome of a culture that uses pictorialism to define people and situations by visible signs. Reading the social descends into a voyeuristic fascination with what happens across the boundaries of social difference and behind the divisions of public and private. Similarly, telling stories gives personal lives public shape and identity. For those bounded by social position, storytelling constructs an imaginary geography allowing autobiographic projection across socially divided spaces. Guy Newall's films are singularly interesting in this respect. As suggested in Chapter 3, his choice of stories, whether as director, scriptwriter or actor, centres on a male hero defined by his marginal social location and personal isolation. Projecting dramas out of an occluded inner life, Newall's oddball character orchestrates real or imaginary encounters at the boundaries of class (*Duke's Son*, 1920); ethnicity (*The Garden of Resurrection*, 1919); regional identity (*Maid of the Silver Sea*, 1922); sexuality and gender (*Testimony*, 1920; *The Lure of Crooning Water*, 1920; *Fox Farm*, 1922); and even the supernatural (*The Ghost Train*, 1927). In all these films (except *Testimony*, in which he did not act), Guy Newall casts himself as a lonely, unlovely, wryly self-deprecating outsider: the archetypal wounded man. At some point, frequently through an encounter with a travelling woman, events bring about a displacement or dislocation, stimulating a projection of a fantasised alternative life story from the one his character is living. In some films the projected story must be given up in a return to the starting point (*The Lure of Crooning Water*); in some the fantasy is materialised in a 'happy ending' that substitutes for the film's 'reality' (*The Garden of Resurrection*, *Maid of the Silver Sea*); in others the Newall protagonist must leave the story for an indeterminate and unimaginable future (*Duke's Son*, *Fox Farm*).

PROJECTING LIFE STORIES: *THE GARDEN OF RESURRECTION*

The Garden of Resurrection, adapted by Newall from E. Temple Thurston's novel and directed by Arthur Rooke, is judged by Rachael Low 'a silly story about a man who wants to commit suicide on account of a girl he hardly knows'.[72] However, she acknowledges the sincere playing by Guy Newall and Ivy Duke, which received warm notice in reviews, and there is no doubt about Newall's commitment to the central protagonist, Bellairs, who shares key features with all his other heroes. If the story seems 'silly', this is perhaps because it takes to extremes, and therefore exposes, the nature of storytelling as a process of fantasising by which the teller seeks to absorb others as players in a self-constructing narrative. Playing at the boundaries of sexuality and race, the film also uncovers the role of storytelling and fantasy in political processes.

Two opening narrator titles establish the Newall persona. 1) 'There is nothing more lonely in this world than a lonely man.' 2) 'Bellairs, obsessed with the idea of his own ugliness, played by Guy Newall.' An iris-out follows on a characteristic British *mise en scène* (stylishly designed by Charles Dalmon). Bellairs enters from a door left front frame and, his back to camera, looks into the picture, through an archway, across the stairs to the front door under another arch at the back of the frame. This shot offers a set of receding spaces and intersections suggesting a complex internal structure. Title 3 tells us: 'But there was one to whom he was as the image of God', and in the next shot a wire-haired terrier runs from the back of the frame. A little comedy follows around the dog, which – given its own dialogue titles, much to the

amusement of reviewers – chases Bellairs's car, ending up in quarantine for its pains as his master takes a trip abroad. This prologue establishes not only Bellairs's loneliness but his dependency on imaginary relationships, thus preparing for the convoluted narrative he constructs for himself on his return.

A title sets the stage: 'Back in London, to this lonely man whom life had never reached there drifted one night an echo of romance.' The scene fades up on exotic palms through a spray of water, dissolving to reveal a violinist and, in a further dissolve, a high-angle view of society people dining in a classy London restaurant. A straight cut to a high-angle medium close-up of Bellairs shows him sitting alone, smoking (Fig. 6.3), followed by a similar shot of a seedy aristocratic-looking man with a cigar holder, holding the hand of a heavy-eyed woman in a plumed headdress. A title indicates that Bellairs is eavesdropping, and the next sequence focuses not on Bellairs but Fennell's conversation with his mistress. This concerns his forthcoming marriage to a cousin he met in Dominica, who, along with a 'coloured strain', has inherited £10,000. Iris-out on the Dominican cousin, played by Ivy Duke, her back to us, relaxing and fanning herself in a cane chair on a leafy verandah. Fennell then enters to embrace her. Back in the restaurant he names her as Clarissa. Cut back to Dominica and forward in time, as Clarissa packs to leave. A geography lesson now ensues as a series of drawn maps, cut-ins, animated arrows and a superimposed image of Clarissa and Fennell on board ship traces her passage from the West Indies to Ireland. This collage is explained in a closing title: 'And so I brought her to my Aunt's house at Ballysheen.' Clarissa's painful introduction to Fennell's two aunts follows, their body language expressing disapproval and distaste for this distant relative. A title reveals Fennell's intention to acquire through marriage Clarissa's dowery. His mistress, looking almost into the camera, does a double take, blurting out the question: 'You don't mean to say she's black?' Clarissa, it appears, conforms to Western ideas of beauty but 'She's got the taste . . . for gaudy things'. She then appears before the aunts in an exotically flowered-print dress, to be looked over, turned around and finally re-clothed in a prim black gown and heavy, studded shoes. Only now do we return to Bellairs in a high-angle close-up as he continues to

Fig. 6.3. Guy Newall as the lonely outsider, Bellairs, weaving his fantasies out of overheard conversation in *The Garden of Resurrection* (1919)

watch, rubbing his hands together nervously. The story of Clarissa's plight darkens cruelly as we learn that she is kept indoors and only allowed to exercise under cover of night, her face hidden by an enveloping veil. Finally, a title comments: 'A sordid little story – brutally told – at which all Bellairs's sense of fair play cried out.'

Given Bellairs's position as eavesdropper, the images represent less Fennell's materialised memory than Bellairs's imaginary projections, constructing a story from overheard scraps. This possibility is stengthened by the filmic narrator addressing us directly: 'You know those little thoughts – perhaps fate ordains them – that stick sometimes for hours afterwards – don't you?' The next sequence fades up on Bellairs, standing rooted in the centre of his sitting room. Absently picking up his cigarette case, he moves to the fire and sits brooding in the firelight, where he summons up in successive and starkly contrasting images the power of Clarissa's otherness. First, exotic native girl, she basks on a sunny vine-

covered verandah, equipped with a parrot. Then dissolving into oppressed prisoner of Irish narrow-mindedness, she is clothed in black, her profile turned in noble suffering against night-time rain. If the first images were not his, their recurrence here belongs to his own imagining, provoking him to weave an extraordinary tale around a woman he has never met, and in which he casts a romantic role for himself.

On the excuse of visiting a former university friend, Bellairs travels to Ballysheen on a self-appointed mission to rescue Clarissa and return her to Dominica, only to have his fantasy rejected by its heroine, who refuses his attempt to enter or deconstruct the story she claims as hers. A convoluted series of plottings now follows, which implicitly links Fennell and Bellairs. Fennell writes letters to his mistress explaining his fake marriage to Clarissa, while Bellairs writes to Clarissa declaring he knows all about her situation. She eventually agrees to a secret meeting, when, summoning up a flashback to his eavesdropping in the restaurant and attempting to alert her to the planned deception, he pitches to her the role she plays in his fantasy. In some ways this both mirrors and relieves his own situation: 'Go back to your home in the sun. Go back and love your love with an aching heart if you like – until there comes along some better man.' An iris opens up on a picture of Clarissa on her Dominican verandah, tickling the head of her parrot. This exotic image, which by now is indubitably Bellairs's construction, transforms through another iris change to factory chimneys and city rooftops. These dissolve to a newsboy holding up a poster that reads, 'Shocking murder in East End'. Over this fades up a title that only makes sense in terms of the imaginary logic of Bellairs's investment in Clarissa's paradisal identity – 'They'll scream at you from the housetops that the world is an ugly place'. Reacting angrily to his story, Clarissa sweeps off.

Back in London, Bellairs attempts to console himself by planting a window box, cross-cut with the image of Clarissa's deteriorating relationship with Fennell, who gambles away her inheritance. Ratcheting up the narrative stakes, Clarissa learns her marriage is a fake. To her demand for the truth, Fennell sneers, 'You're . . . black!' Finally, Clarissa and Bellairs's stories converge. He plans suicide as she, destitute, searches the phonebook for his address. In quick succession, he sits with a gun in his hand, a close-up shows his doorbell ringer vibrating and he finds her standing on the pavement. Taking her in, Bellairs discovers she is pregnant. Now able to take a grip on her story, he bestows his name on her to save embarrassment with the doctor and midwife, and, awaiting her recovery following a miscarriage, lays out the floral dress of Dominican fantasy that he finds among her luggage. As she clutches the dress to her, he declares the completion of the story: 'As soon as you are better I'll send you back to Dominica – to your sunshine.' But as the moment for parting comes, a title comments on the irony of the storyteller: 'Achievement of his object spells the end of romance', and we cut to a wet railway station and the shadowed figure of Bellairs watching her departure. However, Guy Newall, the film story's writer, adds a coda, in which the fantasy is recuperated. His Ballysheen confidante, Belwottle, telegrams Bellairs to return to Ballysheen. She takes him to a thatched cottage, where, pausing, he hallucinates images of Clarissa, calling and then shrinking away inside. Gazing bewildered round the interior, he sees from

behind an armchair a hand carelessly thrown out, holding a flower. Bellairs turns, transfixed. A rose is put into his hand, and his fantasy materialises the happy ending the film's narrator presumes we want: 'And so even as you and I would wish, let us leave the three [Bellairs has been reunited with his dog at the cottage] in their newfound happiness.'

The foregrounding of narrative construction is emphasised by the structural problem of dramatising the story of a character who lives alone, resulting in 'overhearings' projected into fantasised images. The pictorialism of his encounters with Clarissa emphasises her implicit narrated function as an image who provides Bellairs with an identity. The discourse of racism, through which Fennell identifies Clarissa as black under the white skin, links to Bellairs's own self-conception as outcast, and which through her he can reverse. Similarly, Fennell's construction as a sadistic alter ego confirms Bellairs as the romantic hero, recalling the pairing in *The Bargain* (1921) of Henry Edwards's Dennis Trevor with the outcast son, Richard Wentworth. Seen in this perspective, Bellairs's suicide scene, his farewell to his dog and the fortuitous arrival of the abandoned and pregnant Clarissa – 'silly' enough on one level – can be understood as further acts of stage management. The servants – Bellairs's housekeeper and ever loyal butler, Moxon – and his Anglo-Irish friends are commandeered into providing an audience and supporting cast for the enactment in a publicly dramatised story of the otherwise inexpressible personal emotions and ideological repositionings consequent on shifting conceptions of self in a changing world. In this context the role of the mixed-race Clarissa is revealing. For example, her gaudy floral dress would seem to represent an imagined cultural freedom and expressiveness unavailable to the repressed Englishman. Her attack on his vase of lilies when she first arrives at his house – associated with death and the 'war touch'? – and the ultimate replacement of exotic West Indian vegetation by the English country garden, the lily by the rose, would suggest an appropriation and recasting of this 'other' within a 'Garden of Resurrection' no longer to be found in England but sited 'elsewhere' – provocatively, in Ireland. His committed playing suggests Guy Newall's intense belief in the emotions of his protagonist, his script providing occasions for acting them out. In much the same way, his hero, who, as an early title tells us, 'life threatens to pass by', constructs through a series of opportunistic visits, letters, messages, notes and telegrams a story for himself in which others are compelled to serve as a supporting cast.

THE PICTURE'S STORY: DETECTION AND THE IMAGE

Defending his contention noted above that 'British films are almost wholly devoted to the illustration of popular novels', G. A. Atkinson makes three complaints about the highly successful *At the Villa Rose*: first, lack of 'theme'; second, overuse of titles, which he exaggerates as 30 per cent of the film; and last, the divulging of the 'mystery' halfway through. A director of the class of Griffith, he suggests, would have developed 'the subversive moral effects . . . of the cosmopolitan, hectic, gambler-ridden, and moneyed atmosphere of the Riviera'.[73] However, it is less the casino abroad that dominates the film than the fashion at home for the seance, which under detective investigation yields insidious sado-masochistic fantasies circling round female sexuality. Far from an anti-climax, the centre of the film is given over to a breathless, almost title-less enactment before our eyes of what detection has only partially uncovered – Celia's entrapment in a conspiracy involving the brutal murder of a nouveau-riche widow. The journey to this central denouement, however, has been circuitous, and does indeed play off picture and intertitle, for Sinclair Hill's adaptation of A. E. W. Mason's novel tackles the problem of filming the ratiocination of detection by exploiting the tension between pictorial signs and the story*telling*.

The film opens by establishing its authorial and documented authenticity – 'Adapted from the famous novel by A. E. W. Mason', 'Photographed and acted on the Riviera and Mediterranean coast', 'in the actual interior of the world famous casino'. Stylish, successively blue-, pink- and yellow-tinted pictures of landscapes, gracious palm-bedecked interiors and sunlit orangeries follow as introduction to 'Monsieur Hanaud, the great French detective' on holiday in the company of his friend, Julius Ricardo. The story's crux, however, is revealed as the camera closes in on the latter – 'Idler and Philosopher' – eavesdropping on a group of players gathered at the gaming tables. Among them he recognises an old acquaintance, Harry Wethermill, in the company of the vulgar, nouveau-riche Mme Dauvray and her

companion – Harry's fiancee, Celia Harland. Plagued by a troubling but blocked memory stirred by the young woman, Ricardo plays 'the amateur detective', attempting (like Bellairs in *The Garden of Resurrection*) to make sense of overheard scraps of puzzling conversation in titles flashing successively up onto the screen, mimicking his mental struggle. His gaze held by a girl with a past and an intense desire to remember, the amateur detective effectively anticipates – fantasises even – the crime that will constitute the film's mystery. Hence the image, fading out on Ricardo still puzzling, cuts via the title, 'The Villa Rose, home of Madame Dauvray and scene of a terrible tragedy', to a night-time, blue-tinted exterior shot of the villa. Thus, pre-empting suspense, this title boldly reveals the core event, while the looming presence of the villa shifts attention from *what will* happen to anticipation of secrets enclosed within its interior. The villa thus becomes both a portal to, and chief player in, Ricardo's fantasies woven round the hinted mystery of a girl.

Next morning in the prosaic light of day, 'The Amateur Detective is rudely disturbed in his morning toilet' by Harry's arrival with a newspaper report of Mme Dauvray's murder, and the suspect disappearance of Celia. They go immediately to Ricardo's friend, Inspector Hanaud, and the narration is now delivered in a succession of flashbacking stories and pictorial clues through which witnesses, participants and the 'Great Detective' attempt to construct, conceal or reconstruct the secret that lies at the heart of the Villa Rose. In the first half of the film three stories are told: by Perichet, the policeman who discovers the crime, by Mme Dauvray's chauffeur, and by Helene, her maid. Inspector Hanaud's investigation serves as the thread on which to string these successive stories, while, in eliciting reconstructed memories, partial truths, circumstantial evidence and deliberate falsifications, the process of detection foregrounds the constructive work of storytelling. Concern with past events and the testing of stories are, of course, key features of detective fiction and it is no coincidence that this is a dominant genre in British culture, for which the circulation of stories is a crucial form of sociality. Moreover, the discourse of detection emphasises the reading of documents, gestures and visual signs as clues to social and personal identities and events that are frequently opaque and resistant. Here, then, storytelling does not offer the forward trajectory of action ploughing into the future but a process of reverse biography, overdetermined by the grip of the past. Each story construction peels back layers of half-truths until Harry himself is exposed halfway through the film, his confession realising in full action replay the macabre event itself.

The articulation of the reasoning word and the fullness of the image are thus in tension. In the early scenes the dialogue titles that begin the stories produce images as illustration subordinated to the storytelling voice. Thus Perichet's story begins with bare facts: 'Last night I saw a half-open gate.' A blue-tinted medium long shot looks through wrought-iron gates, past palms to steps rising up to the villa. Mounting these, the policeman knocks on the shutters. Hearing nothing further, he departs, shutting the gates behind him, leaving the secret of these images untapped. As we will see during Harry's confession, this was the moment when Celia was in desperate need of rescue. However, as the stories reach deeper into the past, the power of the picture exceeds verbal explanation, contesting the flat, matter-of-fact tone of the storytelling title. On his return beat, the policeman states: 'Passing later, I saw the gates open again.' In a repeat of the previous series, the increasingly ominous villa draws him towards it, an iris shot panning along the frontage to an open shutter, followed by a shot from inside that draws him in further. His torch picks up a luminous globe, mysteriously shining in the gloom, and then a woman slumped dead in her chair, while a noise from above draws him up the stairs to discover the maid, Helene, chloroformed on her bed. Thus the image track hints at the hidden story in the picture, which, expanding through flashback, conceals so much more than it says.

Perichet's story stops here as Hanaud seeks clues to penetrate the secret haunted villa, filled with banal objects that refuse to divulge their meaning. The gap between visual signs – a hair, a shoe, a length of cord, a pot of cold cream – and knowledge is mimicked in the failure of the assembled company (and the audience with them) to see or understand until verbalised by Hanaud. However, despite Hanaud's airy assertion that 'to the trained mind they have much to tell', he is deceived by opaque or duplicitous signs. Declaring Celia's guilt by matching her cast-off shoe with a footprint, we later see the body produce lying signs as Celia is forced to leave her print in the gravel, while Helene, a newspaper headline announces, was 'Actu-

ally Chloroformed to Deceive the Police'. This misrecognition of Celia reinforces her role as a troubling memory in Ricardo's mind. Femininity itself is subject to a cultural investigation, as drawers are pulled open, her clothes examined and a pot of cold cream (sign of a woman's mask and duplicity) appropriated.[74]

In Helene's account of Mme Dauvray's involvement with Celia and spiritualism, transgressive desires and meanings – unperceived in the matter-of-fact titles because unimaginable to the 'trained mind' of the Inspector – come closer to the surface, intensifying their association with aberrant femininity. Her mention of a 'seance' reactivates Ricardo's lost memory, now reprised as a theatrical staging, in lurid yellow and pink-tinted shots, in which Celia performs as a fake medium. In turn, Ricardo's intervention triggers a release of Helene's jealous hatred for the orphaned Celia. Detection shifts from the logic of clues to the allure of feminine psychology and sexuality. Helene tells how she reconstructed the reception room into a space for theatricalised enactment, a black velvet partition concealing behind-the-scenes bondage and erotic and perverse sensation (Fig. 6.4).

Fig. 6.4. Celia, helpless innocent, is subjected to sado-masochistic terror in *At the Villa Rose* (1920). Here Helene checks her gag (see also fig. 2.7)

The murder of a new witness enables Hanaud to declare Celia's innocence, and provoke Harry's exposure. His confession now fills virtually the entire second half of the film, in a breathless enactment that, reprising the half-stories told piecemeal through the circular, disjointed processes of detection, now unfolds as the cumulative, trangressive stages of a criminal conspiracy. Each stage is marked by an illustrative title: 'The Cat's Paw', 'The Suggestion', 'The Conspiracy', 'The First Move' and 'The Trap', the latter repeated three times like a drumbeat as the action gets ever nearer to the heart of the mystery. Announcing, 'At the Villa Rose – the Night of the Tragedy', action replay shifts into Grand Guignol, subjecting Celia, helpless innocent, to sado-masochistic terror (Fig. 6.4; see also Fig. 2.7). In a prolonged bondage sequence, Adele, Harry's mistress and accomplice dressed in an extraordinary sexily rouched, halter-necked and backless taffeta evening gown, makes much of tightly binding first Celia's hands and then, pulling her behind the black velvet curtains, gagging and tying her to a chair. Close-ups on Celia focus on her frightened eyes and fragile white-clothed body, luminous in the darkness. A mirror shot catches Helene's triumph, her clenched fists raised in glee. The sequence culminates in the overheated excitement of the matriarchal Mme Dauvray's murder. Lateral juxtaposition of the curtained-off space where Celia is hidden and the darkened sitting room where the seance is to begin present two pictures. In each a hapless woman is threatened by criminals, who alone have the power to move between the velvet curtain that separates them. Red and blue tinting intensifies the switches between these contrasting pictorial spaces. As Harry glides in behind Mme Dauvray, preparing to strangle her with a cord, a montage of cross-cut close-ups focusing eye communication between the conspirators and Celia's terror-struck 'listening eyes' behind the curtain builds to the climax, played out in their facial reactions.

Thus what starts as the verbalising, circular and title-laden ratiocination of the Inspector ends in full-blooded, gothic melodrama, anticipated in the fantasising of the amateur detective/philosopher, Ricardo. In the process (like many a Hitchcockian hero) he falls in love with his story's victim, object of troubled memory, false incrimination and final exoneration. Close to rescue by Perichet in Harry's story, Celia is again nearly lost, as Hanaud realises that newspaper reports of the recovery of the Dauvray jewels put her life at risk. This enables not only the last-minute rescue of melodrama – when Hanaud's car crawls in long shot, minute and infuriatingly slowly, through a dream-like Mediterranean landscape – but a sado-masochistic finale, in which Celia is sewn into a sack and threatened with vitriol and drowning. This is concluded by a shot of a white door, opening onto the chinoiserie-decorated room to reveal Hanaud, anxiously staring into the camera. Thus the spectator is physically caught between the rationality of law and the perverse tableau revealed in the reverse shot. The next shot returns to the sofa where at an angle across the left bottom frame lies Celia bound in a sack. Helene, the duplicitous maid, startled, looks back over her shoulder as she hovers threateningly over the bound girl. At the sofa head Adele twists to confront Hanaud. Her left arm rises in expostulation as she warns off the intruding inspector, her right hand holding out the open bottle of vitriol. The two playing areas – the confrontation in the background and the foreground pictures of Celia's bondage – are separated by and contained within a frame of hanging curtains, doubled by a Chinese vase on a stand to one side and a pillar to the other. During the stand-off between Adele and Hanaud, Perichet infiltrates the picture, distracting Adele and enabling Hanaud to make his move before Celia is harmed. A brief badinage between Ricardo and Hanaud, both claiming the role of rescuer, shifts the narrative gear back into the make-believe of storytelling and the Inspector hands the troublesome, out-of-place orphan – and effectively the story – over to the romantic, fantasising philosopher for safe keeping.

As suggested in Part One, the interchangeability of picture frame and proscenium arch opens up the picture to incursions facilitated by a three-dimensional space from openings, often obscured, at the back or sides of the frame. The safety of pictorial enclosure is always under threat from theatrical staging. Here, however, the frontal camera is positioned not in the stalls, but rather in a picture gallery, switching back and forth between pictures, closer or further back to catch different views. This construction of shots as pictures, within which camera and figures can move, but which are sandwiched into the various characters' verbal tales, is particularly useful to the detective genre. Evidence builds through the reading of pictures, themselves the products of partial or duplicitous memories offered by apparent 'witnesses'. 'Illustration', then, functions constructively in the relation between pictures and words, rather than as passive support to a verbal story. Significantly, the one figure who has no access to the storytelling process is its object – Celia herself, the innocent misrecognised as guilty and once exonerated nearly lost – whose story is constructed and reconstructed within the circular logistics of detection, enacting the rush to destruction of a melodramatic fantasy crossed with Grand Guignol.

'TELL ME A STORY': A CHILD IN FILMLAND

The whimsical address of the Minerva comedies, the tale-spinning fantasising of the romantic Bellairs and the realisation in *At the Villa Rose* of different characters' recounted 'stories' evoke oral storytelling rather than high literary tradition. The oral tale in modern times is encountered largely in childhood, a connection with film-going that is bluntly asserted by *The Motion Picture Studio*: 'The public is merely a little child. It wants to be told a story.'[75] Towards the end of decade Mary Buxton pleads in *The Bioscope*, 'Let us do what the children ask: "Tell us a story" – Let us tell them as we think them, and to the rest of the world they will not come amiss.'[76] The figure of the child haunts the films of the 1920s, from the children's party game that supplies the title for *General Post* (1920) to the birthday-party opening of *The Queen Was in the Parlour* (1927), from the faux-naive address of the Minerva comedies to the wistful child that haunts Novello's Peter Pannish persona, brought explicitly to the surface on the playing fields of England in *Downhill*. Milne, despite his success as a playwright, is largely remembered for his *Winnie-the-Pooh* stories. Jackie Wullschlager's study, *Inventing Wonderland* (1995), situates Milne at the end of a fifty-year tradition of writing for children that became a major narrative form from the mid-Victorian period to the end of the 1920s – including *Alice in Wonderland*, the nonsense verse of Edward Lear, *Peter Pan* and *Wind in the Willows*.[77] Arising out of the Victorian cult of childhood, this tradition, Wullschlager argues, seeks not its idealisation but the anarchism of the child's literal imagination. Innocently taking adulthood at face value, child heroes expose its pretensions and hypocrisy, while revealing the child in the supposedly grown up. Milne and

Brunel delighted in the semantic oddities of conflicting generational perspectives, from which they produced a charming but doubled-edged wit that pinpointed the absurdities of a decaying class, gender and colonial system. In *The Bump*, for example, the Great Explorer, looking intently through binoculars for the 'Piebald Gorilla', is cut down to size by the panto animal creeping up behind him. Later, he is himself reduced to childhood by a title that archly comments, as he sets out without a train of bearers to find Lillian's home in 'Stuccoway Terrace': 'He feels rather lonely. He has never been on an expedition by himself before.'

However, the touch of childhood in British popular culture of the 1920s goes beyond the parameters of children's stories and comic games. Leisure invokes play rather than, for instance, contemporary DIY hobbies that turn leisure into work. To some the entertainment world offered work as play. As Guy Newall tells his interviewer: 'I would choose film acting as a profession before anything else because it's play to me. Even like it better than golf!'[78] In one sense, play offers a public site, comparable to the stage, the picture and the story, for bounded expressions of personal identity through pleasure and fantasy. Thus star journalism in the 1920s focuses on recreations, hobbies and pastimes – terms that are shared by child and adult – rather than the intimate details of personal life. Alongside Alice's Wonderland, Barrie's Never Never Land and Milne's Hundred Acre Wood at the Top of the Forest, we find newspaper and magazine columns headed 'Notes from Theatreland' or 'Stageland', 'Filmland' or 'Shadowland', while the heroes of picaresque imaginings wander in 'Vagabondia'. In 1923 Herkomer's Lululand is advertised for sale in *The Bioscope*.[79] It is, moreover, striking how many middle-class adult entertainments of this period also partake in what is effectively a reverse biography: from dressing up for *tableaux vivants* at country-house parties to amateur theatricals and film-making; from the charades played, for example, by Novello and his friends into the post-theatre small hours to neighbourhood 'Pooh Parties', to which Milne's unfortunate son contributed as the 'real-life' Christopher Robin. In this respect the 1920s continue what Trewin attributes to Edwardian theatre: 'unrepentant make-believe'.[80]

The demand for story experience so ardently made in the British trade and fan press in the 1920s –

a demand in which 'story' often overrides questions of technique or cinematic specificity – suggests the importance of childhood culture. Re-immersion in storytelling promises a kind of makeover in fantasy of a world that in reality has proved so disillusioning and intractable. This is a world in which nothing can remain the same but which, after the cataclysmic destruction of the Great War, is nervous of radical alternatives. A key feature of child's play, with its dressing up and play-acting, is the possibility of disguise and role change, which, as explored previously, blossomed in the proliferation of costume romances. It is, then, no accident that in *The Bump* Lillian and Freddie meet the Great Explorer at a fancy-dress ball. Nor that it is Freddie rather than Lillian who plays the Cinderella of the piece, raiding a fancy-dress shop for a costume to wear to the ball, while Lillian goes as herself. These two aspects of child's play – the comedy of the absurd and a fantastical imaginary – find rich territory in the heterogeneous conditions of British film-making, not least in the team of contrary talents that came together in the making of Adrian Brunel's *The Man Without Desire* (1923).

A MAKEOVER WORLD: *THE MAN WITHOUT DESIRE*

Brunel describes how *The Man Without Desire* was spun by a group of free-wheeling film-makers abroad, for whom film-making offered a glorious dressing-up box as well as an opportunity to cross temporal and geographic borders, enabling them to film on location in Venice and in Berlin studios.[81] The film made Adrian Brunel's reputation as an emerging director and consolidated Novello's status as film star (it was his third film and he was already a star of the musical world). According to Brunel, the film was commissioned as a combination of costume romance and contemporary drama to hedge the bets of an industry nervous about period pieces. The title belongs to a brief sketch invented one drunken night by Monckton Hoffe.[82] The story's fantastical premise deploys time travel between eighteenth- and twentieth-century Venice, reducing its lovelorn hero, Count Vittorio Dandolo, to childlike dependency after submitting to the experimental drug of an English scientist that puts him into a 200-year sleep. The role is taken by Ivor Novello, the epitome of the desiring-despairing romantic and the ultimate play-actor. Novello's ardent desire to 'perform' on the stage, neither meeting the criteria of underplaying

nor fully committed to rhetorical impersonation, was thwarted until his late twenties. Here, however, the eighteenth-century Venetian romance, in which Vittorio serenades the unhappily married Leonora (played by a splendidly impassive Nina Vanna), allows Novello to 'play-act' to order. Filtering Brunel's love of parody and Novello's love of play-acting through a generic double whammy combining costume romance and a form of contemporary problem picture led to an episodic film of ironic, war-touched child's play.

The romance with Leonora, trapped in marriage to the brutal Count Almaro, implicitly reformulates heterosexuality within a contemporary notion of companionate marriage entailing a female-sympathetic masculinity. The consequent feminisation of Vittorio emphasises the Peter Pannish elements of the Novello persona, which in film roles and biographies link him to older, married or maternal women – Leonora is twice filmed sitting on her son's bed – and plays on the enduring youthfulness and vulnerability of his image. In contrast, the Count's world is represented by elements of sensational Guignol – such as chopping off the fingers of a periodical editor (played by Brunel) for publishing a satire on the Count – and sexual licence. In contrast to the childlike innocence of Vittorio, the irresistibility of parodic reversal for the Brunel team introduces into this licentious world the watchful presence of the dwarves who wait on Almaro's mistress – the scandalous Foscolnia – suggesting an occluded world within a world. This other world reaches materially into the body of the film as the Count, about to take up a poisoned glass of wine, meets in a mirror the watching eyes of a vengeful maid – a distanced image framed in the doorway, waiting intently for him to drink. This encounter in the mirror leads to the exposure of Vittorio's plan to elope with Leonora, resulting in her death and Vittorio's murder of the Count. Taking shelter with an English scientist he had earlier helped, Vittorio agrees to take a coma-inducing drug to escape not simply his pursuers but unendurable loss. Under the hypnotic stare of the scientist, Vittorio/Novello submits to a metaphoric 200-year death with a self-consciously tragic flourish as he enters the laboratory's inner sanctum to be incarcerated in a coffin.

Time shifts between 18th and 20th centuries legitimate Novello's penchant for play-acting, while suggesting that identity is both a temporary staging and subject to change according to shifting cultural values and practices. Thus the outside staircase and balcony of the Almaro mansion are used as theatrical supports to Novello's charade-like performance of a lovelorn serenader, while arches and curtains frame his romantic posing. In the twentieth-century sequences, however, the posing legitimated by costume drama is parodied, the Brunel team's sense of the absurd interlacing romantic fantasy with the satirical sketch.[83] Comically reduced to a state of childish ignorance when confronted with modern technologies and fashions, Vittorio/Novello bows to the telephone voice of Genevia, and, when undergoing a makeover as a modern-day citizen, is caught in a mirror reflection petulantly rejecting the series of ties and hats handed to him.

The device of the will, read out in the film's prologue to the scientist's descendant, serves as a conduit for the play-acting past to enter the present, announced by Novello's haunting, death-like image revealed to his discoverers through a glass panel in his coffin. Left to wake up on his own, Vittorio is instinctively drawn back to the scenes of his last traumatic experience in the 18th century. On encountering the present day Almoras, he mistakes their daughter, Genevia, for Leonora, and the Brunel team play with the incongruities and ambivalences generated by such cross-temporal encounters, heightened by the intertwining of a third figure, the star persona of Novello. The geographic juxtaposition of temporal eras demands the historical figure 'grow up' – which for Vitorrio/Novello means containing expressive performance, flamboyant dress and lifestyle, both as the 'man without desire' – a consequence of the drug – and in conformity to the new conditions of verisimilitude in the postwar 1920s. At the same time, Novello's self-conscious, camp approach to acting draws attention to the star performing the role, yet maintaining through the visibility of the act a space of undisclosed identity and desire not made available in public signs.

While metaphorical death and resurrection entails growing up into present-day adulthood, Brunel's satirical perspective bites again when, after a lacklustre courtship and marriage to Genevia, it becomes clear that Vittorio does indeed 'lack desire'. Novello makes the most of play-acting a restraint undynamised by passion, suggesting yet another version of the 1920s man wounded by war, loss or the repression of a gay identity.[84] In consequence, the modern Genevia begins to philander with an Almaro cousin. Recognising himself as both out of place and out of time, Vittorio seeks to return to the world of costume romance, pulling his cloak from a dressing-up box and taking the pill the scientist had left in his pocket. However, a servant, suspecting the worst, delivers his suicide note earlier than instructed to Genevia, who, on the point of losing him, finds her love rekindled. This permits the playing out of a romantic *Liebestod* as Vittorio dies in her arms – effectively refusing paternalist, heterosexual adulthood – in which 'not having' is enacted as the only triumph allowed a desire without, as yet, a public stage.

FILMLAND AND MODERNITY: THE WOMAN'S STORY

It is notable that the most perceptive critics arguing for cinema as the medium for a modern age are women such as Dorothy Richardson, Iris Barry, Caroline Lejeune and Nerina Shute. Having much at stake in movements for change, they yet respond to cinema as offering not only European sophistication in a new art form but the chance of a return to the imagination of childhood – as a source of new stories indulging basic human needs for fun, dreams, escape and comfort. Thus Dorothy Richardson, in a now celebrated passage, records her response to a Monday afternoon at the pictures:

> Tired women, their faces sheened with toil, and small children, penned in the semi-darkness and foul air on a sunny afternoon. There was almost no talk. Many of the women sat alone, figures of weariness at rest. Watching these I took comfort. At last the world of entertainment had provided, for a few pence, tea thrown in, sanctuary for mothers, an escape from the everlasting qui vive into eternity on a Monday afternoon.[85]

Similarly, Iris Barry, responding ambivalently to the routinised lives produced by the regime of the machine, delights in films that take us back to the naive bedrock of the story experience as a source of renewal:

> Now the shadows on the screen have something happen to them all the time . . . It is all very nice, it is *something*; whereas making the beds and shopping, or

taking shorthand, or covering jam-pots is, by repetition, less than nothing. So there the girl sits in the cinema and feels that life after all is not so dreary: even if nothing happens to her, it happens to other people.[86]

Inveighing against the intrusion of 'uplift' in *The Thief of Bagdad* (1924), Barry hopes 'the film was a failure . . . because it cheated us of our real Fairbanks, the cheery fellow who leaps about in such a jolly way'.[87] The nursery language Barry uses so self-consciously suggests a cinema that as a new entertainment medium offers the possibility of stripping away both postwar resignation to a mundane, threadbare reality and the pseudo-sophistication of the adult world. The basic tropes of childlike fantasy revived by cinema suggest a point to things that replaces perhaps the moral certainties of melodrama offered to earlier generations. Such perception provides a reflexive moment in Anthony Asquith's *Shooting Stars* (1928), when film star soon to become film director, Julian Gordon (Brian Aherne), visits the cinema to watch himself and his increasingly estranged wife play in their latest film. Sitting behind two entranced small boys, Julian is as engrossed and identifying as they are with the exploits of his character on screen. Dependent on its appeal to a harassed mass audience and in Britain located on the lowbrow side of an embattled cultural divide, the cinema's identification with childhood imagination asserts, for Barry, the right to dream:

> It is not merely that the cinema is cheap, accessible . . . and that you don't have to put your best clothes on to see Harold Lloyd fall off a sky-scraper. After the agitation of a day which includes catching buses, trams or tubes, manipulating typewriters or telephones or lathes or the machines . . . a rest in the picture-house with all its flattering dreams is better for one . . . We get too much actual experience and not enough dreams.[88]

Significantly it is American cinema, unencumbered with past traditions and established cultural priorities that can unabashedly embrace the new world of shiny, noisy, speedy modernity. Barry is not so liberated from her cultural roots not to register some ambivalence about its brash commercialism or to forgo making claims for the more complex artistic practices that European cinemas exemplify. However, it is the mass audience that both makes the capital-intensive film industry possible and whose pleasures, fostering a return to the story world of childhood, provide the possibility of recoil to origins the better to leap forward: 'The cinema . . . is not designed to be an art but a comforter . . . for the huge audience that the cinema has created would never have come into existence otherwise, and it is the great audience which makes all things possible.'[89] Barry's iconoclastic insistence on cinema as 'drug', 'sedative', source of the recuperative power of dreaming illuminates the tendency towards the fey and whimsical peculiar to the British cultural imaginary of the 1920s. This underpins the huge appeal of Ivor Novello as the eternally wistful youth of Arcadian fantasy, or of Betty Balfour as the plain-speaking East End flower girl of Victorian imagination. Alongside such popular personae, Barry's perception applies to the impulse to revive the pageants, harlequinades and pierrot acts of fast disappearing tradition, not to mention the pastoralism of image and story with which 1920s British cinema is so liberally endowed. It is in such a context that George Pearson's *The Little People* (1926) can be revisited as a meditation on modernity and culture that takes advantage of 'the small place' allowed 'for genuine merit' within the 'adulterate mixture of many improperly allied things' that necessarily grounds cinema as a mass medium.[90]

A HEROINE WHO DOES 'BIG THINGS': GEORGE PEARSON'S *THE LITTLE PEOPLE*

The pressbook for the now lost *Réveille* includes an appreciation of George Pearson penned by the company's newly acquired publicity officer H. Rowan Walker, which claims:

> Pearson is one of the few . . . who dares talk of his Art with a capital A . . . He believes in the cinema as an art-form complete in itself, with possibilities . . . few have envisaged . . . Yet he is . . . apart from the highbrow . . . [having that] vein of sanity . . . which tells him how far he can experiment without being precious or obscure . . . [he is] a master of entertainment.[91]

The Little People, as an original film story, realises Pearson's belief in 'the film prepared directly for the cinema screen, told not merely *on* it, but *by* it'. Underpinning this ambition lay Pearson's rejection of established canons – he left his position as headmaster and eventually teaching in protest at its rigid curriculum. He conceived cinema as both a populist and innocent medium, capable of starting afresh: 'the cinema, if true to itself, should be as free as the vision of the human eye'.[92] In this respect, *The Little People* is one of the few surviving works of the British filmmaker with most claim on 'art cinema' – he was held in high respect, if also at some distance, by the trade. The trade press did not really know what to make of the film, but recognised that its 'simple story' was very 'unusually' and 'amazingly' treated. In fact the film was withdrawn after its first press show and re-edited, to the satisfaction of many reviewers. The *Daily Mail* suggested that in its greater attention to character, it 'displayed virtues which are peculiarly British',[93] while a significant feature noted by Michael Orme in *The Illustrated London News*, and proudly quoted by Pearson in his autobiography, is the film's 'merging the real and the unreal'.[94]

On one level the film documents through its framing device the dilemmas of English cultural and intellectual life in the mid-1920s, with the displaced intellectual, Lyn (Randle Ayrton), and high-society dilettante, Walery (Gerald Ames), wandering abroad in search of, respectively, inspiration and sensation. They happen on a precious survival of a fast disappearing way of life represented by the puppet show. A crucial element binding travelogue and story fantasy is the documenting of the captivated wide-eyed faces of the puppet play's audience, particularly the children, grounding the fantasy in a strong sense of the culture and rituals that separate the two different societies. Along with the much praised and infectious performances of Frank Stanmore (Paolo), Harry Furniss (Gian) and Mona Maris (Lucia) as the puppeteering family, this embedding of the tale in the responses of a live audience contributes much to what the *Daily Sketch* notes as the film's 'human-beingness'.[95]

The arrival of English tourists in a small southern Italian town intervenes in the film's central story of the puppeteer family's struggle to maintain its audience in a modernising world and to ride out generational and gender conflicts. Gian argues with his father about updating the show and with his cousin, Lucia, who, trapped in the female roles allowed by traditional stories, is seduced by Walery's promise of Mayfair stardom. Out of the imagery of the puppets and the cross-cultural adventures of its protagonists, the film develops a poetically imaged meditation on the conflict between home and otherness in the search for personal identity. Contrasting the significance of Italian peasant life for the urbanising, society-bound English with the oppression of past tradition on the young puppeteers, tied to and bored by the rituals of their elders, the film also acknowledges a gendered struggle around patriarchal authority based on female compliance. In this sense, the film resonates with demands for autonomous experience fielded by a postwar generation of British women not yet fully enfranchised. Pearson, noting in his scrapbook audience applause for Janet Gaynor's declaration that she too will be a 'very fine fellow' in Borzage's *Seventh Heaven*,[96] adapts the lines for Lucia. In response to Gian's 'Don't worry Lucia . . . I've got dreams too . . . when we're married and happy, I'LL DO BIG THINGS', Lucia replies, 'That's just it – YOU'LL do big things . . . YOU'RE A MAN . . . but I want to do big things MYSELF!'

The oppressiveness of Lucia's role in the puppet show is forcefully enacted through repetitions of the opening big close-ups of the drum that calls the audience and whips up the frenetic energy of the coming dramatic ritual. Its impact on Lucia is emphasised when in a montage of close-ups of sticks beating the drum and Lucia shrinking back, hands to her ears, the camera suddenly homes in on its surface, blurring the focus in a visual suggestion of its sickening reverberation in Lucia's head. As the drum strives to dictate and control Lucia's energies, she clenches her fists, again covering her ears and resisting Gian's demand that she come to the stage. Paolo, endearingly tries to placate her restlessness by pointing out that 'Man must always be the master', but next morning Lucia has gone. However, in London she is no less a 'puppet on a string', either dancing to Walery's ambition as star-maker or idealised by the elderly Lyn, who sets her photograph in front of his typewriter as a more 'authentic' muse than that offered by London society women. His preface begins: 'My play tries to show that happiness consists of two things only: Firstly, *Be* Yourself, Secondly . . . ' It proves impossible, however, to transplant to England the qualities in Lucia that each man desires to appropriate. London society is inhospitable. The uninhibited wrangles and bonding of the Italian village community are displaced by society gatherings rendered in close-ups of repressive glances and whispers as gossip spreads about Lucia's irregular relation to Walery. In the end, Lucia performs in earnest a 'dance of the dying puppet' as she collapses on her opening night in a Mayfair nightclub. Subjected to a sadistic high-angle shot from behind the spectators leaning over a balustrade above the dance floor, Lucia turns, almost looking into the camera, to accuse her audience: 'Laugh Puppets . . . what do you care!'

Pearson uses puppetry for a range of purposes in an intricate interplay between puppets and humans. They suggest parallels to human life, as in the dance of the dying puppet; they return adults to the innocence of childhood; they represent companions to the puppeteers more loyal than humans can be; or, like the medieval fool, they serve as ironisers and forewarners of impending hubris, as when a female puppet falls on Paolo's head after his claim to patriarchal authority. Occasionally, they offer their human counterparts images of manipulation and emptiness, as in Lucia's accusation to her audience. Most crucial, in their connection with childhood and ancient rituals of the past, they represent the ambivalent pull of home, which holds back the ambitions of future generations but also represents sustaining roots. In London Lucia is sad to encounter a pathetic little puppet on strings displayed by a party reveller as an insignificant tourist memento.

The film's ending cannot fully resolve the tensions it has highlighted at work in a society undergoing rapid and disorienting change. Lucia's departure destroys Paolo's anarchic show life, and he succumbs to the wiles of the widow, Aunt Sala (Barbara Gott), who seeks to entrap him into a bullying matriarchal domestic order. Gian, however, works feverishly on, seeking to prove to the absent Lucia that even without her he can 'turn dreams into reality'. For Lucia, gazing into her mirror after her failed attempt at stardom, dreams have been destroyed by reality. Positioned between her mirror reflection and the modernist paintings of peasant dancers and musicians on her apartment walls, her gaze calls up a ballerina pirouetting along the mirror top, dissolving into and back from a disfigured puppet, until a solution strikes her. Inspired, she understands how she can take home what she has learned. The film concludes with Lucia creeping back through the window into her bedroom, now occupied by Gian and his designs. She sits in front of the model theatre and, pushing his hand out of the way, takes a pencil and reworks what he has done. Aunt Sala is ejected, Paolo rein-

vigorated and the show starts up again, to the delight of the community and its children.

In the end it is unclear what she has learned, or how tradition and modernity are to be reconciled. The concluding shot repeats one from the opening: Paolo counting out the evening's take, followed by a big close-up of a puppet head looking up at him. What this image seems to represent is something akin to Raymond Williams's notion of culture as 'a whole way of life', an image that combines economic sustainability with the direct relation of entertainers to the show and its audience, a relation lost in the negative parallel offered in London. The difference, however, between the ending of the film and the ending of the earlier puppet tale, which demonstrated to the erring wife that 'finest love is found at home', is that now the woman is regained as a co-creator of the show.

BRITISH CINEMA GOES TO THE BALL: *PALAIS DE DANSE*

Encountered some eighty years later, the fantasising of 1920s popular culture may feel 'strange' in its unabashed embrace of child's play – the fantastical seemingly reduced to whimsy, a term detested by A. A. Milne. For Jackie Wullschlager, the Pooh stories represent a taming of Wonderland. For if, she argues, Milne offers a more realistic approach to childhood than his predecessors, ironically exposing the presumptions of both child and adult, the toys, no longer 'real' animals, are themselves the subject of mockery, diminishing childhood's power to undermine the adult world.[97] However, in filmland – as a place of regressive play with all forms the culture throws up – no place is secure from the mockeries and self-conscious parodies so easily generated by the posing of play-acting, dressing up and picture-making. Pantomime and fairy tale, with their devices for manipulating class, gender, ethnic and national representations, make a game of generational transformations. Such transformations in perspective and meaning are eloquent in a society in which an evolving social democracy demands closer social class interaction; for which postwar paternalist authority is at issue; for which the question, 'What do women want?' presses; and for which Britain's imperial mission is beginning to show strains. For a society scarred by war and historically and ideologically resistant to revolution, the new institutions of storytelling provided by the mass media offer relatively 'safe space' in which to make acculturated signs play off each other, to try on different costumes and try out different roles.

By the end of the decade a formidable film-making practice had emerged, melding the range of transformational pictorial, performing and story-telling practices identified in this study as the bedrock of a distinctive cinematic poetics. Maurice Elvey's *Palais de Danse* (1928) is exemplary, based on a script he developed with his co-producer, V. Gareth Gundrey, from an 'original story' devised by Jean Jay, wife of John Longdon, who also plays its identity-switching villain. Taking *Cinderella* as its starting point, the film both declares itself to be about 1928 and employs a fairy tale structure of cross-class courtship. As the parent-defying Tony (Robin Irvine) declares, 'times have changed' – the term 'palais de danse' first appeared in the English language in 1926. Making the Tottenham Palais[98] its setting, the film uses its story of romance, double-dealing and black-mail to offer pointed slidelights on an incipient sex industry. The film stars Mabel Poulton as a delicately luminous but resilient East End Cinderella, playing against Chili Bouchier as the sceptical, gum-chewing cockney hostess.

The film's opening skilfully weaves together such heterogeneous cultural sources – including powerful American signifiers – both to establish familiar story territory and introduce, through pointed montage juxtapositions, perspectives on modernity. The first shot fades up on the arrival of a taxi outside the brightly lit dancehall. It dissolves into a tracking shot across the neon sign, 'Palais de Danse', which prom-ises 'Romance by Chance, where every girl thinks she has "It" and every boy believes he's the son of a Sheik'. After shots of dancers, we cut to a close-up of a young girl seated on a stool, watching wistfully from across the road. A figure on crutches, her wid-owed, near immobilised war-veteran father, sits close by in his role as night watchman. The camera pans across her view of the dancehall and down to a poster. Tonight, at a 'Grand Ball in aid of Local Hos-pitals', a 'special Cinderella Tableau' is to be staged, in which 'well-known members of society', including Lady King and her son, Mr Anthony King, will sup-port 'Miss Trixie Braganza of the Follies Theatre' in the lead role. Thus is economically put in place a potentially conflictual melange of class-cultural prac-tices, attitudes and values along with signs of extreme social contrast. As the nightwatchman's daughter wishes she could go to the ball, members of the King party cross to light cigarettes at her father's brazier, among them the shadowy figures of Harlequin and Pierrot, who laughingly enact a mock fight, using umbrellas as swords. One of the girls, glancing in our nameless heroine's direction, comments casually, 'Doesn't she look like a real Cinderella?' In the mean-time, Lady King is told that the star is unable to appear, so after some demurring the nightwatchman's daughter is summoned.

These elements of fairy tale, *tableau vivant*, har-lequinade and dancehall – touched by the mercurial presence of Harlequin, instigator of the traditional pantomime's transformation scene[99] – are orches-trated to produce cross-class, sexual encounters, gen-erating melodrama's conflicts between contrary desires, identities and social values. In their hurry to prepare their substitute Cinderella, the King girls cut up her dress to make her more 'realistic', and after-wards completely forget their promise to replace it. The *tableau vivant* is played for humour and romance, picking up the near mishaps and awkward-nesses of amateur dramatics and juxtaposing Mabel Poulton's nervous giggles when Prince Charming/ Tony King tries the slipper on her foot with big close-ups that focus his admiring glances and too prolonged kiss. Into this is cut Cinderella's frontal glance to us – an acknowledgment of inevitable cross-class attraction, perhaps, or a plea for help? At the very least, this use of the close-up frame creates a space for the release of private communication, feel-ings and meanings into otherwise strictly public materials and images.

However, the sado-sexual undertones registered in the scissors that lacerate Cinderella's clothing return when she is interviewed for a job as a dancing partner by 'The Head Professional . . . almost a gen-tleman thanks to his tailor'. This ambiguous class identity is emphasised by a big close-up of a No. 1 stitched to his lapel while he casually buffs his nails. The camera pans from this action to his sultry look of contempt, linking 'The Head Partner' with the class-sex services of the gigolo – another term that comes into the English language in 1927.[100] The threat to Cinderella by a modern, commodified sex-uality is registered in a dissolve that merges the No. 1 on the Head Professional's lapel with his saturnine frontal gaze, into which her own face is absorbed. Then a series of dissolves and pans draws numbers pinned to female bosoms across her own face, ending with a close-up on the resistant, large-eyed, gum-chewing Chili Bouchier. New 'pictures' from an emergent sex industry flick past us, as a parade of men's and women's feet leave their separate changing rooms at the beginning of a new day's work. Shots of the dancing partners follow, as they doze, awaiting clientele to buy tickets for their services, each identified in turn by a superimposed number – the last, No. 16, now worn by Cinderella (Fig. 6.5).

The basic cultural-pictorial building blocks established, Elvey creates a montage of class-conflicting protagonists and story elements, images and performance gestures as the inevitable melodrama unfolds. Thus, in the dancing that follows, we cut between a happily waltzing Cinderella and Prince

Charming to shots of Lady King, haughtily erect in her silver-lamé sheath dress, watching in high displeasure. The call-girls lean against a barrier, laughing raucously, Chili Bouchier, still chewing away, mockingly wiping her nose on her fingers in response to their introduction by the manager as 'our young lady dancing partners'. No. 1 hastily conceals himself behind a carnival mask to avoid encountering Lady King, mistress of his duplicitous aristocratic persona, Count Alban. Two photographs make the link to the following sequences. One is a newspaper photograph of Lady King performing 'fairy godmother' to No. 16, which she later signs for her secret lover, Count Alban, now her partner at the roulette tables. The second, a photograph of Cinderella's father in serviceman's uniform placed on top of the note she leaves him announcing her new job. This juxtaposition of contrasting, 'telling' documents could not be

Fig. 6.5. Cinderella (Mabel Poulton) joins the line of dancing partners as No. 16 under the scrutiny of the Head Professional (John Longdon) in Elvey's *Palais de Danse* (1928)

more pointed, while also driving the story – Lady King's photograph will become a mechanism of later blackmail.

Crucially, the dissolute aimlessness of the King crowd is paralleled by the sexploitation of the dancehall, where men – and women – buy tickets for a partner at a shilling a time, intercut with images of cheerfully cynical or exhausted human beings delivering up their commodified bodies and services. These economic signs of a sex-class system become potent mechanisms for the romantic melodrama. As in Victor Saville's *Kitty* (1928), which developed a similar theme the following year, the cross-class romance between Cinderella and Tony King is blocked by a powerful mother exerting control in the interests of family lineage over a debilitated only son. But whereas Kitty, as her shopkeeper mother points out, can respectably earn her own as well as her war-crippled husband's living, Cinderella is compromised by her position in the dancehall. Tony's only access to her is through the ticket system, a point humorously made when he buys up a whole reel. Lady King finally confronts Cinderella in a series of aggressive shot/reverse shots. To Cinderella's twice-posed question 'Why?' when Lady King asserts the impossibility of marriage, the camera, following Lady King's hooked finger downwards, cuts into a big close-up as her finger slips behind the incriminating No. 16 on her blouse. But Lady King shortly finds the signs working in reverse. While she is preparing to leave, the door to the manager's office opens, and, head down, busy reading some papers, in walks No. 1, aka Count Alban.

Meanwhile, browbeaten by Lady King, Cinderella attempts, in an unusual private moment, to break with Tony. However, her line, 'you musn't see me', is immediately contradicted by a big close-up on her face turned up in profile and collaged across his, cutting into the left frame. Responding to his 'Why? don't you love me?', her hand touches his face. 'Love you . . . ?', and, turning, she throws her head back as they fall into a dance hold and he swings her onto the floor, she leaning back in ecstatic abandon. In a shot from the rig above, the lighting man picks them out with his spotlight. Soon this private moment becomes a public spectacle as the other couples stop their own dancing, first entrapping the couple in an enclosing circle that threatens to crush them and then, as they try to escape, dragging them apart. Film itself becomes choreographed dance designed to carry, impede and sometimes release the romantic desires generated at the boundaries that block social change. The force of the story realised through moving, dancing pictures carries us to the desired happy ending, involving the rehabilitation of the mother (as also in *Kitty*) and the spectacular death of the ruthless blackmailing No. 1. The last shudder of his clenched fist dissolves into a wedding photograph. But true to the dynamic of a popular culture constructed from a montage of traditional story elements and contemporary signs, a concluding close-up of the wedding couple dissolves into a tear-dropping but still gum-chewing Chili Bouchier – a reminder that the girls of the Palais de Danse yet await their rescue.

For a society that has learned to contain social difference through representation, filmland offers a space of fantasy in which the transformations of role-playing, picture-making and storytelling bring the signs and documents of culture into strange conjunctures. Playing them off against each other in new ways, such films open up a small cultural path for social change.

In Conclusion: The Cultural Poetics of British Cinema

Palais de Danse (1928) exemplifies the cultural work of British cinema's mixed sources, which span a continuum running between the classic text at one end, through an array of middlebrow print stories, novelettes and magazine fictions, to the oral fairy tale, poetic quotation, nursery rhyme, music-hall routine and pub joke at the other. This heterogeneity has been largely lost to a critical view dominated by literary assumptions at the expense of the profligate medium-crossing story. The regulatory codes developed in numerous screenplay manuals and the later critical model of the 'classical narrative text' have emphasised a literary concept of film narrative, based on causality and character motivation, while, paradoxically, excluding the literate word from the body of the film. This homogenising conception of film is intensified with the increasing grip of copyright laws, enshrining concepts of originality and of intellectual or creative ownership, and underpinning 'adaptation' as the dominant understanding of the relationship between a film and its sources. 'Adaptation', however, is a limiting critical concept, focusing either on how faithful a film is to a supposed original or on how far it transforms its source into something else – into cinema. In either case, the dynamics of the *relationship* with a source is lost: we either admire the old work or revel in a new. Recovery of the history of the 'realisation' suggests heuristically the particular significance of this relationship for British popular culture. In the first place, the realisation highlights the nature of the media as cultural spaces open to each other's products and practices. In the story as on the stage many things can happen, including the appearance of artefacts or practices interpolated from other entertainment forms. Second, what is made 'real' through the increment of 'reality' offered by the new medium is not some aspect of the real world (although plentiful illusory realism is attempted in the process), but itself a representation, a cultural

product. This shifts the notion of representation from 'reflection' of an unmediated reality to the fact of its own construction. As an artefact, it becomes in its turn a signifier in the making of further representations.

As noted in Chapter 1, the heterogeneity of nineteenth-century theatrical and subsequent British cinematic practice fostered the reproduction not only of feted paintings and literary texts but topical events, archaeological research, historical and mythical personages, social documents, news items, songs, sensations, and so on. Born of commercial exploitation, the realisation contributes to the circulation of cultural and creative signifiers from one entertainment form and – crucial for British culture – from one social arena to another. In this respect, reproduction circulates acts, pictures and stories as signifiers in the expansion of public discourse that contributes to democratisation in an increasingly mass-mediated society. At the turn of the 19th century the established arts retreat from this popular cultural sphere, asserting their unique automony and/or critical function. If, however, as a consequence the realisation as a specific theatrical practice dies out, the conditions for heterogeneity remain in the mixed-media exhibition context of British cinema, while the habit of reproduction, recycling and cross-media circulation is established as the common sense of its film-making practices. It is then but a short step for Maurice Elvey to invent the film biography, woven from the extraordinary melange of stories, historical documents, pictorial realisations and performances in, for example, *Florence Nightingale* (1915), *Nelson* (1918) and *The Life Story of David Lloyd George* (1918); or for Bruce Woolfe and Walter Summers to develop the part-dramatised documentary reconstruction exemplified by *Zeebrugge* (1924) and *Ypres* (1925); or for George Pearson to mix music-hall turn and social document in the Squibs films. Thus the stories and acts, the character types and popular stereotypes out of which such films are fabricated circulate as acculturated representations. Such heterogeneity can be accommodated within the performative geography of storytelling as digression, encounter and boundary-crossing. But it contradicts the notion of cinema as a purely visual medium and undermines the demand for story unity, continuity and the causal logic necessary to the linear trajectory of a heroic biography.

Although the realisation is not an interpretation, neither is it an inert copy. In reproducing an existing work, the realisation functions much like an 'attraction',[1] cut from its original place and displayed in a new context for our appreciation as both aesthetic event and cultural document. Thus a kind of cultural reflexivity comes into play – a constructive reflexivity rather than the deconstructive kind associated with modernist practice. The appeals of British cinema's cultural poetics derive not from social reflections or distortions, but from the performance of certain acculturated representations, skills and aesthetic pleasures: picturing, role-playing, storytelling – performances that at the same time foreground cultural signifiers in order to demarcate and identify their protagonists and stories. For a society founded in social difference, which requires both maintenance of social boundaries but also an increasing degree of negotiation across those boundaries, the production and circulation of such signifiers is of key importance. In the context of a widening public sphere, British popular culture requires a diversity of protagonists and performers to present themselves at the boundaries of cultural difference. Realisation and reproduction produce pictures, stories and acts as public signs meeting at, sometimes negotiating, sometimes transgressing, these boundaries. In this sense, performances are class acts. The recognisable character actor and familiar tale function as signposts in a social topography. The pictorial frame produces landscapes or architectural gems as views onto the ambivalent intersection of history and the future. Stories, recited or enacted within a film, rehearse familiar cultural beliefs through which protagonists test and sometimes contest the limits of the prevailing cultural imaginary of popular fiction.

In this sense, to draw on Bakhtinian concepts, cinema offers British culture a heteroglossic story space that ingests all manner of theatrical enactments, pictures and storytellings, encouraging the collaborative, and potentially dialogic, interchange between word, performance, picture and document, and not least between the tastes and perspectives of different social audiences brought to the cinema. For if the literary text based on written traditions of cultural 'heritage' addresses us as *readers*, 'story' invokes oral traditions carried through the storyteller's voice and performer's gestures, calling on a listening, participatory audience presence. Realise-ation, thus, contributes a double meaning – to make real is also to understand, to understand makes real. This suggests the role of the act, the picture and the story in the construction and reconstruction of the social world. It is this process that we find curiously, richly, marginally or blatantly at work in so many films of the 1920s, from *General Post* (1920), *Duke's Son* (1920) and *A Daughter of Love* (1925) to *Underground* (1928), *Palais de Danse* and *Kitty* (1928).

CINEMA'S SPACE FOR CULTURAL FANTASY

The impulse of the realisation is underpinned, in Martin Meisel's terms, by the tension between the idealism of the imagination and demand for the real. Cinema brings this paradox to a head with a fresh piquancy for cultural observers such as Dorothy Richardson, Iris Barry and the many female film columnists who, like Nerina Shute, enfant terrible of *Film Weekly*, were looking to escape the Doll's House, while recognising the role of cultural fantasy in the making and living of people's lives.[2] In this sense, the cinema is the most intense realiser of all media. *The Picturegoer*, in a 1921 article headed, '?Anything But the Truth', goes to the heart of the conundrum provoked by cinema's extension of the ideology of realisation and the frisson of recognition it offers in the play between cultural construction, fantasy and reality:

> The castles of the screen are real castles, right enough; but still they are *castles in the air* . . . You sit back in your ninepenny (with tax) plus tip-up and you look at him and you smile. *You have recognised him*. Douglas Fairbanks? not a bit of it. He's – *YOU*! THAT'S WHY THE MOVIES ARE POPULAR.
>
> *The Same Old Reason*. Castles in the air. Day-dreams. Cinderella. The GIRL who's of another world. The boy you'll never meet. *You* – YOURSELF – if things had been as they never can be . . .
>
> In the Book you hear about it. On the Stage you are shown a shoddy imitation. But on the Silver Sheet you

get the real thing, the *real* UNREAL *thing*. Life as it *is*? Never! Life as it would be if it was as it should be – which it never will be. Things as they are – *not* (original emphasis).[3]

Although focused on Hollywood and the figure of the star-struck adolescent, this acutely perceptive piece of journalism implicitly recognises the never-ending play-off between the real and storytelling in the cultural processes of identity and reality construction.

To many twentieth-century minds, bent on abolishing Victorian values and social organisation, the boundary-obliterating heroes and heroines of the Hollywood screen promised escape from the Doll's House that was class-bound England. For those whose imaginations also wandered in home territory and for those who from the 21st century make the journey back to the Vagabondia of 1920s British Filmland, the film story opens onto a world of make-believe in which performers, picture-makers and storytellers shake the kaleidoscope of familiar cultural representations, producing, if not visions of a new world, then sometimes fey, sometimes paradoxical and often covertly disturbing configurations that mark the first steps in loosening old relationships. In their desire to compete in the new medium of film and to engage with a newly configuring world, many film-makers and commentators struggled to escape the grip of the old. Thus *Kinematograph Weekly* suggests that 'when cinema is a novelty it can make money by presenting old material in an old form by means of a new medium . . . but now it must modernise'.[4] But while Henry Edwards greets *The Picturegoer* interviewer with a hungry demand for new plots and original stories, he also ruefully quotes the adage that there are only seven plots in history of storytelling: 'The old ideas over and over again . . . What you want to invent . . . is a new kind of kinematography – stereoscopic, or something like that. Then we can start all over again and re-film all the old stories'.[5] Kenelm Foss similarly warns in *The Picturegoer* that 'it is only entirely new and different angles on the old and well-worn problems of life that are at all likely to intrigue the fancy of either producer, player, or picturegoer'.[6] Implicitly, these different takes on the problem suggest that modernist practice in an old culture is not free to start again, but must reinvestigate its starting points. G. A. Atkinson, reviewing *This Freedom* (1923) – a *cause célèbre*

for the debates it provoked about the wife who treats career as of equal importance to home and children – uncovers surprising parallels, exposed through recycling, between the originating author, A. S. M. Hutchinson, and the now venerable Thomas Hardy:

> Each takes freakish and extraordinary people, places them in abnormal situations, swings the heaviest hammers of fate over them and says in effect, 'How like real life!' . . . The screen ruthlessly sweeps all this literary integument aside and reveals Hardy and Hutchinson as the ringmasters of a marionette show, working the same old melodramatic puppets for the same old melodramatic ends.[7]

Despite his modern impatience with 'Hutchinson's flatulent revival of the futile sex-conflict', Atkinson finds the film 'enthralling', a 'glowing photoplay' offering 'spell-binding' performances from Fay Compton and Clive Brook. While the loss of the film makes it difficult to assess, its reanimation of a familiar family plot and set of protagonists contributes to the continuing social debate that can be followed in the review press about the role of woman and female sexuality dramatised by the sensation novelists and genre painters of the 19th century and earlier realised in Elvey's *The Fallen Idol* (1913).

The metaphor of the ringmaster of the marionette show not only captures the productivity of 1920s British cinema but is itself the trope used by George Pearson to imagine its engagement with modernity in *The Little People* (1926). Significantly, as described in Chapter 6, it is Lucia who makes the bid for freedom by coming to London to seek stardom in a Mayfair nightclub. It is Lucia, who after the failure of her debut and her realisation that to the Englishman she is merely a puppet dancing on the strings of his ambitions, gazes into the mirror to discover a solution for the stymied Italian puppet show. If the nature of her discovery is never made explicit, the precise detail is unimportant. The significance of this moment of epiphany is that, having refused to allow her puppeteer family to write her story at home, and rejecting the stories on offer in England, she is now able to rejoin Gian on equal terms, as a co-producer rather than construct of the show.

In Britain, cinema is a space of capturing, replaying and retelling. The mass audience does not only in Iris Barry's terms offer marketing opportunities: it keeps open a vital cultural space of imagination and fantasy, for it is in the Vagabondia of filmland that travelling protagonists may unfix for a moment the tropes and figures of the cultural jigsaw. For this reason, perhaps, George Pearson, jibbing like many British film-makers against the constraints of American continuity, claims cinema as a 'lawless medium, as free as the vision of the human eye'.[8] And Iris Barry also responds to the new freedom of cinematic imagining: 'There are no laws or canons for the making of films: you can mix up any ingredients.'[9] British cinema, if not quite in the way Barry meant, provides a heteroglossic space for mixing contradictory ingredients. It is true we do not in these films find dramas of the General Strike and of the social conflicts that such an exemplary historical moment represents. It is, however, significant that in the fragment remaining of Kenelm Foss's *No. 5 John Street* a tramp and a factory owner change costumes, enabling the latter to visit his own works and join a Communist Party meeting. Make-believe, play-acting, dressing up, picture-making and child's play are the aesthetic instruments of a culture operating within cultural division, and which knows itself through its entertainment practices and representations. If, as Christopher Williams suggests, British cinema is an insistently social cinema, and yet also, in Charles Barr's account, equally a self-reflexive cinema, the source of this paradox lies in these deeply acculturated processes of imagination and representation that emerge from the habit of reproduction and recycling so visibly manifested in the realisation.[10] Contemporary British cultural criticism remains as obsessed as the 19th century with the representation of reality, if inflected through the neo-Marxist concern with ideology as its misrepresentation that dominated film theory through the 1970s and 1980s. For a theoretical movement so concerned with the power of form, of the signifier, of process, it seems now with hindsight astonishing how strongly the desire for an original innocence remains hooked on the notion of an uncontaminated 'real'. In an age of postmodern consciousness we can perhaps be more tolerant of a culture that delights in the realisation of pre-existing representations and artefacts; a culture that keeps the signs by which we recognise – and contest – our reality on the surface as signs.

British cinema of the 1920s commits itself with such apparently whimsical abandon to escapist fantasies of class and sexual transmutation – the tailor or chauffeur become general and marrying the titled daughter – because, paradoxically, it operates on such public terrain, working with the signs produced by self-evidently ritualistic modes of performance, character typage, picturisation and tale-telling. However, despite the publicness of British cinema's cultural poetics, which demand, as the condition of passion, underplaying, bounded character types, class-accented staging, locations and imagery, such films are neither repressed films nor, in Andy Medhurst's terms, films about repression – whether of class, sexual identity, gendered or ethnic otherness.[11] These films *use* repression – the constraints of performance, the act, the type, social coded behaviour and gesture, the articulating word – as concomitant of a public stage or story space. Here, behind the acts, between performers, in the point of contact at the boundary, running between storyteller and listening viewer, suggestions of different perceptions, contradictory desires and wayward imaginings are glimpsed or explode into melodramatic enactment.

A powerful metaphor explains America as the 'melting pot' of the world. American cinema's investment in the biographic trajectory of the hero who can cross and conquer both geographic and cultural spaces produces a strong forward narrative drive that integrates divergent elements. A culture that is invested in the preservation of cultural boundaries cannot produce the homogenising ideal represented, for example, by the WASP. While the geographic imagination may use its boundaries and social codes of performance to locate and contain, it is precisely because this cinema needs to demarcate social difference that difference is kept *in* play and *on* screen. A culture of realisation, recycling, adaptation, deploying existing artefacts and cultural practices as material for new configurations, both commands recognition – pleasurable and resistant – from a diverse and divided audience and keeps the processes of cultural construction on the surface, visibly at work: as acting, as picture-making, as storytelling. But precisely because these forms and practices are foregrounded as a public surface, they gesture to another as yet occluded, space, in which other identities and acts are hinted at, and may in the future, when difference is at stake, construct different stories for public circulation.

Revisited in this perspective, within the context of the cultural traditions and practices on which they draw, the oddities and aberrations of British films of the 1920s reveal both aesthetic delights, quirks, surprises generating insight into the movements, hesitant perceptions and retreats of shifting imaginaries at work in the new cultural space offered by cinema. These films speak of their times not in representations reflecting an external reality, but in the processes of play-acting, storytelling, trying on another's costumes, listening to another's stories, representing another's cultural practices. Not all stories wield the same social power: hegemonic narratives control story outcomes; resisting stories must negotiate their space; some are perceived as dangerous and are silenced. But as a mass medium, cinema accelerates the rate of circulation, intensifying the dialogic possibilities at the boundaries of cultural difference both in the body of the film and among audiences gathered in the picture house. Unearthing and revaluing these films is more than an archival exercise. In a society undergoing intensive social change, the fantasising and representational practices of popular culture come under pressure from above and below: for example, the current injunction on national and local authorities to produce policies that address cultural and ethnic diversity. Reframing British cinema as a whole in the light of the emergent and volatile practices of the 1920s highlights the degree to which its productivity lies in idiosyncrasies of play-acting, picture-making and storytelling. For example *Educating Rita* (1983), *The Company of Wolves* (1984), *My Beautiful Laundrette* (1985), *High Hopes* (1988), *Brassed Off* (1996), *The Full Monty* (1997), *Billy Elliot* (2000) and *Once Upon a Time in the Midlands* (2002), to name a few, belong to a cinema of circulating stories and character types, of game-playing, role-swapping, dressing up and make-believe, of quotation, parody and pastiche. This is a cinema that in delineating social boundaries and clearly defined cultural types, signs and documents is capable of generating new and highly charged encounters across divisions. In the process, then, of preserving the contours of social difference, British cinematic poetics makes possible the reconfiguration of boundaries, experimental border-crossings and the recasting of social types in a much needed recognition of the plural identities of the postmodern world.

Notes

These notes use a short-note system for books, chapters and scholarly journal articles, referring the reader to the Select Bibliography for full publication details. Christian names are supplied with the first entry in each chapter of an author's name; thereafter only the surname is used. Trade, fan and newspaper press references are supplied here in full.

Reference to BFI Special Collections are abbreviated as follows:

Betty Balfour	BB/SC
Clive Brook	CB/SC
Adrian Brunel	AB/SC
Sidney Carroll	SC/SC
George Pearson	GP/SC
Mabel Poulton	MP/SC
Harry Rowson	HR/SC
Victor Saville	VS/SC

INTRODUCTION

1. This project begins with the Melodrama Study Group, which, emerging from a BFI/London University extra-mural class, pursued the melodramatic imagination into Hollywood and then British cinema in NFT seasons and related events held in 1988 and 1989. It continued through BFI summer schools on Melodrama and British Cinema, held respectively in 1988 and 1989.
2. Quoted in Charles Barr, 1977, p. 13.

1 – THEATRICALISING BRITISH CINEMA

1. Unless, that is, adopted for specific artistic or experimental purposes, for example Olivier's *Henry V* (1944).
2. Hugh Hunt (1978) in Hunt, Richards and Russell Taylor, p. 7.
3. Paul Fussell, 1975, pp. 197–8.
4. This is declared an 'incalculable good' for the theatre by Mrs Forbes-Robertson, driving it 'to adopt original plots and intellectual ideas'. The *Newcastle Clarion*, 27 August 1926, SC/SC. Basil Dean argues that 'the kinema had taken away from [the theatre] . . . the whole range of spectacle and most of melodrama'. *The Stage*, 3 February 1927, p. 17. See also W. A. Darlington, 1950, pp. 316–20.
5. James Agate, 1924a, pp. 44–5.
6. *The Bioscope*, 6 November 1919, p. 58.
7. See *The Bioscope*, 1 December 1927, p. 44; Rachael Low, 1971, p. 153.
8. Michael Sanderson, 1984, pp. 120–30. See also Jonathon Burrows, 2000.
9. John Stokes, 1972, p. 127. Stanley Houghton's *Hindle Wakes* made an almost instantaneous transfer to London from Annie Horniman's Gaiety Theatre, Manchester, committed to new drama (Rex Pogson, 1952, pp. 125–34).
10. Lillah McCarthy, 1933, pp. 34 and 52–5; Matheson Lang, 1940, p. 25.
11. Denis Gifford, 1997, p. 81.
12. Sanderson, 1984, pp. 20–1 and Darlington, 1950, pp. 269–75.
13. Brian Aherne, 1969, pp. 14 and 30–2.
14. See Noel Coward, 1937; Herbert Wilcox, 1967; Harry Rowson, n.d., HR/SC.
15. See Burrows, 2000, and Sanderson, 1984, pp. 210–13.
16. *The Picturegoer*, August 1927, pp. 16–17.
17. Rachael Low, 1950, pp. 18–19.
18. Low, 1971, p. 38 and MP/SC.
19. *Kinematograph Weekly*, 25 March 1920, p. 130, and 8 April 1920, supp., p. xii for photographic illustrations.
20. Wilcox, 1967, pp. 52–3; *Kinematograph Weekly*, 2 November 1922, p. 47.
21. *Kinematograph Weekly*, 12 February 1925, p. 76. See also *The Bioscope*, 4 September 1924, p. 44.
22. See 'Artistic Prologue at Sunderland', *Kinematograph Weekly*, 7 May 1925, p. 64. See also

the *Manchester Chronicle*, 18 August 1923, CB/SC; *The Bioscope*, 31 January 1924, p. 52, and 3 January 1927, supp., p. xv; *Kinematograph Weekly*, 8 January 1925, p. 77; *The Motion Picture* Studio, 17 November 1923, p. 12; *The Cinema*, 8 February 1923, CB/SC; *Daily Mail*, 8 October 1926, SC/SC; *The Stage*, 11 November 1926, SC/SC; *Kinematograph Weekly*, 4 May 1929, pp. 53–4.

23. *Kinematograph Weekly*, 3 December 1925, p. 28. Leon Pollock, the theatrical booking chief of PCT, had come from the 'legitimate' theatre and is credited by *Kinematograph Weekly* as being responsible for the 'first big prologue at a Trade Show in this country': First National's *Man, Woman, Marriage* (1921).

24. *The Stage*, 3 February 1927, p. 15.

25. *Daily Herald*, 24 June 1926, SC/SC.

26. *Theatre World*, 25 November 1925, p. 80.

27. *The Stage*, 3 February 1927, p. 15.

28. *The Kine Year Book 1929*, p. 16. See also *The Bioscope*, 7 October 1926, p. 38; 28 October 1926, p. 61; and 3 March 1927, p. xi.

29. Low, 1971, p. 39. De Groot was, according to *The Bioscope*, Director of Music at the Piccadilly Hotel (18 October 1923, p. 52).

30. Ibid., p. 38.

31. *Kinematograph Weekly*, 29 January 1925, p. 47.

32. *Daily News*, 12 October 1926, SC/SC. Film was used for a sequence in a motor car – 'the characters speaking their parts as the film unwound. The car comes to a stop, the actors alight, there is a momentary "black out", during which the screen is raised and there are the characters still continuing their conversation actually on the stage.'

33. *The Bioscope*, 13 October 1927, p. 40.

34. David Mayer, 1997, pp. 106–8.

35. *Daily Sketch*, 25 June 1926 SC/SC.

36. *The Motion Picture Studio*, 21 April 1923, p. 3. This weekly journal was an enterprising and lively off-shoot of *Kinematograph Weekly*, dedicated to raising the standard of intellectual and artistic debate for creative film workers.

37. *Kinematograph Weekly*, 12 February 1925, p. 76. See also the *Evening Standard*, 10 August 1926, SC/SC, whose critic reports that Sidney Bernstein was commissioning Komisarjevsky 'to devise prologues for his shows, a matter with which I have no interest whatsoever'.

38. *Daily Mail*, 23 October 1926, SC/SC.

39. See the *Mansfield Reporter*, 11 January 1924, CB/SC.

40. Desmond MacCarthy, 1954, p. 11.

41. Mayer, 1997, pp. 92–114.

42. Of *Chu-Chin-Chow* the writer explains: 'In its kaleidoscopic *mise-en-scene*, tiny inset scenes showing two or at most three figures were disclosed by exactly the same means as those in use for film "fade-ins" and "fade-outs". The moving structure of black cloth was nothing but the well-known 'mask', of which every camera-man carries a stock in a little tin box in his pocket, enlarged and utilised to make a stage novelty' (*The Picturegoer*, January 1926, p. 21). The National Theatre's production of Mike Alfreds and Michelene Wandors' new adaptation of Eugene Sue's *The Wandering Jew* (1987) employed the same techniques using black curtains and spotlights brought onto stage. See also Chapter 2.

43. Cecil Hepworth, 1951, p. 193.

44. Ibid., p. 194.

45. See Low Warren: 'the cinema is doing pioneer work for legitimate theatre among the masses . . . cultivating a taste for drama' (*The Era*, 2 January 1918, p. 34). Also *The Bioscope*, 6 November 1919, p. 65; *Stoll's Editorial News*, 1 July 1920, p. 1.

46. This practice, Sanderson notes, continues into television shows to this day (1984, p. 129).

47. *Westminster Gazette*, 7 July 1926, SC/SC.

48. See the BBFC's concern at the 'undress habit' of increasing numbers of cabaret scenes reported in the *Daily Herald*, 3 November 1926, SC/SC, and *The Times* report of Iris Barry's claim to the Faculty of Arts that 'the British public [are] sick of cabaret scenes', 6 December 1926, SC/SC.

49. For shadows/flesh and blood opposition, see *The Bioscope*, 22 July 1920, p. 14; *The Motion Picture Studio*, 23 September 1922, p. 5. For cinema and the soul, see Michael Orme in *The Illustrated London News*, 26 June 1926, SC/SC, and 11 September 1926, SC/SC. See also Chapter 3.

50. George Rowell, 1985, pp. 22–9.

51. Thomas Postlewait, 1997, pp. 39–60.

52. Phyllis Hartnoll, 1985, p. 32.

53. *The Bioscope*, 31 January 1924, p. 52.

54. See Michael Booth, 1981, Chapter 1.

55. See Thomas Elsaesser, 1987, p. 48.

56. As Martha Vicinus notes (1981, pp. 129–30), melodrama sides with 'the helpless and unfriended against the rich and powerful'.

57. See Daniel Gerould, 1994, pp. 185–98.

58. *All Sorts and Conditions of Men* is the title of a novel published by Walter Besant in 1882, which was filmed in 1921 by Georges Treville from a script by Colden Lore for Ideal, and later an opening subtitle in Asquith's *Underground* (1928).

59. Steve Neale (1990, pp. 46–8) defines 'verisimilitude' as that which is generally agreed is or should be the case. 'Truth' as an idealist goal reaches beyond the social or material world, while 'realism' is claimed by those who wish to challenge the definition of either. These distinctions are conceptually useful, but in practice, of course, popular and much critical discourse confuses them.

60. Rowell, 1985, p. 83.

61. Sanderson, 1984, pp. 18–19.

62. G. H. Lewes, reprinted in George Rowell, 1971, p. 206.

63. Lewes, 1875, p. 64.

64. William Archer, 1923, p. 259.

65. Sanderson, 1984, p. 179.

66. Martin Meisel, 1983, Chapter 1.

67. Charles Barr (1986, pp. 23–4) discusses the contrasting use of space between persons in English and American film-making, drawing on Daniel Snowman's comparative study of the two national cultures.

68. Church steps or porches provided powerful settings for Victorian melodramas and paintings turning on fateful encounters between the poor and middle classes – see, for example, the Notre Dame set for *The Two Orphans* 1874, utilised by D. W. Griffith for *Orphans of the Storm* (1921).

69. After Novello and Adrian Brunel had failed to find backers for a film (Adrian Brunel, 1949, p. 102).

70. See Low, 1971, p. 247.

71. *The Bioscope*, 11 March 1920, pp. 50–1.

72. *Kinematograph Weekly*, 11 March 1920, p. 88.

2 – GOING TO THE – BRITISH – PICTURES

1. Indeed, the title was changed for the American reprint, *Let's Go to the Movies* (New York: Arno Press, 1972). However, significant to discussion of pictorial collage below and of Elvey's 'flicker-book' editing strategies in Chapter 4 is the term 'flicks', which the Oxford English Dictionary dates from 1926. It appeared perhaps earlier than this, given the Sunday press column headed 'Flickers' – see unidentifiable clipping in Clive Brook's scrapbook for 21 May 1922 (CB/SC).

2. George Sadoul, 1948, p. 3.

3. 'Many amateurs joined photographic clubs. Up to World War I Great Britain retained its position as the country most active in photography, and by 1900 had no fewer than 256 clubs as against 99 in the United States and only 23 throughout the whole of the Continent' (Helmut Gernsheim and Alison Gernsheim, 1971, p. 168).

4. For a fascinating development of the link between motor transport and film, see Lynda Nead, 2002, pp. 240–55.

5. Michael Booth, 1981, p. 8.

6. Martin Meisel, 1983.

7. Ibid., p. 69.

8. See Patricia Warren, 1995, pp. 21–2; John Stokes, 1972, Chapter 3; Nead, 2002, pp. 240–55.

9. Meisel, 1983, p. 68.

10. Ibid., p. 12.

11. In relation to pictorialism in photography, see John Taylor (ed.), 1978.

12. Christopher Wood, 1999; Lionel Lambert, 1999.

13. Paul Martin, 1939, p. 18. Martin records his early days in wood engraving, which, he suggests, as an early means of recording news events based on artists' drawings, influenced early photographers. Depending on the wood engraver for reproduction, they sought to provide photographs that replicated the quality of the artist's sketch (p. 11).

14. Ibid., p. 23.

15. G. H. Martin and David Francis (1978, p. 234) note that Henry Mayhew's *London Life and London Poor* (1852–62) 'increasingly used photographs as the basis of engraved illustrations', as did *The Illustrated London News*, founded in 1842.

16. Peter Brooks, 1976, p. 9.

17. Walter Scott, 1819, p. 385.

18. W. P. Frith, 1888, p. 164.

19. Julian Treuherz, 1987, pp. 10–11.

20. Raymond Williams, 1977, pp. 61–74.

21. Frith, 1888, pp. 193–5.

22. H. P. Robinson, 1896, p. 65.

23. Meisel, 1983, pp. 11 and 162.

24. *The Bioscope*, 20 November 1919, p. 98.

25. Ibid., 5 January 1920, review of *The Elusive Pimpernel*, pp. 56–7.

26. Ibid., 31 January 1924, p. 52.

27. *Stoll's Editorial News*, 1 July 1920, p. 8 and 7 August 1919, p. 6. This magazine reproduced all reviews of Stoll films whether good or bad and encouraged debate, presumably as valuable publicity. This review is a reprint from *Films*.

28. *Kinematograph Weekly*, 22 April 1920, p. 88. This was Ivor Novello's first film.

29. Kenelm Foss, *c.* 1919, pp. 13–14.

30. *Pictures and the Picturegoer*, 20 September 1919, p. 356.

31. Meisel, 1983, pp. 29–30 and 91–5.

32. See Denis Gifford 1997, p. 85.

33. *The Picturegoer*, January 1924, p. 42. The Charles II portraits are attributed to Velázquez, presumably a slippage from the use of this artist in a scene from *The Wandering Jew* also referenced in this article.

34. *The Bioscope*, 16 June 1921, p. 44.

35. Ibid., 22 November 1923, p. 63.

36. *The Picturegoer*, January 1924, p. 43.

37. *Westminster Gazette*, 4 October 1926, SC/SC.

38. *Cinema World*, November 1928, BB/SC.

39. *The Picturegoer*, January 1924, p. 4.

40. *The Motion Picture Studio*, 15 April 1922, p. 12.

41. *The Bioscope*, 21 February 1921, CB/SC.

42. Ibid., 31 January 1924, p. 52.

43. *Daily News*, reprinted in *Stoll's Editorial News*, 15 January 1920, p. 8.

44. *The Bioscope*, 1 July 1920, supp., p. xv.

45. *The Sphere*, 31 July 1926, SC/SC.

46. *The Bioscope*, 20 November 1919, p. 98.

47. Ibid., 6 November 1919, p. 67.

48. Ibid., 3 January 1924, supp., p. xvi.

49. Frederick Talbot, 1923, p. 377.

50. Edward Carrick, 1972, p. 28.

51. *The Bioscope*, 18 June 1927, p. 171.

52. Andrew Higson, 1995, pp. 53–4.

53. Meisel, 1983, Chapter 4.

54. See Brooks, 1976; Richard Dyer, 1991.

55. Colden Lore, 1923, pp. 9 and 13.

56. George Pearson, typescript of lecture, 'First and Foremost the Actor', to a film class at RADA, 21 May 1929, GP/SC.

57. Meisel, 1983, pp. 8–11.

58. Ibid., pp. 38–9.

59. Ibid., p. 8.

60. Henry Neville, 1875, p. 74.

61. Brochure for Victoria School of Cinema Acting, *c.* 1915–17, p. 5.

62. Louis James, 1981, p. 12; Meisel, 1983, p. 44.

63. David Mayer, 1997, p. 100.

64. Booth, 1981, Chapter 4; Meisel, 1983, Chapter 19.

65. Quoted in Booth, 1981, p. 121.

66. *The Bioscope*, 22 July 1920, p. 14.

67. *Aberdeen Evening Press*, 19 April 1921, CB/SC.

68. *Dundee Argos*, 14 April 1921, CB/SC. According to the *Aberdeen Evening Press* (19 April 1921, CB/SC), Stewart Rome's costume was identical to the one worn by Henry Irving in this role.

69. *The Bioscope*, 15 January 1920, p. 57, on *The Elusive Pimpernel*.

70. *The Motion Picture Studio*, 27 May 1922, p. 13. For Netterville Barron, see Chapter 3, note 147.

71. James, 1981, p. 12. Similarly, Martin Meisel argues that the stage-picture aims not only at spectacle but contributes to a particular form of dramatic structure (1983, pp. 38–9).

72. See Redgrave's painting, *The Outcast* (1851), and D. W. Griffith's *Way Down East* 1920, for the currency of this gesture across painting and film.

73. Meisel, 1983, p. 38.

74. Desmond MacCarthy, 1954, p. 142.

75. Meisel, 1983, pp. 24–8 and 143–8.

76. Brooks, 1976, pp. 31–2.

77. Dion Boucicault, 1926, p. 34. Reprint of a lecture delivered at the Lyceum Theatre and subsequently published in *The Era*, 29 July 1882.

78. Neville, 1895, p. 121.

79. Lore, 1923, p. 12.

80. See Brooks, 1976; James, 1980; Meisel, 1983; Amy Sargeant, 2000a.

81. See Sargeant, 2000a, 2000b; Joe Kember, 2001.

82. See, for example, 'The Expressions of Clive Brook', *Picture Show*, 28 January 1922, p. 7, and 'The Expressions of Guy Newall', ibid., 27 March 1920, p. 7. The latter issue carries an article, 'Character as Told by the Face', which dissects the meaning of Alma Taylor's features, including eyebrows, inquisitive nose, the eye, mouth and chin (p. 21).

83. See James, 1981; Meisel, 1983; David Mayer, 1999.

84. Leman Thomas Rede, 1827, p. 77.

85. *The Motion Picture Studio*, 27 May 1922, p. 13.

86. Mayer, 1999, pp. 17–18.

87. Meisel, 1983, pp. 38–9.

88. Brooks, 1976, pp. 66–7.

89. Henry Siddons, 1822, p. 22.

90. Neville, 1895, pp. 148–9.

91. Siddons, 1822, pp. 27 and 33.

92. Lore, 1923, p. 10.

93. Boucicault, 1882, pp. 32–3.

94. Mayer, 1999, pp. 17–18.

95. G. H. Lewes, 1875, pp. 98–9.

96. Ibid., pp. 100 and 124.

97. Meisel, 1983, pp. 351–72.

98. Ibid., p. 354. H. P. Robinson similarly turns to the Pre-Raphaelites for their exemplary reconciliation of the new photographic possibilities of fidelity to nature with the artistic perception that establishes significance. He quotes Millais's *The Huguenot* (1852) and Holman Hunt's *Claudio and Isabella* (1850), both of which, as Martin Meisel shows, depend on the small, incidental gesture as an index of more complex political or psychological conflicts. The fingers of the Huguenot tug gently on the white armband, sign of Catholic allegiance, that his fiancée is slipping round his arm, while both concentrate on their parting embrace. Claudio fiddles with the chain around his foot braced against his prison wall while asking his sister nun to save his life by sleeping with his captor. Crucially, Hunt accesses inner drama through the perception dawning in the nun's eyes.

99. *Blackwood's Edinburgh Magazine*, 1856, p. 218.

100. William Archer, 1923, p. 260.

101. William Archer, 1886, p. 335.

102. Lore, 1923, p. 13.

103. *The Motion Picture Studio*, 11 June 1921, p. 13.

104. Griselda Pollock (1988), in an unpublished public lecture for a BFI Education day school, *Hollywood's Victorian Legacy* (National Film Theatre, January 1988), suggested the bridge offered by the Pre-Raphaelites between melodramatic gesture and film acting.

105. Rede, 1827, p. 78.

106. Violet Hopson, *c.* 1919, p. 22.

107. Ibid.

108. Neville, 1895, pp. 128–9.

109. Ibid., pp. 134–5.

110. Ibid., p. 138.

111. *The Bioscope*, 6 October 1913, p. 241.

112. Lewes, 1875, pp. 98–9, quoted in Pearson's notebooks, GP/SC.

113. Boucicault, 1882, p. 32.

114. Neville, 1895, p. 157.

115. Lilian Bamburg, 1929, p. 106.

116. Neville, 1895, p. 124.

117. Mayer, 1999, p. 22.

118. *The Bioscope*, 22 November 1923, p. 63.

119. See advertisements in *Kinematograph Weekly* for *Call of the Blood* (15 April 1920, p. 89); *Gwyneth of the Welsh Hills* (3 November 1921, pp. 33 and 36); a B & C Series promoting Jose Collins Dramas (24 January 1924, p. 15); and *The Bioscope* for George Clark Productions (1 July 1920, pp. 77 and 80). For Berstein's article on cinema design see *Kinematograph Weekly*, 3 January 1924, p. 123.

120. *The Motion Picture Studio*, 13 October 1923, p. 7.

121. Meisel, 1983, p. 80. In 1919, a reader writes to *The Kinematograph and Lantern Weekly* to praise the introduction of 'titling . . . pictures on films by means of a frame or border' as 'a national trait' stamping the film as "British and Best" '. Not only does this practice afford 'an additional beauty', it also ensures efficient narrative (6 February 1919, p. 96).

122. L. C. MacBean (1922, p. 65) defines a circular mask with softened, fuzzy edges as a 'spot-iris'.

123. *The Motion Picture Studio*, 13 October 1923, p. 7.

124. Robinson, 1896, p. 146.

125. Higson, 1985, pp. 54–8.

126. *The Bioscope*, 21 October 1920, p. 70.

127. The stage play, *Waiting for the Verdict, or; Falsely Accused* (1859) by Colin Hazelwood realised Solomon's paintings. See section on 'realisations', pp. 34–6.

128. Meisel, 1983, p. 53.

129. Ibid., p. 36.

130. The *Daily Telegraph* review of *Henry Dunbar* (1865, Tom Taylor from Mrs Braddon's novel), quoted in Donald Mullin (ed.), 1983, p. 354.

131. Neville, 1895, p. 128.

132. Meisel, 1983, pp. 53–5.

133. Ibid., pp. 38, 56 and 80.

134. Ibid., Chapter 13.

135. The term 'intertextual relay' is discussed in Steve Neale, 1990, p. 49.

136. Stephen Humphries, 1989, pp. 24–32; Mervyn Heard, 1996, pp. 15–26.

137. Frederick Alderson, 1970, Chapter 1.

138. James Fenton, 1990, p. 40.

139. Humphries, 1989, pp. 53–8.

140. Alderson, 1970, p. 17.

141. Humphries, 1989, p. 160.

142. *The Bioscope*, 17 February 1921, p. 72.

143. Ibid., 24 November 1921, p. 72.

144. Ibid., 3 January 1924, supp., p. xvi.

145. Denis Gifford, 1997, p. 83.

146. *Around the Town*, 5 January 1923, CB/CB.

147. *Films*, reprinted in *Stoll's Editorial News*, 7 August 1919, p. 5.

148. *Films*, reprinted in *Stoll's Editorial News*, 1 April 1920, p. 4.

149. *Kinematograph Weekly*, 11 March 1920, pp. 34–5.

150. *Daily Express*, 3 December 1926, SC/SC. This despite Atkinson's severe stricture that 'patriotism is not enough where entertainment is concerned' and that 'the stereotypes need revising'. G. A. Atkinson had been review editor for *Kinematograph Weekly* and from April 1920 film critic for both the *Daily* and *Sunday Express*.

151. *Pictures and the Picturegoer*, 20 September 1919, p. 356.

152. *The Bioscope*, 20 November 1919, p. 98.

153. Ibid., 24 November 1921, p. 72, finds Elvey's *Romance of Wastedale* 'a rather conventional melodrama' with unclear narrative that nevertheless yields 'some really excellent pictures of mountain climbing'.

154. *The Motion Picture Studio*, 3 August 1921, p. 5.

155. *The Bioscope*, 11 March 1920, p. 50.

156. Ibid., 4 September 1924, p. 44.

157. See Janet Staiger, 1985, pp. 147–9; Rachael Low, 1971, pp. 243–8.

158. See Low, 1971, pp. 37–8.

159. Kristin Thompson, 1985, pp. 163–70.

160. See Talbot, 1923, pp. 218–19. For complaints about British film-makers' conception of editing, see Adrian Brunel, 1949, pp. 117–22 and 132–3.

161. *Kinematograph Weekly*, 25 May 1922, p. 55.

162. Ibid., 10 February 1921, p. 78.

163. *The Motion Picture Studio*, 17 November 1923, CB/SC.

164. *Weekly Dispatch*, 11 November 1923, CB/SC.

165. *Kinematograph Weekly*, 16 November 1922, p. 51; 25 October 1923, p. 60; *The Motion Picture Studio*, 3 June 1922, p. 4. The problem of continuity is discussed further in Chapter 6.

166. *The Motion Picture Studio*, 3 June 1922, p. 4. See also the *Yorkshire Western Post*, 7 August 1926, SC/SC, for praise of Griffith's introduction of 'that mystic thing "continuity"', which overcomes the mere 'succession of scenes' that painfully 'retard' a story. The emphasis in British use of continuity is its service to 'story' rather than the technicalities of scene dissection. See the 'full and clever continuity'

attributed to *General Post* (*Kinematograph Weekly*, 3 November 1920, p. 88), or Daisy Martin's 'ingenious continuity' for *The Broken Road* (*Kinematograph Weekly*, 23 June 1921, p. 37).

167. *Kinematograph Weekly*, 10 February 1921, p. 78.

168. Pearson, typescript of public lecture given on 14 October 1923, GP/SC.

169. *Daily Sketch, c.* 30 November 1926, SC/SC.

170. Robinson, 1896, pp. 90–1.

171. Meisel, 1983, pp. 60–4; Grahame Smith, 2003.

172. Hopson, *c.* 1919, p. 22. See Sargeant (2000b) for this common training task.

173. James, 1981, pp. 11–13.

174. *The Picturegoer*, July 1921, p. 10.

175. Ibid., January 1922, BB/SC.

176. Hopson, *c.* 1919, p. 22.

177. *The Bioscope*, 1 July 1920, supp., p. xxix.

178. *Picture Show*, 17 March 1923, CB/SC.

179. Pearson, 1957, p. 140.

180. Ibid.

181. *Sunday Express*, 4 July 1926, SC/SC.

182. Pearson, notebooks, GP/SC.

183. Pearson, synopsis for *Réveille*, GP/SC.

184. Ibid.

185. Pearson, 1957, p. 140.

186. See Kenton Bamford (1999) on Pearson, and Higson (2001) on Hepworth's *Tansy* for opposing views on the degree of regression or modernity in their respective outlooks.

187. Robinson, 1896, p. 146.

188. Christopher Hussey, 1927, p. 4.

189. Cecil Hepworth, 1951, p. 123.

190. Robinson, 1896, pp. 31 and 65.

191. Ibid., pp. 87–8.

192. Ibid., p. 31.

193. Ibid., p. 48.

194. Pictorial values were found in the apparent natural disorder of, for example, rocky outcroppings, falling torrents, tree clumps, folding hills, animal groupings, the disposition of castles, cottages and village spires. See Hussey, 1927.

195. John Taylor, 1990, p. 181.

196. Ibid.

197. *The Bioscope*, 20 November 1919, p. 98.

198. *The Picturegoer*, January 1924, pp. 41–4.

199. *The Bioscope*, 23 October 1913, pp. 304–5; *Kinematograph Weekly*, 3 January 1924, p. 123.

200. I am indebted for this distinction to Alan Appleby, *A Step Too Far? A Kantian Look at Godard's Counter-*

Cinema (1999), unpublished dissertation, Staffordshire University.
201. Robinson, 1896, p. 58 and Chapter 13 on models.
202. This ambivalence is found in Higson, 1995, pp. 50–1 and 54. The criticism of pictorialism for its inhibition on spectator involvement also neglects the narrative dimension of the picture itself – which is never 'quite complete without mystery . . . [and] . . . must draw you on to admire it, not show you everything at a glance'. Robinson, 1896, p. 58.
203. Higson, 1995, p. 51; *Kinematograph Weekly*, 3 April 1924, p. 69.
204. Treuherz, 1987; Peter Keating, 1976. Of the social-realist painters, Julian Treuherz notes: 'The greater emphasis on social realism in the 1870s and 1880s has more to do with developments in illustrated journalism (the commissioning of artists to provide illustrations) than with any intensification of social problems at that time' (p. 12).
205. Humphries, 1989, pp. 86–90. In *Comrades* (1989) Bill Douglas dramatises the role of the lanternist in circulating social ideas along with his entertainments.
206. *The Bioscope*, 11 March 1920, pp. 50–1.
207. Ibid., 8 August 1928, p. 61. Earlier, the Boer War, according to Stephen Humphries (1989, pp. 160–1), was a fertile source of slide sets for many years after.
208. See Colin Mercer, 1988; Pollock, 1988; Robert Colls and Philip Dodd, 1985.
209. Humphries, 1989, p. 86.
210. Brooks, 1976, p. 9.
211. Meisel, 1983, p. 282.
212. Ibid., p. 11.
213. *Kinematograph Weekly*, 11 March 1920, p. 88.
214. Ibid. This last episode is missing from the print preserved in the NFTVA.
215. See *Comradeship* (1919) and *Blighty* (1927) for similar First World War cross-class marriages at the centre of cohering communities.
216. Iris Barry, 1926, p. 234.
217. Hubert von Herkomer, *Sunday at Chelsea Hospital* (*The Graphic*, 1871), developed as the oil painting, *The Last Muster* (1875).
218. *The Bioscope*, 16 October 1913, p. 241.

3 – PERFORMING BRITISH CINEMA

1. G. H. Lewes, 1875, p. 61.
2. J. T. Grein in George Rowell (ed.), 1971, p. 221.
3. William Archer, 1888, p. 58.
4. J. T. Grein, 1924, pp. 152–3.
5. Archer, 1888, pp. 56–7.
6. *The Bioscope*, 21 October 1920, p. 71.
7. Ibid., 31 January 1924, p. 52.
8. Ibid., 8 November 1923, CB/SC.
9. *Westminster Gazette*, 15 September 1926, SC/SC.
10. *Weekly Dispatch*, reviewing a reissue, 11 November 1927, CB/SC.
11. *The Motion Picture Studio*, 17 November 1923, CB/SC.
12. *Picture Show*, 12 November 1921, CB/SC.
13. Ibid., April 1923, CB/SC.
14. *Morning Post*, 29 September 1927, BB/SC.
15. *The Bioscope*, 6 October 1927, p. 31.
16. *Western Dispatch*, 5 September 1926, SC/SC.
17. *Western Morning News*, 14 September 1926, SC/SC.
18. *Film Weekly*, 6 May 1929, p. 16.
19. *The Motion Picture Studio*, 17 February 1923, p. 14. Similar complaints were made against the American *The Unknown Soldier*. See Chapter 5, p. 132 and note 49.
20. George Pearson, notebooks, GP/SC.
21. Archer, 1888, pp. 70–1.
22. *Stoll's Editorial News*, 7 July 1919, p. 3.
23. *The Bioscope*, 22 November 1923, pp. 23–4.
24. See *Variety*, 31 December 1924, reprinted in R. R. Bowker (ed.), 1983, vol. 2, no page nos.
25. See Michael Sanderson, 1984, Chapters 2 and 7.
26. *The Picturegoer*, July 1921, p. 20.
27. Lewes in Rowell (ed.), 1971, p. 206.
28. J. L. Styan, 1981, p. 69.
29. Sanderson, 1984, pp. 188–9.
30. A. E. Matthews, 1952, pp. 93–4. The play in which Hawtrey appeared was *Harvest*, adapted from a novel by John Strange Winter, pen name for Henrietta Eliza Vaughan Stannard, Eliot Stannard's mother.
31. Ibid.
32. Denis Gifford, 1997, p. 89.
33. Hugh Hunt, 1978, p. 127.
34. Sanderson, 1984, p. 188.
35. See *Glasgow Evening News*, 7 May 1924, CB/SC, quoted below.
36. *Kinematograph Weekly*, 6 May 1920, p. 109.
37. *The Motion Picture Studio*, 8 September 1923, p. 12.
38. *Northern Mail and Newcastle Clarion*, 2 January 1928, BB/SC.
39. Clive Brook, *c.* 1970, p. 34. See also W. A. Darlington, 1950, p. 349.

40. *Film Weekly*, 3 December 1928, p. 15.
41. Archer, 1988, pp. 55–6.
42. Archer in Rowell (ed.), 1971, p. 230.
43. See Alison Light, 1991; Janice Winship, 1996.
44. *The Motion Picture Studio*, 25 February 1922, p. 7.
45. Ibid., 21 October 1922, p. 13.
46. *Morning Post*, 29 June 1926, SC/SC.
47. Ibid. Michael Sanderson argues that the role played during and after the First World War by dramatic training – which included elocution and deportment – represented a cheaper form of social 'finishing' for the daughters and sometimes younger sons of the declining upper classes or upwardly mobile *nouveau riche* (1984, pp. 44 and 189).
48. *Morning Post*, 29 June 1926, SC/SC.
49. Ibid.
50. Ibid.
51. *The Bioscope*, 8 July 1926, p. 49.
52. Ibid.
53. William Gillette, 1915.
54. Richard Dyer, 1991, pp. 132–40.
55. Matheson Lang, 1940, p. 20.
56. Dion Boucicault, 1926, pp. 50–2.
57. Lewes, 1875, pp. 102–3.
58. Ibid., p. 105.
59. Archer, 1888, p. 26.
60. Grein, 1924, p. 155.
61. Lang, 1940, p. 82.
62. Ibid., pp. 115–16.
63. J. T. Grein, 1921, p. 36.
64. *Picture Show*, 1 July 1922, p. 19, CB/SC.
65. *The Bioscope*, 17 February 1921, p. 72.
66. Peter Noble, 1951, p. 89; *The Bioscope*, 15 September 1921, p. 43.
67. Pearson's notebooks, GP/SC.
68. Louis James (1981), Martin Meisel (1983), David Mayer (1999) and Amy Sargeant (2000a) refer to the work of Charles Darwin and Charles Bell.
69. Henry Neville, 1895, p. 122.
70. Ibid., pp. 112–14.
71. Boucicault, 1926, p. 49.
72. William Archer, 1923, p. 258.
73. Raymond Williams, 1977.
74. Jan McDonald, 1986, p. 29; John Stokes, 1972, p. 127.
75. Styan, 1981, p. 5; McDonald, 1986, p. 8.
76. McDonald, 1986, pp. 7–9; see also Styan, pp. 5–6.
77. Sanderson, 1984, pp. 12–20 and 179–82.
78. Violet Hopson, *c.* 1919, p. 26.
79. *The Picturegoer*, February 1921, p. 12.
80. Stewart Rome, *c.*, 1919, pp. 7–8.
81. Ibid., p. 12.
82. Ibid., p. 9.
83. See the double spread in *The Kinematograph Year Book* for 1928, illustrating his 1928 releases together with press comments over the caption 'Moore Marriott an Actor – Not a Type' (pp. 274–5). 'Type' here is shifting towards 'stereotype', which would preclude acting.
84. Both reviews were reprinted as an advertisement for Artistic Films in *The Bioscope*, 6 December 1923, p. 18.
85. See Jane Cowl (American actress in London to play in *Easy Virtue*), in *The Bioscope*, 15 July 1926, p. 17; *Stoll's Editorial News*, 8 April 1920, pp. 3 and 7.
86. Albert Chevalier, in *The Bioscope*, 22 July 1920, p. 14. Through this debate run conflicting arguments about the role of gesture and speech in relation to the virtues and deficiencies of either medium. According to some arguments, larger movements are required on stage in order to be visible throughout the theatre, while the slightest movement of body or facial muscles registers on film, and sudden or enlarged movements look exaggerated and degenerate into 'overacting'. According to others, film requires pantomime in order to compensate for lack of dialogue, while on the stage minimal gesture only is needed in support of the human voice. See: *The Motion Picture Studio*, 25 March 1922, p. 13; *The Bioscope*, 22 July 1920, p. 14; 2 December 1926, p. 30; 20 March 1929, p. 29; *The Picturegoer*, January 1926, p. 26; August 1927, pp. 16–17; *Yorkshire Post*, 6 December 1926 (SC/SC); Lilian Bamburg, *c.* 1927, pp. 32, 56, 96, 106; Hopson, *c.* 1919, pp. 18–19.
87. *Kinematograph Weekly*, 11 March 1920, p. 88.
88. *The Bioscope*, 15 December 1921, p. 32.
89. *Northern Weekly Telegraph*, 24 November 1923, CB/SC.
90. *Kinematograph Weekly*, 1 December 1921, p. 70.
91. *Glasgow Evening News*, 7 May 1924, CB/SC.
92. *Leeds Mercury*, 7 October 1926, SC/SC.
93. *Leicester Mercury*, 9 October 1926, SC/SC.
94. Bamburg, *c.* 1927, pp. 20–1.
95. Kenelm Foss, *c.* 1919, p. 25.
96. Ibid., p. 26.
97. *The Illustrated London News*, 26 June 1926, SC/SC.
98. *Film Weekly*, 7 January 1929, p. 14.
99. See Adrian Brunel, 1949, p. 128.
100. J. T. Grein, 1924, p. 179.

101. Ibid., pp. 158–9.

102. Rachael Low, 1971, p. 262.

103. *The Bioscope*, 18 June 1927, p. 139, and 4 July 1928, p. 28.

104. *Evening News* for 9 August 1926 calculates that there are '25 women and 89 men from Britain working in important roles in Hollywood' (SC/SC).

105. On the use of stage names, see: *Stoll's Editorial News*, 29 July 1920, p. 6; *The Motion Picture Studio*, 3 June 1922, p. 4; and 21 October 1922, p. 11; *Theatre World*, October 1925, p. 88; *The Bioscope*, 3 January 1924, supp., p. xv, and 18 June 1927, p. 139. In 1921 *The Motion Picture Studio* warns, 'The public only cares for big names when their owners do big things. It has an awkward habit of making its own stars. And it soon refuses to accept a "name" if it is not accompanied by an equally prominent performance' (11 June 1921, p. 7).

106. Advice included the necessity of publicity as the means of bonding stars and their public. *Film Weekly* cites Victor McLaglen as a star lost through 'publicity starvation' (29 October 1928, p. 10).

107. *The Motion Picture Studio*, 25 February 1922, p. 7.

108. Ibid., 26 August 1922, p. 5.

109. *Film Weekly*, 5 November 1928, p. 8.

110. *The Bioscope*, 6 February 1919, p. 8. Terris writes: 'as an Englishman . . . of a well-known theatrical family' and now 'director-general of the oldest and best established cinematographic firm extant – to wit, the Greater Vitagraph Company of America'.

111. *Kinematograph Weekly*, 26 June 1924, p. 31.

112. *The Bioscope*, 4 November 1926, p. 37.

113. *The Motion Picture Studio*, 25 February 1922, p. 7.

114. *Stoll's Editorial News*, 5 August 1920, p. 7.

115. *The Picturegoer*, February 1921, p. 40.

116. *Film Weekly*, 21 January 1929, p. 11.

117. Ibid., 5 November 1928, p. 12.

118. Foss, *c.* 1919, p. 26.

119. *Stoll's Editorial News*, 12 August 1920, pp. 9–10.

120. *The Motion Picture Studio*, 22 October 1921, p. 7.

121. Ibid.

122. Bamburg, *c.* 1927, pp. 114–15.

123. *The Bioscope*, 16 February 1928, supp., p. iii.

124. See Christine Gledhill, 1991, pp. 207–29.

125. *The Motion Picture Studio*, 11 February 1922, p. 14.

126. *The Bioscope*, 23 July 1925, p. 45.

127. *Picture Show*, 21 August 1926, p. 19.

128. *The Picturegoer*, March 1921, p. 14.

129. *Film Weekly*, 26 November 1928, p. 12.

130. Reprinted in *Stoll's Editorial News*, 5 February 1920, p. 8.

131. Ibid., 1 July 1920, p. 9.

132. *Kinematograph Weekly*, 1 November 1923, p. 67.

133. *Film Weekly*, 26 November 1928, p. 12.

134. *Around the Town*, 5 January 1923, CB/SC, on *This Freedom*.

135. *Film Weekly*, 26 November 1928, p. 12.

136. Ibid., 13 May 1929, p. 20.

137. Ibid., 28 January 1929, p. 13.

138. *Cinema Chat*, no. 24, 1920, p. 21.

139. *Daily News*, 26 November 1923, CB/SC.

140. Hopson, *c.* 1919, pp. 6–7.

141. *Kinematograph Weekly*, 9 February 1922, p. 38.

142. *The Picturegoer*, March 1921, p. 41.

143. *The Bioscope*, 5 January 1928, p. 40.

144. *Film Weekly*, 26 November 1928, p. 20.

145. *The Motion Picture Studio*, 25 February 1922, p. 7. See also Sanderson, 1984, p. 189.

146. *The Motion Picture Studio*, 23 September 1922, p. 5.

147. *The Motion Picture Studio* introduces Barron as follows: 'Colonel Barron is a physician and dramatist and is a Fellow of the Royal Society of Medicine. He is the author of *The Three Brothers* and other wordless plays, and founded the Windsor Forest School of Physical Culture. He is well known as a lecturer on the Art of Dramatic Expression' (27 May 1922, p. 13). Barron belonged to a convergence of medical science with the dramatic arts around voice production and speech that had been set in motion by Elsie Foggerty, founder of the Central School of Speech and Drama in 1904.

148. Colden Lore, 1923, p. 12.

149. Pearson, unpublished RADA lecture, 'First and Foremost an Actor', 21 May 1929, GP/SC.

150. *The Motion Picture Studio*, 27 May 1922, p. 12.

151. Ibid., 24 June 1922, p. 13. Barron explains how actors of one class and nationality frequently misunderstand the movements appropriate to a character of another – in particular, the Americans get British customs wrong. William MacDougall's *Introduction to Social Psychology* was first published in 1908 by Methuen & Co. In 1912, a fifth revised edition was published with a supplementary chapter on theories of action. The last, twenty-third enlarged edition was published in 1960 by Methuen & Co. in London, and by Barnes & Noble in New York.

152. Hopson, *c.* 1919, p. 24.

153. Annette Kuhn, 1996, pp. 177–92.
154. *Film Weekly*, 7 January 1929, p. 20.
155. Ibid., 14 January 1929, p. 5.
156. Noble, 1951.
157. *Picture Show*, 13 November 1926, p. 13.
158. James Agate, 1926, pp. 84–7.
159. See Michael Williams, 2001.
160. *Variety*, 25 February 1921, in Bowker (ed.), 1983, no page nos.
161. *The Cinema*, and *The Film Renter*, reprinted in *Stoll's Editorial News*, 1 July 1920, pp. 8–9.
162. *Daily News*, reprinted in *Stoll's Editorial News*, 1 July 1920, p. 8.
163. *Kinematograph Weekly*, 3 August 1922, p. 44.
164. Desmond MacCarthy in a 1930 radio talk, published in 1954, p. 17.
165. *The Bioscope*, 11 December 1919, p. 96.
166. *The Film Renter*, reprinted in *Stoll's Editorial News*, 1 July 1920, p. 8.
167. *The Times*, reprinted in *Stoll's Editorial News*, 29 January 1920, p. 4.
168. *The Bioscope*, 1 July 1920, supp., p. xxiv.
169. See *The Bioscope*, 3 January 1924, supp., p. xv; 8 July 1926, p. 33; and 5 March 1928, p. 42; and readers letters to *The Picturegoer*, April 1924, CB/SC, and *Film Weekly*, 28 January 1929, p. 13.
170. Foss, *c.* 1919, p. 26.
171. *The Motion Picture Studio*, 22 October 1921, p. 7.
172. *The Picturegoer*, April 1924, CB/SC.
173. Foss, *c.* 1919, p. 26.
174. Ibid., pp. 26–7.
175. *Kinematograph Weekly*, 23 June 1923, p. 30.
176. Hopson, *c.* 1919, p. 26.
177. *Lloyds Weekly News*, 27 June 1926, SC/SC.
178. *Film Weekly*, 7 January 1929, p. 20.
179. *The Picturegoer*, September 1927, p. 16.
180. Ibid., pp. 16–17.

4 – DIRECTORS' PICTURE STORIES

1. Rachael Low, 1971, p. 114.
2. See Cecil Hepworth, 1951, p. 178; Andrew Higson, 1995, p. 54.
3. See Jonathon Burrows, 2000.
4. *The Bioscope*, 1 March 1923, p. 61. See also *Pictures and the Picturegoer*, 20 September 1919, p. 356 and January 1924, pp. 41–4.
5. Hepworth, 1951, p. 123.
6. Ibid., p. 30.
7. Ibid., pp. 30–1.
8. Ibid., pp. 35–6. The *Evening Standard* is similarly unimpressed by the news that Komisarjevsky had been commissioned by Sidney Berstein not only to devise prologues but 'to treat the cramping black border which so cribs and cabins the white screen which is always struggling to be unconfined'. He was 'to make a pretty frame (sometimes thought to be so artistic, like a picture gallery). He will contrive a surrounding to suit the atmosphere of the picture' (10 August 1926, SC/SC).
9. Ibid., p. 140.
10. Ibid., pp. 139–40. Hepworth was not a great inventor of stories, writing only one screenplay.
11. Ibid., pp. 114–15.
12. Ibid., p. 139.
13. Higson, 1995, pp. 85–6.
14. Hepworth, 1951, p. 137.
15. Ibid., p. 138.
16. Ibid., p. 137.
17. Ibid., p. 143.
18. See Iris Barry, 1926, pp. 240 and 241; Kenton Bamford, 1999, p. 10.
19. Raymond Williams (1973), Julian Moynahan (1972), and Fred Inglis (1990) pay respect to the complexity and diversity of the pastoral tradition and its meanings.
20. See Higson, 1995, pp. 41–3, and John Taylor (1990) in S. Pugh, pp. 188–91. English Heritage was founded in 1983.
21. See discussion of populist aesthetics in Chapter 2.
22. Terry Morden, 1983.
23. Higson, 1995, pp. 28–30.
24. Martin Meisel, 1983, p. 27. Meisel here refers to Egg's triptych, *Past and Present* (1858), described in its original arrangement that made the two 'after' pictures pendants to the centrepiece depicting the marital crisis. Thus, rather than offering causal linearity, the narrative circles back on itself, to the consequences already prefigured in the initiating situation. See also Meisel, p. 145, for pastoralism, the past and genre painting.
25. See David Peters Corbett, 1997.
26. See, for example, *Pictures and the Picturegoer*, 20 September 1919, p. 356 and January 1924, pp. 41–4.
27. Andrew Higson (2001), in an interesting analysis of *Tansy*, takes up similar themes, arguing the pictorial presentation of landscape as a kind of 'performance' of Englishness.

28. See Julian Moynahan's 1972 analysis of the 'maiden' in novelistic pastoralism.

29. Peter Brooks, 1976, p. 32.

30. *The Bioscope*, 15 December 1923, p. 32.

31. Hepworth (1951, p. 150) records that Alma Taylor went to stay with a shepherd's family for several weeks in order to learn their skills, bringing the acting dog to live with her so that they built up a working relationship.

32. This symbolism has been recently re-articulated in the socialist pastoral of Ken Loach's *Land and Freedom* (1995) and, more tenuously perhaps, in *Brassed Off* (1996).

33. Geoffrey Faithful orchestrated a seven-minute continuous take of this scene, which at the trade show drew 'a round of applause from the audience, hard-boiled as most of them were' (Hepworth, 1951, p. 151).

34. *The Bioscope*, 15 December 1921, p. 32.

35. Ibid., 1 March 1923, p. 61.

36. H. P. Robinson, 1896, p. 97.

37. Hepworth, 1951, p. 149. See Laurence Napper (2001, p. 43) who explains that *The Piper of Dreams* 'was painted by Estella Canziani and exhibited at the Royal Academy in 1915. The reproduction rights were acquired by the Medici Society and the postcard became an instant success, selling an astonishing 250,000 copies in the first year.' Napper suggests the postcard was carried by soldiers at the front as a form of talisman.

38. Hepworth, 1951, p. 150.

39. Conan Doyle's uncle, Richard Doyle, had been one of the most popular of the Victorian fairy painters. According to Lionel Lambourne (1999, p. 205), he achieved 'magical effects of diminution in scale'. He juxtaposed fairy activities with 'natural forms', relying 'compositionally on the self-imposed constraints provided by the insertion either of the branches of a tree or its gnarled roots'. Such 'natural forms' are used also by Hepworth in these woodland sequences. Conan Doyle's father was also in his spare time a fairy painter, whose fantasies took on a different dimension as he succumbed to alcoholism and epilepsy, ending up in an asylum.

40. Ibid., 1999, p. 192.

41. Christopher Wood, 1999, p. 42.

42. The connection between the fairy and pastoral is exploited in an advertisement for Delectaland sweets, featuring a fairy scattering bon-bons against a radiant sunrise – 'Heralding . . . the awakening of a new industrial era, where ideal conditions of light, cleanliness, and fresh air remove from work the taint of drudgery, and inspire in all a spirit of loyal co-operation to accomplish each day something better than the day before.' *Royal Academy Illustrated*, 1919, p. 23. The need for 'belief' is taken up in Guy Newall's novel and play adaptation, *Husband Love* (1924, a & b). Referencing the Cottingley fairies, the story pits Professor Adam Budd – who is determined to prove or disprove the existence of fairies through the materialising power of photography – against the imaginary child/creature, Rubber Face, invented by Jim and Paula as their means of marital communication. Jim's later attempt to 'realise' Rubber Face by taking under his protection a poverty-stricken and persecuted Italian dwarf, Baptista, destroys the power of 'Imagination' for Paula, and their marriage is threatened until the dwarf is repatriated and Rubber Face returned.

43. *The Motion Picture Studio*, 24 February 1923, p. 8.

44. *The Bioscope*, 14 July 1927, p. 27.

45. *The Bioscope*, 9 July 1914, p. 171, on *The Suicide Club*; *Stoll's Editorial News*, 30 October 1919, p. 7 on *Mr Wu*; *Kinematograph Weekly*, 6 May 1920, pp. 92 and 97, on *At the Villa Rose*; *The Motion Picture Studio*, 8 October 1921, p. 3, on *The Fruitful Vine*, 10 March 1923, p. 7, on *The Royal Oak*, and 24 March 1923, p. 7, on *The Wandering Jew*.

46. Including in the 1920s, Estelle Brody, John Longdon, Jameson Thomas, Basil Rathbone, Brian Aherne, John Gielgud, Madeleine Carroll and Jessie Matthews. See Victor Saville, nd., VS/SC, p. 33; Low, 1971, p. 173.

47. *The Picturegoer*, June 1927, pp. 8–9; Denis Gifford, 1997, p. 79.

48. Linda Wood, 1987, p. 11.

49. *The Cine-Technician*, May–June 1947, pp. 67–8; also, the transcript of a radio interview, 'Maurice Elvey in Conversation with John Sharp', tx 29 November 1963, p. 3/8. Held in BFI Library.

50. Gifford, 1997, p. 81.

51. See David Berry and Simmon Horrocks (eds), 1998.

52. Gifford, 1997, p. 87.

53. Transcript, 'Maurice Elvey in Conversation with John Sharp', tx 29 November 1963, pp. 2/3. Held in the BFI Library.

54. *The Picturegoer*, June 1927, p. 9.

55. Gifford, 1997, p. 83.

56. *The Motion Picture Studio*, 21 July 1923, p. 5. Elvey, however, distinguishes 'real' history from the official propaganda taught in schools.

57. *The Bioscope*, 3 January 1924, supp., p. xvi.

58. *The Motion Picture Studio*, 5 May 1923, p. 9.

59. Gifford, 1997, p. 83.

60. *The Bioscope*, 1 July 1920, supp., p. iv.

61. A forgivable foible according to *Kinematograph Weekly*, 6 May 1920, p. 92.

62. Jay Winter, 1995.

63. Low, 1971, pp. 172–3; Wood, 1987, pp. 14–16; and Saville, nd., VS/SC, pp. 32–42.

64. Saville, nd., VS/SC, p. 33. See also: *Sunday Pictorial*, 4 July 1926; *Evening News*, 26 July 1926; *Competitions*, 31 July 1926; *Observer*, 8 November 1926 – all in SC/SC, and all dealing with the question of a British answer to *The Big Parade*.

65. James Agate, 1927, p. 357.

66. *Daily News*, 14 September 1926, SC/SC.

67. *Evening Standard*, 14 September 1926, SC/SC.

68. *Westminster Gazette*, 15 September 1926, SC/SC. Similarly, the *Daily Mirror* declares 'it grinds no axe of patriotism . . . [but] . . . has the unmistakable stamp of British nationality all over it' (15 September 1926, SC/SC). The *Daily Mail* thinks it 'a film of real war, real soldiers, real impulses, all the more enchanting when genuinely English' (14 September 1926, SC/SC). A production note in *The Bioscope* tells of its deployment of British veterans among producers, lead actors and extras (8 July 1926, p. 35). In fact, this was not true of Elvey himself.

69. *Daily Telegraph*, 14 September 1926, SC/SC.

70. Saville, nd., VS/SC, p. 31.

71. *Yorkshire Observer*, 30 July 1926, SC/SC.

72. *Evening News*, 14 September 1926, SC/SC.

73. Paul Fussell, 1975.

74. James Agate, 1927, p. 357.

75. Fussell, 1975; Winter, 1995.

76. I use collage to refer to the abutment of images in an imaginary spatial plane, creating a variety of relationships, while montage refers to serial organisation that focuses the effects of juxtaposition between two specific images.

77. Charles Barr, 2002, pp. 227–41.

78. Sergei Eisenstein, 1963, pp. 195–255.

79. *The Kinematograph and Lantern Weekly*, 23 May 1918, p. 76.

80. Ibid., 12 July 1917, p. 108.

81. Ibid., 26 July 1917, p. 79.

82. *The Bioscope*, 19 July 1917, p. 925.

83. Ibid., 15 January 1920, pp. 56–7.

84. Transcript, 'Maurice Elvey in Conversation with John Sharp', pp. 3/1 and 3/7.

85. Charles Barr, 1986, p. 24.

86. *The Motion Picture Studio*, 17 November 1923, p. 10.

87. *Bromley News*, 1 March 1924, CB/SC.

88. *Daily Express*, 13 November 1923, CB/SC.

89. Unidentifiable clipping, 17 November 1923, p. 46, CB/SC.

90. *The Film Renter and Moving Picture News* (17 November 1923, p. 46, CB/SC).

91. George Pearson's notebooks, GP/SC.

92. Henry Neville, 1895, p. 149.

93. Herbert Wilcox, 1967, p. 51.

94. Low, 1971, p. 133.

95. *Daily Mail*, 18 August 1926, SC/SC.

96. Michael Balcon, 1969, p. 26.

97. In an interview with Low (1971, p. 167), A. V. Bramble claimed that Gainsborough was founded on Cutts's work, while there is evidence in the trade press of the respect with which he was regarded by the industry. Low also suggests that Wilcox suppressed his debt to Cutts (p. 133).

98. *Kinematograph Weekly*, 1 June 1922, p. 56.

99. Ibid., 13 March 1924, CB/SC.

100. Ibid., 22 October 1925, p. 44.

101. Unidentified clipping, 1 November 1923, CB/SC.

102. *Westminster Gazette*, 8 February 1924, CB/SC.

103. *Evening Standard*, 21 August 1926, SC/SC.

104. See the organisation and publicity material of Hitchcock's Pordonone and National Film Theatre centenary retrospectives, 2000.

105. *Kinematograph Weekly*, 23 July 1925, p. 49; *Daily News*, 1 December 1926, SC/SC.

106. See *Picture Show*, 1 July 1922, CB/CB: 'I expect . . . readers will be thrilled by the news that "Cocaine" was banned by the censor. Of course, Hilda Bayley was the dope fiend, the woman led astray into the land of darkness. There are few actresses . . . who can play such a realistic part and yet keep the sympathy of the audience.' Is Edith Nepean writing tongue in cheek? See also *Kinematograph Weekly*, 11 May 1922, p. 64, and 6 July 1922, p. 51, on the rerelease, retitled, *While London Sleeps*: 'To the ordinary man there was nothing to give offence before.' Also, *The Bioscope*, 6 July 1922, p. 56: 'the

story is somewhat frank melodrama with the perils of dancing painted in lurid colours'.

107. *Kinematograph Weekly*, 1 June 1922, p. 56.
108. Ibid., 16 November 1922, p. 51.
109. *The Picturegoer*, August 1927, p. 17.
110. *Daily Mail*, 18 August 1926, SC/SC.
111. *Westminster Gazette*, 11 September 1926, SC/SC.
112. *The Bioscope*, 13 August 1925, p. 53.
113. See *Westminster Gazette*, 7 July 1926, SC/SC; *Morning Post*, 10 July 1926, SC/SC; *The Star*, 11 September 1926, SC/SC; *Kinematograph Weekly*, 9 September 1926, p. 52; *The Bioscope*, 9 September 1926, p. 36.
114. *Theatre World*, February 1925, p. 29.
115. Ibid., October 1925, p. 39.
116 *Daily Mail*, 18 August 1926, SC/SC.
117. *The Star*, 11 September 1926, SC/SC.
118. Low, 1971, pp. 167–8.
119. *Kinematograph* Weekly, 1 June 1922, p. 56.
120. *Westminster Gazette*, 11 September 1926, SC/SC.
121. *Birmingham Dispatch*, 20 February 1924, SB/SC.
122. Low, 1971, p. 168.
123. *The Bioscope*, 18 February 1926, p. 44. Hitchcock was to attempt to undermine the Balfour ebullience two years later in *Champagne*.
124. This NFTVA Dutch-titled print is missing its last reel, but is otherwise well worth viewing.
125. Meisel, 1983, p. 368.
126. Barr, 1986, p. 17.
127. Michael Allen, 1999.

5 – CLASS ACTS: GENRES, MODES AND PERFORMERS

1. Rachael Low, 1971.
2. See Andrew Higson and Richard Maltby (eds), 1999.
3. Denis Gifford, 2000.
4. Michael Williams, 2001.
5. See Steve Neale 1990; Christine Gledhill 2000.
6. See Mrs Forbes-Robertson, reported in the *Newcastle Clarion*, 27 August 1926, SC/SC; Basil Dean in *The Stage*, 3 February 1927, p. 17; and W. A. Darlington, 1950, pp. 316–20.
7. Desmond MacCarthy, 1954, pp. 15 and 19.
8. *Kinematograph* Weekly, 5 May 1920, p. 109.
9. See Chapter 3, note 147.
10. The impact of pantomime on certain strands of British film-making has been extensively researched by Jonathon Burrows (2000 and 2002a).
11. See Phyllis Hartnoll (ed.), 1985, pp. 621–2 and 639.
12. *Pictures – The Screen Magazine*, March 1922, p. 57.
13. According to the *Kinematograph Weekly* synopsis, 25 October 1923, p. 62. *The Bioscope* records that special music was supplied by De Groot, mentioned in Chapter 1 (18 October 1923, p. 52).
14. For example, Frank Benson, Herbert Tree, Ellen Terry and John Martin-Harvey.
15. Matheson Lang, 1940, pp. 76 and 82–3.
16. Low, 1971, p. 262.
17. The *Daily News* 1924 British Film Stars Competition records Lang as the most popular male star (11 April 1924, BB/SC; see also Peter Noble, 1951, p. 115). Sidney Bernstein's 1927 international star poll showed that for women Lang came fourth and for men fifth (unidentified cutting, BB/SC). *Picturegoer's* 1928 International Star Popularity Competition lists Lang fourth (Noble, 1951, p. 136). A correspondent's challenge to readers of *Film Weekly* to name twenty stars to match America's put Lang in sixteenth position, while a reader writes: 'John Barrymore . . . leaves me cold. We can produce as fine a character actor – Matheson Lang' (14 January 1929, p. 5). The *Northern Evening Dispatch* critic writes that 'although a brilliant stage actor, Mr Lang soon adapted himself to film technique and I have not yet seen an American leading man who can equal him in character portrayals' (18 February 1929, BB/SC). The *Daily Mirror*, explaining the concept of a bankable star, lists Matheson Lang as one of only six British stars in this category – the others are Ivor Novello, Betty Balfour, Mabel Poulton, Estelle Brody and Henry Edwards. Jameson Thomas is tipped to join them (18 February 1929, BB/SC).
18. J. C. Trewin et al., 1958, p. 13.
19. *Manchester Guardian*, 13 April 1948 (BFI personality microfiche).
20. Trewin et al., 1958, p. 13.
21. See *The Motion Picture Studio*, 2 February 1924, p. 8.
22. *Kinematograph Weekly*, 1 December 1921, p. 63.
23. Ibid., 1 January 1923, p. 58.
24. *The Motion Picture Studio*, 14 July 1923, p. 10.
25. *Kinematograph Weekly*, 1 January 1923, p. 58.
26. *Pictures and the Picturegoer*, February 1924, p. 40.
27. *The Sphere*, 10 July 1926, SC/SC. See Sue Harper (1994) for extended discussion of the continuation of this debate in British cultural politics and of its impact on British film-making.
28. *Evening News*, September 1926, SC/SC.

29. *Kinematograph Weekly*, 1 March 1923, p. 58.
30. Ibid., 23 June 1921, p. 25. These comments are made about the imperial saga, *The Broken Road*.
31. Lilian Bamburg, *c.* 1927, p. 98.
32. *The Picturegoer*, January 1929, p. 62.
33. Sue Harper, 1987, p. 174, and 1994, p. 1.
34. Lang, 1940, p. 85.
35. *The Bioscope*, 23 October 1919, supp., pp. iv–v.
36. Ibid.
37. Low, 1971, p. 262.
38. Lang, 1940, p. 112.
39. *Stoll's Editorial News*, 17 July 1919, p. 1.
40. *The Cinema*, reprinted in *Stoll's Editorial News*, 23 October 1919, p. 3.
41. *Kinematograph Weekly*, reprinted in *Stoll's Editorial News*, 17 July 1919, p. 4.
42. Harold Wimbury, *Stoll's Editorial News*, 17 July 1919, p. 4.
43. Trewin et al., 1958, p. 13.
44. Ibid.
45. For example, *The Bioscope* reviewer quoted in Chapter 3 responding to St John Ervine's attack on impassive English actresses (8 July 1926, p. 49).
46. *The Picturegoer*, June 1927, p. 9.
47. *The Motion Picture Studio*, 24 June 1922, p. 13.
48. *Evening Standard*, 20 July 1926, SC/SC. There is an echo here of Walter Scott's complaint quoted in Chapter 3.
49. Respectively, *The Referee*, 11 July 1926, SC/SC, and *Daily News*, 10 July 1926, SC/SC. See also Chapter 3, notes 15, 16 and 17.
50. *The Motion Picture Studio*, 3 June 1922, p. 15. The Melville Brothers were 'for 25 years joint proprietors of the Lyceum where they produced annually a spectacular pantomime', and 'were also successful writers of highly coloured melodramas, simple, direct stories with virtue triumphant' (Hartnoll (ed.), 1985, p. 540).
51. *The Motion Picture Studio*, 3 June 1922, p. 6.
52. *The Referee*, 5 December 1926, SC/SC.
53. *The Bioscope*, 28 June 1917, p. 1296.
54. *Evening News*, 20 July 1926, SC/SC.
55. Attacking the play *What Money Can Buy* (1923), James Agate writes: 'Now I take it that the good ship Melodrama may sail what outrageous waters she please provided she steer clear of the snag of silliness . . . Be it noted that melodrama is, in all soberness and not in mockery, to be accounted a good ship. Only she must be stageworthy' (1924b,

pp. 257–8). Similarly, Shaw's attack on *True Blue* (1896) begins: 'I am often told by people who never go to the theatre that they like melodramas, because they are so funny. Those who do go know better than that. A melodrama must either succeed as a melodrama or else fail with the uttermost ignominies of tedium' (in George Rowell [ed.], 1971, p. 215).
56. *The Bioscope*, 6 May 1920, p. 60. 'Transpontine' refers to the Surrey, and therefore working-class, side of the Thames.
57. Noble, 1951, p. 114.
58. *Yorkshire Post*, 4 October 1926, SC/SC.
59. *The Bioscope*, 26 November 1914, p. 913, reviewing *Her Luck in London* (1914).
60. Harry Rowson, ' "Ideals" of Wardour Street', unpublished autobiography, HR/SC.
61. Low, 1971, p. 119.
62. Frustratingly, both films are lost, existing only in their enthusiastic reviews. See besides references below, *The People*, 11 February 1923, CB/SC, and *The Sketch*, 21 February 1923, CB/SC.
63. *Kinematograph Weekly*, 23 August 1923, CB/SC; *Grimsby* Telegraph, 1 April 1924, CB/SC. *Out to Win* was a stage success through 'the torrid summer of 1921' (*News of the World*, 6 January 1924, CB/SC) and a newspaper serial before that (*Westminster Gazette*, 18 August 1923, CB/SC).
64. *The Film Renter*, 11 September 1923, CB/SC.
65. *The Cinema*, 8 February 1923, CB/SC.
66. *The Studio*, 10 February 1923, CB/SC.
67. *Westminster Gazette*, 18 August 1923, CB/SC.
68. *Kinematograph Weekly*, 23 August 1923, CB/SC.
69. *The Motion Picture Studio*, 25 August 1923, CB/SC.
70. *The Film Renter*, 5 January 1924, CB/SC.
71. Ibid.
72. *The Motion Picture Studio*, 25 August 1923, CB/SC.
73. Ibid., 17 November 1923, CB/SC.
74. See note 56.
75. *The Bioscope*, 1 December 1927, p. 44.
76. Low, 1971, p. 153.
77. Daniel Gerould, 1980, pp. 43–8. Such revivals might be serious or 'hammed-up' for laughs.
78. 'It will be recalled that Mr Baughan gave a really impressive performance of Sweeney himself in the Critics' Film at the 1926 Trade Garden Party'. *Kinematograph Weekly*, 5 April 1928, p. 24. Baughan uses this experience to advise film-makers in the *Daily News* (14 July 1926, SC/SC).

79. If not so odd a choice, Herbert Thompson, writing a production note for *The Bioscope*, recognises the challenge of modernising melodrama: 'I wonder what the critics will think of the lesser artists who will follow in their footsteps' (8 December 1927, p. 40).

80. *Kinematograph Weekly*, 5 April 1928, p. 24.

81. See Gerould, 'Toddography', 1980, p. 46. Anne Cox reported at the 5th British Silent Film Event at Nottingham Broadway, 2002, that George Dare, in whose company she acted, was still touring with *Sweeney Todd* and other melodramas through East Anglia in the 1950s.

82. At this point, the NFTVA print is badly damaged by nitrate burns.

83. Louis James, 1974, p. 190.

84. See David Mayer, 2002, pp. 26–33.

85. *Kinematograph Weekly*, 10 November 1921, p. 67.

86. In British films, colonial postings, while they freeze time, also bring about a dissolution of white masculinity – for example, in *The Broken Road* (1921), *A Romance of Old Baghdad* (1922), *The Pleasure Garden* (1926), *One Colombo Night* (1926), *The Blue Peter* (1929) and *The First Born* (1928).

87. See Robert Colls and Philip Dodd, 1985, pp. 22–3.

88. *Illustrated London Chronicle*, 22 March 1924, CB/SC.

89. The roles of the two tailors are similarly inflected and developed with comic irony in *General Post* (1920), a film also attuned to shifting class identities attending the First World War, if different in outcome.

90. The *Nottingham Weekly Guardian* reported that the filming of returning troops at Waterloo brought crowds out to participate in this 'recrudescence of history' (14 April 1924, CB/SC).

91. See David Mayer, 2001, pp. 21–7; Michael Sanderson, 1984, pp. 120–30; Burrows, 2000, pp. 283–91.

92. Sanderson, 1984, p. 118.

93. See Michael Chanan, 1980; Andy Medhust, 1986; Richard Dacre, 2001.

94. *The Cinema*, 6 October 1921, p. 17, CB/SC.

95. George Pearson, 1957, p. 95.

96. Ibid.

97. Pearson notebooks, GP/SC.

98. The stardom of Gracie Fields and Diana Dors is similarly grounded.

99. An unidentified clipping, dated 11 April 1924 in the Betty Balfour Special Collection, names her 'Britain's Queen of Happiness'. *Picture Show*, 9 June 1928, BB/SC, prints a reader's poem that begins, 'B is for Betty and B is for Balfour' and ends, 'B is for Beautiful, British and Best'. See Kenton Bamford (1999) for an appreciative chapter on Betty Balfour.

100. For the text of her British Film Weeks broadcast, see *The Bioscope*, 31 January 1924, pp. 34b–34c. For press reports of her holding foreign producers at bay, see: *The Picturegoer*, June 1926, p. 52; *Morning Post*, 31 July 1926, SC/SC; *Westminster Gazette*, 15 October 1927, BB/SC; *Daily News*, 15 January 1927, BB/SC – where she is reported as saying: 'I am a British film artist . . . I don't want to deprive 1000s of film-goers in England who support British films of my services.'

6 – THE STORIES BRITISH CINEMA TELLS

1. *Stoll's Editorial News*, 5 August 1920, p. 7.

2. *The Motion Picture Studio*, 20 August 1921, p. 5. See also 25 June 1921, p. 5 and 17 February 1923, p. 6.

3. *The Picturegoer*, February 1921, p. 62.

4. *The Yorkshire Weekly Post*, 2 October 1926, SC/SC.

5. *Daily Express*, 2 July 1926, SC/SC.

6. *The Bioscope*, 1 December 1927, p. 41.

7. Ibid., 18 June 1927, p. 153.

8. G. K. Chesterton, assigning 'stories of a rowdy or romantic sort' to cinema while preserving for literature those of a 'subtle and intellectual' kind, claims that 'no form of art can replace any other form of art'. Extract from *The Illustrated London News* reprinted in *Stolls' Editorial News*, 1 July 1920, p. 2.

9. *The Motion Picture Studio*, 21 October 1922, p. 13.

10. *Picture Show*, 24 January 1925, CB/SC.

11. *Stoll's Editorial News*, 29 January 1920, p. 13.

12. *The Bioscope*, 18 June 1927, p. 153.

13. *Stoll's Editorial News*, 5 August 1920, p. 7.

14. Brian McFarlane, 1986, p. 134.

15. Jane Bryan, 2003.

16. *Kinematograph Weekly*, 14 October 1920, pp. 50–2.

17. *Picture Show*, 1 July 1922, p. 19, CB/SC.

18. *The Motion Picture Studio*, 17 February 1923, p. 6.

19. *The Bioscope*, 8 February 1923, p. 71.

20. *The Motion Picture Studio*, 17 February 1923, p. 6.

21. Ibid., pp. 6 and 11.

22. Jon Burrows, 2002b.

23. *The Bioscope*, 21 February 1921, CB/SC.

24. *Kinematograph Weekly*, 1 January 1925, p. 68.

25. *The Bioscope*, 30 October 1919, p. 59.
26. *Stoll's Editorial News*, 14 August 1919, pp. 5–6.
27. *The Cinema*, 19 May 1921, CB/SC.
28. *Pictures and the Picturegoer*, 17 March 1917, p. 513.
29. *Stoll's Editorial News*, 14 August 1914, p. 5.
30. *Kinematograph Weekly*, 6 May 1920, p. 93.
31. *Stoll's Editorial News*, 5 August 1920, pp. 7–8.
32. Ibid., 14 August 1919, p. 6.
33. *Kinematograph Weekly*, 11 March 1920, pp. 34–5.
34. *Stoll's Editorial News*, 13 May 1920, p. 5. Similar points are made by Kenelm Foss in *The Picturegoer*, April 1921, p. 49, and by *Kinematograph Weekly*, 15 April 1920, p. 154.
35. *Pictures and the Picturegoer*, December 1923, p. 43.
36. *Stoll's Editorial News*, 13 May 1920, p. 5.
37. *Around the Town*, 5 January 1923, CB/SC.
38. *Kinematograph Weekly*, 19 June 1924, p. 68.
39. *The Motion Picture Studio*, 20 August 1921, p. 5.
40. Ibid., 6 January 1923, p. 10.
41. *The Author*, July 1926, SC/SC.
42. *The Bioscope*, 1 July 1920, supp., p. viii.
43. Ibid. *Kinematograph Weekly* declares: 'It is America . . . which realises that . . . the soul of a photoplay resides in its scenario', 1 April 1920, p. 83. See also: *Kinematograph and Lantern Weekly*, 12 July 1917, p. 76; *Kinematograph Weekly*, 24 November 1921, p. 68; *The Bioscope*, 28 June 1927, p. 155.
44. *The Motion Picture Studio*, 5 November 1921, p. 7.
45. *Stoll's Editorial News*, 3 June 1920, p. 2.
46. *Sunday Express*, 22 April 1923, CB/SC.
47. *Daily Express*, 2 July 1926, SC/SC, and *Sunday Express*, 4 July 1926, SC/SC.
48. *The Motion Picture Studio*, 30 July 1921, p. 8.
49. Ibid., 17 June 1922, p. 6.
50. *Spectator*, 7 August 1926, SC/SC.
51. Ibid.
52. Ibid.
53. *Sunday Express*, 4 July 1926, SC/SC.
54. *Spectator*, 7 August 1926, SC/SC.
55. *The Bioscope*, 6 May 1920, p. 60.
56. *The Motion Picture Studio*, 31 December 1921, p. 14.
57. Ibid., 12 August 1922, p. 10.
58. For example, John Everett Millais's, *The Boyhood of Raleigh* (1870) and Daniel Maclise's *A Winter Night's Tale* (c. 1867). More contemporary examples are found in the Royal Academy's wartime exhibitions: e.g. Andrew Gow's *The Survivor's Story* (1917) or Septimus Power's *A Canteen: Some Story* (1918).
59. Denis Gifford, 2000.
60. Martin Meisel, 1983, p. 32.
61. David Peters Corbett, 1997, pp. 32–8.
62. Minerva Films publicity brochure, AB/SC.
63. Jackie Wullschlager, 1995, p. 181.
64. Adrian Brunel, 1949, p. 61.
65. *The Motion Picture Studio*, 6 January 1923, p. 10.
66. *Kinematograph Weekly*, 1 December 1921, p. 65.
67. Ibid., 1 April 1920, p. 94.
68. *The Motion Picture Studio*, 30 July 1921, pp. 6–7.
69. Ibid., 23 July 1921, p. 6.
70. *Kinematograph Weekly*, 1 June 1922, p. 56.
71. Herbert Wilcox, 1967, pp. 26–7.
72. Rachael Low, 1971, p. 147.
73. *Stoll's Editorial News*, 13 May 1920, p. 5.
74. This moment is repeated with similar aesthetic and ideological effects thirty-odd years later in *Sapphire* (1957).
75. *The Motion Picture Studio*, 13 August 1921, p. 5.
76. *The Bioscope*, 18 June 1927, p. 156.
77. Wullschlager, 1995.
78. *Stoll's Editorial News*, 15 April, 1920 p. 5.
79. *The Bioscope*, 1 November 1923, p. 73.
80. J. C. Trewin et al., 1958, p. 3.
81. Brunel, 1949, pp. 91–101.
82. Ibid., pp. 91–2.
83. Brunel preferred the more comedy-likely title, *It Happened in Venice*, but was overruled by his production team (ibid., p. 91).
84. For a complex exploration of these links in Novello's star image, see Michael Williams, 2001.
85. Dorothy Richardson, 1998, p. 160.
86. Iris Barry, 1926, pp. 8–9.
87. Ibid., pp. 55–6
88. Ibid., pp. 31–2.
89. Ibid., pp. 53–4.
90. Ibid., p. 54.
91. Pressbook for *Réveille*, p. 1, GP/SC.
92. George Pearson, 1957, p. 140.
93. Pressbook for *The Little People*, GP/SC.
94. Pearson, 1957, p. 143.
95. Pressbook for *The Little People*, GP/SC.
96. Pearson notebooks, GP/SC.
97. Wullschlager, 1995, Chapter 6.
98. *The Bioscope*, 17 May 1928, p. 37; *Kinematograph Weekly*, 3 May 1928, p. 47.
99. My thanks to David Mayer for pointing this out to me.

100. Although this role is already imaged as part of French culture in Ivor Novello's *Downhill* and Hitchcock's film of that play.

IN CONCLUSION: THE CULTURAL POETICS OF BRITISH CINEMA

1. The concept is developed by Tom Gunning, 1990, pp. 56–62.
2. Nerina Shute, 1973, pp. 27–32.
3. *The Picturegoer*, March 1921, p. 7.
4. *Kinematograph Weekly*, 1 April 1920, p. 83.
5. *The Picturegoer*, February 1921, pp. 12–13.
6. Ibid., April 1921, p. 49.
7. *Sunday Express*, 23 April 1923, CB/SC.
8. George Pearson, 1957, p. 140.
9. Iris Barry, 1926, p. 53.
10. Christopher Williams, 1996, pp. 191–3; Charles Barr, 1986, pp. 1–29.
11. Andy Medhurst (1986), quoted in Barr, p. 25.

Filmography

This filmography lists all films mentioned in the text. Information includes trade-show date, production company and director. Country of origin is British, unless otherwise indicated. First names are included for first director entry, and surnames thereafter. Films for which there is some extended discussion or analysis are shown in bold. Most of the titles listed for the 1920s may be viewed in the National Film and Television Archive, although some prints may be damaged, incomplete or fragmentary.

Alf's Button, 1920, Hepworth Manufacturing Co., Cecil Hepworth

The Apache, 1925, Millar-Thompson, Adelqui Millar

At the Villa Rose, 1920, Stoll, Maurice Elvey

Battling Bruisers, 1925, Gainsborough Burlesques, Adrian Brunel

The Bargain, 1921, Hepworth Manufacturing Co., Henry Edwards

The Beloved Vagabond, 1923, Astra-National, Fred LeRoy Granville

The Bigamist, 1921, George Clark Productions, Guy Newall

The Big Parade, 1926, USA, MGM, King Vidor

Billy Elliot, 2000, Tiger Aspect Productions, Stephen Daldry

The Blackguard, 1925, Gainsborough/UFA, Graham Cutts

Black Narcissus, 1947, Archers Film Productions, Michael Powell and Emeric Pressburger

Bleak House, 1920, Stoll, Elvey

Blighty, 1927, Gainsborough, Brunel

The Blue Peter, 1929, British Filmcraft, Arthur Rooke

Boadicea, 1926, Stoll, Sinclair Hill

The Bohemian Girl, 1922, Alliance, Harley Knoles

Bookworms, 1920, Minerva Films, Brunel

Brassed Off, 1996, Prominent Features, Mark Herman

Brief Encounter, 1945, Cineguild, David Lean

The Broken Road, 1921, Stoll, René Plaisetty

The Bump, 1920, Minerva Films, Brunel

The Call of the Blood, 1920, France, Louis Mercanton

Call of the Road, 1920, I. B. Davidson, A. E. Coleby

Carnival, 1921, Alliance, Knoles

Champagne, 1928, BIP, Alfred Hitchcock

Christie Johnston, 1921, Broadwest, Norman McDonald

Cocaine, 1922, Master Films (Astra), Cutts

Comin' thro' the Rye, 1923, Hepworth Manufacturing Co., Hepworth

The Company of Wolves, 1984, Palace Productions, Neil Jordan

Comrades, 1989, Skreba/NFFC/FilmFour, Bill Douglas

Comradeship, 1919, Stoll, Elvey

Daniel Deronda, 1921, Master, W. Courtenay Rowden

A Daughter of Love, 1925, Stoll, Walter West

Decameron Nights, 1924, Graham-Wilcox, Herbert Wilcox

The Devil, 1921, Phillips Film Company, James Young

Don Quixote, 1923, Stoll, Elvey

Downhill, 1927, Gainsborough, Hitchcock

Duke's Son, 1920, George Clark Productions, Franklin Dyall

East Is East, 1916, Turner Film Company, Edwards

Easy Virtue, 1927, Gainsborough, Hitchcock

Educating Rita, 1983, Acorn Pictures, Lewis Gilbert

The Elusive Pimpernel, 1920, Stoll, Elvey

The Face at the Window, 1920, British Actors Film Company, Wilfred Noy

The Fallen Idol, 1913, Motograph Film Co., Elvey
The Farmer's Wife, 1928, BIP, Hitchcock
The First Born, 1928, Gainsborough, Miles Mander
The Flag Lieutenant, 1926, Astra-National, Elvey
Flames of Passion, 1922, Graham-Wilcox, Cutts
Florence Nightingale, 1915, British & Colonial
  Kinematograph Co., Elvey
Four Men in a Van, 1921, Direct, Hugh Croise
Fox Farm, 1922, George Clark Productions, Newall
The Full Monty, 1997, Redwave Films Production,
  Peter Cattaneo

The Garden of Resurrection, 1919, George Clark
  Productions, Rooke
General Post, 1920, Ideal, Thomas Bentley
The Ghost Train, 1927, Gainsborough, Geza Von
  Bolvary
A Girl of London, 1925, Stoll, Edwards
The Glorious Adventure, 1922, J. Stuart Blackton
  Photoplays, J. Stuart Blackton
God's Good Man, 1919, Stoll, Elvey
The Great Gold Robbery, 1913, Motograph Film
  Co., Elvey
The Green Goddess, 1923, USA, MGM, Sidney
  Olcott
Guns at Loos, 1928, Stoll, Hill

Henry V, 1944, Two Cities, Laurence Olivier
Her Luck in London, 1914, B&C, Elvey
High Hopes, 1988, Portman Productions, Mike
  Leigh
High Treason, 1929, Gaumont, Elvey
Hindle Wakes, 1927, Gaumont-British, Elvey
A Honeymoon for Three, 1915, B&C, Elvey
The Hound of the Baskervilles, 1921, Stoll, Elvey
The House of Peril, 1922, Astra, Kenelm Foss
Human Law, 1926, Astra-National, Elvey

If Youth But Knew, 1926, G. B. Samuelson, George
  Cooper

Justice, 1917, Ideal, Elvey

Kitty, 1928, Gaumont, Victor Saville

Lady Audley's Secret, 1920, Ideal, Jack Denton
Lady Clare, 1919, British Actors Film Company, Noy
Land and Freedom, 1995, UK/Spain/Germany,
  Parallax Pictures, Ken Loach

The Life Story of David Lloyd George, 1918, Ideal,
  Elvey
The Little People, 1926, Welsh-Pearson, George
  Pearson
The Lodger, 1926, Gainsborough, Hitchcock
London Love, 1926, Gaumont, Manning Haynes
The Loss of the Birkenhead, 1914, B&C, Elvey
Love, Life and Laughter, 1923, Welsh-Pearson,
  Pearson
The Lure of Crooning Water, 1920, George Clark
  Productions, Rooke
The Lyons Mail, 1917, Ideal, Fred Paul

Madame Pompadour, 1928, British International
  Pictures, Wilcox
Mademoiselle d'Armentières, 1926, Gaumont, Elvey
Maid of the Silver Sea, 1922, George Clark
  Productions, Newall
The Man Who Forgot, 1919, Harma, F. Martin
  Thornton
The Man Without Desire, 1923, Atlas Biocraft,
  Brunel
Man, Woman, Marriage, 1921, USA, First National,
  Allen Holubar
The Manxman, 1929, BIP, Hitchcock
Mr Wu, 1919, Stoll, Elvey
Monkey's Paw, 1923, Artistic, Haynes
Monte Carlo, 1925, Gaumont-Phocea, Mercanton
My Beautiful Laundrette, 1985, Working Title,
  Stephen Frears

Narrow Valley, 1921, Hepworth Manufacturing
  Co., Hepworth
Nell Gwynne, 1926, British National, Wilcox
Nelson, 1918, International Exclusives, Elvey
Nobody's Child, 1919, B&C, G. Edwardes Hall
No. 5 John Street, 1921, Astra, Foss
Nothing Else Matters, 1920, Welsh-Pearson,
  Pearson

Once Upon a Time in the Midlands, 2002, Big Arty,
  Shane Meadows
One Columbo Night, 1926, Stoll, Edwards
The Only Way, 1925, Graham-Wilcox, Wilcox
Out to Win, 1923, Ideal, Denison Clift

Paddy-the-Next-Best-Thing, 1923, Graham-Wilcox,
  Cutts
Palais de Danse, 1928, Gaumont, Elvey

Paradise, 1928, BIP, Clift

The Passionate Adventure, 1924, Gainsborough, Cutts

Passionate Friends, 1921, Stoll, Elvey

Piccadilly, 1929, BIP, E. A. Dupont

The Pipes of Pan, 1923, Hepworth Manufacturing Co., Hepworth

The Pleasure Garden, 1926, Gainsborough/Emelka, Hitchcock

The Prodigal Son, 1923, Stoll, Coleby

The Prude's Fall, 1924, Gainsborough, Cutts

The Queen Was in the Parlour, 1927, Gainsborough, Cutts

The Rat, 1925, Gainsborough, Cutts

The Return of the Prodigal, 1923, Stoll, Coleby

The Return of the Rat, 1929, Gainsborough, Cutts

Réveille, 1924, Welsh-Pearson, Pearson

The Reverse of the Medal, 1923, Quality Plays/Gaumont, Cooper

The Ring, 1927, BIP, Hitchcock

Rob Roy, 1922, Gaumont, Will Kellino

The Rocks of Valpre, 1919, Stoll, Elvey

A Romance of Old Baghdad, 1922, H. W. Thompson, Foss

A Romance of Wastedale, 1921, Stoll, Elvey

The Royal Oak, 1923, Stoll, Elvey

Sapphire, 1959, Artna Films, Basil Dearden

The Sea Urchin, 1926, Gainsborough, Cutts

Second to None, 1926, Britannia, Dinah Shurey

She, 1925, G. B. Samuelson, Leander de Cordova

Shooting Stars, 1928, British Instructional Films, Anthony Asquith

The Sign of the Four, 1923, Stoll, Elvey

Squibs, 1921, Welsh-Pearson, Pearson

Squibs Wins the Calcutta Sweep, 1922, Welsh-Pearson, Pearson

Sweeney Todd, 1928, OTS Productions/Ideal, West

Tansy, 1921, Hepworth Manufacturing Co., Hepworth

Testimony, 1920, George Clark Productions, Newall

The Thief of Bagdad, 1925, USA, Douglas Fairbanks Picture Corporation, Raoul Walsh

This Freedom, 1923, Ideal, Clift

Through Fire and Water, 1923, Ideal, Bentley

The Triumph of the Rat, 1926, Gainsborough, Cutts

Underground, 1928, British Instructional Films, Asquith

The Unknown Soldier, 1926, USA, Charles R. Productions/Renaud Hoffman Productions, Renaud Hoffman

Vaudeville, 1925, Germany, Ufa, Dupont

The Victim, 1917, USA, Fox, Will S. Davis

The Wandering Jew, 1923, Stoll, Elvey

Woman to Woman, 1923, Balcon, Freedman & Saville, Cutts

The Wonderful Story, 1922, Graham-Wilcox, Cutts

The Wonderful Year, 1921, H. W. Thompson, Foss

Young Lochinvar, 1923, Stoll, Kellino

Ypres, 1925, British Instructional Films, Walter Summers

Zeebrugge, 1924, British Instructional Films, H. Bruce Woolfe and A. V. Bramble

Sources and Select Bibliography

BFI SPECIAL COLLECTIONS
Betty Balfour
Clive Brook
Adrian Brunel
Sidney Carroll
George Pearson
Mabel Poulton
Harry Rowson
Victor Saville

JOURNALS OF THE 1910s AND 1920s
The Bioscope
The Cinema
Cinema Chat
The Film Renter
The Film Renter and Moving Picture News
The Film Weekly
The Kinematograph and Lantern Weekly
Kinematograph Weekly
Kine Year Books
The Motion Picture Studio
The Picturegoer
Pictures and the Picturegoer
Picture Show
Pictures – the Screen Magazine
The Royal Academy Illustrated
The Stage
Stoll's Editorial News
Theatre World
Variety

References to newspapers and general interest magazines are largely derived from the scrapbooks of key players housed in BFI Special Collections, or from reprints in *Stoll's Editorial News*.

SELECT BIBLIOGRAPHY
Since a comprehensive bibliography for the early period of British cinema to 1930 has been constructed for Andrew Higson's *Young and Innocent? The Cinema in Britain 1896–1930*, what is listed here represents all books and articles mentioned in the course of this study.

Agate, James (1924a), 'A Private Show', in *On an English Screen* (London: John Lane/The Bodley Head).
—— (1924b), *The Contemporary Theatre, 1923* (London: Leonard Parsons).
—— (1925), *The Contemporary Theatre, 1924* (London: Chapman & Hall).
—— (1926), *The Contemporary Theatre, 1925* (London: Chapman & Hall).
—— (1927), *The Contemporary Theatre, 1926* (London: Chapman & Hall).
Aherne, Brian (1969), *A Proper Job: The Autobiography of an Actor's Art* (Boston: Houghton Mifflin).
Alderson, Frederick (1970), *The Comic Postcard in English Life* (Newton Abbot, Devon: David Charles).
Allen, Michael (1999), *Family Secrets: The Films of D. W. Griffith* (London: BFI).
Archer, William (1886), *About the Theatre: Essays and Studies* (London: T. Fisher Unwin).
—— (1888), *Masks or Faces? A Study in the Psychology of Acting* (London: Longmans, Green, & Co.).
—— (1923), *The Old Drama and the New: An Essay in Re-Valuation* (London: William Heinemann).
Balcon, Michael (1969), *Michael Balcon Presents . . . A Lifetime of Films* (London: Hutchinson).
Bamburg, Lilian (1927), *Film Acting As a Career* (London: W. Foulsham & Co.).
Bamford, Kenton (1999), *Distorted Images: British National Identity and Film in the 1920s* (London: I. B. Tauris).
Barr, Charles (1977), *Ealing Studios* (London and Newton Abbot, Devon: Cameron & Tayleur/David & Charles).

—— (1986), 'Amnesia and Schizophrenia', in Barr (ed.), *All Our Yesterdays* (London: BFI).

—— (2002), 'Writing Screen Plays: Stannard and Hitchcock', in A. Higson (ed.), *Young and Innocent? The Cinema in Britain 1896–1930* (Exeter: University of Exeter Press).

Barry, Iris (1926), *Let's Go to the Pictures* (London: Chatto & Windus).

Berry, David, and Horrocks, Simon (eds) (1998), *David Lloyd George: The Movie Mystery* (Cardiff: University of Wales Press).

Booth, Michael (1981), *Victorian Spectacular Theatre: 1850–1910* (London: Routledge & Kegan Paul).

Bouchier, Chili (1995), *Shooting Star: The Last of the Silent Film Stars* (London: Atlantis).

Boucicault, Dion (1926), *The Art of Acting* in Dramatic Museum of Columbia University *Papers on Acting 1*, fifth series, no. 1 (New York: Columbia University Press).

Bowker, R. R. (ed.) (1983), *Variety's Film Reviews, 1921–1925* (New York: Reed Publishing).

Brook, Clive (*c.* 1970), *The Eighty Four Ages* (unpublished autobiography, Item no. 38, CB/SC).

Brooks, Peter (1976), *The Melodramatic Imagination: Balzac, Henry James, Melodrama, and the Mode of Excess* (New Haven, CT: Yale University Press).

Brunel, Adrian (1949), *Nice Work: The Story of Thirty Years in British Film Production* (London: Forbes Robertson).

Burrows, Jonathan (2000), *'The Whole English Stage to Be Seen for Sixpence!' Theatrical Actors and Acting Styles in British Cinema 1908–1918* (Norwich: unpublished PhD thesis, University of East Anglia).

Burrows, Jon (2002a), 'It Would Be a Mistake to Strive for Subtlety of Effect': Richard III and Populist, Pantomime Shakespeare in the 1910s', in A. Higson (ed.), *Young and Innocent? The Cinema in Britain 1896–1930* (Exeter: University of Exeter Press).

—— (2002b), 'The Mark of Caine on British Cinema, 1915–1929' unpublished paper given at the Fifth British Silent Cinema Weekend: 'Scene Stealing: Investigating British Silent Cinema and its Sources', Broadway, Nottingham, April 2002.

—— (2003), *Legitimate Cinema: Theatre Stars in Silent British Films 1908–1918* (Exeter: University of Exeter Press).

Bryan, Jane (2003), 'From Film Stars to Film Stories: The Beginnings of the Fan Magazine in Britain', in A. Burton and L. Porter (eds), *Scene-Stealing: Sources for British Cinema before 1930* (Trowbridge, Wiltshire: Flicks Books).

Carrick, Edward (1972), *Art and Design in the British Film: A Pictorial Directory of British Art Directors* (New York: Arno Press/New York Times).

Chanan, Michael (1980), *The Dream that Kicks* (London: Routledge & Kegan Paul).

Colls, Robert, and Dodd, Philip (1985), 'Representing the Nation: British Documentary Film, 1930–45', *Screen*, vol. 26 no. 1, January/February, pp. 21–33.

Cook, Pam (1996), *Fashioning the Nation: Costume and Identity in British Cinema* (London: BFI).

Coward, Noel (1937), *Present Indicative* (London: William Heinemann).

Dacre, Richard (2001), 'Traditions of British Comedy', in R. Murphy (ed.), *The British Cinema Book* (London: BFI); second edn.

Darlington, W. A. (1950), *I Do What I Like* (London: Rockliff); second edn.

Doré, Gustave, and Jerrold, Blanchard (1872), *London, A Pilgimage* (London: Grant & Co.).

Dyer, Richard (1991), '*A Star is Born* and the Construction of Authenticity', in C. Gledhill (ed.), *Stardom: Industry of Desire* (London: Routledge).

—— (1992), *Only Entertainment* (London: Routledge).

Eisenstein, Sergei (1963), 'Dickens, Griffith and the Film Today', in Eisenstein, *Film Form: Essays in Film Theory* (London: Dennis Dobson).

Elsaesser, Thomas (1987), 'Tales of Sound and Fury: Observations on the Family Melodrama', in C. Gledhill (ed.), *Home Is Where the Heart Is: Studies in Melodrama and the Woman's Film* (London: BFI).

Fenton, James (1990), 'The Evolution of Photographic Lantern Slides', in D. Crompton, D. Henry and S. Herbert (eds), *The Art of Hand-Painted and Photographic Lantern Slides* (London: Magic Lantern Society of Great Britain).

Foss, Kenelm (*c.* 1919), *The Work of the Film Producer*, Lesson 3 of *Cinema: A Practical Course in Ten Lessons* (London: Standard Art Book Company).

—— (1920), *The Dead Pierrot*, with decorations by T. C. Gilson (London: Erskine Macdonald).

Frith, W. P. (1888), *My Autobiography and Reminiscences* (London: Richard Bentley & Son).

Fussell, Paul (1975), *Modern Memory and the Great War* (Oxford: Oxford University Press).

Gernsheim, Helmut, and Gernsheim, Alison (1971), *The History of Photography* (London: Thames & Hudson).

Gerould, Daniel (1980), 'A Toddography', in D. Gerould (ed.), *Melodrama* (New York: New York Forum).

—— (1994), 'Melodrama and Revolution', in J. Bratton, J. Cook and C. Gledhill (eds), *Melodrama: Picture, Stage, Screen* (London: BFI).

Gifford, Denis (1997), 'The Early Memories of Maurice Elvey', *Griffithiana*, nos. 60–1, October, pp. 76–125.

—— (2000), *British Film Catalogue*, vol. 1 (London: Fitzroy Dearbon); third edn.

Gillette, William (1915), *The Illusion of the First Time* (New York: Dramatic Museum of Columbia University).

Gledhill, Christine (ed.) (1987), *Home Is Where the Heart Is: Studies in Melodrama and the Woman's Film* (London: BFI).

—— (1991), 'Signs of Melodrama', in C. Gledhill (ed.), *Stardom: Industry of Desire* (London: Routledge).

—— (1992), 'Between Melodrama and Realism: Anthony Asquith's *Underground* and King Vidor's *The Crowd*', in J. Gaines (ed.), *Classical Hollywood Narrative: The Paradigm Wars* (Durham, NC: Duke University Press).

—— (2000), 'Rethinking Genre', in L. Williams and C. Gledhill (eds), *Reinventing Film Studies* (London: Arnold).

Grein, J. T. (1921), *The World of the Theatre: Impressions and Memoirs, 1920–1921* (London: William Heinemann).

—— (1924), *The New World of the Theatre, 1923–1924* (London: Martin Hopkinson & Co.).

Gunning, Tom (1990), 'The Cinema of Attractions: Early Film, its Spectator and the Avant-Garde',

in T. Elsaesser and A. Barker (eds), *Early Cinema: Space, Frame, Narrative* (London: BFI).

Harper, Sue (1987), 'Historical Pleasures: Gainsborough Costume Melodrama', in C. Gledhill (ed.), *Home Is Where the Heart Is: Studies in Melodrama and the Woman's Film* (London: BFI).

—— (1994), *Picturing the Past: The Rise and Fall of the British Costume Film* (London: BFI).

Hartnoll, Phyllis (ed.) (1985), *The Oxford Companion to the Theatre* (Oxford: Oxford University Press); fourth edn, corrected.

Heard, Mervyn (1996), 'The Magic Lantern's Wild Years', in C. Williams (ed.), *Cinema: The Beginnings and the Future* (London: University of Westminster Press).

Hepworth, Cecil (1951), *Came the Dawn* (London: Phoenix House).

Higson, Andrew (1995), *Waving the Flag: Constructing a National Cinema in Britain* (Oxford: Oxford University Press).

—— (ed.) (1996), *Dissolving Views: Key Writings on British Cinema* (London: Cassell).

—— and Maltby, Richard (eds) (1999), *'Film Europe' and 'Film America'* (Exeter: University of Exeter Press).

—— (2001), 'Figures in a Landscape: The Performance of Englishness in Cecil Hepworth's Tansy (1921)', in A. Burton and L. Porter (eds), *The Showman, the Spectacle and the Two-Minute Silence: Performing British Cinema before 1930* (Trowbridge, Wiltshire: Flicks Books).

—— (ed.) (2002), *Young and Innocent? The Cinema in Britain 1896–1930* (Exeter: University of Exeter Press).

Hopson, Violet (*c.* 1919), *Hints for the Cinema Actress*, Lesson 9 of *Cinema: A Practical Course in Ten Lessons* (London: Standard Art Book Company).

Humphries, Stephen (1989), *Victorian Britain Through the Magic Lantern* (London: Sidgwick & Jackson).

Hunt, Hugh (1978), 'The Social and Literary Context', in H. Hunt, K. Richards and J. Russell Taylor (eds), *The Revels History of Drama in English, Volume VII – 1880 to the Present Day* (London: Methuen).

Hussey, Christopher (1927), *The Picturesque: Studies in A Point of View* (London and New York: G. P. Puttnam).

Inglis, Fred (1990), 'Landscape as Popular Culture', in S. Pugh (ed.), *Reading Landscape: Country – City – Capital* (Manchester: Manchester University Press).

James, Louis (1974), *Fiction for the Working Man 1830–50: A Study of the Literature Produced for the Working Classes in Early Victorian Urban England* (Harmondsworth: Penguin University Books).

—— (1981), 'Was Jerrold's Black Ey'd Susan More Popular than Wordsworth's Lucy?', in D. Bradby, L. James and B. Sharrat (eds), *Performance and Politics in Popular Drama: Aspects of Popular Entertainment in Theatre, Film and Television, 1800–1976* (Cambridge: Cambridge University Press).

Keating, Peter (1976), *Into Unknown England, 1866–1913: Selections from the Social Explorers* (London: Fontana).

Kember, Joe (2001), 'Face-to-Face: The Facial Expressions Genre in Early British Films', in A. Burton and L. Porter (eds), *The Showman, the Spectacle and the Two-Minute Silence: Performing British Cinema before 1930* (Trowbridge, Wiltshire: Flicks Books).

Kuhn, Annette (1996), 'Cinema Culture and Femininity in the 1930s', in C. Gledhill and G. Swanson (eds), *Nationalising Femininity: Culture, Sexuality, and British Cinema in the Second World War* (Manchester: Manchester University Press).

Lambourne, Lionel (1999), *Victorian Painting* (London: Phaidon Press).

Lang, Matheson (1940), *Mr Wu Looks Back: Thoughts and Memories* (London: Stanley Paul & Co.).

Lewes, G. H. (1875), *On Actors and the Art of Acting* (London: Smith, Elder & Co).

Light, Alison (1991), *Forever England: Feminism, Literature and Conservatism Between the Wars* (London: Routledge).

Lore, Colden (1923), *The Modern Photoplay and its Construction* (London: Chapman & Dodd).

Low, Rachael (1950), *The History of the British Film 1914–18* (London: George Allen & Unwin).

—— (1971), *The History of the British Film 1918–28* (London: George Allen & Unwin).

MacBean, L. C. (1922), *Kinematograph Studio Technique* (London: Sir Isaac Pitman & Sons).

MacCarthy, Desmond (1954), *Theatre* (London: Macgibbon & Kee).

McCarthy, Lillah (1933), *Myself and My Friends* (London: Thornton Butterworth).

McDonald, Jan (1986), *The 'New Drama' 1900–1914: Harley Granville-Barker, John Galsworthy, St. John Hankin, John Masefield* (Houndmills, Basingstoke, Hampshire and London: Macmillan).

McFarlane, Brian (1986), 'A Literary Cinema? British Films and British Novels', in C. Barr (ed.), *All Our Yesterdays* (London: BFI).

Martin, G. H., and Francis, David (1978), 'The Camera's Eye', in H. J. Dyos and M. Wolff (eds) (1978), *The Victorian City: Images and Realities*, vol. 1: *Shapes on the Ground and a Change of Accent* (London: Routledge & Kegan Paul).

Martin, Paul (1939), *Victorian Snapshots* (London: Country Life).

Matthews, A. E. (1952), *Matty. An Autobiography* (London: Hutchinson).

Mayer, David (1997), 'Learning to See in the Dark', *Nineteenth Century Theatre*, vol. 25 no. 2, Winter, pp. 92–114.

—— (1999), 'Acting in Silent Film: Which Legacy of the Theatre?', in A. Lovell and P. Kramer (eds), *Screen Acting* (London: Routledge).

—— (2001), 'Eighteen Minutes', in A. Burton and L. Porter (eds), *The Showman, the Spectacle and the Two-Minute Silence: Performing British Cinema before 1930* (Trowbridge, Wiltshire: Flicks Books).

—— (2002), 'Doubles: Lesurques and Dubosc, Jekyll and Hyde, Svengali and Trilby', in A. Burton and L. Porter (eds), *Crossing the Pond: Anglo-American Film Relations before 1930* (Trowbridge, Wiltshire: Flicks Books).

Medhurst, Andy (1986), 'Music Hall and British Cinema', in Charles Barr (ed.), *All Our Yesterdays* (London: BFI).

Meisel, Martin (1983), *Realizations: Narrative, Pictorial and Theatrical Arts in Nineteenth-Century England* (Princeton, NJ: Princeton University Press).

Mercer, Colin (1988), 'Entertainment, or the Policy of Virtue', *New Formations*, no. 4, Spring, pp. 51–73.

Minney, R. J. (1973), *Puffin Asquith: A Biography of the Hon. Anthony Asquith* (London: Frewin).

Morden, Terry (1983), 'The Pastoral and the Pictorial', *Ten:8*, no. 12, pp. 18–25.

Moynahan, Julian (1972), 'Pastoralism as Culture and Counter Culture in English Fiction, 1800–1928: From a View to a Death', *Novel*, vol. 6 no. 1, Autumn.

Mullin, Donald (ed.) (1983), *Victorian Actors and Actresses in Review: A Dictionary of Contemporary Views of Representative British and American Actors and Actresses, 1837–1901* (Westport, CT: Greenwood Press).

Napper, Laurence (2001), 'The Middlebrow, "National Culture" and British Cinema, 1920–1939' (Norwich: unpublished PhD thesis, University of East Anglia).

Nead, Lynda (2002), 'Paintings, Films and Fast Cars: A Case Study of Hubert von Herkomer', *Art History*, vol. 25 no. 2, April, pp. 240–55.

Neale, Steve (1990), 'Questions of Genre', *Screen*, vol. 31 no. 1, Spring, pp. 45–66.

Neville, Henry (1875), *The Stage, its Past and Present in Relation to Fine Art* (London: Richard Bentley & Son).

—— (1895), 'Gesture', in H. Campbell, R. F. Brewer and H. Neville, *Voice, Speech and Gesture: Practical Handbook to the Elocutionary Art* (London: Charles William Deacon & Co.).

Newall, Guy (1924a), *Husband Love* (London: Constable).

—— (1924b), *Husband Love* (Lord Chamberlain's playscript collection, 20–10–24).

Noble, Peter (1951), *Ivor Novello, Man of the Theatre* (London: The Falcon Press); third rev. edn.

Pearson, George (1957), *Flashback* (London: Allen & Unwin).

Peters Corbett, David (1997), *The Modernity of English Art: 1914–30* (Manchester: Manchester University Press).

Pevsner, Nikolaus (1993), *The Englishness of English Art* (London: Penguin).

Pogson, Rex (1952), *Miss Horniman and the Gaiety Theatre, Manchester* (London: Rockliff).

Pollock, Griselda (1988), 'Vicarious Excitements: *London: A Pilgrimage* by Gustave Doré and Blanchard Jerrold, 1872', *New Formations*, no. 4, Spring.

Postlewait, Thomas (1997), 'From Melodrama to Realism: The Suspect History of American Drama', in Michael Hays and Anastasia Nikolopoulou (eds), *Melodrama, The Cultural Emergence of a Genre* (New York: St Martin's Press).

Rede, Leman Thomas (1827), *The Road to the Stage; or, the Performer's Preceptor* (London: Joseph Smith).

Richardson, Dorothy (1998), 'Continuous Performance', in J. Donald, A. Friedberg and L. Marcus (eds), *Close Up: Cinema and Modernism* (London: Cassell).

Robinson, Henry Peach (1896), *The Elements of a Pictorial Photograph* (Bradford, Yorkshire: Percy Lund & Co. The Country Press).

Rome, Stewart (*c.* 1919), 'The Value of Specialisation', Lesson 7 of *Cinema: A Practical Course in Ten Lessons* (London: Standard Art Book Company).

Rowell, George (ed.) (1971), *Victorian Dramatic Criticism* (London: Methuen).

—— (1985), *The Victorian Theatre, 1792–1914* (Cambridge: Cambridge University Press); second edn.

Rowson, Harry (n.d.),*"IDEALS" OF WARDOUR STREET* (unpublished memoirs held in BFI Special Collections).

Sadoul, George (1948), *British Creators of Film Technique* (London: BFI).

Sanderson, Michael (1984), *From Irving to Olivier: A Social History of the Acting Profession in England 1880–1983* (London: Athlone).

Sargeant, Amy (2000a), 'Darwin, Duchenne, Delsarte', in L. Fitzsimmons and S. Street, *Moving Performance: British Stage and Screen, 1890s–1920s* (Trowbridge, Wiltshire: Flicks Books).

—— (2000b), 'On Receiving Letters from Despised Lovers', in Toulmin and Popple (eds), *Visual Delights: Essays on the Popular and Projected Image in the Nineteenth Century* (Trowbridge, Wiltshire: Flicks Books).

Saville, Victor (n.d.), *SHADOWS ON A SCREEN* (unpublished memoirs held in BFI Special Collections).

Scott, Walter (1819), 'Essay on the Drama', in Supplement to *The Encyclopaedia Britannica*.

Shute, Nerina (1973), *The Escapist Generations: My London Story* (London: Robert Hale & Co.).

Siddons, Henry (1822), *Practical Illustrations of Rhetorical Gesture and Action; Adapted to the English Drama: From a Work on the Same Subject by M. Engel* (London: Richard Phillips).

Sims, George (1883), *How the Poor Live* (London: Chatto & Windus).

Smith, Grahame (2003), *Dickens and the Dream of Cinema* (Manchester: Manchester University Press).

Staiger, Janet (1985), 'The Division and Order of Production: the Subdivision of the Work from the First Years through the 1920s', in D. Bordwell, J. Staiger and K. Thompson, *The Classical Hollywood Cinema: Film Style and Mode of Production to 1960* (New York: Columbia University Press).

Stokes, John (1972), *Resistable Theatres: Enterprise and Experiment in the Late Nineteenth Century* (London: Paul Elek Books).

Styan, J. L. (1981), *Modern Drama in Theory and Practice!: Realism and Naturalism* (Cambridge: Cambridge University Press).

Talbot, Frederick (1923), *Moving Pictures: How They Are Made and Worked* (London: William Heinemann); rev. edn.

Taylor, John (ed.) (1978), *Pictorial Photography in Britain, 1900–1920* (London: Arts Council of Great Britain in association with the Royal Photographic Society).

—— (1990), 'The Alphabetic Universe: Photography and the Picturesque Landscape', in S. Pugh (ed.), *Reading Landscape: Country – City – Capital* (Manchester: Manchester University Press).

Thompson, Kristin (1985), 'The Formulation of the Classical Style, 1909–28', in D. Bordwell, J. Staiger and K. Thompson, *The Classical Hollywood Cinema: Film Style and Mode of Production to 1960* (New York: Columbia University Press).

Thwaite, Ann (1990), *A. A. Milne: His Life* (London: Faber & Faber).

Treuherz, Julian (ed.) (1987), *Hard Times: Social Realism in Victorian Art* (London: Lund Humphries in association with Manchester City Art Galleries).

—— (1993), *Victorian Painting* (London: Thames & Hudson).

Trewin, J. C., Mander, Raymond and Mitchenson, Joe (1958), *The Gay Twenties: A Decade of the Theatre* (London: MacDonald).

Vernon, Frank (1923), *Modern Stage Production* (London: 'The Stage' Office).

Vicinus, Martha (1981), 'Helpless and Unfriended: Nineteenth-Century Domestic Melodrama', *New Literary History*, vol. 3 no. 1, Autumn, pp. 127–43.

Warren, Patricia (1995), *British Film Studios: An Illustrated History* (London: Batsford).

Wilcox, Herbert (1967), *Twenty-Five Thousand Sunsets: The Autobiography of Herbert Wilcox* (London: Bodley Head).

Williams, Christopher (1996), 'The Social Art Cinema: A Moment in the History of British Film and Television Culture', in C. Williams (ed.), *Cinema: The Beginnings and the Future* (London: University of Westminster Press).

Williams, Michael (2001), ' "England's Apollo": Ivor Novello – Post-War Icon, Matinee-Idol and "Ambassador of the British Film" ' (Norwich: unpublished PhD thesis, University of East Anglia).

—— (2003), *Ivor Novello: Screen Idol* (London: BFI).

Williams, Raymond (1973), 'Between Country and City', in S. Pugh (ed.), *Reading Landscape: Country – City – Capital* (Manchester: Manchester University Press).

—— (1977), 'A Lecture on Realism', *Screen*, vol. 18 no. 1, Spring, pp. 61–74.

Winship, Janice (1996), 'Women's Magazines: Times of War and Management of the Self in *Woman's Own*', in C. Gledhill and G. Swanson, *Nationalising Feminity: Culture, Sexuality and British Cinema in the Second World War* (Manchester: Manchester University Press).

Winter, Jay (1995), *Sites of Memory, Sites of Mourning* (Cambridge: Cambridge University Press).

Wood, Christopher (1999), *Victorian Painting* (London: Weidenfeld & Nicolson).

Wood, Linda (1987), *The Commercial Imperative in the Film Industry: Maurice Elvey, a Case Study* (London: BFI).

Wullschlager, Jackie (1995), *Inventing Wonderland: The Lives and Fantasies of Lewis Carroll, Edward Lear, J. M. Barrie, Kenneth Grahame and A. A. Milne* (London: Methuen).

Index

Italicised page numbers denote illustrations; those in **bold** indicate detailed analysis.
n = endnote (indexed only for background information, not citations).
Names of people are indexed at every reference. Production companies are indexed only where some information is given beyond their having produced a particular film.
Titles of works are of films unless otherwise stated; where reference is made to both a stage play and its cinematic adaptation only the date of the film is given. Literary/pictorial works are listed under the author/artist's name.